Automating
Active Directory®
Administration with
Windows PowerShell® 2.0

Automating Active Directory® Administration with Windows PowerShell® 2.0

Ken St. Cyr
Laura E. Hunter

WILEY

Wiley Publishing, Inc.

Acquisitions Editor: Agatha Kim
Development Editor: Kim Beaudet
Technical Editor: Steve Patrick
Production Editor: Dassi Zeidel
Copy Editor: Tiffany Taylor
Editorial Manager: Pete Gaughan
Production Manager: Tim Tate
Vice President and Executive Group Publisher: Richard Swadley
Vice President and Publisher: Neil Edde
Book Designer: Maureen Forys, Happenstance Type-O-Rama
Proofreader: Rebecca Rider; Paul Sagan, Word One, New York
Indexer: Ted Laux
Project Coordinator, Cover: Katie Crocker
Cover Designer: Ryan Sneed
Cover Image: © Andrey Volodin / iStockPhoto

Dear Reader,

Thank you for choosing *Automating Active Directory Administration with Windows PowerShell 2.0*. This book is part of a family of premium-quality Sybex books, all of which are written by outstanding authors who combine practical experience with a gift for teaching.

Sybex was founded in 1976. More than 30 years later, we're still committed to producing consistently exceptional books. With each of our titles, we're working hard to set a new standard for the industry. From the paper we print on, to the authors we work with, our goal is to bring you the best books available.

I hope you see all that reflected in these pages. I'd be very interested to hear your comments and get your feedback on how we're doing. Feel free to let me know what you think about this or any other Sybex book by sending me an email at nedde@wiley.com. If you think you've found a technical error in this book, please visit http://sybex.custhelp.com. Customer feedback is critical to our efforts at Sybex.

Best regards,

Neil Edde
Vice President and Publisher
Sybex, an Imprint of Wiley

ACKNOWLEDGMENTS

There's no way I could have written this book without my tremendous support system. At the head of that system is my best friend and amazing wife, Brenna. She has the patience of a saint and is wise beyond her years. It's through her support and help that I was able to have the time to take on this project and the encouragement to finish. Alongside her are my brilliant and adorable children, Lincoln and Nora. Their helpfulness was manifested in their cuteness and willingness to let me write.

When I first entertained the thought of taking on this book, I looked at the timeline and realized that it was impossible for me to go about this one alone. My first choice for a coauthor was the obvious one; Laura Hunter's name is almost synonymous with Active Directory. Thankfully, when I asked her to coauthor this book with me, she was happy to do it. So, a big thanks goes out to Laura for helping me write this. Along with Laura, we had two contributors working on this book, Chas Jeffries and Nick DiCola. Both Chas and Nick bring an incredible amount of experience and expertise in security and Active Directory, and I am thankful that they were able to help.

It was a great pleasure to work with the wonderful group of professionals at Wiley. In particular, I would like to thank the development editor, Kim Beaudet; the production editor, Dassi Zeidel; editorial manager, Pete Gaughan; copy editor Tiffany Taylor; and the compositors at Laserwords. I would also like to thank my good friend and technical editor, Steve Patrick, who is one of the deepest Active Directory guys on the planet. And I would like to give an extra-special thanks to my acquisitions editor, Agatha Kim, who, as always, was a real treat to work with.

I also need to thank my wonderful friends and coworkers at Microsoft. A big thanks goes out to my fellow Directory Masters and members of the product group who answered my questions and gave me great insight. I would also like to thank my many teachers, mentors, and encouraging friends: Abe Berlas, Aaron Isom, Darryl Schaffer, Alex Bogdanovsky, Heath Aubin, Ben Drake, Joe Fox, Jim Hale, and the members of the Microsoft OCTO team.

And finally, I would like to give a special thanks to my wonderful friends and family at Grace Baptist Church in Bowie, MD, who offered their prayers and encouragement for me throughout this process. The Godly direction given by my pastors and mentors has been invaluable: Steve Lane, Dr. George Harton, Mark Tanious, and Larry Olson. There's no group of people more loving and caring than those at Grace.

Ken St. Cyr

As always, my thanks go out to my friends and family for their support in my pursuit of this project, especially Megan Kristel, Brian Puhl, Dean Wells, Brian Desmond, Gil Kirkpatrick, and Stuart Kwan.

Laura E. Hunter

ABOUT THE AUTHORS

Ken St. Cyr is a solution architect at Microsoft in the Public Sector Services CTO organization. Ken's primary areas of technical expertise are in directory services and identity systems. Ken is a 14-year industry veteran, consulting to a broad range of organizations to design and deliver numerous large and complex identity solutions. In addition to being a Microsoft Certified Master in Directory Services and Advanced Infrastructure, Ken has written for *TechNet Magazine* and *Windows IT Pro* magazine.

In his leisure time, Ken enjoys spending time with his wife, Brenna, and two children, Lincoln and Nora. As a lifelong learner and avid technology enthusiast, Ken enjoys researching the latest technologies and attempting to understand how they work. Aside from that, Ken is most enthusiastic about teaching and instructing others to realize their passion through the magic of software. You can visit Ken's blog at www.theidentityguy.com and follow him on Twitter at @kenstcyr.

Laura E. Hunter is a principal technology architect for Microsoft IT's Identity and Access Management team, responsible for determining architecture and strategy for Microsoft deployments of products and services across the IAM suite. In previous lives, she has been an identity management consultant, the Active Directory architect for a global engineering firm, IT project leader for the University of Pennsylvania, and director of computer services for a regional headquarters of the Salvation Army. Laura has a bachelor's and master's degree from the University of Pennsylvania, is an unrepentant ADFS technology zealot, and likes to talk about herself in the third person when providing autobiographical information. She blogs at www.shutuplaura.com, and Twitters (tweets? She's not cool enough to know the verb form of Twitter) @adfskitteh.

ABOUT THE CONTRIBUTING AUTHORS

Chas Jeffries is a security architect in Microsoft Services. Before joining Microsoft Services, Chas was a lead program manager in the Windows Core Operating System Division (COSD) at Microsoft, where he contributed to the design and development of BitLocker as well as a number of other security features in the Windows operating system. Chas is a CISSP with over 10 years in the computer security industry and 20 years in software engineering and information technology. Chas holds an MBA from Seattle University and an MS in computer science from the University of Nebraska—Omaha.

Nicholas DiCola is a senior consultant for Microsoft Consulting Services and has designed and implemented directory solutions based on Active Directory for over 12 years. He is one of the few Microsoft Certified Masters for Directory Services.

CONTENTS AT A GLANCE

TABLE OF CONTENTS

INTRODUCTION

The goal of this book is to give you the information you need to know in order to use PowerShell for managing, configuring, and scripting tasks in Active Directory. In many cases, we didn't seek to answer your deepest and darkest questions about Active Directory. Instead, our attempt is to give you a practical guide that you'll refer to frequently and that will become your administrative companion.

You'll find that this book contains a lot of information that is useful for Active Directory (AD) administration even outside of the PowerShell world. We've brought many years of AD experience to the table, and I'd venture to say that among all the authors, we've probably seen about every AD scenario there is. Most of us regularly give training on these topics and are members of an elite community known as the Directory Masters, where we've been put through the wringer to prove our abilities and knowledge in AD. In reading this book, you're gaining our collective experience in this technology.

One of the things that we really wanted to focus on in this book is giving you lots of sample scripts. So as you read through these pages, you'll find dozens of scripts and examples that you can use verbatim or modify to put to work in your domain. Whether you're a one-person team in a small organization or a member of a larger team, this book is your own personal guide to automating AD.

If you're new to AD or PowerShell and are using either technology for the first time, you can start at the first chapter and read through the book to learn the technologies. Each chapter of this book deals with a different area of AD administration, from deployment to security. Our hope is that you'll keep coming back to this book and use it as a reference for how to use PowerShell to accomplish a given task for AD or how to write that one script that does your job for you. We look forward to being a well-used tool in your AD administration toolbox.

Who Should Read This Book

Although many ranks of IT professionals can get something out of this book, our target audience is primarily administrators who manage Microsoft Active Directory Domain Services environments running on Windows Server 2008 R2. Whether or not you have experience with previous versions of AD server, you can use this book.

In order to use this book to the fullest, you should possess:

- ► Some level of familiarity with Windows Server 2008 or Windows Server 2008 R2

- ► A basic understanding of Windows networking

This book may also prove useful to people who want to use hands-on examples with relevant narratives to play with AD in a lab environment. If you fall into this category, you can start at the first chapter and read your way through the book, following the examples and steps as you go along.

What Is Covered in This Book

To make this book easy to consume, we've broken it into three parts with a total of 11 chapters. As you progress through this book, you start by picking up the essential knowledge required to begin PowerShell 2.0 and then move into various aspects of AD administration. Although there is value in reading this book cover to cover in sequential order, it also serves those well who prefer to flip around from chapter to chapter. At the very least, however, we recommend that everyone read Chapter 1 first, even if you're a PowerShell 2.0 guru. Doing so will reinforce your understanding of the basics and ensure that our terminology and scripting style is in sync with yours.

Part 1: Administering Service Delivery

Chapter 1, "Using PowerShell with Active Directory," serves as your guide for understanding the essentials of Windows PowerShell. We'll take you through the basics, from cmdlets to scripts, and then to some advanced techniques. We'll also explain how PowerShell is used to interact with AD and how to prepare your AD environment to get it ready for PowerShell 2.0.

Chapter 2, "Managing Domains and Forests," is intended to help you manage two of the high-level containers in AD: domains and forests. We'll walk you through the process of adding and removing domains, as well as configuring domain- and forest-wide settings. In this chapter, we'll also spend some time helping you understand how to manage trust relationships between different domains and forests.

Chapter 3, "Managing Sites and Replication," is about managing your site topology and making sure your domain controllers replicate properly. Here, you'll learn how to use PowerShell to automate your site settings, replication settings, and even the process of ensuring that replication is healthy in your environment.

Chapter 4, "Managing Domain Controllers," focuses on all things that are specific to the configuration of a domain controller (DC). This includes the promotion and demotion of a DC, managing the Global Catalog settings, and even the FSMO roles. In addition, we'll show you how to use PowerShell to manage other configuration settings on your DC, such the configuration of the AD database.

Part 2: Managing Active Directory Data

Chapter 5, "Configuring Active Directory Dependencies," is about working with two of the primary dependencies for a healthy AD: name resolution and the system time. We'll show you how to use PowerShell to configure and manage the Domain Naming System (DNS) as well as managing the system time service across your forest.

Chapter 6, "Administering User and Group Accounts," will probably be one of the most used chapters in the book. This chapter teaches you how to use PowerShell for automating basic and advanced operations for both users and groups in your domain. We'll provide lots of PowerShell guidance in this chapter, and these practices will instantly become part of your toolbox for working with AD in your lab environment as well as your production forest.

Chapter 7, "Managing Computer Accounts, Objects, and Organizational Units," guides you through managing those non-user and non-group objects. We'll walk you through using PowerShell to manage computer accounts and organizational units specifically, but we'll also spend some time showing you how to use PowerShell to manage all types of objects in the forest.

Chapter 8, "Managing Group Policies," will help you use PowerShell to automate the creation, modification, and application of Group Policy Objects in your domains. You'll also use PowerShell scripts to perform some other useful Group Policy management functions, such as generating an automated report of the Group Policy settings and linking Group Policy Objects to organizational units (OUs), sites, and domains.

Part 3: Protecting Your Investment in Active Directory

Chapter 9, "Automating Active Directory Security," is a rare chapter that you'll likely not find anywhere else. Here, we'll show you how to use PowerShell to manage AD security settings across your forest. Also in this chapter, you'll learn how to use PowerShell to manage BitLocker settings and recovery passwords. This special content was written and contributed to this book by a BitLocker program manager at Microsoft.

Chapter 10, "Backing Up Data and Recovering from Disasters," is one of those chapters that you can't survive without. We'll explain how to use PowerShell to both back up and restore AD data. In this chapter, we'll cover automating the backup and restore process for directory data, SYSVOL data, Group Policies, and certificates.

Chapter 11, "Monitoring Health and Performance," wraps up this book by helping you use PowerShell to keep your AD environment healthy and performing at an optimum level. Not only will we show you what to monitor on your DCs, but we'll also spend time explaining what all the data means.

How to Contact the Author

I welcome feedback from you about this book or about books you'd like to see from me in the future. You can reach me by writing to ken@theidentityguy.com. For more information about my work, please visit my blog at www.theidentityguy.com.

Sybex strives to keep you supplied with the latest tools and information you need for your work. Please check their website at www.sybex.com, where we'll post additional content and updates that supplement this book if the need arises. Enter **Active Directory** in the Search box (or type the book's ISBN—**9781118027318**), and click Go to get to the book's update page.

Administering Service Delivery

Using PowerShell with Active Directory

IN THIS CHAPTER, YOU WILL LEARN TO:

S ince the dawn of the information technology age, administrators have been continually searching for ways to make their jobs easier. Rather than spending time performing the same or similar tasks repeatedly, many administrators have taken to adopting some form of automation. Throughout the years, you've witnessed many advances in automation, from the early days of DOS batch files to VBScripts and Windows Management Instrumentation (WMI). These advances come out of the desire for things to happen on their own—to use the computing power available at the fingertips of administrators to make their lives easier.

The next generation of automation technology was officially released for Windows environments in 2006. PowerShell (formerly referred to as Monad in the beta release years) promised to deliver an extremely powerful and flexible scripting environment complete with access to standard object models and programming interfaces. PowerShell has certainly lived up to the promise over the years, but adoption by Microsoft products has been slow. Until Windows Server 2008 R2, there was no out-of-the-box PowerShell extension for Active Directory. However, the adoption of PowerShell has now become mainstream, and Active Directory has a built-in module for PowerShell. In this chapter, you'll learn the basics of PowerShell and understand how Active Directory and PowerShell work together.

Understand the Basics of PowerShell

PowerShell version 1 debuted as a web download and as part of Windows 2008, although you had to install it through the Add Features Wizard in the Server Manager. PowerShell v2 is installed by default in Windows Server 2008 R2. At its core, PowerShell is a command interpreter. Much as with the command prompt, you type in a command and press Enter, and the command executes. But beyond that, PowerShell has some amazing scripting capabilities that really take it to the next level in terms of administrative usefulness. Because of this, it's becoming increasingly more common to see people replacing the command prompt with PowerShell. In fact, most of the things that you can do at a command prompt can be done by default with PowerShell using the same commands. Figure 1.1 shows a comparison of the dir command run in a traditional command prompt (top) and PowerShell (bottom).

One of the things you'll notice in Figure 1.1 is that the information PowerShell exposes by default looks more structured. The entries in the output have headings attached to them, similar to how a spreadsheet might look. This is because PowerShell isn't a text-based command interpreter like the Windows command prompt and other command shells. Standard text-based interpreters can take a text string as input and return a text string as output. PowerShell is based on the .NET Framework. Rather than using text, PowerShell takes .NET objects as input and returns .NET objects as output. So, when the `dir` command is run, PowerShell enumerates the files and folders on disk and treats each file and folder as a separate object. Each object is composed of a variety of properties that describe it, which are exposed as the headings across the top of the output. This object model is unique to PowerShell and is one of the primary things that elevates it above other commonly used shells.

FIGURE 1.1   PowerShell can do just about anything that the command prompt can do.

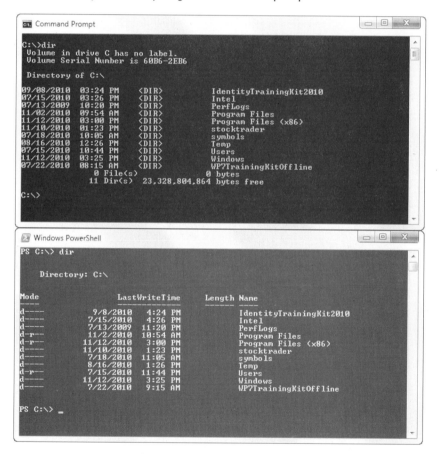

Before you begin using PowerShell to automate Active Directory, you must first understand some of the fundamentals. The essential components are used as building blocks for creating the commands and scripts that you'll use in your automation tasks. Without this base knowledge, your commands and scripts will be limited, and you won't be able to take advantage of the true power of PowerShell. In this section, we'll take a closer look at these components.

Use the Shell

The shell is the primary way that you'll interact with PowerShell. The shell is very similar to the Windows command prompt. You can type in commands and have some output returned to you. You can launch the shell by clicking the Start menu and selecting All Programs ➢ Accessories ➢ Windows PowerShell ➢ Windows PowerShell. If you're on a 64-bit operating system, then you may notice that there are two PowerShell options: Windows PowerShell and Windows PowerShell (x86). The x86 version is the 32-bit version of PowerShell. Unless you need to run a command in a 32-bit environment, we recommend using the 64-bit version of the shell. This will allow you to use additional memory beyond 4 GB if you're caching lots of data in the shell. And with Active Directory, this could actually be a possibility if you have a large forest. In Windows Server 2008 R2, PowerShell is pinned to the taskbar by default, so you can launch it by clicking the PowerShell icon. You can also choose to launch it by typing **powershell.exe** in the Run dialog or at the command prompt.

Sometimes, you'll have to launch PowerShell in administrator mode. This may be required when you're making system-level changes through PowerShell. To use PowerShell in administrator mode, you can right-click the PowerShell executable and select Run As Administrator from the menu. Depending on your system's configuration, you may be prompted with a User Account Control dialog. If you're prompted, click Yes to continue. The shell will launch, and it will look similar to the window in Figure 1.2.

FIGURE 1.2   The PowerShell shell

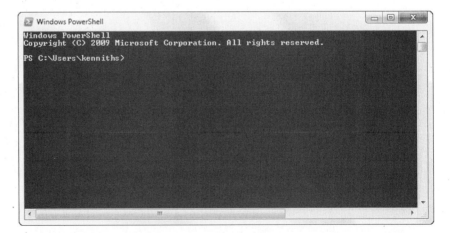

When you're working with the shell, you can use some shortcuts to make your job easier. Each command that you type in is kept in memory. Therefore, you can cycle through commands that you typed earlier by using the up and down arrow keys.

You can use the right arrow key to retype the previous command one character at a time. You also have the option of accessing a list of the previous 50 commands by pressing the F7 key, as shown in Figure 1.3. Navigate through this list by using the arrow keys and pressing Enter on the command you want to execute, or type the command number that you want to execute and press F9. To close the list without executing a command, press the Esc key.

FIGURE 1.3   PowerShell command history

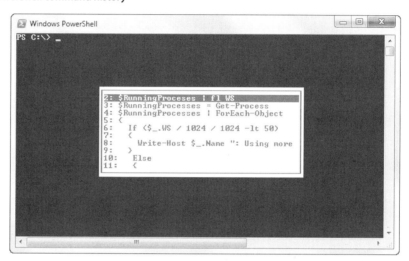

One of the lesser-known customizations of PowerShell is the ability to change the look at and feel of the shell itself. You can do this via the Get-Host cmdlet in PowerShell (more on cmdlets later in this chapter). You modify certain components of the shell by changing the properties in the console. For example, to change the text color to green, you can use the following command:

```
(Get-Host).UI.RawUI.ForegroundColor = "Green"
```

Table 1.1 outlines some properties that you may want to change in the console.

TABLE 1.1   Console Properties

Property	Description	Example Command
ForegroundColor	The color of the text	`(Get-Host).UI.RawUI ↵` `.ForegroundColor = "Green"`
BackgroundColor	The color of the background	`(Get-Host).UI.RawUI ↵` `.BackgroundColor = "Black"`
WindowTitle	The text that is displayed in the title bar of the PowerShell window	`(Get-Host).UI.RawUI.WindowTitle ↵` `= "Ken's PowerShell Window"`

Use the Scripting Environment

PowerShell 2.0 provides a new Integrated Scripting Environment (ISE) for writing PowerShell scripts with more ease. The ISE provides some great capabilities that are typically found in expensive development environments. Full development environments offer additional features that justify the cost if you'll be writing a lot of code; but if you're just looking for basic debugging and script writing, you need look no further than the ISE.

The PowerShell ISE isn't installed by default on Windows Server 2008 R2, so you'll need to add it if you want to use it. You can install the PowerShell ISE through Server Manager, using the `Add-WindowsFeature` PowerShell cmdlet. This cmdlet isn't registered by default, so you must first import the Server Manager module in PowerShell:

```
Import-Module ServerManager
```

After the module is imported, you have access to the `Add-WindowsFeature` cmdlet. You can run the following command to add the PowerShell ISE:

```
Add-WindowsFeature PowerShell-ISE
```

The 3.5.1 version of the .NET Framework is required for the ISE, so you may notice that installing as well if it's not already installed on your server. After you install the ISE, you can launch it by clicking the Start menu and selecting All Programs ➢ Accessories ➢ Windows PowerShell ➢ Windows PowerShell ISE.

The ISE will be launched as shown in Figure 1.4. It consists of three panels that assist you in writing scripts:

Script Editor   The script editor is the top panel of the ISE. You can have multiple scripts open at the same time, and each script will have its own tab in the editor. You can run your script and test it in the editor by clicking the green arrow in the toolbar.

Command Pane   The bottom panel is called the command pane. This pane provides you with an interactive PowerShell command interface just as if you were using the shell itself. You can type in commands freehand and see the results. This is especially useful when determining the syntax of your command before inserting it into a script.

Output Pane   The output pane is the middle pane in the ISE. When you run the script you're writing or execute a command in the command pane, the output is displayed in the output pane.

FIGURE 1.4   The PowerShell Integrated Scripting Environment

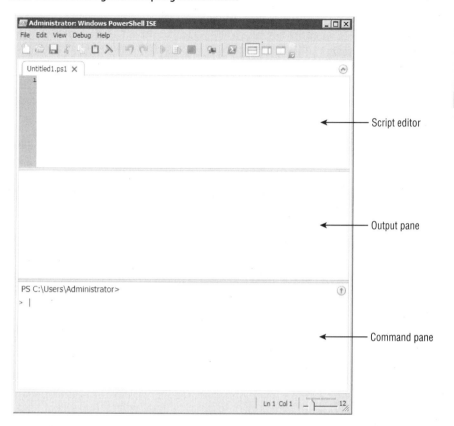

 NOTE   It's important to understand that the ISE isn't the only way to create PowerShell scripts. PowerShell scripts can be created with any text editor, including built-in utilities like Notepad and WordPad, along with third-party development environments.

Understand Profiles

PowerShell also has a concept of *profiles*. Profiles in PowerShell are similar to profiles in Windows. When you log on to Windows, your user profile is loaded, which loads all of your Windows customizations, such as your desktop items and wallpaper. Likewise, PowerShell profiles save your PowerShell customizations. When you open PowerShell, your profile will load, and your customizations will be loaded as well.

Profile Scripts

The PowerShell profile is really a script that runs automatically when you open PowerShell. PowerShell scripts are covered in more detail later in this chapter, but for now just know that you can execute various PowerShell commands, save variables, and define functions in your PowerShell profile. For example, suppose you frequently put your computer into Hibernate mode. You can create a custom function (functions are also covered later in this chapter) that puts the computer in Hibernate mode by typing in a simple command. To do this, add the following line to your PowerShell profile:

```
function hib { shutdown -h -t 0 }
```

This function tells PowerShell to run the `shutdown` command with the -h (hibernate) switch whenever you type in **hib**. Because your PowerShell profile is loaded every time you open PowerShell, the `hib` command will always be available to you.

Creating a Profile

By default, you have a PowerShell profile defined, but the file doesn't exist and therefore isn't executed. You determine what your current profile script is by displaying the contents to the `profile` variable. To see the `profile` variable, type the following command:

```
$profile
```

You can determine whether the profile script exists by the running the `Test-Path` cmdlet, which returns true if the file exists and false if it doesn't:

```
Test-Path $profile
```

If the profile script doesn't exist, you can create it using any text editor, such as `Notepad .exe`. You can also run the `New-Item` command to create the profile script file:

```
PS C:\Users\Administrator> New-Item -Path $profile -ItemType File -Force


    Directory: C:\Users\Administrator\Documents\WindowsPowerShell


Mode             LastWriteTime    Length Name
----             -------------    ------ ----
-a---        11/29/2010    3:29 PM        0 Microsoft.PowerShell_profile.ps1
```

After the profile script is created, you can use Notepad to edit it:

```
PS C:\Users\Administrator> notepad.exe $profile
```

If you try to create a profile script now, you may receive the error shown next when PowerShell attempts to load the profile script. This is a security measure put in place by PowerShell to ensure that only trusted scripts are run. You'll learn how to create a trusted script later in this chapter in the "Create PowerShell Scripts" section:

```
Windows PowerShell
Copyright (C) 2009 Microsoft Corporation. All rights reserved.


File C:\Users\Administrator\Documents\WindowsPowerShell\Microso
ft.PowerShell_profile.ps1 cannot be loaded because the executio
n of scripts is disabled on this system. Please see "get-help a
bout_signing" for more details.
At line:1 char:2
+ . <<<<  'C:\Users\Administrator\Documents\WindowsPowerShell\M
icrosoft.PowerShell_profile.ps1'
    + CategoryInfo          : NotSpecified: (:) [], PSSecurity
  Exception
    + FullyQualifiedErrorId : RuntimeException
```

Work with Cmdlets

In PowerShell, a cmdlet (pronounced *command-let*) is a small, lightweight command. Each cmdlet is self-contained, meaning that you can run it by itself as its own command. For example, you can execute the get-process cmdlet, and it will return the list of processes currently running on the computer, as shown in Figure 1.5.

FIGURE 1.5   Running the Get-Process cmdlet returns the list of processes currently running on the computer.

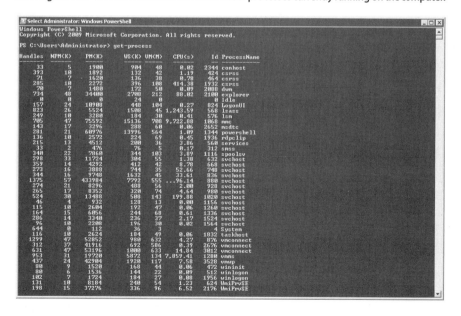

Cmdlets are precompiled and can be run from the PowerShell command interpreter directly or be used in a script. They're surprisingly flexible and can be used in a variety of ways.

PowerShell has several cmdlets built in, and applications can provide their own cmdlets as well. For example, Active Directory adds 76 additional cmdlets to PowerShell when the module is installed. In fact, anyone can write a cmdlet to be used in PowerShell; the process for writing a cmdlet is well documented by Microsoft.

Execute Cmdlets

When it comes down to it, executing cmdlets is as easy as opening PowerShell and typing in the name of the cmdlet, as was demonstrated in Figure 1.5.

Basic Cmdlet Structure

When you work with cmdlets long enough, you'll start to notice some similarities between them. Most cmdlets start with a verb, such as Get, Set, Add, or Remove. Usually following the verb is a noun, such as Process. This common structure used in cmdlets is referred to as a *verb-noun pair*. For example, in the Get-Process cmdlet, the verb (Get) tells the cmdlet that it's retrieving information for the noun (Process). All cmdlets are singular, so you'll never see a cmdlet called Get-Processes.

Executing a cmdlet is as simple as opening up PowerShell and running the cmdlet:

1. Open PowerShell by choosing Start ➤ All Programs ➤ Accessories ➤ Windows PowerShell ➤ Windows PowerShell.

   You can also launch PowerShell by clicking the icon in the taskbar, as shown in Figure 1.6. After PowerShell loads, you're presented with the cursor, ready to accept your command.

FIGURE 1.6   Launching PowerShell via the icon in the taskbar

2. Type in the cmdlet, and press Enter. For example, to get a list of the services currently installed on the computer, you can run the Get-Service cmdlet.

Parameters

You can also feed a cmdlet parameters that influence the behavior of the cmdlet when it's run. To specify a parameter, append it to the end of the cmdlet. For example, if you want to get information about a specific service on your computer, you can run the same `Get-Service` cmdlet that you just ran, but this time specify the name of the service as a parameter. Figure 1.7 shows the output of the `Get-Service` cmdlet run against the Windows Update service.

FIGURE 1.7   Adding a parameter to a cmdlet

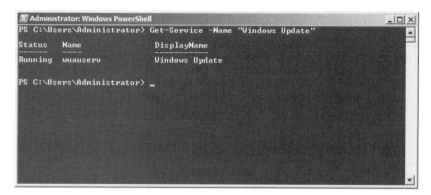

The -Name parameter shown in Figure 1.7 is a positional parameter. This means you don't have to specify -Name when using the parameter. If you ran the same cmdlet but didn't include -Name in the command, the cmdlet would assume that the first unnamed parameter was the -Name parameter. That makes the following two commands identical:

```
Get-Service -Name "Windows Update"
Get-Service "Windows Update"
```

This next command is also identical to the first two:

```
Get-Service -ComputerName localhost "Windows Update"
```

In the previous command, the first parameter used (-ComputerName) is a named parameter, because the parameter is specified by using -ComputerName in the command, followed by the name of the computer (localhost in this case). The second parameter wasn't named. However, because it's the first unnamed parameter in the command, the cmdlet assumes that it's the -Name parameter. It's the same as using the following command:

```
Get-Service -ComputerName localhost -Name "Windows Update"
```

You'll learn how to find out which parameters are positional or named, along with their default values, later in this chapter.

Each cmdlet has a different set of parameters that it recognizes. The -ComputerName parameter in the previous example is only relevant for the Get-Service cmdlet. If you tried to pass it into the Get-ChildItem cmdlet, an error would be thrown:

```
PS C:\> Get-ChildItem -ComputerName localhost
Get-ChildItem : A parameter cannot be found that matches parameter name 'Comput
erName'.
At line:1 char:28
+ Get-ChildItem -ComputerName <<<<  localhost
    + CategoryInfo          : InvalidArgument: (:) [Get-ChildItem], ParameterB
   indingException
    + FullyQualifiedErrorId : NamedParameterNotFound,Microsoft.PowerShell.Comm
   ands.GetChildItemCommand
```

However, PowerShell implements some parameters that are common to all cmdlets. These are referred to as *common parameters*. You can retrieve a list of common parameters in PowerShell by running the following command:

```
Get-Help about_CommonParameters
```

Table 1.2 lists the common parameters and describes what each does.

TABLE 1.2   **Command Parameters**

Name	Description
-Verbose	Includes detailed information in the output of the cmdlet. This is typically in-depth information that may not be commonly used.
-Debug	Includes programmer-level detail in the output of the cmdlet. In most day-to-day administration tasks, the -Debug parameter is rarely used.
-WarningAction	Specifies what the cmdlet should do if it encounters a warning. The possible values are SilentlyContinue (continue executing the cmdlet without notification), Continue (display a notification and then continue executing the cmdlet), Inquire (ask the user whether to stop or keep going), and Stop (stop execution of the cmdlet).
-WarningVariable	Specifies a variable to which warning information can be written. You can use this variable later in other commands or scripts.
-ErrorAction	Specifies what the cmdlet should do if it encounters an error. The possible values are SilentlyContinue (continue executing the cmdlet without notification), Continue (display a notification and then continue executing the cmdlet), Inquire (ask the user whether to stop or keep going), and Stop (stop execution of the cmdlet).
-ErrorVariable	Specifies a variable to which error information can be written. You can use this variable later in other commands or scripts.

Name	Description
-OutVariable	Specifies a variable to which you want to write the output objects.
-OutBuffer	Determines how many objects are in the output buffer before the objects are passed through the pipeline. This is an advanced parameter that you probably won't use frequently, if at all.

NOTE   Cmdlets and their parameters aren't case sensitive. However, it's a good practice to use capitalization for cmdlets that other people might read, such as when writing scripts. This increases the readability of the command without affecting the syntax of the cmdlet.

Aliases

If you've already been using PowerShell, you may have noticed that not all of the cmdlets you've run have conformed to the structure discussed earlier. For example, the dir command doesn't conform to the verb-noun pair syntax. The reason for this is that dir is really an alias. In PowerShell, an *alias* is an alternate name that you can give to command elements, such as cmdlets and scripts, to make them easier for users to run. When you execute the dir alias, the cmdlet that is really being run is Get-ChildItem. You don't have to use an alias; if you wanted to, you could run the Get-ChildItem cmdlet directly. However, the dir alias saves you time; and if you're used to typing dir into a Windows command prompt to get a listing of files and directories, then this alias makes PowerShell a little more intuitive and uses the muscle memory you've built up over the years.

You aren't limited to one alias per command. If you have a Unix or Linux background, then you're probably more likely to use the ls command for listing files and directories. For this reason, ls is also an alias to the Get-ChildItem cmdlet.

To create your own alias, you can run the New-Alias cmdlet. You'll need to pass in the name for the alias and the command element for which you're creating the alias. The following example creates an alias called d for the Get-ChildItem cmdlet. If you create this alias, then you only need to type d instead of dir or ls to get a listing of files and directories in PowerShell:

```
New-Alias -Name d -Value Get-ChildItem
```

Earlier in this chapter, you learned about using profiles to customize the PowerShell environment for different users. You can add your commonly used aliases to your profile so that your aliases are loaded every time you open PowerShell.

String Cmdlets Together

When used alone, a cmdlet can be a powerful tool. However, you can use cmdlets more efficiently by stringing multiple cmdlets together using a process called *pipelining*. When you pipeline two cmdlets, the results from the first cmdlet are fed into the second cmdlet. In order to perform a pipeline, you use the pipe character (|). For example, if you want to kill every Internet Explorer process running on your computer, you can use the Get-Process cmdlet and pipe its output into the Stop-Process cmdlet. The command to accomplish this looks like this:

```
Get-Process iexplore | Stop-Process
```

A pipelined cmdlet is also sometimes referred to as a *one-liner*. Some advanced administrators pride themselves on the length of their one-liners. Some consider a long one-liner that performs a complex task an administrative badge of honor. One-liners can get complex, but when you start using PowerShell regularly, they will become second nature. Some of the complex one-liners can be good substitutes for administrative tasks that require multiple steps. For example, the following one-liner will look in the Application Event Log, find all the error and warning events, put them in a CSV file, and then open the file with Microsoft Excel:

```
Get-EventLog Application -EntryType Error | Export-Csv errors
.csv -NoTypeInformation | Start-Process excel.exe errors.csv
```

At first, it may seem complex, but you could easily create a function for this one-liner, put it in your profile, and have an easier and more flexible way to view your critical system events. Or imagine running this command on each of your domain controllers every day using the Task Scheduler and outputting your errors and warnings into a shared folder.

Get Help on a Cmdlet

You can get help executing any cmdlet by using a special PowerShell cmdlet called Get-Help. When you execute Get-Help, you must specify the name of the cmdlet that you want help on as the first parameter. For example, if you're stuck on how to use the Get-Process cmdlet, you can run the following command to learn how to use it:

```
Get-Help Get-Process
```

Figure 1.8 shows the output of this command.

FIGURE 1.8   The output of the `Get-Help` cmdlet

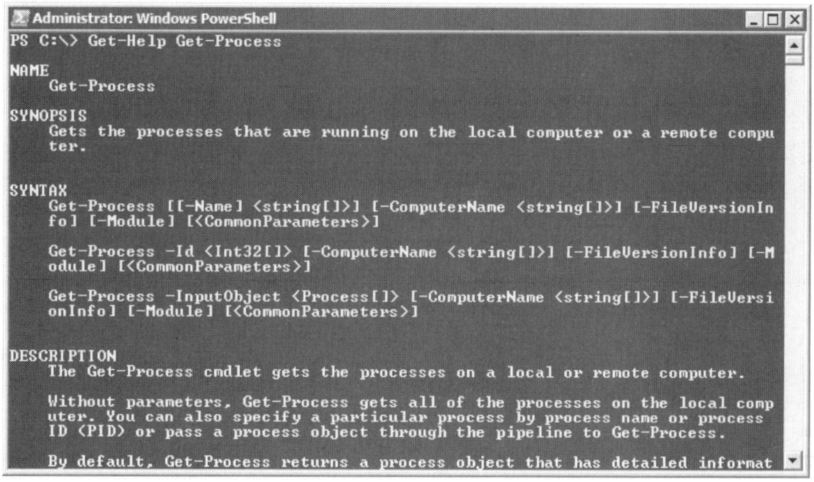

Various types of help are available for cmdlets. If you don't want to read through
a large screen full of text just to find out the syntax for a particular command, you
can add the `-Examples` parameter to the `Get-Help` cmdlet. This will only display
the examples for the cmdlet. Figure 1.9 demonstrates the output of `Get-Help` with
the `-Examples` parameter.

FIGURE 1.9   Using `Get-Help` with the `-Examples` parameter

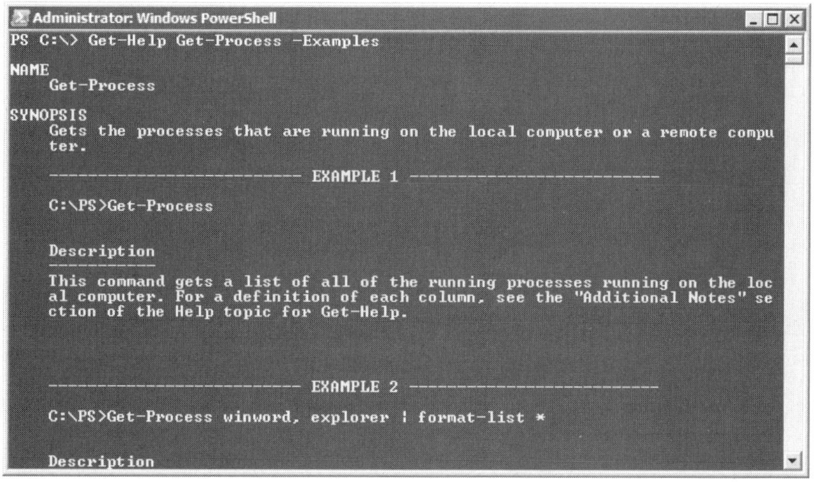

Table 1.3 outlines the various parameters available for use with the `Get-Help` cmdlet.

TABLE 1.3   Parameters for the `Get-Help` Cmdlet

Parameter	Description
-Examples	Displays various examples that demonstrate the use of the cmdlet
-Detailed	Displays detailed information on the cmdlet, including a description of each parameter that is accepted
-Full	Displays the full output of the technical information for the cmdlet

Format the Output of a Command

Sometimes, when you run a command, the output is difficult to read or you don't get all the information you wanted. You can change the output of the cmdlets that you run in various ways. This is accomplished using cmdlets beginning with `Format-`.

There are multiple `Format-` cmdlets that will format the output into multiple views. To use them, you simply pipeline the output from one cmdlet into the appropriate format cmdlet. For example, if you want to view the running processes as a list, you can pipeline the output to the `Format-List` cmdlet:

```
Get-Process | Format-List
```

To view the list of available format cmdlets, you can run the `Get-Command` cmdlet:

```
PS C:\> Get-Command format-*


CommandType     Name                    Definition
-----------     ----                    ----------
Cmdlet          Format-Custom           Format-Custom [[-Property] <...
Cmdlet          Format-List             Format-List [[-Property] <Ob...
Cmdlet          Format-Table            Format-Table [[-Property] <O...
Cmdlet          Format-Wide             Format-Wide [[-Property] <Ob...
```

Test What a Command Will Do

There may be times when you just want to see the output of a particular command to make sure you have it right, without making the actual change to the system. This is especially useful when you're writing scripts, as covered in the next section, "Script Administration Tasks." To find out what is affected by a command without actually running it, you can use the `-WhatIf` parameter.

Perhaps you're trying to figure out if you have the syntax of a cmdlet right, but you don't want to accidently run the cmdlet if you happen to get it right. In this case, you can use the `-Confirm` parameter. Doing so adds a confirmation prompt to your command that requires additional input by the executor before it continues.

Script Administration Tasks

In addition to offering a robust environment for executing cmdlets, PowerShell also provides an integrated environment for writing scripts. Like one-liners, scripts allow you to execute a series of commands all at once, without having to enter each command individually. For example, if you have a list of commands that you run every time a server is promoted to a domain controller, you can put those commands into a script. Then, the next time you install Active Directory on a server, you run the script once instead of executing each command.

Scripts are also useful if you want to apply some logic to a series of commands. For example, you could write a script to determine the last time your users logged in and then disable the accounts and move them to a different Organizational Unit (OU) if it's been over 90 days. In this case, the script would make the decisions about what to do with the user accounts.

Create PowerShell Scripts

You can create a script using any standard text editor that you're comfortable with. However, there are advantages to using the built-in PowerShell ISE discussed earlier. If you have the ISE available to you, it makes sense to use it rather than a standard text editor.

When you create scripts, you type in the commands just as you would if you were typing them directly into the shell. You have the option of inserting comments into your scripts by placing a pound symbol (#) in front of the comment, as shown in the following snippet:

```
# This is a comment.
Get-Process
```

In PowerShell v2, you also have the ability to use block comments. This allows you to comment out large portions of text in your script files. To use a block comment, you start the comment with <# and end it with #>. Everything in between is considered a comment, as demonstrated in the following snippet:

```
<#
This is a block comment.
The next line of code will execute the Get-Process cmdlet
which will display a list of running processes on the screen
#>
Get-Process
```

When you're done creating your script, save it with a `.ps1` extension, and the script will be executable in PowerShell.

Execution Policy

With great power comes great responsibility. Being the robust scripting environment that PowerShell is, its capabilities could potentially be misused. There has been a lot of scripting misuse in the past with other scripting languages. Multiple vulnerabilities, viruses, and malware have used script-based exploits to engrain themselves on users' machines. To prevent this from happening in PowerShell, an execution policy defines if and how scripts can run.

By default, the execution policy is configured to not allow any scripts to run. This security enhancement is meant as a failsafe to prevent users from accidently executing malicious code and isn't intended as a fully vetted security architecture. Users can easily overcome the limitations of the execution policy by manually typing the script into PowerShell line by line or by copying and pasting it in.

You can use six different settings for the PowerShell execution policy. Table 1.4 describes each of these settings.

TABLE 1.4   **Execution Policy Settings**

Setting	Description
`Restricted` (Default)	Prevents all scripts from executing.
`AllSigned`	Allows only scripts that are signed with a trusted certificate.
`RemoteSigned`	Allows scripts written locally to execute, but scripts downloaded from a nonlocal source (such as a website or email) must be signed with a trusted certificate.
`Unrestricted`	Allows unsigned scripts to execute but warns the user about scripts that were not created from the local machine.
`Bypass`	No scripts are blocked, and no warnings are generated.
`Undefined`	No execution policy is specifically defined.

You can determine what the current execution policy is by running the `Get-ExecutionPolicy` cmdlet:

```
PS C:\> Get-ExecutionPolicy
Restricted
```

If you're running scripts that you wrote for computer administration, then using the `RemoteSigned` setting will be ideal in most cases. However, you do have the option of signing the scripts that you create for additional security. If you're going to be using PowerShell scripts for Active Directory administration and storing the scripts on a network share or somewhere that other people may have write access to, then it's a good idea to sign the scripts. Signing the scripts will ensure that no one can tamper with them. If you choose to sign the scripts that you write locally, then using the `AllSigned` execution policy is recommended.

To configure the execution policy setting, use the `Set-ExecutionPolicy` cmdlet:

```
Set-ExecutionPolicy RemoteSigned
```

Script Signing

When you sign a script, you put a digital signature on the script that can be traced back to the owner of the signature. The script is run through a mathematical algorithm that generates a unique value (called a *hash*) that is based on the contents of the script. If the script is changed, a different hash value is generated. The process that is executing the script can run the script through the same algorithm that was used to sign it, and if the resulting hash value is different than the one the script is signed with, the process knows the script has been tampered with.

This hash value isn't stored in plain text, though, because someone could potentially change the script and then change the hash value to reflect the script's new hash. To prevent this from happening, the hash value is encrypted with a public/private key pair. The idea behind a public/private key pair is that data can be encrypted with one of the keys and can only be decrypted using the other. When a user obtains a Public Key Infrastructure (PKI) certificate, two keys are associated with the certificate: the public key and the private key. The private key is only available to the owner of the certificate. In fact, most of the time, this key is automatically generated and stored in a protected manner in the local certificate store of the computer. The public key, however, is usually given to other people in a publically available certificate.

To illustrate this, consider two people, Alice and Bob. Alice created a script, and Bob is using it. When Alice signs the script that she created, the script's hash gets encrypted with Alice's private key. When Bob uses the script, he decrypts the hash with Alice's public key before checking whether the hash is valid. By doing this, Bob is assured that Alice really created the script, because she is the only person who has her private key. Bob doesn't manually validate Alice's script against her public key, however. This process is handled by PowerShell when Bob attempts to run the script.

To be able to sign scripts, you first need to obtain a code-signing certificate with a private key. This certificate must be trusted by the computer that the script is executing on in order for it to be considered valid. There are a few different ways that you can obtain a trusted certificate:

Use an Internal Public Key Infrastructure   Some organizations have their own certificate authorities (CAs) for creating and validating PKI certificates. If your organization has its own CA, you can probably request a code-signing certificate from it. When using an internal PKI, you run a good chance that your certificate will be trusted by the computers your PowerShell scripts might run on. However, this isn't always the case, because the trust configuration is heavily dependent on how the organization configured the PKI.

Use a Publically Trusted Certificate Authority   If you don't have an internal PKI, then you can buy a trusted certificate from a well-known Internet CA such as VeriSign or Go Daddy. Many of these CAs are trusted by default in Windows. Therefore, if you obtain a code-signing certificate from one of them, you'll almost be guaranteed that the certificate is trusted by any computer on which you run the PowerShell script. The downside to this method is that it's going to cost you money.

Use a Self-Signed Certificate   You can also obtain a self-signed certificate, which means that you create the certificate yourself. The drawback to self-signed certificates is that the certificate is only trusted by the computer on which it was created. This means that if you create a script and sign it with a self-signed certificate that was issued by one computer, the script will only be considered valid on that computer. You can get around this, however, by adding the self-signed certificate to the list of trusted certificates on your other computers. If you decide to use a self-signed certificate for scripts that you use for Active Directory administration, you should ensure that the self-signed certificate is trusted by each domain controller. The good news is that you can do this rather easily with a Group Policy Object (GPO).

To create your own self-signed certificate signing PowerShell scripts, you can use the `makecert.exe` utility included in the Windows SDK. You can download this SDK from `http://msdn.microsoft.com/en-us/windows/bb980924.aspx`. After you install the SDK, use the following command to create a self-signed certificate:

```
makecert.exe -r -pe -n "CN=PowerShell Signing Cert" -ss MY -a sha1 -eku ↵
1.3.6.1.5.5.7.3.3
```

You can then run the following PowerShell command to verify that the certificate was successfully created:

```
PS C:\> Get-ChildItem cert:\currentuser\my -codesigning
    Directory: Microsoft.PowerShell.Security\Certificate::currentuser\my
Thumbprint                                Subject
----------                                -------
DA747C75B468FCF2701FC844799B3DCE44B5F512  CN=PowerShell Signing Cert
```

Now that you've obtained your certificate, you can use the `Set-AuthenticodeSignature` cmdlet to sign your PowerShell script. You'll need to pass the certificate object as a parameter in the cmdlet. You can do this by assigning the certificate to a variable and then referencing the variable in the `Set-AuthenticodeSignature` cmdlet. For example, if you wanted to sign a script called `UpdateSiteTopology.ps1`, you would run the following commands:

```
PS C:\> $certificate = Get-ChildItem cert:\currentuser\my -codesigning
PS C:\> Set-AuthenticodeSignature UpdateSiteTopology.ps1 $certificate
```

After you sign the script, you'll notice that a signature block has been added to the end of the file. This block represents the encrypted hash. If you modify the script, be sure to re-sign it so this encrypted hash value is updated.

Use Variables in a Script

You could write scripts to execute one command after another, but PowerShell scripts can be more than mere substitutes for batch files. In order to take your scripting to the next level and write more powerful scripts, you need to learn some of the basics of scripting, starting with variables.

Variables are nothing more than a way to temporarily store data for later use. In PowerShell, variables are easy to work with because they can hold any type of data, such as text, numbers, or whole objects.

NOTE Some other development languages require you to define what kind of data your variables will hold up front, but this isn't the case with PowerShell.

Variables in PowerShell all begin with a dollar sign ($). For example, if you wanted to create a variable and hold a sentence in it, you would use the following PowerShell command:

```
$MySentence = "Active Directory Rules!"
```

This example stores the text string "Active Directory Rules!" into the variable called $MySentence. You can name variables anything you want, as long as they begin with a dollar sign. Here's another example, except this time we'll store a number:

```
$MyInteger = 1234567890
```

Notice that we didn't use the quotation marks this time. You only use quotation marks for text strings—you have to use quotation marks for text so PowerShell knows you're using text and not trying to run a PowerShell cmdlet instead.

You can store data other than text and numbers in variables. For example, the following command is valid in PowerShell:

```
$DirectoryListing = dir
```

This command runs the PowerShell command dir, which lists the files and folders in the current directory and stores the output in the variable called $DirectoryListing. $DirectoryListing doesn't contain the text of the output from the dir command. Instead, $DirectoryListing stores each of the files and folders as objects with their own properties. This allows you to do some interesting things. For example, you could go through the file and folder objects in the $DirectoryListing variable and rename them.

Variables can contain many types of objects. The type of object that is stored in the variable depends on the output of the command that is populating the variable. The dir command we used in the example works with files and folders, so it stored file and folder objects. If you used another command, such as Get-Service, it would store the objects that represent the computer's services and their associated properties into the variable.

You can see what variables are currently being used by running the Get-Variable cmdlet as shown in Figure 1.10.

FIGURE 1.10   Listing the currently used variables

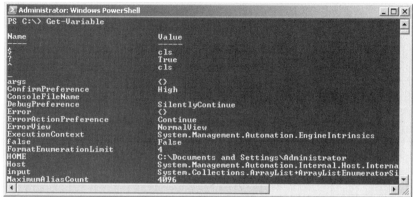

In addition to variables that you define yourself, there are special variables called *shell variables* built into PowerShell. Shell variables are automatically created by PowerShell. An example of a shell variable is $null, which always means that something has no value. For example, if you had an Active Directory user object and you wanted to clear the Description attribute, you could set the Description property to $null. This can be accomplished with the following command:

```
Set-ADUser "Lincoln Alexander" -Description $null
```

There are many other shell variables in PowerShell. Table 1.5 lists some of the more common shell variables you'll encounter.

TABLE 1.5   Common Shell Variables

Variable	Description
$_	Refers to the current object that is being processed in a pipeline or a loop.
$Error	When an error is encountered in the command, the error is stored here.
$Home	The home directory of the current user.
$true	Represents the condition True.
$false	Represents the condition False.
$null	Represents a null entry, meaning the property is blank.

Add Logic to a Script

Logic allows your scripts to do things to the variables you're using and make decisions about what to do. You need to know two basic logic concepts in order to write PowerShell scripts: loops and conditionals.

Loops

Loops allow you to go through a collection of items and do something to each item. For example, if you run the Get-Process cmdlet on one of your servers, PowerShell displays a list of processes that are currently running on that server. However, you can assign the output of Get-Process to a variable, using the following command:

```
$RunningProcesses = Get-Process
```

In the $RunningProcesses variable, each process is represented by a different object. You could loop through the objects in this variable and do something to each object, such as display the process ID of each process. One way to accomplish this is with the ForEach-Object cmdlet:

```
$RunningProcesses | ForEach-Object { Write-Host $_.Name : $_.Id }
```

By piping the $RunningProcesses variable into the ForEach-Object cmdlet, the ForEach-Object cmdlet can cycle through all the objects. The command inside the curly brackets ({ . . . }) is executed for each of the objects processed by the loop. You may recognize the $_ variable from Table 1.5. The $_ variable references the current object that the loop is processing. So when $_.Id is used, you're working with the Id property on each of the objects in the variable. In this case, we're calling the Write-Host cmdlet to output the Name and Id of each process to the screen.

Another type of loop you can use is Do. The Do loop allows you to loop until a specific condition is met. There are two types of Do loops: Do . . . While and Do . . . Until.

In a Do . . . While loop, a block of script code is executed over and over again as long as something is happening. For example, consider the following script code snippet:

```
$counter = 0
Do
{
    Write-Host "Current Number: $counter"
    $counter++;
} While ($counter -lt 3)
```

If you were to run this code in a PowerShell script, the output would read

```
Current Number: 0
Current Number: 1
Current Number: 2
```

The Do statement loops through the code inside the curly brackets for as long as the condition specified in the While statement is valid. In this example, the Do loop will keep going as long as the $counter variable is less than 3 (-lt 3). After $counter reaches 3, the loop stops, and therefore only the numbers 0, 1, and 2 are displayed. With a Do ... While loop, the code inside the curly brackets is executed first, and then the condition determining whether it should keep going is evaluated.

On the other hand, a Do ... Until loop processes the condition first. To understand this, we'll turn the previous code into a Do ... Until loop:

```
$counter = 0
Do
{
    Write-Host "Current Number: $counter"
    $counter++;
} Until ($counter -gt 3)
```

This time, the Do loop will continue to process until $counter is greater than 3. Before the code in the Do loop is processed even once, the condition is evaluated to make sure $counter is still 3 or less. The following is the output if this code is run in a script:

```
Current Number: 0
Current Number: 1
Current Number: 2
Current Number: 3
```

After the script displays that the current number is 3, $counter is incremented to 4. This causes the condition ($counter -gt 3) to be met because 4 is greater than 3, and the Do loop is no longer processed.

Conditionals

In addition to loops, you can use conditionals to make decisions inside your scripts. One conditional that you'll probably use often is If ... Else. The If statement tests whether something is true. If it is, it executes some code. If not, the If statement can either end or test to see if something else is true. For example, consider the following If statement:

```
$RunningProcesses = Get-Process
$RunningProcesses | ForEach-Object {
  $MemUsageMB = $_.PrivateMemorySize / 1024 / 1024
  If ($MemUsageMB -lt 50)
  {
    Write-Host $_.Name ": Using less than 50MB of memory"
  }
  Else
  {
    Write-Host $_.Name ": Using " $MemUsageMB "MB of memory"
  }
}
```

If you execute this script, the output lists every running process and, if it's using more than 50 MB of memory, displays the amount of memory that the process is using. The ForEach-Object command loops through all the processes. For each process, the If statement is evaluated. The If statement checks to see whether the amount of memory is less than 50. If so, it writes to the screen that the process is using less than 50 MB of memory. If the process is using more than 50 MB, the Else statement is executed, and instead, the script outputs to the screen the name of the process and the amount of memory that it's using.

The -lt parameter indicates that the If statement is checking whether $MemUsageMB is less than 50. In typical programming languages, this is usually accomplished with the symbol <. Instead, PowerShell uses the comparison operators listed in Table 1.6.

In addition to the If statement, you can use the Where-Object command. Where-Object evaluates the objects that are piped into it and filters out everything that doesn't meet the expression you set. For example, you can use the following Where-Object command in a script to filter out all processes that are using less than 50 MB of memory:

```
Get-Process | Where-Object { $_.PrivateMemorySize / 1024 / 1024 -gt 50 }
 | ForEach-Object { Write-Host $_.Name }
```

In this command, the Where-Object cmdlet is passing through every process that is using more than 50 MB of memory. The processes that are passed through the filter are piped into the ForEach-Object cmdlet so they can be further processed, and the information is displayed on the screen.

TABLE 1.6   PowerShell Comparison Operators

Comparison Operator	Description	Example
`-eq`	Determines if expression1 is equal to expression2	`[PS] C:\> "Active Directory" -eq "AD"` `False`
`-ne`	Determines if expression1 isn't equal to expression2	`[PS] C:\> "Active Directory" -ne "AD"` `True`
`-gt`	Determines if expression1 is greater than expression2	`[PS] C:\> 1000 -gt 50` `True`
`-ge`	Determines if expression1 is greater than or equal to expression2	`[PS] C:\> 1000 -ge 1000` `True`
`-lt`	Determines if expression1 is less than expression2	`[PS] C:\> 1000 -lt 50` `False`
`-le`	Determines if expression1 is less than or equal to expression2	`[PS] C:\> 1000 -le 1000` `True`

`-like`	Determines if expression1 is equal to expression2 using the wildcard character (*)	`[PS] C:\> "Active Directory" ↵`
		`-like "Act*"`
		`True`

`-notlike`	Determines if expression1 isn't equal to expression2 using the wildcard character (*)	`[PS] C:\> "Active Directory" ↵`
		`-notlike "Ac*ry"`
		`False`

`-match`	Uses a regular expression to determine if expression1 matches expression2	`[PS] C:\> "Active Directory" ↵`
		`-match "[abc]"`
		`True`

`-notmatch`	Uses a regular expression to determine if expression1 doesn't match expression2	`[PS] C:\> "Active Directory" ↵`
		`-notmatch "[abc]"`
		`False`

`-contains`	Determines if a specific item is in a group of items	`[PS] C:\> "AD DS", "AD LDS" ↵`
		`-contains "AD DS"`
		`True`

`-notcontains`	Determines if a specific item isn't in a group of items	`[PS] C:\> "AD DS", "AD LDS" ↵`
		`-notcontains "AD FS"`
		`True`

Accept Script Parameters

When you write a PowerShell script, there are times when you may want the user to feed some information into the script. There are two ways to handle this. The first way is to allow the user to edit the script and add their information directly. If your script was signed, however, this will break the signature. The second way is for your script to accept command parameters.

Command parameters can be passed into the script when the user runs the script's command in PowerShell. For example, the following command uses a parameter to tell the Get-Process cmdlet which computer to execute on:

```
Get-Process -ComputerName BAL-DC01
```

You'll be working with two types of parameters in your PowerShell scripts: positional parameters and named parameters. Positional parameters are used based on where they show up in the command. For example, you could have a positional parameter specified that uses the first parameter in the command as the -FirstName parameter. The user can choose to run the script in one of the following ways. Both are functionally equivalent:

```
MyScript.ps1 -FirstName Brenna
MyScript.ps1 Brenna
```

Use Named Parameters

Named parameters, on the other hand, require that the user indicates the parameter name before specifying the value. If the FirstName parameter in the previous example was a named parameter, the following command would be invalid:

```
MyScript.ps1 Brenna
```

When configuring your scripts to accept parameters, you must include some code at the beginning of your script consisting of the keyword param, the type of parameter (for example, string), and the variable to which the parameter will be passed. By default, the name of the variable becomes the name of the parameter, but without the dollar sign that prefixes the variable name. Consider the following parameter declaration in a script:

```
param([string]$FirstName)
```

This specifies that the script will accept a string parameter called -FirstName that gets passed into the $FirstName variable inside the script. When the script is run, the user executes it with the following command:

```
MyScript.ps1 -FirstName Brenna
```

Use Positional Parameters

When using a parameter as a positional parameter, you need to specify the parameter's position in the parameter declaration. Expanding on the previous example, the following command declares the FirstName parameter as a positional parameter that is accepted as the first parameter in the script's command:

```
param([Parameter(Position=0)][string]$FirstName)
```

When the user runs the script, the FirstName parameter can be specified as either a positional or a named parameter. Because we included the name of the parameter in addition to its position, both commands are valid.

Other Parameter Settings

You should be aware of a couple of other parameter settings. Optionally, you can specify a default value for a parameter in case the user decides not to pass a value in. The following parameter declaration assigns a default value of Ben to the FirstName parameter:

```
param([string]$FirstName = "Ben")
```

You can also decide whether a parameter is mandatory for the script or whether it's optional. To declare a parameter as mandatory, set the mandatory property to $true in the script's parameter declaration. The following example sets the FirstName parameter as mandatory:

```
param([Parameter(Mandatory=$true)][string]$FirstName)
```

There are many other properties that you can set for a parameter as well. Table 1.7 describes some of the common properties that you might use when writing your PowerShell Scripts.

TABLE 1.7   Parameter Properties

Property Name	Purpose
Mandatory	A Boolean property that determines whether the parameter is mandatory in order for the script to run.
Position	An integer property that identifies the position in which a positional parameter should appear.
ValueFromPipeline	A Boolean property that indicates whether this parameter can accept an object that is pipelined in from another script or cmdlet.
ValueFromPipelineByPropertyName	A Boolean property that indicates whether this parameter can accept data being pipelined in from another command. The difference between this and the ValueFromPipeline property is that this property specifies that the parameter accepts a single parameter from the pipelined command. The ValueFromPipeline property applies to an entire object. If this property is used, the parameter that is accepted from the pipelined command is the parameter that uses the same name defined in this command.
HelpMessage	A String property that allows you to specify a help message for a mandatory parameter. If the user runs the script and doesn't include the mandatory parameter, this help message is displayed.

Use Functions in a Script

Functions give you the ability to take a block of script code and assign a name to it. There are quite a few benefits to using functions inside your scripts. First, functions allow you to organize scripts into executable chunks, which makes the scripts easier to edit and troubleshoot. By isolating a block of code into a function, you can make sure that particular block of code works apart from the rest of your script code. Another benefit of functions is that they sandbox the scope of your scripts. A variable that is declared and used inside a function is only valid to that function. And finally, functions let you write a block of code once and call it as many times as you like, making your script code more reusable. Functions are very helpful, so you'll notice that throughout this book, we make generous use of them in our sample scripts.

Define Functions

To declare a block of code as a function, you can place the code between opening and closing curly brackets and prefix it with the following declaration:

```
Function <FunctionName> (<Parameters>)
```

For example, if you were to create a function called `DisplayMessage` that displays "Hello, Ken!" it would look like the following:

```
Function DisplayMessage ()
{
    Write-Output "Hello, Ken!"
}
```

In this function, the message that is displayed is hard-coded. When you call the `DisplayMessage` function, it will display the same message every time. You can modify this behavior by configuring a parameter that the user can pass in. There are two different ways to define parameters in functions. If you've developed scripts or applications in other languages, then you're probably familiar with defining parameters in functions using the parentheses in function declarations. Here's an example of how this might look:

```
Function DisplayMessage($name)
{
    Write-Output "Hello, $name!"
}
```

This function allows you to pass in the name that you want displayed in the message. In the parentheses following the name of the function, we specified a variable called $name. By doing this, we told the function that the first parameter that we send to it will be kept in the $name variable. You can also add additional variables for other parameters. When doing so, you need to separate them inside the parentheses with commas.

You can also specify parameters on functions using the same method that we described for using parameters in scripts. Refer to the section "Accept Script Parameters" earlier in this chapter to learn how to use this method. When you're defining parameters on functions with this method, you follow the same process, but your parameter declaration happens on the first line of the function rather than the first line of the script. For example, the following function uses this method and is equivalent to the `DisplayMessage` function that we defined earlier:

```
Function DisplayMessage
{
        param([string]$name)
        Write-Output "Hello, $name!"
}
```

Call Functions

If you want to use a function that you've defined in your script, you have to call the function. To call the function, you simply need to type in the name of the function, similar to how you might execute a cmdlet in PowerShell. To call the DisplayMessage function, you can use the following line in a script:

```
DisplayMessage "Brenna"
```

When this line of the script executes, the DisplayMessage function is called and "Brenna" is passed in as a parameter. The function will then execute and output the message "Hello, Brenna!" One important thing to note is that in order to call a function, the function must be defined at the beginning of the script. If you attempt to call a function before it has been defined, you'll receive an error because the function doesn't exist yet.

The sample script in Listing 1.1 puts these concepts together so you can better understand how to use a function. This script creates and calls the DisplayMessage function used as an example throughout this section.

LISTING 1.1: **SayHello.ps1**

```
## File Name: SayHello.ps1
## Description:
## Demonstrates the use of functions by outputting a simple
## hello message.
##
Function DisplayMessage_Paren($name)
{
    Write-Host "Hello, $name!"
}
Function DisplayMessage_Param
{
    param([string]$name)
    Write-Host "Hello, $name!"
}
Write-Host "Calling the function that uses parentheses..."
DisplayMessage_Paren "Lincoln"
Write-Host
Write-Host "Calling the function that uses param..."
DisplayMessage_Param "Nora"
```

Run a Script Outside of PowerShell

When you write a `.ps1` script, you can run that script anytime you're in a PowerShell session. But you can also run scripts without opening PowerShell manually. The process is similar to running a batch file outside of the command prompt. You can double-click the script, and PowerShell will be automatically opened, your script will run, and then PowerShell will close.

By default, when you double-click a PowerShell `.ps1` script file, the file opens in Notepad. You can use the following procedures to launch the file in PowerShell:

1. Browse to the PowerShell `.ps1` script file that you want to launch.

2. Right-click the file, and select Run With PowerShell from the drop-down menu as shown in Figure 1.11.

FIGURE 1.11   Launching a PowerShell script outside of PowerShell

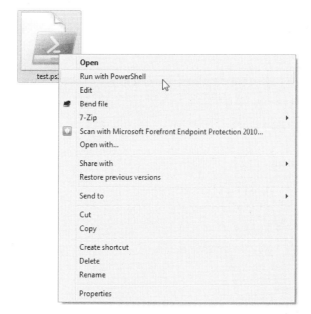

The PowerShell script will launch and run in PowerShell. PowerShell will be closed when the script completes.

You can also change the file association to PowerShell instead of Notepad. This will ensure that when you double-click the script, it opens in PowerShell automatically.

To change the `.ps1` file association, do the following:

1. Open the Control Panel, and run the Default Programs applet.

2. When the Default Programs applet launches, select the option Associate A File Type Or Protocol With A Program.

3. Scroll down to the `.ps1` file extension, and click it to select it. Click the Change Program button above the list of file types, as shown in Figure 1.12.

FIGURE 1.12   Changing the default program for PowerShell scripts

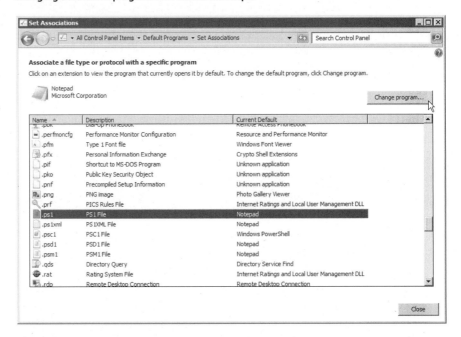

4. When the Open With dialog opens, click the Browse button to locate the PowerShell executable. This executable is stored at `C:\Windows\System32\WindowsPowerShell\v1.0\powershell.exe`. Select the `powershell.exe` file, and click Open to choose it.

5. Click OK in the Open With dialog to choose Windows PowerShell and set the file association.

6. Close the Default Programs applet and any remaining windows. Now, when you double-click a `.ps1` file, it will launch with PowerShell instead of Notepad.

Schedule a Script to Run Automatically

Sometimes you'll want to create a script and have it run repeatedly at a specified interval. Windows has a powerful Task Scheduler service that allows you to set up programs to launch in a very flexible manner. If you want to schedule a script to run at a later time or after a specified interval, you can schedule the script to run with the Task Scheduler. In order to execute a PowerShell script via Task Scheduler, you need to associate your PowerShell `.ps1` script file with the `PowerShell.exe` program or have the scheduler execute the command `PowerShell.exe MyScript.ps1` to launch the script in the scheduled task.

There are multiple ways to schedule a task with the Windows Task Scheduler. The easiest way is to use the Task Scheduler snap-in. In this example, you'll use the Task Scheduler to create a task that does the following things:

- ► Runs a script every night that collects user statistics to determine who has not logged on in the past 90 days. In this example, the script is named `GetLogonStats.ps1`. This is a script that we created ourselves; it isn't installed with Active Directory. In the fake script, the statistics are saved in the file `C:\Stats\LogonStats.log`.

- ► Emails the statistics file to the mail-enabled distribution group called `ADTeam@contoso.com`.

To create the scheduled task, follow these steps:

1. Click the Start menu, and select Administrative Tools ➢ Task Scheduler. The Task Scheduler launches.

2. In the Action Pane on the right side of the Task Scheduler snap-in, choose the option Create Task. The Create Task dialog box opens.

3. On the General tab, give the task a name, and choose the option Run Whether User Is Logged On Or Not. Set the account that you want the script to run under using the Change User Or Group button. Ensure that the account running the script has the appropriate permissions. Figure 1.13 shows these options.

4. Click the Triggers tab, and click the New button to create a new trigger for the task. Set this task to run every night at 1:00 a.m.

FIGURE 1.13   Selecting the appropriate permissions for scheduling a script

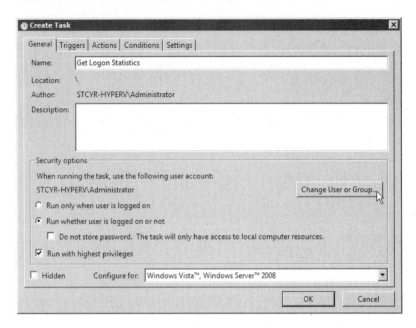

5. Click the Actions tab, and click the New button to create a new action for this task to perform. In the Action drop-down list, choose Start A Program. In the Program/script text box, type **powershell.exe**. In the Add Arguments text box, type the location of the script:

   ```
   C:\Scripts\GetLogonStats.ps1
   ```

   These options are shown in Figure 1.14.

6. Click the OK button in the Edit Action dialog.

7. When you're back on the Action tab, click the New button to add another action. In the New Action dialog select Send An E-mail from the Action list. Fill out the options for the email message. Type **C:\Stats\LogonStats .log** in the Attachment text box, and enter your SMTP server name in the SMTP Server text box. Click OK to add the action.

8. Back in the Create Task dialog, click OK to create the task. You may be prompted to enter the password for the account under which the task will run.

FIGURE 1.14   Selecting the appropriate action for running a PowerShell script

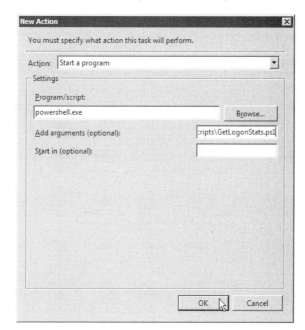

Understand How PowerShell and Active Directory Work Together

Now that you have a basic understanding of PowerShell, let's take a closer look at how Active Directory and PowerShell work together. First we're going to look at the different ways you can interact with Active Directory using PowerShell, and then we'll discuss what you have to do to configure your environment so you can use the scripts and techniques discussed in this book.

Interact with Active Directory Using PowerShell

Active Directory provides several different protocols and methods for users to interact with it. Traditionally, when you used other scripting and programming languages to interact with Active Directory, you had a choice of techniques. In PowerShell, there are two ways to go about it: using the Active Directory Services Interface or using the Active Directory module. Depending on your Active Directory implementation, you may be limited to only one of the two ways.

Use the Active Directory Services Interface

Prior to Windows Server 2008 R2, if you wanted to manage Active Directory with PowerShell, you were limited to using the Active Directory Services Interface (ADSI). ADSI is a set of Common Object Model (COM) interfaces that allow you to programmatically work with directory services such as Active Directory. ADSI is very flexible, and once you get the hang of it, it's actually quite easy to work with. However, there is a learning curve involved, and sometimes your results can be inconsistent depending on the environment you're working in.

In Windows Server 2008 R2, you're provided with the Active Directory module, which simplifies a lot of tasks for which you previously needed ADSI. Even though there are many new Active Directory cmdlets, ADSI will still be needed for more complex tasks that you'll want to perform. Therefore, a solid understanding of how to work with ADSI is necessary.

When you work with ADSI to manage objects in Active Directory, you'll be doing one of the following things: reading an object, updating an object, creating an object, or deleting an object. All of ADSI's functionality revolves around these operations.

Retrieve an Object

The first step to any ADSI task is to bind to the object that you're working with. For example, if you want to read a user's logon name, then you first need to bind to the user's object. You can use ADSI to bind to an object using the following PowerShell command:

```
$user = [ADSI]"LDAP://cn=Nora Shea,cn=users,dc=contoso,dc=com"
```

In this example, the user variable is being populated with Nora Shea's user object. In this command, the distinguished name of Nora's user object (cn=Nora Shea, cn=users,dc=contoso,dc=com) is used to identify which object to retrieve. By specifying LDAP:// at the beginning of the path, you tell ADSI that the provider is an LDAP-capable directory service such as Active Directory. It's important to note that this provider name is case sensitive. If you used ldap:// instead of LDAP://, you would get an error. The [ADSI] statement at the beginning of the command is called a *type adapter*. Its purpose is to ensure that the object retrieved conforms to a specific object type, which ensures consistency across the objects you work with. By specifying ADSI as the type adapter, you're telling PowerShell that the object is a System.DirectoryServices.DirectoryEntry object. This means the object will have the properties and methods that all DirectoryEntry objects have. In fact, if you pipe the user object into the Get-Member cmdlet, you can retrieve a listing of the object's properties and methods:

```
PS C:\> $user | Get-Member


    TypeName: System.DirectoryServices.DirectoryEntry

Name                      MemberType Definition
----                      ---------- ----------
ConvertDNWithBinaryToString CodeMethod static string ConvertDNWithBinaryToSt...
ConvertLargeIntegerToInt64  CodeMethod static long ConvertLargeIntegerToInt6...
accountExpires            Property   System.DirectoryServices.PropertyValu...
badPasswordTime           Property   System.DirectoryServices.PropertyValu...
badPwdCount               Property   System.DirectoryServices.PropertyValu...
cn                        Property   System.DirectoryServices.PropertyValu...
codePage                  Property   System.DirectoryServices.PropertyValu...
countryCode               Property   System.DirectoryServices.PropertyValu...
description               Property   System.DirectoryServices.PropertyValu...
distinguishedName         Property   System.DirectoryServices.PropertyValu...
dSCorePropagationData     Property   System.DirectoryServices.PropertyValu...
instanceType              Property   System.DirectoryServices.PropertyValu...
isCriticalSystemObject    Property   System.DirectoryServices.PropertyValu...
lastLogoff                Property   System.DirectoryServices.PropertyValu...
lastLogon                 Property   System.DirectoryServices.PropertyValu...
lastLogonTimestamp        Property   System.DirectoryServices.PropertyValu...
logonCount                Property   System.DirectoryServices.PropertyValu...
logonHours                Property   System.DirectoryServices.PropertyValu...
memberOf                  Property   System.DirectoryServices.PropertyValu...
name                      Property   System.DirectoryServices.PropertyValu...
nTSecurityDescriptor      Property   System.DirectoryServices.PropertyValu...
objectCategory            Property   System.DirectoryServices.PropertyValu...
objectClass               Property   System.DirectoryServices.PropertyValu...
objectGUID                Property   System.DirectoryServices.PropertyValu...
objectSid                 Property   System.DirectoryServices.PropertyValu...
primaryGroupID            Property   System.DirectoryServices.PropertyValu...
pwdLastSet                Property   System.DirectoryServices.PropertyValu...
sAMAccountName            Property   System.DirectoryServices.PropertyValu...
sAMAccountType            Property   System.DirectoryServices.PropertyValu...
```

Administering Service Delivery

PART I

userAccountControl	Property	System.DirectoryServices.PropertyValu...
uSNChanged	Property	System.DirectoryServices.PropertyValu...
uSNCreated	Property	System.DirectoryServices.PropertyValu...
whenChanged	Property	System.DirectoryServices.PropertyValu...
whenCreated	Property	System.DirectoryServices.PropertyValu...

You can work with any of those properties in PowerShell by referencing the object, followed by a dot, followed by the property name. For example, if you want to view the logon name of the user, run the following command in PowerShell and press Enter:

```
PS C:\> $user.samAccountName
```

Change Object Properties

After you bind to the object, you have a copy of it in PowerShell. If you were to change any of the properties, it would change your local copy. For example, if you change the user's first name to Charlie, the change is made on the PowerShell object but not in Active Directory:

```
PS C:\> $user.givenName = "Charlie"
```

In order to make the change take effect in Active Directory, you need to call the CommitChanges method. When you call this method, PowerShell commits the changes that you made on its local copy of the object into Active Directory. The following command ensures that the user's object is updated in Active Directory:

```
PS C:\> $user.CommitChanges()
```

The parentheses after the method name indicate that you're calling a method rather than referencing a property. Properties only contain data that you can read or write, but a method actually executes some code. Because you know that the user object is being used in PowerShell as a System.DirectoryServices.DirectoryEntry object, you can see a listing of all the methods this object supports by looking at Microsoft's documentation online: http://msdn.microsoft.com/en-us/library/system.directoryservices.directoryentry_methods.aspx.

Create New Objects

As shown earlier, when you want to work with an object via ADSI, you first have to bind to it. But what do you do if the object doesn't exist yet? Consider the situation where you want to create an object in Active Directory. In this case, you'll need to bind to the parent of the object that you creating. When creating a user, for example, the parent will either be an organizational unit (OU) or a container. Assuming that you're creating a user in the Users container, you bind using the following command:

```
PS C:\> $container = [ADSI]"LDAP://cn=users,dc=contoso,dc=com"
```

After you bind to the container, you can create the child object by calling the Create method. For this example, you'll pass in the type of the child object being created (user) and the common name of the object (cn=Nora Shea):

```
PS C:\> $user = $container.Create("user", "cn=Nora Shea")
```

In a manner similar to changing an object's properties, this user is only created locally in PowerShell's memory. Therefore, you need to call the same CommitChanges method as you did previously when you were modifying a property. This instructs ADSI to write the changes into Active Directory:

```
PS C:\> $user.CommitChanges()
```

If you were to now look in Active Directory, you would see Nora Shea's account created and in a disabled state. You'll learn how to work with users in more detail in Chapter 6, "Administering User and Group Accounts."

Delete Objects

Deleting an object requires an approach similar to creating an object. You can't bind directly to the object that you're deleting because after you delete it, it will be gone. Therefore, you need to bind to the parent of the object. To delete the object that you just created, first bind to the Users container:

```
PS C:\> $container = [ADSI]"LDAP://cn=users,dc=contoso,dc=com"
```

Then, call the Delete method and pass in the object type and the common name of the object you're deleting:

```
PS C:\> $container.Delete("user", "cn=Nora Shea")
```

As in the past few examples, this object is only deleted from the local copy of the object in PowerShell. Therefore, you need to call the CommitChanges method again to make the change in Active Directory:

```
PS C:\> $container.CommitChanges()
```

Beyond the Basics

You now have an overview of the basics of using ADSI to manage Active Directory. Throughout the remainder of this book, you'll see many more examples using both ADSI and the new Active Directory PowerShell module. If you understand the basics as they're outlined here (working with objects, properties, and methods) then you're well equipped to handle some of the more advanced ADSI operations discussed later.

Use the Active Directory Module

The Active Directory module for PowerShell is a new feature of Windows Server 2008 R2. As discussed earlier, prior to Windows Server 2008 R2, you had to use the ADSI interfaces for using PowerShell with Active Directory. Windows Server 2008 R2 provides you with several cmdlets for Active Directory administration. The Active Directory module groups these cmdlets together into a package. In order to use the Active Directory module, you have to install it on the computer from which you're performing the administration and then load the module in PowerShell.

The Active Directory module will only run on Windows Server 2008 R2 and Windows 7. The following editions of Windows are capable of running the module:

► Windows 7 (all versions)

► Windows Server 2008 R2 Standard

► Windows Server 2008 R2 Enterprise

► Windows Server 2008 R2 Datacenter

It's important to understand that the Active Directory module can only be used with domain controllers running the Active Directory Web Services (ADWS) component or the Active Directory Management Gateway (ADMG). Table 1.8 lists the domain controller operating system requirements for each.

TABLE 1.8   Requirements for ADWS and ADMG

Component	Domain Controller OS
Active Directory Web Services	Windows Server 2008 R2
Active Directory Management Gateway	Windows Server 2003 SP2
	Windows Server 2003 R2
	Windows Server 2008 SP2

These components provide a web services interface to Active Directory. The Active Directory PowerShell module uses SOAP-based web services protocols to communicate with the domain controller. If you don't have ADWS or ADMG installed on at least one domain controller in your environment, then you won't be able to use the Active Directory PowerShell module.

Load the Active Directory Module

After you've installed the Active Directory module, you can use the cmdlets in PowerShell. To use the cmdlets, you'll need to import the module. Use the following PowerShell command to import the Active Directory module:

```
PS C:\> Import-Module ActiveDirectory
```

As mentioned earlier, the AD PowerShell module requires either a Windows Server 2008 R2 domain controller or a Windows Server 2003/2008 domain controller running ADMG. If there are none available, you'll receive an error when attempting to import the module stating that a server with ADWS can't be found.

After the module loads successfully, you can begin using the Active Directory cmdlets. To view a listing of the Active Directory cmdlets added by the module, run the following PowerShell commands:

```
PS C:\> $module = Get-Module ActiveDirectory
PS C:\> $module.ExportedCmdlets | ft Key

Key
---
Add-ADComputerServiceAccount
Add-ADDomainControllerPasswordReplicationPolicy
Add-ADFineGrainedPasswordPolicySubject
Add-ADGroupMember
Add-ADPrincipalGroupMembership
Clear-ADAccountExpiration
Disable-ADAccount
Disable-ADOptionalFeature
Enable-ADAccount
Enable-ADOptionalFeature
Get-ADAccountAuthorizationGroup
Get-ADAccountResultantPasswordReplicationPolicy
Get-ADComputer
Get-ADComputerServiceAccount
Get-ADDefaultDomainPasswordPolicy
Get-ADDomain
Get-ADDomainController
Get-ADDomainControllerPasswordReplicationPolicy
Get-ADDomainControllerPasswordReplicationPolicyUsage
Get-ADFineGrainedPasswordPolicy
Get-ADFineGrainedPasswordPolicySubject
Get-ADForest
Get-ADGroup
Get-ADGroupMember
Get-ADObject
Get-ADOptionalFeature
Get-ADOrganizationalUnit
Get-ADPrincipalGroupMembership
```

```
Get-ADRootDSE
Get-ADServiceAccount
Get-ADUser
Remove-ADComputer
Remove-ADComputerServiceAccount
Remove-ADDomainControllerPasswordReplicationPolicy
Remove-ADFineGrainedPasswordPolicy
Remove-ADFineGrainedPasswordPolicySubject
Remove-ADGroup
Remove-ADGroupMember
Remove-ADObject
Remove-ADOrganizationalUnit
Remove-ADPrincipalGroupMembership
Remove-ADServiceAccount
Remove-ADUser
Rename-ADObject
Reset-ADServiceAccountPassword
Restore-ADObject
Search-ADAccount
Set-ADAccountControl
Set-ADAccountExpiration
Set-ADAccountPassword
Set-ADComputer
Set-ADDefaultDomainPasswordPolicy
Set-ADDomain
Set-ADDomainMode
Set-ADFineGrainedPasswordPolicy
Set-ADForest
Set-ADForestMode
Set-ADGroup
Set-ADObject
Set-ADOrganizationalUnit
Set-ADServiceAccount
Set-ADUser
Uninstall-ADServiceAccount
Unlock-ADAccount
```

Most of the cmdlets are self-explanatory. If you can't figure out what some of them do by looking at the names, don't worry—you'll be working with many of them throughout the remainder of this book.

Use the Active Directory Drive

In addition to providing the Active Directory cmdlets, the Active Directory module for PowerShell also provides a new drive called the *AD drive*. With the AD drive, you can navigate Active Directory in a manner similar to the way you would navigate the file system on your hard drive. To use the AD drive, first make sure the Active Directory module is loaded, and then run the following command:

```
PS C:\> cd AD:
```

This changes the working context of your PowerShell session to the Active Directory drive. The default location is the rootDSE, which is the top-level entry in the domain controller itself. A listing of the objects in the default path is as follows:

```
PS AD:\> dir


Name             ObjectClass       DistinguishedName
----             -----------       -----------------
contoso          domainDNS         DC=contoso,DC=com
Configuration    configuration     CN=Configuration,DC=contoso,DC=com
Schema           dMD               CN=Schema,CN=Configuration,DC=contoso,DC=com
DomainDnsZones   domainDNS         DC=DomainDnsZones,DC=contoso,DC=com
ForestDnsZones   domainDNS         DC=ForestDnsZones,DC=contoso,DC=com
```

From here, you can change the path just as you would change directories in the filesystem. To do so, you can use the cd command followed by the distinguished name of the path. To navigate to the contoso.com domain, use the following command:

```
PS AD:\> cd "dc=contoso,dc=com"
PS AD:\dc=contoso,dc=com> dir


Name                ObjectClass         DistinguishedName
----                -----------         -----------------
Builtin             builtinDomain       CN=Builtin,DC=contoso,DC=com
Computers           container           CN=Computers,DC=contoso,DC=com
Contacts            organizationalUnit  OU=Contacts,DC=contoso,DC=com
Domain Controllers  organizationalUnit  OU=Domain Controllers,
                                        DC=contoso,DC=com
ForeignSecurityPr...  container         CN=ForeignSecurityPrincipals,
                                        DC=contoso,DC=com
```

Infrastructure	infrastructureUpdate	CN=Infrastructure,DC=contoso, DC=com
Jenny Smith	contact	CN=Jenny Smith,DC=contoso, DC=com
Jim Johnson	user	CN=Jim Johnson,DC=contoso, DC=com
Joe User	contact	CN=Joe User,DC=contoso,DC=com
LostAndFound	lostAndFound	CN=LostAndFound,DC=contoso, DC=com
Managed Service A...	container	CN=Managed Service Accounts, DC=contoso,DC=com
NTDS Quotas	msDS-QuotaContainer	CN=NTDS Quotas,DC=contoso, DC=com
Program Data	container	CN=Program Data,DC=contoso, DC=com
Sara Smith	user	CN=Sara Smith,DC=contoso, DC=com
Sara Smith2	user	CN=Sara Smith2,DC=contoso, DC=com
Sara Smith3	user	CN=Sara Smith3,DC=contoso, DC=com
System	container	CN=System,DC=contoso,DC=com
temp	organizationalUnit	OU=temp,DC=contoso,DC=com
Template	user	CN=Template,DC=contoso,DC=com
Users	container	CN=Users,DC=contoso,DC=com

You'll be using the AD drive throughout the remainder of this book, so you may want to take a few minutes now and become familiar with navigating around the AD drive in PowerShell.

Use Windows Management Instrumentation

When you automate Active Directory with PowerShell, you'll use one additional technique: the Windows Management Instrumentation (WMI) interface. WMI isn't used for interacting with Active Directory per se; rather, it's used for interacting with the Windows operating system. This is important because you may have to do some things to Windows that affect its interaction with Active Directory, even though you're not touching Active Directory itself. For example, in Chapter 5,

"Configuring Active Directory Dependencies," we'll look at how to automate DNS. The majority of the ways you'll interact with DNS will use WMI.

WMI Basics

WMI provides an object-oriented way to manage Windows. WMI uses the concept of *classes*, which define different types of objects that WMI can interact with. Similar to how .NET classes work, WMI provides *methods* (pieces of executable code) and *properties*.

Windows provides a series of classes out of the box for interacting with core Windows components. For example, the `Win32_Service` class provides a way to interact with Windows services. The methods in the class allow you to do things like start or stop a service, while the properties define the different attributes of the service, such as its name.

Several classes are packaged together to form *namespaces*. Namespaces can be provided by both Microsoft applications and third-party applications. This speaks to the extensibility of WMI and is one of the reasons why WMI is so widely used not only in PowerShell scripting, but in other scripting languages as well. The Windows operating system places its core classes in the namespace `root\cimv2`.

WMI also uses instances. An *instance* is an instantiation (an actual object) of a class. For example, if you have 20 services running on your computer, then you have 20 instances of the `Win32_Service` class. You can connect to each instance (each service) and modify it or perform one of its methods.

Another thing you should know about WMI is that there is a query language built around it. You can use this WMI Query Language (WQL) to search for WMI instances. Without WQL, you would have to list the instances of a class and then enumerate through each instance to find the one you want. With WQL, you can search for that particular instance and work with it directly.

WMI PowerShell Cmdlets

PowerShell can interact with WMI in a couple of different ways. Similar to how PowerShell uses ADSI to interact with Active Directory, there is a WMI provider. This allows you to use the following method of interacting with WMI:

```
$objReg = [WMICLASS]"\\.\root\cimv2:StdRegProv"
```

This example connects to the root\cimv2 namespace and uses the class StdRegProv, which provides access to the system's registry.

In addition to using the WMI provider, PowerShell provides a series of cmdlets you can use to interact with WMI. You can view these cmdlets by running the following command:

```
PS C:\> get-command -Noun *wmi*

CommandType      Name                    Definition
-----------      ----                    ----------
Cmdlet           Get-WmiObject           Get-WmiObject [-Class] ...
Cmdlet           Invoke-WmiMethod        Invoke-WmiMethod [-Clas...
Cmdlet           Register-WmiEvent       Register-WmiEvent [-Cla...
Cmdlet           Remove-WmiObject        Remove-WmiObject [-Clas...
Cmdlet           Set-WmiInstance         Set-WmiInstance [-Class...
```

The two WMI cmdlets you'll be primarily working with in this book are Get-WmiObject and Set-WmiObject. These cmdlets are respectively used for retrieving WMI information and configuring WMI information. We'll be discussing how to use these cmdlets throughout the remainder of this book.

Prepare Your Environment for the Active Directory Module

Before you can begin using the Active Directory module to manage Active Directory, you'll need to take some steps to prepare the environment. Depending on your current Active Directory configuration, you may need to make changes on a domain controller in your forest.

Configure Domain Controllers

As mentioned in the previous section, the Active Directory module requires that at least one domain controller be running ADWS or ADMG.

Install Active Directory Web Services

ADWS will run only on your Windows Server 2008 R2 domain controllers. When you promote a Windows Server 2008 R2 member server to a domain controller, the ADWS component is automatically installed and enabled. One situation you may encounter is that if there is a firewall between your domain controller and the computer from which you're running the Active Directory PowerShell module, the module may not be able to connect to ADWS. To fix this, you should ensure that you allow traffic on TCP port 9389 to communicate with the domain controller.

Install the Active Directory Management Gateway

If you don't have a Windows Server 2008 R2 domain controller, you can still use the Active Directory PowerShell module by installing ADMG on one of your domain controllers. ADMG is supported on the following domain controller operating systems:

- Windows Server 2003 SP2

- Windows Server 2003 R2

- Windows Server 2008 SP2

As a prerequisite, the ADMG requires the .NET Framework 3.5 Service Pack 1. You'll need to install it before you can install ADMG. Follow these steps to install ADMG on a legacy domain controller:

1. Download the appropriate ADMG installation package from the Microsoft website at the following URL: `www.microsoft.com/downloads/en/details.aspx?displaylang=en&FamilyID=008940c6-0296-4597-be3e-1d24c1cf0dda`.

2. Launch the installation package that you downloaded to start the installation.

3. On the opening screen of the installation wizard, click the Next button.

4. On the License Agreement screen, read the license and then choose I Agree (assuming that you agree with the terms of the license). Click Next to continue.

5. ADMG will be installed. After the installation is finished, click the Finish button.

6. You can verify that ADMG was installed by opening the Services MMC (Microsoft Management Console) snap-in and checking to see that the ADWS service is installed and running, as shown in Figure 1.15.

FIGURE 1.15   ADWS Running on a Windows 2003 domain controller

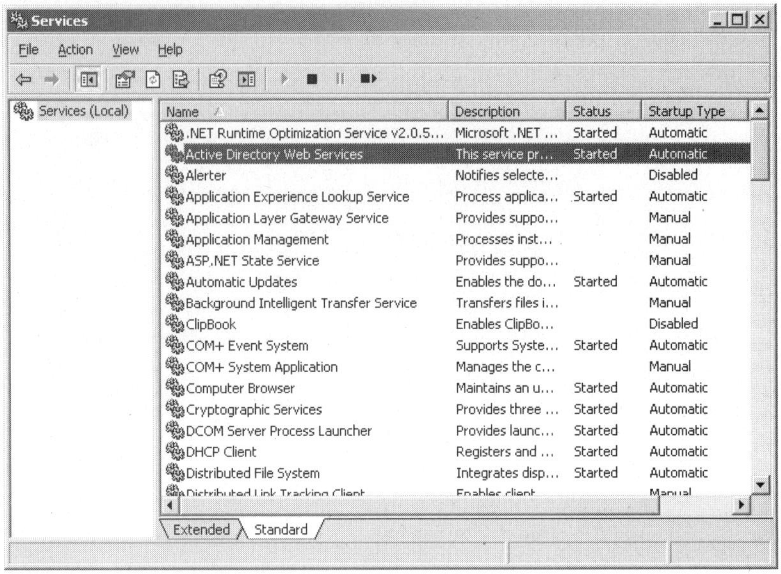

Use Windows 7 or Windows Server 2008 R2 for Administration

When you promote a Windows Server 2008 R2 server to a domain controller, the Active Directory module is installed by default. Therefore, you can use the Active Directory PowerShell module on the domain controller without additional configuration. However, if you want to use PowerShell to administer Active Directory with the Active Directory module from Windows Server 2008 R2 member servers or Windows 7 workstations, you'll need to install the modules separately.

The Active Directory module is included in the Remote Server Administration Tools (RSAT). In Windows Server 2008 R2, this doesn't require a separate download. You can install the Active Directory module by running the following series of commands in PowerShell:

```
PS C:\> Import-Module ServerManager
PS C:\> Add-WindowsFeature RSAT-AD-PowerShell
```

One of the prerequisites for using the Active Directory module is version 3.5.1 of the .NET Framework. Therefore, if you don't already have the .NET Framework 3.5.1 installed, it will be installed automatically when the Active Directory module is installed.

Windows 7 doesn't include the RSAT feature by default. Therefore, you'll need to download and install these tools before you can enable the Active Directory module on Windows 7. You can download RSAT from Microsoft's website at the following URL: `www.microsoft.com/downloads/en/details.aspx?FamilyID=` `7d2f6ad7-656b-4313-a005-4e344e43997d`.

After you install RSAT, you can use the following steps to install the Active Directory module in Windows 7:

1. Click the Start menu, and select Control Panel.

2. In the Control Panel, click Programs and then Turn Windows Features On Or Off. The Windows Features dialog opens.

3. In the Windows Features dialog, browse to Remote Server Administration Tools ➢ Role Administration Tools ➢ AD DS And AD LDS Tools. Select the Active Directory Module For Windows PowerShell check box, and then click OK.

Use an Older Client for Administration

The Active Directory module can only be installed on Windows 7 and Windows Server 2008 R2. However, because of the remoting capabilities in PowerShell v2, you can use an older client operating system to manage Active Directory with the Active Directory PowerShell module.

To accomplish this, you'll still need a computer in the environment with the Active Directory PowerShell module installed. On your older client machine, you'll need to install PowerShell 2.0 and Windows Remote Management 2.0, which you can download from Microsoft's website at the following URL: `http://support` `.microsoft.com/kb/968929`. Establish a remote PowerShell session between your older client and the server that has the Active Directory module installed, and the Active Directory module cmdlets will be proxied on your client. This means you'll type the command into your client, but it will really execute on the computer with the Active Directory module.

Follow these steps to administer Active Directory with an older client:

1. Create a remote session from your client by executing the following command:

   ```
   $session = New-PSSession -ComputerName MgtServer01
   ```

2. Import the Active Directory module into the remote session:

   ```
   Invoke-Command { Import-Module ActiveDirectory } -Session ↵
   $session
   ```

3. Export the AD cmdlets from the remote session into a local copy of the module. The following example references all the cmdlets that contain `-AD` in the name:

```
Export-PSSession -Session $session -CommandName *-AD* ↵
-OutputModule LocalADModule -AllowClobber
```

4. Import the local module that you just created:

```
Import-Module LocalADModule
```

After you follow these steps, you should be able to execute the Active Directory cmdlets from your older Windows client. Remember, though, that the cmdlet itself will really be run from the machine with which you establish the remote session.

Managing Domains and Forests

IN THIS CHAPTER, YOU WILL LEARN TO:

Determining the number of Active Directory domains and forests to be created is typically performed early on in the AD design process, based on the number of users and physical locations within an environment as well as the physical and logical security requirements of the organization. When you install the first Active Directory domain controller (DC) in an environment, you're creating a new AD domain within a new AD forest. Additional domains and forests may be added to the environment during the initial AD deployment, or later on as part of a merger, an acquisition, or a divestiture.

Manage AD Domains

When planning your AD environment, the number of forests and domains you select will be based on the security and administrative requirements of your organization. Within AD, the AD *forest* constitutes the security boundary within AD—AD administrators from one forest can't exert administrative privileges within a separate AD forest (unless a trust relationship is in place). Conversely, if you have multiple domains within a single AD forest, the Enterprise Admins group in the forest root domain has default administrative privileges across the entire forest, including all child domains. In fact, Domain Admins in any child domains can potentially (although not by default) escalate their privileges so that they can access any domain in the forest, including the forest root domain.

THE FOREST AS THE SECURITY BOUNDARY

There are numerous misconceptions on the Internet about this matter, because when AD was first released in Windows 2000, the initial documentation from Microsoft indicated that the domain, rather than the forest, was the AD security boundary. This has been proven not to be the case because of the potential escalation of privileges; when determining the security boundary for your AD environment, always remember that it's the forest that is the security boundary.

Within a single forest, you may still wish to configure multiple domains for purposes of administrative separation. The AD domain is the fundamental unit of

Administering
Service Delivery

PART I

administration within AD—all users, groups, and other security principals are created within the *domain-naming context* and are replicated only to other DCs within the same domain: an AD user, group, or other security principal may only exist within a single domain at any one time. (Other data regarding the AD schema and other configuration information such as IP addressing and site information is replicated forest-wide.) In a multidomain environment, the first domain that you install in the forest will be the *forest root domain*; this domain contains such built-in security groups as the Enterprise Admins and Schema Admins groups. Although you may use tools like the Active Directory Migration Tool (ADMT) to restructure or consolidate an AD forest after it has been created, the forest root domain must always remain the forest root domain—the only way to configure a "new" forest root domain within an AD forest is to decommission the entire forest and begin again from scratch.

In a multidomain environment, you may have one or more *domain trees* that follow a contiguous naming convention: a forest root domain called contoso.com with two child domains called west.contoso.com and east.contoso.com, for example, as shown in Figure 2.1.

FIGURE 2.1   A multidomain forest

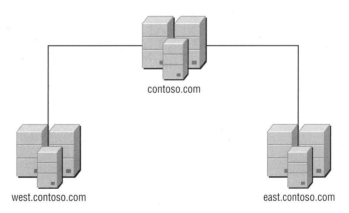

contoso.com

west.contoso.com

east.contoso.com

You can also configure multiple domain trees that use noncontiguous naming conventions. You may have a domain tree called contoso.com and a second domain tree within the same forest called adatum.com, as shown in Figure 2.2.

FIGURE 2.2   Multiple domain trees in a forest

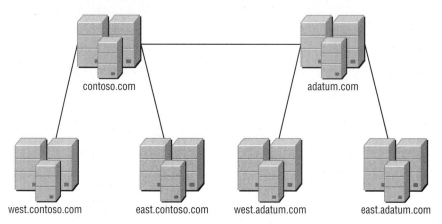

Whatever the structure of your forest, if you have multiple trees or domains in your forest, then each domain in the forest has a two-way, transitive trust relationship with every other domain in the forest. This means that, by default, a user in any domain in the forest may authenticate to a resource in any other domain in the forest. (Obviously, you may still lock down access to specific resources through the use of Access Control Lists [ACLs].) This transitivity is created as follows:

- ▶ When a new child domain is added to an existing domain tree, a two-way transitive trust is created between the child domain and its parent domain. This works recursively, so that a "grandchild" domain has a two-way trust with the child domain, which has a two-way trust with the root domain.

- ▶ When a new domain tree is added to an existing forest, a two-way transitive trust is created between the root domain of the new tree and the root domain of every other tree in the forest.

Through the use of these two trust configurations, each new domain that is added to an AD forest has an automatic trust with every other domain in the forest, as shown in Figure 2.3.

If your AD design extends to multiple forests, or if you need to expand your AD environment to extend to other organizations, you'll sometimes need to create *trust relationships* between one AD domain or forest and others. Depending on the nature of the environments, a number of different types of trusts may be created to meet the needs of the scenario. If two separate AD forests are running at least Windows Server 2003, you can create a *forest trust* between the two forests. A forest trust takes the two-way transitive trust web within each forest and extends it across the trust relationship, so that each domain in ForestA has a two-way transitive trust with each domain in ForestB, and vice versa, as shown in Figure 2.4.

FIGURE 2.3 The default trust configuration

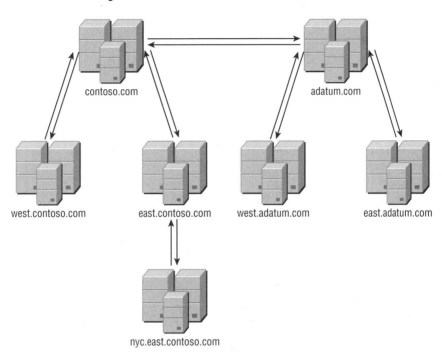

FIGURE 2.4 Cross-forest trusts

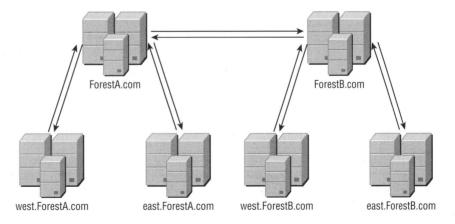

If this level of trust transitivity isn't desired, you can instead create an *external* trust between one specific domain and another specific domain; the trust relationship won't extend to any other domains in either forest, as shown in Figure 2.5.

FIGURE 2.5 **External trust**

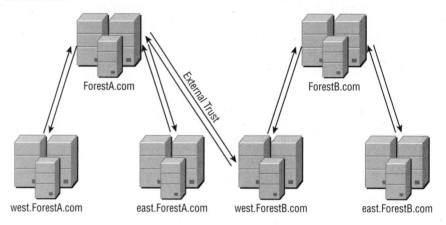

You can also create a *realm trust* between an AD domain and a third-party realm based on the MIT Kerberos protocol, or a *shortcut trust* to improve the efficiency of cross-domain access within a single AD forest.

Within an AD environment, the AD domain is the primary unit of administration—the domain represents a single cohesive unit of administration that can correspond to a geographical area, a business unit, or an entire company. Although a significant number of organizations have deployed their AD environments as a single domain within a single forest, you also have the option to deploy multiple domains or domain trees within a single forest, or even multiple separate forests.

Add and Remove Active Directory Domains

Whether you're creating a brand-new domain in a brand-new forest or creating a new domain or domain tree within an existing forest, you create a new AD domain by promoting a single server as the first DC in the new domain; this may be automated by using the dcpromo.exe command-line tool.

The dcpromo.exe tool contains a significant number of command-line switches that you can use to customize its behavior. In this section, you'll see examples using many of them. The complete list of available parameters for dcpromo.exe in Windows Server 2008 R2 is as follows:

▶ AllowDomainControllerReinstall specifies whether to install the DC even if another DC computer account with the same name is detected.

▶ AllowDomainReinstall specifies whether an existing domain may be re-created when promoting this DC.

▶ ApplicationPartitionsToReplicate specifies which partitions should be replicated.

▶ ChildName specifies the single-label DNS name of the child domain if the promotion is creating a child domain.

▶ ConfirmGc specifies whether the DC should be configured as a global catalog server.

▶ CreateDNSDelegation specifies whether to create a DNS delegation for the new DNS server that you're creating.

▶ CriticalReplicationOnly specifies whether only critical replication should be performed prior to the final reboot of the promotion process.

▶ DatabasePath specifies the filesystem path that should contain the AD database.

▶ DelegatedAdmin specifies the name of the delegated administrator or group when installing a read-only domain controller (RODC).

▶ DNSDelegationPassword specifies the password used to create a DNS delegation.

▶ DNSDelegationUserName specifies the username used to create a DNS delegation.

▶ DNSOnNetwork specifies whether DNS is available elsewhere on the network, or if DNS will be installed on the DC itself to be used for name resolution.

▶ DomainLevel specifies the domain functional level of the new AD domain.

▶ DomainNetBiosName specifies the NetBIOS name of a newly created domain.

▶ ForestLevel specifies the forest functional level of a newly created forest.

▶ InstallDNS specifies whether the DNS server service should be installed on this DC.

► `LogPath` specifies the filesystem path that should contain the AD log files.

► `NewDomain` specifies whether you're creating a new forest, a new domain tree within a forest, or a new child domain within an existing domain tree.

► `NewDomainDNSName` specifies the fully qualified domain name (FQDN) of a newly created domain.

► `ParentDomainDNSName`, if creating a child domain, specifies the DNS name of the new child domain's parent domain.

► `Password` specifies the password of the account credentials to be used to install the DC.

► `PasswordReplicationAllowed` specifies the names of security principals whose passwords may be replicated to an RODC.

► `PasswordReplicationDenied` specifies the names of security principals whose passwords may not be replicated to an RODC.

► `RebootOnCompletion` specifies whether the DC should reboot on completion of the `dcpromo` operation: `{<Yes> | No}`.

► `RebootOnSuccess` specifies that the DC should reboot at the end of the `dcpromo` operation only if the operation completes successfully.

► `ReplicaDomainDNSName`, if installing an additional DC in an existing domain, specifies the DNS name of the AD domain in question.

► `ReplicaOrNewDomain` specifies whether you're creating a new AD domain or adding a new DC to an existing domain.

► `ReplicationSourceDC`, if installing an additional DC in an existing domain, specifies the name of the DC from which information will be replicated.

► `ReplicationSourcePath` specifies the location of Install From Media (IFM) files, if these are being used.

► `SafeModeAdminPassword` specifies the password to be used when the DC is started in Directory Services Restore Mode.

► `SiteName` specifies the name of the site where the new DC should be installed (the site name must already exist within AD).

► `SkipAutoConfigDns` skips the automatic configuration of DNS if the DNS service has already been installed on the server.

► `SysVolPath` specifies the filesystem path used to store the `SYSVOL` directory.

▶ UserDomain specifies the domain of the user credentials being used to install the DC.

▶ UserName specifies the username of the credentials being used to install the DC.

Creating a New Domain

Dcpromo.exe possesses a significant number of command-line options that allow you to customize the behavior of the domain-creation process to fit your needs. You can enter the necessary parameters on the same command line as dcpromo, or you may record the parameters into a separate text file for reuse in subsequent domain promotions.

In our first example, you see the command-line switches necessary to create a brand-new AD forest with a single domain called contoso.com. The new domain has a domain NetBIOS name of CONTOSO, with a forest and domain functional level of Windows Server 2008 R2 (denoted by the number 4). The available settings for domain and forest functional levels are as follows:

▶ Windows2000: 0

▶ Windows Server 2003 Interim: 1

▶ Windows Server 2003: 2

▶ Windows Server 2008: 3

▶ Windows Server 2008 R2: 4

You can see that the AD database, log files, and SYSVOL directories have been separated onto three separate drives; the AD database is stored at d:\ntds, the AD logs are stored at e:\ntdslogs, and SYSVOL is stored at f:\sysvol. Also notice that the DNS Server service will be installed on this DC during the dcpromo process:

```
dcpromo /unattend /replicaOrNewDomain:domain /NewDomain:Forest
/NewDomainDNSName:contoso.com /DomainNetbiosName:contoso /
InstallDns:yes /databasePath:"d:\ntds" /logPath:"e:\ntdslogs" /
sysvolpath:"f:\sysvol" /safeModeAdminPassword:DS%sdr5!@V8d3 /
forestLevel:4 /domainLevel:4 /rebootOnCompletion:yes
```

The next example creates a new child domain within an existing AD forest. The name of the existing forest is contoso.com, and the new domain being created is called corp.contoso.com, with a domain NetBIOS name of corp. Notice again that the AD database, log files, and SYSVOL directories are separated onto three separate drives, and the domain functional level of the new domain is Windows Server 2008 R2, denoted by the number 4:

```
dcpromo /unattend /adv /replicaOrNewDomain:domain /NewDomain:
child /ParentDomainDNSName:contoso.com /newDomainDnsName:corp
.contoso.com /childName:corp /DomainNetbiosName:corp /
InstallDns:yes /databasePath:"d:\ntds" /logPath:"e:\ntdslogs"
/sysvolpath:"f:\sysvol" /safeModeAdminPassword:FD^#cdsr1
2CSD%sd /domainLevel:4 /ReplicationSourcePath:g:\ntds\ /
rebootOnCompletion:yes
```

Listing 2.1 uses the /unattend:<filename> switch to force dcpromo to reference an external text file for its command-line parameters. In this case, you're creating a new domain tree within an existing AD forest. The format of the answer file begins with [DCINSTALL] in Listing 2.1.

LISTING 2.1: Creating a New Domain Tree Using an **unattend.txt** File

```
dcpromo /unattend:answer.txt

[DCINSTALL]
UserName=administrator
UserDomain=WORKGROUP
Password=P@ssw0rd1
replicaOrNewDomain=domain
newDomain=tree
ParentDomainDNSName=contoso.com
NewDomainDnsName=contosocorp.com
DomainNetbiosName=contosocorp
InstallDns=yes
databasePath="d:\ntds"
logPath="e:\ntdslogs"
sysvolPath="f:\sysvol"
safeModeAdminPassword=FSD#%$Tfe23
domainLevel=4
rebootOnCompletion=yes
```

Decommissioning a Domain

You can also customize the dcpromo.exe command-line tool to decommission an existing AD domain. In order to decommission an AD domain using the syntax shown in the following example, you must first demote any other DCs in the domain:

```
dcpromo /unattend /UserName:contosoadmin /UserDomain:contoso.com
/Password:#$%CVSER$% /AdministratorPassword:%#Q@DCed23
/AdministratorPassword:%#Q@DCed23 /DemoteFSMO:Yes /IsLastDc
InDomain:Yes /IgnoreIsLastDcInDomainMismatch:Yes /IgnoreIsLastDN
SServerForZone:Yes /RebootOnCompletion:Yes
```

When demoting an existing DC, dcpromo performs a number of safety checks before allowing the demotion to continue. One of these checks is to determine whether the DC in question holds one or more Flexible Single Master of Operation (FSMO) roles for the domain or forest. If you don't specify the /demoteFSMO switch with a value of Yes, you'll be prompted by dcpromo as to whether you wish to continue the demotion. You can also see the /IsLastDcInDomain switch, which denotes that this is the last DC in this domain and that this operation will decommission this domain.

In some cases, you may not be able to demote all other DCs before decommissioning the domain. The /IgnoreIsLastDcInDomainMismatch switch allows the domain decommission to continue even if the AD database still contains references to remaining DCs. Likewise, the /IgnoreIsLastDNSServerForZone switch allows the operation to continue even if this DC is the last holder of a DNS zone such as DomainDNSZones or ForestDNSZones.

Upgrading an Active Directory Domain

Whenever a new version of the Windows operating system is released, administrators of existing AD forests need to plan how they will introduce the new OS into their environment. The process of upgrading from one OS to the next has remained largely the same when upgrading from Windows 2000 to Windows Server 2003, from Windows Server 2003 (including 2003 R2) to Windows Server 2008, and most recently from Windows Server 2008 to Windows Server 2008 R2.

Broadly speaking, the steps needed to upgrade an existing AD domain to a new version of the Windows operating system are as follows:

1. Assign appropriate credentials to the users who will be preparing the forest and domain for the upgrade.

2. Introduce a member server running the new version of the Windows OS.

3. Inventory existing DCs, and determine whether each DC may be upgraded in place, or if it needs to be reinstalled or replaced. (A Windows 2000 DC can't be

upgraded directly to Windows Server 2008, for example.) Determine whether the existing hardware of each DC is capable of running the new version of the operating system, or if upgrades are required to RAM, hard drive space, and so on.

4. Create a test plan for your domain upgrade, including steps needed to recover from any failures. Ensure that you have tested and verified backups of your AD in place.

5. Upgrade your AD schema by running `adprep.exe /forestprep` from the DC that holds the Schema Master FSMO for the forest.

6. Prepare each domain by running `adprep /domainprep /gpprep`.

7. If you plan to install RODCs, run `adprep /rodcprep` in each domain that will contain an RODC.

8. If the domain was upgraded from Windows 2000, run the `GrantPermissions OnAllGPOs.wsf` script. This resolves a backward-compatibility issue in which the Enterprise Domain Controllers security group doesn't have read access to the Group Policy Objects (GPOs) in each domain.

The following example shows the commands described in this checklist, for the `contoso.com` domain:

```
adprep /forestprep
adprep /domainprep /gpprep
adprep /rodcprep
cscript GrantPermissionOnAllGPOs.wsf "Enterprise Domain
Controllers" /permission:read /domain:contoso.com /Replace
```

Cleaning Up Old Domain Controllers

You've already seen the process of demoting DCs in the "Decommissioning a Domain" section, because decommissioning a domain is done by demoting the last DC in that domain. If your aim is to decommission a single DC without decommissioning the entire domain, you can use a much simpler syntax for dcpromo, as shown in the following example. The most interesting syntax here is the /DemoteFSMO switch, which allows a DC to be automatically demoted without prompting the administrator, even if that DC holds one or more FSMO roles for the domain or forest:

```
dcpromo /unattend /UserName:contosoadmin /UserDomain:contoso
.com /Password:#$%CVSER$% /AdministratorPassword:%#Q@
DCed23 /AdministratorPassword:%#Q@DCed23 /DemoteFSMO:Yes /
RebootOnCompletion:Yes
```

Manage Domain Settings

After an AD domain has been created, a number of domain- and forest-wide settings need to be managed on an ongoing basis. For example, in order to enable additional functionality in a domain or forest, you need to raise the domain or forest functional level to reflect the OS level of its DCs: a forest whose DCs are all running the latest version of the Windows OS can support new functionality because it no longer needs to maintain backward compatibility with legacy DCs.

It's also critical to configure an authoritative time source to ensure time synchronization across all computers within an AD forest. In large or complex environments, you may also need to configure additional UPN suffixes for use across your AD forest, or modify the default tombstone lifetime to manage how AD handles the deletion of objects.

Retrieving the Domain and Forest Functional Level

Within a single AD domain, it's possible to have DCs running many different versions of the Windows Server OS. Reflecting this, AD domains and forests have *functional levels* that indicate which OS versions are running on the DCs in the domain or forest. The functional level of a domain or forest dictates which advanced features are available in that domain or forest—a higher functional level allows additional functionality to be enabled because there is less need for backward compatibility with older OSs. This allows administrators to perform phased upgrades of DCs when a new version of the Windows OS becomes available, rather than requiring an all-or-nothing approach.

It's important to note that changing the domain or forest functional level requires positive action on the part of the administrator, because raising the functional level prevents additional downlevel DCs from being added to a domain or forest. For example, even if all DCs in a domain have been upgraded from Windows Server 2003 to Windows Server 2008, changing the domain functional level to Windows Server 2008 requires additional configuration; the functional level doesn't change automatically.

Currently, six domain functional levels are available in AD:

- ► *Windows 2000 mixed:* Allows all versions of AD DCs, as well as Windows NT 4.0 DCs. This is the default domain functional level in Windows Server 2003.

- ► *Windows 2000 native:* Allows all versions of AD DCs, but no Windows NT DCs.

- ► *Windows Server 2003 interim:* Allows only Windows NT 4 and Windows Server 2003 DCs. This functional level is selected automatically when you're upgrading a Windows NT 4 domain to Windows Server 2003. You can't specify this functional level manually.

► *Windows Server 2003:* Allows Windows Server 2003 or higher DCs only. No Windows NT or Windows 2000 DCs may be added to a domain at this functional level.

► *Windows Server 2008:* Allows only Windows Server 2008 and Windows Server 2008 R2 DCs. No Windows NT, Windows 2000, or Windows Server 2003 DCs may be added to a domain at this functional level.

► *Windows Server 2008 R2:* Allows only Windows Server 2008 R2 DCs. No downlevel DCs of any kind may be added to a domain at this functional level.

Similarly, five forest functional levels are currently available:

► *Windows 2000:* Allows DCs of any OS within the forest. This is the default forest functional level for Windows Server 2003 and Windows Server 2008.

► *Windows Server 2003 interim:* Similar to the domain functional level, allows only Windows NT 4 and Windows Server 2003 DCs within the forest. This functional level is selected automatically when upgrading a Windows NT 4 domain to Windows Server 2003; you can't specify this functional level manually.

► *Windows Server 2003:* Allows only Windows Server 2003 or higher DCs within the forest. All domains in the forest must be running at least the Windows Server 2003 DFL. This is the default forest functional level for Windows Server 2008 R2 forests.

► *Windows Server 2008:* Allows only Windows Server 2008 or higher DCs within the forest. All domains in the forest must be running at least the Windows Server 2008 DFL.

► *Windows Server 2008 R2:* Allows only Windows Server 2008 R2 DCs within the forest. All domains in the forest must be running the Windows Server 2008 R2 DFL.

You can obtain the domain and forest functional levels for a particular domain or forest by querying a DC's `RootDSE` object; Domain Functional Level and Forest Functional Level information is stored as properties on this object. Querying `RootDSE` is a convenient way to query for active directory information without hard-coding the name of a specific DC. `Get-ADRootDSE` queries the `RootDSE` object of whichever DC the user is currently connected to.

You can query `RootDSE` for properties such as the following:

- ► ConfigurationNamingContext

- ► CurrentTime

- ► DefaultNamingContext

- ► DnsHostName

- ► DomainControllerFunctionality

- ► DsServiceName

- ► HighestCommittedUSN

- ► IsGlobalCatalogReady

- ► IsSynchronized

- ► LdapServiceName

- ► NamingContextsRoot

- ► DomainNamingContext

- ► SchemaNamingContext

- ► ServerName

- ► SubschemaSubentry

- ► SupportedCapabilities

- ► SupportedControl

- ► SupportedLDAPPolicies

- ► SupportedLDAPVersion

- ► SupportedRootDSEOperations

- ► SupportedSASLMechanisms

The example in this section demonstrates the Get-ADRootDSE PowerShell cmdlet, which allows you to quickly obtain the domainFunctionality and forestFunctionality properties.

```
Get-ADRootDSE -Server dc1.contoso.com | Format-Table
defaultNamingContext, domainFunctionality, forestFunctionality
```

Changing the Domain and Forest Functional Level

When a particular domain or forest meets the requirements of a new domain or forest functional level, you need to issue a specific command to change the functional level to its new value. Before AD will commit the new functional level, it performs safety checks to ensure that the new functional level is supported. In the case of a domain functional level, all DCs in the domain are enumerated to confirm that they're running the appropriate OS level; for upgrades to the forest functional level, all domains in the forest are checked to ensure that they're running the appropriate domain functional levels. Only after these safety checks have passed will the functional level be committed.

In this section, you'll use `Set-ADDomainMode` to upgrade the domain functional level for a specific domain. You can specify the domain to be upgraded using the `-Identity` parameter, which can take one of the following types of arguments:

- ► Fully qualified domain name (FQDN), such as `corp.contoso.com`

- ► Distinguished name (DN), such as `dc=corp,dc=contoso,dc=com`

- ► Domain NetBIOS name, such as CORP

- ► Domain GUID (`objectGUID`), such as 599c3d2e-f72d-4d20-8a88-030d99495f20

- ► Domain Security Identifier (`objectSid`), such as S-1-5-21-3165297888-301567370

You can specify any of the following values for the `-DomainMode` parameter:

- ►   Windows2000Domain or 0

- ►   Windows2003InterimDomain or 1

- ►   Windows2003Domain or 2

- ►   Windows2008Domain or 3

- ►   Windows2008R2Domain or 4

MIXING FUNCTIONAL LEVELS

It's possible to have a domain with a higher domain functional level than the forest functional level, but never the reverse. So the `contoso.com` forest may be at the Windows Server 2003 forest functional level while the `east.contoso.com` domain has been raised to the Windows Server 2008 domain functional level. However, it isn't possible for the `contoso.com` forest to be configured at the Windows Server 2008 functional level if any of the domains within the forest are running at the Windows Server 2003 functional level.

In Figure 2.6, you can see examples of domain and forest functional levels at work.

FIGURE 2.6   Domain and forest functional levels

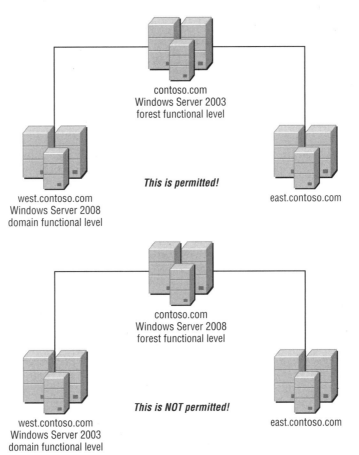

The following example uses Set-ADDomainMode to set the domain functional level of the child.contoso.com domain to Windows Server 2008 R2:

```
Set-ADDomainMode -Identity child.contoso.com -DomainMode
Windows2008R2Domain
```

The next example uses the Set-ADForestMode cmdlet to upgrade the forest functional level. The -Identity parameter specifies the distinguished name of the contoso.com forest and specifies a forest functional level of 3, which denotes the Windows Server 2008 forest functional level:

```
Set-ADForestMode -Identity dc=contoso,dc=com -ForestMode 3
```

Creating and Removing UPN Suffixes

In AD, each user account that you create has a user logon name, such as *administrator*, a pre-Windows 2000 logon name like *CONTOSO\administrator*, and a UPN logon name such as *administrator@contoso.com*. The second part of the UPN logon name, called the *UPN suffix*, is made up of the DNS domain name of the user's logon domain by default. The UPN suffix can also be configured as the DNS name of any domain within the forest, or it can be configured as an alternative DNS name that has been created by an administrator.

Using alternative domain names as the UPN suffix can help you to simplify the names that users rely on to log on to other domains in the forest. For example, if your organization has a domain structure containing numerous domain trees and child domains, it can be confusing for users to remember what their UPN suffix has been set to. Creating a single common UPN suffix for all users lets users log on using a much simpler logon name, possibly corresponding to the domain of their email address, regardless of which AD domain their account was created in. UPN suffixes are configured on a per-forest basis; when you add a new UPN suffix, it's available forest-wide.

You can modify the list of configured UPN suffixes for a forest by using the `Set-ADForest` cmdlet with the `–UPNSuffixes` argument. The list of UPN suffixes for a forest is a multivalued array; you'll need to use a `@{...}` syntax for the values you wish to modify. The following example illustrates how to add the `headquarters.fabrikam.com` UPN suffix to the existing list of UPN suffixes for a forest. This adds the new UPN suffix without affecting any suffixes that have already been configured:

```
Set-ADForest -UPNSuffixes @{Add="headquarters.fabrikam.com"}
```

In the next example, you can see how to use the `Remove` verb to remove the `headquarters.fabrikam.com` UPN suffix. This removes only the specified UPN suffix without affecting any other UPN suffixes configured for the forest:

```
Set-ADForest -UPNSuffixes @{Remove="headquarters.fabrikam.com"}
```

Next, you'll use the `Replace` verb to remove all existing UPN suffixes and replace them with UPN suffixes that you specify. You separate multiple entries with commas. Finally, you use the `$null` keyword to remove all configured UPN suffixes and insert an empty list:

```
Set-ADForest -UPNSuffixes @{Replace="headquarters.fabrikam
.com","corp.fabrikam.com"}

Set-ADForest -UPNSuffixes $null
```

You can also perform more than one operation at a time by separating multiple @ { . . . } entries with semicolons, like this:

```
@{Add=value1,value2,...};@{Remove=value3,value4,...}
```

Configuring an Authoritative Time Source

AD is a distributed directory service that must replicate and manage directory data across multiple DCs, often spanning significant geographic areas, including the ability to process authentication requests and apply directory changes that originate from any available DC. In order to perform this task correctly, AD relies heavily on all DCs, member servers, and client computers maintaining accurate time on the network; by default, all domain-joined computers (including DCs) must be accurate to within 5 minutes of one another. In the case of user authentication, accurate time synchronization ensures the security of the user's authentication request by preventing replay attacks. Within an AD environment, all Kerberos tickets are time-stamped using the local time of the client computer, translated to Zulu Time, or UTC. When the authentication request is received by a DC, the DC confirms that the timestamp falls within this 5-minute *clock skew*; if not, the authentication request is rejected.

Within an AD domain, time synchronization occurs using a particular hierarchy, in which the PDC emulator in the forest root domain is considered the authoritative time source for the whole forest. The PDC emulators in any child domains receive their time from the PDC emulator in the forest root domain. All other DCs within a particular domain receive their time from the PDC emulator of their own domain, whereas member servers and client computers receive their time from the DC that authenticated them.

In order to maintain authoritative time for a forest, the W32Time service on the PDC emulator in the forest root domain should be configured to obtain its time from an external time source, typically a time source on the Internet such as one run by NIST or the U.S. Navy.

The first example shows the commands required to configure the PDC emulator in the forest root domain to receive its time from an external time source. The <peers> placeholder should be replaced with the fully qualified domain name of an Internet time source such as time.nist.gov:

```
w32tm /config /manualpeerlist:<peers> /syncfromflags:manual /
reliable:yes /update
Stop-Service w32time
Start-Service w32time
```

The next example shows the commands required to configure all other computers in an AD forest to receive their time using the default AD time-synchronization hierarchy:

```
w32tm /config /syncfromflags:DOMHIER /reliable:no /update
Stop-Service w32time
Start-Service w32time
```

Retrieving and Setting the Tombstone Lifetime

Because AD is a distributed directory service, object deletions require special handling so that all DCs can be notified correctly that a particular object has been deleted. In order to achieve this, when a user or administrator deletes an object within an AD domain, the object isn't completely deleted; rather, the object is placed into a tombstoned state for a period of time called the *tombstone lifetime*. This tombstone lifetime allows the deletion of the object to be replicated to all DCs before the object is removed from the AD database entirely. The tombstone lifetime needs to be configured with enough time for deletions to be replicated to all DCs within an AD forest.

In Windows 2000, the default tombstone lifetime was set to 60 days; subsequent versions of the OS increased the default tombstone lifetime to 180 days. After an AD forest has been created, the tombstone lifetime remains as is unless it's modified by an administrator. If a Windows 2000 AD is upgraded to Windows Server 2003, the tombstone lifetime remains at 60 days unless it's updated manually.

The following example uses the Get-ADObject cmdlet to retrieve the current tombstone lifetime for the contoso.com AD forest:

```
Get-ADObject -Identity "CN=Directory Service,CN=Windows NT,CN=
Services,CN=Configuration,DC=contoso,DC=COM" -Partition "CN=
Configuration,DC=contoso,DC=COM" -Properties tombstoneLifetime
```

In the next example, you can see how to modify the tombstone lifetime for the contoso.com domain to a setting of 210 days:

```
Set-ADObject -Identity "CN=Directory Service,CN=Windows NT,CN=
Services,CN=Configuration,DC=contoso,DC=COM" -Partition "CN=
Configuration,DC=contoso,DC=COM" -Replace @{tombstoneLifetime='210'}
```

Manage Active Directory Trusts

An AD trust relationship that you establish between two domains or two forests makes it possible for users in one domain to be authenticated by a DC in the other domain, thus allowing users to access resources in the other domain (subject to any ACLs or other authorization controls that have been placed on the remote resource).

An AD trust may be *one-way* or *two-way* in direction, and *transitive* or *nontransitive* in nature. Each trust relationship consists of a *trusted* domain (or forest) and a *trusting* domain (or forest). The trusted domain in a trust relationship is the one that contains the user objects, whereas the trusting domain is the one that contains the resources to be accessed. When you see trust relationships depicted graphically, they're indicated by an arrow between the two domains. In the case of a one-way trust, the arrow always points toward the trusted domain, as shown in Figure 2.7.

FIGURE 2.7   Trusted and trusting domains

ForestA.com
resource forest

ForestB.com
user forest

TRUSTED AND TRUSTING DOMAINS

A simple mnemonic for remembering the difference between the trusted and trusting domains, and the direction of the arrow, is this: *trusted* ends with the word *Ed*, like the man's first name. Trusting rhymes (loosely) with *thing*. The trusting domain contains the things (resources), whereas the trusted domain contains Ed (the people.) When you draw the arrows that depict the direction of the trust, the arrow always points toward Ed.

In the case of a *two-way* trust, this means users on either side of the trust relationship may be authenticated by DCs on either side of the trust and access resources on either side of the trust. When you see a two-way trust depicted in a diagram, it's illustrated using a two-way arrow as shown in Figure 2.8.

FIGURE 2.8   A two-way AD trust

ForestA.com
users and resources

ForestB.com
users and resources

TRUST DIRECTIONS

In effect, a two-way trust is two one-way trusts, one in each direction.

In addition to the direction of the trust, one-way or two-way, an AD trust may be either *transitive* or *nontransitive*. A transitive trust allows a trust relationship to extend beyond the trusted and trusting domains and allows users to access resources in other domains further along the trust path. For example, if DomainA has a transitive trust relationship with DomainB, and DomainB has a transitive trust with DomainC, then users in DomainA can authenticate to DomainC, as shown in Figure 2.9.

FIGURE 2.9   Transitive trust relationships

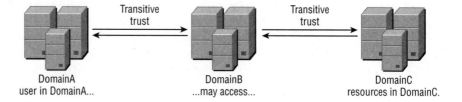

DomainA
user in DomainA...

DomainB
...may access...

DomainC
resources in DomainC.

Conversely, a nontransitive trust relationship doesn't allow the trust to extend beyond the specific trusted and trusting domain that you specified when you created the trust, as shown in Figure 2.10.

FIGURE 2.10 Nontransitive trust relationship

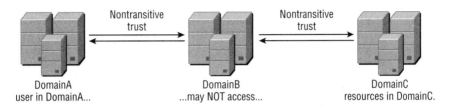

Create and Remove Active Directory Trusts

Depending on the business and technical requirements of the trust relationship, you can create several different types of AD trusts:

▶ A *cross-forest trust* creates a two-way transitive trust between two AD forests, each of which must be running at least the Windows Server 2003 forest functional level. This trust creates an effective mesh of trusts so that each domain in the trusted domain has an implicit trust relationship with, and thus can access resources within, each domain in the trusting domain. Figure 2.11 illustrates a cross-forest trust that has been configured between the contoso .com and adatum.com AD forests.

FIGURE 2.11 A cross-forest AD trust

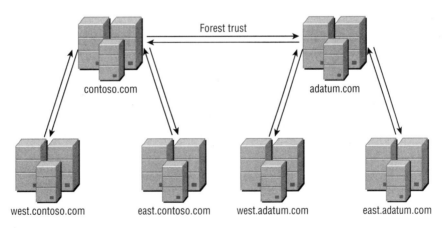

Figure 2.12 and 2.13 illustrate additional examples of cross-forest trust configurations.

FIGURE 2.12 Transitivity of cross-forest trusts

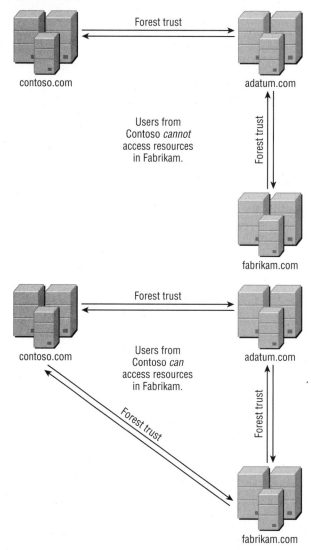

TRANSITIVITY OF FOREST TRUSTS

The transitivity of a forest trust doesn't extend beyond the two forests that have been configured for the trust. So a forest trust between ForestA and ForestB creates a two-way transitive trust between all domains in both trusts. But if you have a forest trust between ForestA and ForestB, and a second forest trust between ForestB and ForestC, this doesn't allow users from ForestA to access resources in ForestC, unless you explicitly create a second forest trust between ForestA and ForestC.

FIGURE 2.13 A one-way external trust

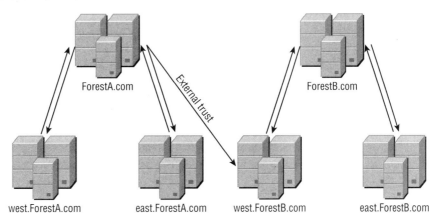

► An *external trust* can be created with a single AD domain if a cross-forest trust isn't desired or feasible. Instead of a transitive mesh of trusts, an external trust creates an explicit trust relationship with only the specific domain in question. An external trust is only ever nontransitive, but you may create either a one-way or a two-way external trust. You can see a one-way external trust illustrated in Figure 2.13. In this example, users from the west.ForestB.com domain *only* may access resources in the ForestA.com domain *only*; if a user from east.ForestB.com tried to access resources anywhere in the ForestA.com forest, they would be denied access.

► A *realm trust* may be created between an AD domain and a Unix Kerberos realm, enabling interoperability with third-party environments.

► A *shortcut trust* doesn't create a new trust relationship, per se; rather, it optimizes access between two domains within an existing cross-forest trust, which is often required in large environments with deeply nested child domains that may be connected by slow or overloaded WAN links. A shortcut trust is transitive in nature, and it may be one-way or two-way in direction.

Creating Trusts with Other Forests

Beginning in Windows Server 2003, AD administrators have the ability to create a cross-forest trust with other AD forests, as long as both forests are running at least the Windows Server 2003 forest functional level. This trust type creates an effective mesh of trusts between all domains in each forest, by creating a transitive trust between the forest root domains of each forest. Cross-forest trusts may be one-way or two-way in direction—in the case of a two-way cross-forest trust, a user in any domain in the trusted forest can access resources in any domain in the trusting forest, and vice versa. It's important to remember that this trust transitivity doesn't extend beyond the two forests: If a cross-forest trust exists between ForestA and ForestB, and a second cross-forest trust exists between ForestB and ForestC, users in ForestA can't access resources in ForestC unless a trust is explicitly created between ForestA and ForestC.

A cross-forest trust can't be automated through the use of the `netdom` command-line tool. Cross-forest trusts may only be created using the Active Directory Domains and Trusts graphical user interface.

Creating External Trusts with a Remote AD Domain

For scenarios in which a cross-forest trust isn't possible or isn't desired, you can create an external trust between two specific AD domains. Unlike the cross-forest trust, which creates a mesh of trusts between two entire forests, an external trust is a non-transitive trust that only permits users from one single domain to be able to access resources within a single remote domain. So, an external trust between the `contoso.com` and `adatum.com` domains allows users from `contoso.com` to access resources in the `adatum.com` domain, but it does *not* allow `contoso.com` users to access resources in the `corp.adatum.com` child domain without another explicit trust being configured between `contoso.com` and `corp.adatum.com`. External trusts may be one-way or two-way, and may be created from the command line using the `netdom.exe` utility.

The following example creates a one-way trust with `fabrikam.com` as the trusting domain and `contoso.com` as the trusted domain. This trust may be created as a two-way trust by adding the `/twoway` switch to the syntax. You'll be prompted for administrative credentials in both the trusting and the trusted domain to be able to create a two-way trust within a single operation:

```
netdom trust fabrikam.com /d:contoso.com /add
```

Creating Realm Trusts with a Non-Windows Kerberos Realm

Because AD is based on Kerberos, an industry standard, you can create trust relationships between AD domains and forests with a remote realm based on Kerberos V5. This realm trust allows cross-platform access to resources and services hosted in Unix and other third-party environments. Realm trusts may be transitive or non-transitive, and may be configured as one-way or two-way trusts.

In the following example, the `netdom` command-line tool is configuring a realm trust with the ATHENA Kerberos realm as the trusting domain and `contoso.com` as

the trusted domain. Because this is a realm trust, the command specifies a
trust password that will need to be entered identically when the trust is configured
from a server in the ATHENA realm, on the Unix side of the trust relationship. As
written, the following example configures a one-way, non-transitive trust relationship. You can add the /twoway switch to configure this as a two-way trust, and the
/transitive:YES switch to configure a transitive trust:

```
Netdom ATHENA /d:contoso.com /add /realm /
PasswordT:TrustPA$$w0rd
```

Creating Shortcut Trusts

In a large AD environment with multiple domain trees, or child domain structures
nested several layers deep, or both, users may encounter slowness when authenticating to resources nested deep within the forest structure. This is because of the
default trust path used to authenticate users in a trusted domain to a resource in a
remote trusting domain. In a single AD forest, each child domain has a two-way
transitive trust with its parent domain, whereas in a forest trust between two separate AD domains, a two-way transitive trust is configured between the forest root
domain of each forest.

Consider a user account in the sales.east.us.contoso.com child domain who
wishes to access a resource in the payroll.finance.de.emea.adatum.com
domain within the adatum.com domain tree. In order for the user to access the
desired resource, they need to walk the default trust path from the sales domain
to the east domain, to the us domain, to the contoso.com root domain. From
there the authentication path continues to the adatum.com root domain, to emea,
to de, to finance, and finally to the payroll domain, which contains the resource
the user is attempting to access. Particularly if the DCs in any of these domains are
connected via slow links, this can create delays in allowing users to access desired
resources. You can see this default trust path illustrated in Figure 2.14.

You can improve the performance of resource access across deeply nested trusts
(across a particular path that is frequently used, for example) by creating a shortcut
trust to optimize the authentication path that's used between domains. Shortcut
trusts are transitive in nature, meaning that they also confer access to additional
domains on the trusting side of the trust; and shortcut trusts can be one-way or
two-way. In the previous example, you could configure a shortcut trust between
the sales and payroll domains, which would create a trust path consisting of a
single hop whenever a user in the sales domain needed to access a resource in the
payroll domain. If the shortcut trust is one-way in nature, the optimized trust path

wouldn't apply to users in the payroll domain who attempt to access resources in sales; the longer default trust path would apply in that case unless the shortcut trust was configured as a two-way trust. You can see this illustrated in Figure 2.15.

FIGURE 2.14 The default trust path

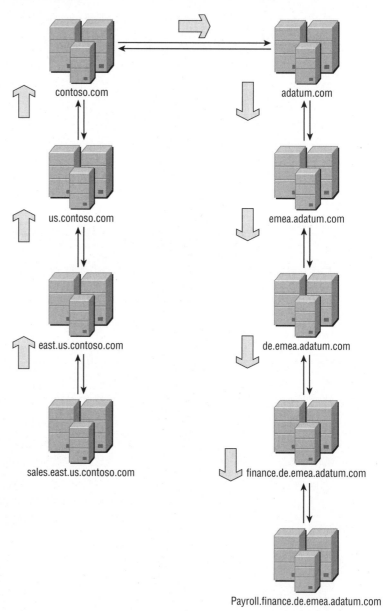

FIGURE 2.15 Using a shortcut trust

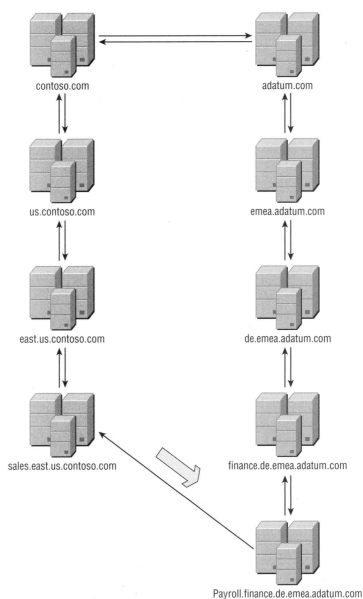

contoso.com

adatum.com

us.contoso.com

emea.adatum.com

east.us.contoso.com

de.emea.adatum.com

sales.east.us.contoso.com

finance.de.emea.adatum.com

Payroll.finance.de.emea.adatum.com

The following example uses the `netdom` command-line tool to create a two-way shortcut trust between the `ma.finance.corp.contoso.com` domain and the `sales.contoso.com` domain. (If required, you can also include the `/UserD` and

/PasswordD switches to specify a username and password with administrative credentials in the sales.contoso.com domain.)

```
netdom ma.finance.corp.contoso.com /d:sales.contoso.com /add /twoway
```

Removing a Trust

You can remove an AD trust relationship at any time using the /remove switch for netdom. In the following example, fabrikam.com denotes the trusting domain, whereas /d:contoso.com denotes the trusted domain. The /UserD switch indicates that CONTOSO\ContosoAdmin is a user account that has administrative privileges in the CONTOSO domain to remove the trust, whereas /PasswordD:* indicates that the user will be prompted to enter the password for CONTOSO\ContosoAdmin before the netdom command will run:

```
netdom trust fabrikam.com /d:contoso.com /remove /UserD:CONTOSO\
ContosoAdmin /PasswordD:*
```

Manage Active Directory Trusts

Once a trust relationship has been created, there are a number of administrative tasks that may need to be performed on an ongoing basis. Depending on the security requirements of a particular trust, you may need to fine-tune the ability of trusted users to access trusting resources, either by modifying SID Filtering settings or by enabling selective authentication across the trust. In large or complex environments, it may also be necessary to manage the list of UPN suffixes that may be routed for authentication requests across a particular trust.

Retrieving a List of Trusting and Trusted Domains

When an administrator creates a trust relationship in an AD domain or forest, that trust is represented by a trusted domain object (TDO) on both sides of the relationship. The TDO is a specific object class in AD that contains a number of mandatory and optional attributes, including the name of the trust partner, and the type and direction of the trust.

Using PowerShell, you can obtain a list of trusted and trusting domains for a particular domain by querying AD for a list of TDOs using the Get-ADObject cmdlet as shown here:

```
Get-ADObject -Filter {objectClass -eq "trustedDomain"}
-Properties TrustPartner,TrustDirection,trustType | FT Name,
TrustPartner,TrustDirection,TrustType
```

Verifying a Trust Relationship

After an AD trust relationship has been established, you may need to verify the secure channel on which it's based as part of troubleshooting or ongoing monitoring of your AD environment. This can be performed at the command line using the `netdom` command-line tool, as demonstrated here:

```
Netdom trust fabrikam.com /d:contoso.com /verify
```

In this command, `fabrikam.com` denotes the trusting domain, and `/d:contoso .com` denotes the trusted domain.

Configuring SID History

Each security principal in AD (user, group, or computer object) possesses a numeric security identifier known as an SID. This SID is unique within a single AD domain and doesn't change even if the security principal is renamed or moved to another container or OU in the same domain. (The SID isn't retained if an object is deleted and re-created with the same display name; the re-created object is a brand-new object with a completely different SID.) All Windows ACLs configured on files, folders, and other resources such as SharePoint document libraries use this SID to determine whether a particular user or computer should be granted or denied access to that resource.

This becomes potentially problematic, though, if you ever need to migrate a security principal from its current AD domain into a new AD domain or forest, as often happens during mergers, acquisitions, or divestitures in the business world. Because the SID is only unique within a single domain, migrating a security principal into a new domain creates a new SID for the object that doesn't correspond to the SID that is present in any existing ACLs. As a convenience measure during AD migrations, AD security principals also possess an attribute called SID History, which allows migrated user objects to retain records of any old SIDs they once possessed. This lets a migrated object continue to access a resource that used its premigration SID in an ACL. If a user attempted to access a resource with their new SID and was denied access, for example, Windows would check the SID History attribute to determine whether any previous SIDs were listed in the ACL that would allow or deny access.

You can enable SID History on any AD trust using the `netdom.exe` command, as shown here:

```
Netdom trust fabrikam.com /d:contoso.com /EnableSIDHistory:Yes
```

In this example, you can see how to list the SID History setting on an existing trust relationship without changing the setting:

```
Netdom trust fabrikam.com /d:contoso.com /EnableSIDHistory
```

The SID History is a great convenience measure, but it should be clear that it has the potential to be misused. If a malicious user in the source domain were able to find the SID of an administrative user in the target domain and inject that SID into their SID History attribute, this would create an elevation-of-privilege attack when their account was migrated into the target domain. So, if you have a trust relationship with users in `contoso.com` and resources in `adatum.com`, and a `contoso.com` user is able to inject the SID corresponding to `ADATUM\Administrator` into their SID History attribute, this user will have the same privileges as `ADATUM\administrator` within the `adatum.com` domain. This occurs because, without further restrictions, the SID History feature will process *all* entries contained in an object's SID History attribute without performing any sort of sanity check to determine whether the SID History entry might be malicious or forged.

You can mitigate this security risk through the use of *SID filtering*, which creates a kind of whitelist of domains whose SIDs are honored in the SID History attribute. This is possible because all security identifiers contains two components: the domain SID that is common to all security principals in a single domain, and the relative identifier (RID) that is unique to the individual object. Put another way: Domain SID + Relative Identifier = Security Identifier. The SID Filtering feature enumerates the list of trusted domains for a particular trust and disregards any SID History entries that don't contain the domain SID corresponding to one of those domains. In the previous example, if a `contoso.com` user attempts to access an `adatum.com` resource, SID Filtering filters out the `ADATUM\Administrator` entry in the user's SID History because `adatum.com` isn't in the list of trusted domains for that trust.

SID Filtering is enabled automatically on any trust relationship created in Windows Server 2003 or later. To enable SID Filtering on an existing trust, you run the `netdom.exe` command and *disable* the SID History feature. (Likewise, enabling SID History on a trust relationship disables SID Filtering.) The following example shows how to enable SID Filtering on a trust relationship by disabling SID History:

```
Netdom trust fabrikam.com /d:contoso.com /EnableSIDHistory:No
```

Configuring Selective Authentication

When you configure a trust relationship between two AD domains or forests, by default the Authenticated Users group in the trusted domain possesses all the permissions of the Authenticated Users group in the trusting domain. This includes the ability to authenticate to any domain-joined computer in the trusting domain. If you want to restrict the computers in the trusting domain to which trusted users are able to authenticate, in high security and/or restricted-use environments, for example, you can configure selective authentication on the trust relationship. Doing so forces administrators in the trusting domain to specify computers to which users from the trusted domain can authenticate. This additional permission is assigned through the use of the Allowed to Authenticate extended right that exists on each computer account. (Chapter 10, "Backing Up Data and Recovering from Disasters," will include scripts to automate the ability to assign this extended right on one or several computer accounts.) The following example demonstrates how to enable selective authentication on an AD trust relationship:

```
Netdom trust fabrikam.com /d:contoso.com /SelectiveAuth:Yes
```

Configuring Name-Suffix Routing

When two AD forests are connected via a forest trust, you can configure name-suffix routing to control how authentication requests are managed across the trust relationship. When you create a new forest trust, AD automatically adds a new name-suffix route to both sides of the trust in a format that allows authentication requests to be routed to the trusted and trusting forests, as well as to all child domains. If a forest trust has been configured with the contoso.com forest, a name suffix route of *.contoso.com is added dynamically to both sides of the trust. This simplifies administration of authentication requests by allowing all unique name suffixes to be routed across the forest trust.

In more complex environments, you may need to add additional name suffixes to a particular trust relationship, or you may need to exclude a particular name suffix from the wildcard routing created by the use of the *. You can use the netdom command-line tool to list all routed name suffixes and to enable or disable routing for particular name suffixes, NetBIOS names, and SIDs.

For example, you may wish to create a forest trust between two forests, adatum.com and contoso.com, both of which contain a child domain with a NetBIOS name of SALES—if the ussales.adatum.com and sales.contoso.com child domains both possess the same NetBIOS name, this creates a conflict across the forest trust. In this example, after you create the new trust to contoso.com, users in the Adatum forest can't route authentication requests to the sales.contoso.com domain using the SALES NetBIOS name, but users in contoso.com can still access resources in sales.contoso.com using its NetBIOS name. If you need to allow users to use the NetBIOS name SALES to route to the `contoso.com` forest instead, you can use `netdom` to disable SALES in `adatum.com` and then enable it in `contoso.com`.

The following example details all name suffixes that are currently configured over the forest trust between `fabrikam.com` and `contoso.com` (sample output is listed following the `netdom` command syntax):

```
Netdom trust fabrikam.com /namesuffixes:contoso.com

Name, Type, Status, Notes

1. *.contoso.com, Name Suffix, Enabled

2. *.child.contoso.com, Name Suffix, Enabled

3. CHILD, Domain NetBIOS name, Enabled, For child.contoso.com

4. s-1-5-21-1550512861-723516995-420396236, Domain SID, Enabled,
For child.contoso.com
```

In order to enable or disable a particular suffix, you need to run the first command from the following example and take note of the number assigned to the suffix that you want to enable (if currently disabled) or disable (if currently enabled). When you have the number, run the `netdom` command a second time using the `/togglesuffix` argument, as shown here:

```
Netdom trust fabrikam.com /namesuffixes:contoso.com
netdom trust fabrikam.com /namesuffixes:contoso.com /
togglesuffix:3
```

In the case of a forest trust with a non-Windows realm, you can also use `netdom` to add additional name suffixes to and remove them from the forest trust, as well as add specific exclusions to and remove them from the forest trust. (Note that this may only be performed using `netdom` in the case of a forest-transitive, non-Windows realm trust. For a cross-forest trust between two AD forests, name suffixes and name suffix exclusions must be added or removed using the Active

Directory Domains and Trusts user interface.) The following examples demonstrate how to add and remove a name suffix, as well as how to add and remove a name-suffix exclusion:

```
Netdom trust fabrikam.com /d:contoso.com /
AddTln:contosoresearch.com
Netdom trust fabrikam.com /d:contoso.com /
RemoveTln:contosoresearch.com
Netdom trust fabrikam.com /d:contoso.com /
AddTlnEx:contosoresearch.com
Netdom trust fabrikam.com /d:contoso.com /
RemoveTlnEx:contosoresearch.com
```

CHAPTER 3

Managing Sites and Replication

IN THIS CHAPTER, YOU WILL LEARN TO:

n Active Directory, sites are the only view that your domain controllers (DCs) have into your physical network infrastructure. Active Directory is optimized to take advantage of this knowledge. The more accurately your site topology reflects what your network is like, the better Active Directory will perform. For example, if Active Directory knows that the network link between your Chicago site and your Seattle site is faster than the link between your Chicago site and your Baltimore site, then DCs will prefer to replicate data to your Chicago DCs from Seattle rather than from Baltimore.

Your site topology affects things other than replication as well. There are some services on your network whose behavior you determine by using the site topology. One such case is client logon traffic. Clients prefer to perform their logon sequence against DCs that have good physical connectivity. Another example of a server that relies on the site topology is the Distributed File System (DFS). DFS can provide a virtual namespace for file shares. When a client accesses the namespace, DFS can use the site topology to determine whether the user accesses the copy of the file hosted in Baltimore or Seattle. DFS is just one of example of this. The site topology information can be made available to any application or service on your network that wants to take advantage of it. Because of this, it's sometimes difficult in complex enterprise environments to understand the impact that a site topology change may have. Managing your site topology is of utmost importance. In this chapter, you'll learn how to manage this site topology and also be introduced to the various factors that affect replication.

Manage the Site Topology

The site topology can be broken down into a few different components. Consider the site topology diagram in Figure 3.1.

In the figure, the larger circles represent the sites themselves. Typically, a *site* is a collection of well-connected networks. These are usually local area networks (LANs) with connection speeds ranging from 10 Mbps to multiple Gbps. More often than not, the circle in Figure 3.1 also represents a geographic boundary; that's why you'll sometimes see sites named after physical locations or office building codes. However, there is no requirement for the networks in a site to be in the same building.

The primary design considerations are typically client logon and Active Directory replication. Client computers will attempt to process their logon against a DC in the same site; if this site is in the same physical building on the same physical network, then the result will be a much better experience for the end users. Also, when Active Directory sees that two DCs are in the same site, it assumes that the network connection is faster and more reliable and therefore optimizes replication traffic between those DCs.

FIGURE 3.1   An example site topology

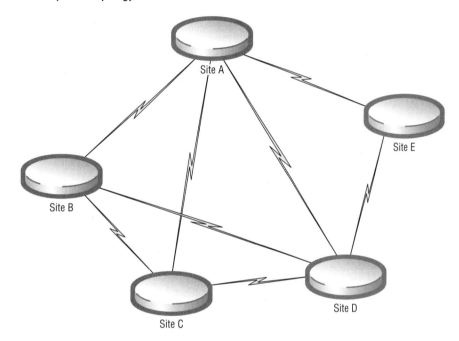

You'll also notice in Figure 3.1 that lines connect some of the sites together. These are called *site links*. Site links represent physical network connections between sites. When you tell Active Directory that one site is linked to another, then Active Directory knows that when a DC in one site talks to another, it has to traverse the network. Because of this, Active Directory may optimize the traffic between those two DCs. For example, in some cases Active Directory compresses replication data. Doing so results in higher CPU utilization on the DC but increases network efficiency.

When you define a site link in Active Directory, you give the site link an arbitrary number, referred to as the *cost*. This gives Active Directory some insight into the conditions of the connection as compared to other connections. We'll give you some guidance for specifying this cost later in this chapter.

Edit Sites, Site Links, and Subnets

When you define what a site is in Active Directory, you give the site a name, a list of subnets in the site, and a list of other sites that it can talk to directly. When these components come together, you can paint an accurate picture of what your network looks like and give that picture to Active Directory. As time moves on, however, things tend to change. This will include the addition or removal of sites, subnets, and site links. Therefore, as an Active Directory administrator, it's important to ensure that you're aware of the changes occurring on your network. If a physical connection between sites is removed from your network, you'll want to reflect this change in your Active Directory site topology to ensure that Active Directory is making the right decisions.

The information about your site topology is unique for each Active Directory forest. So if you have two separate forests in your environment, you'll need to update the site topology in each forest independently. Information about the site topology is stored in Active Directory itself. The directory contains multiple partitions, each with its own purpose. The site topology is stored in the configuration partition, whose purpose is to store configuration data about the forest. For more information about directory partitions, refer to Chapter 2, "Managing Domains and Forests."

Manage Sites

When managing your site topology, you should ensure that you first have an accurate representation of your sites. As stated earlier, a site ideally consists of a collection of well-connected networks with good bandwidth and low latency. Here, we'll look at how to manage the `site` objects themselves, determine which ones exist, remove old ones, and create new ones. Later in this chapter, we'll explore some of the additional settings that can be configured for each site that affect your end-user's and application's experience.

List All the Sites in a Forest

Each site has a unique object in Active Directory's configuration partition. You can view what sites exist in your forest by connecting to the configuration partition and listing each of the `site` objects. If you're using ADSI, you can use the following steps in PowerShell to obtain a list of sites in your forest:

1. Obtain the Distinguished Name (DN) of the configuration partition. The following PowerShell command retrieves the DN of the configuration partition for the domain that your computer is currently a member of. Here, the DN is stored in the $cnfg variable.

```
$cnfg = ([ADSI]"LDAP://RootDSE").configurationNamingContext
```

2. Connect to the Sites container. This container is the parent for each of the site objects in the forest. The DN of the Sites container is CN=Sites, CN=Configuration, <domain DN>. For example, in the contoso.com domain, the DN of the Sites container is CN=Sites, CN=Configuration, DC=contoso, DC=com:

```
$sites = [ADSI]"LDAP://CN=Sites,$cnfg"
```

3. List the site objects by passing the children to the ForEach-Object cmdlet. By default, this list includes objects that aren't sites. Therefore, you need to filter the list so that only site objects are displayed. In the following command, this is accomplished by using the Where-Object cmdlet:

```
$sites.children | where-object {$_.objectcategory -like ↵
"CN=Site*"} | ForEach-Object { $_.Name }
```

Rather than running these steps each time, you can use the script in Listing 3.1, which combines them.

LISTING 3.1: ListSites-ADSI.ps1

```
## File Name: ListSites-ADSI.ps1
## Description: Uses ADSI to print a list of sites in the forest
# Get the DN of the configuration partition in the current forest
$cnfg = ([ADSI]"LDAP://RootDSE").configurationNamingContext
# Get the DN of the Sites container
$sites = [ADSI]"LDAP://CN=Sites,$cnfg"
# Loop through each object in the Sites container
foreach ($site in $sites.children)
{
    # If the object is a site object, display its information
    if ($site.objectcategory -like "CN=Site*")
    {
        $site.Name
    }
}
```

There is no specific set of cmdlets in the Active Directory module for working with sites. However, you can use the Get-ADObject cmdlet to view site objects. The Get-ADObject cmdlet can be used to search through an Active Directory subtree and return objects that meet the conditions set in the filter. The following PowerShell one-liner uses the Get-ADObject cmdlet to display a list of sites in the forest to which you're currently logged in:

```
Get-ADObject -Filter 'objectclass -eq "site"' -SearchBase ↵
(Get-ADRootDSE).ConfigurationNamingContext' | ft name
```

Remove a Site

When you remove a site, you're not only removing the site object itself, but also its association with any site links as well as the list of subnets that was assigned to the site. If the site still physically exists in your environment, then you should ensure that the subnets associated with the site are associated with a different site. You can use the following steps to remove a site with ADSI in PowerShell:

1. Retrieve the DN of the forest's configuration partition. The following command stores the configuration partition DN for the current forest in the $cnfg variable:

   ```
   $cnfg = ([ADSI]"LDAP://RootDSE").configurationNamingContext
   ```

2. Build out the DN of the site that you want to delete. You can do this by prepending the configuration partition DN with the common name of the site followed by the common name of the Sites container. For example, the Baltimore site in the contoso.com domain has the following DN: CN=Baltimore, CN=Sites, CN=Configuration, DC=contoso, DC=com. The following command builds out the site's DN and places it in $site:

   ```
   $site = [ADSI]("LDAP://cn=Baltimore,cn=sites,$cnfg")
   ```

3. Call the DeleteTree method on the site to delete the site object and its associated child objects:

   ```
   $site.DeleteTree
   ```

The script in Listing 3.2 uses ADSI to delete the site that you pass in as the first script parameter.

LISTING 3.2: RemoveSite-ADSI.ps1

```
## File Name: RemoveSite-ADSI.ps1
## Description: Uses ADSI to remove the site specified in the command.

## Prints out information for how to use the script
$script_name = $MyInvocation.MyCommand.Name
function print_usage
{
    Write-Host "You must specify the site name that you would like
    to `remove."
    Write-Host
    Write-Host "Example:"
    Write-Host "    $script_name Baltimore"
}
## Removes the site
function remove_site($sitename)
{
    # Add cn= to the site name to make it a common name
    $sitename = "cn=$sitename"
        # Get the configuration partition
    $cnfg = ([ADSI]"LDAP://RootDSE").configurationNamingContext
    # Delete the site object
    $site = [ADSI]("LDAP://$sitename,cn=sites,$cnfg")
    $site.DeleteTree()
}
# Ensure that a site name was passed into the script. If not, show
# an example of how to use the script and then exit. Else, remove
# the site
if ($args.Length -eq 0)
{
    print_usage
    Exit
}
else
{
    # Get the name of the site from the first command line argument
    $sitename = $args[0]
```

(continues)

LISTING 3-2 *(continued)*

```
        try
        {
            remove_site($sitename)
            Write-Host "The site $sitename was successfully deleted."
        }
        catch
        {
            Write-Host "The site $sitename could not be deleted:"
            Write-Host "    $_"
        }
    }
```

When using the Active Directory PowerShell module, you can use the Remove-ADObject cmdlet to delete a site. You'll need to pass in the DN of the site and specify the -Recursive option to ensure that the NTDS Site Settings and Servers containers are both deleted as well. If you know the site's DN, you can use the following one-liner to delete the site:

```
Remove-ADObject <SiteDN> -Recursive
```

For example, to delete the Baltimore site in the contoso.com forest, the command would resemble the following:

```
Remove-ADObject "CN=Baltimore,CN=Sites,CN=Configuration, ↵
DC=contoso,DC=com" -Recurse
```

If you don't know the DN of the site and would rather use the name, you can use the script in Listing 3.3. Remember that this script uses the Active Directory module, so you need to have the module imported before you can use it. Pass the name of the site into the script as the first parameter. Note that this script won't prompt you for confirmation before deleting the site.

LISTING 3.3: RemoveSite-ADModule.ps1

```
## File Name: RemoveSite-ADModule.ps1
## Description: Uses the AD Module to remove the site specified in
## the command.
## Prints out information for how to use the script
$script_name = $MyInvocation.MyCommand.Name
function print_usage
{
```

```
        Write-Host "You must specify the site name that you would like" +
            "to remove."
        Write-Host
        Write-Host "Example:"
        Write-Host "    $script_name Baltimore"
}
## Removes the site
function remove_site($sitename)
{
    # Get the DN of the Site object
    $rootdse = Get-ADRootDSE
    $cnfg = $rootdse.ConfigurationNamingContext
    $sitedn = "CN=$sitename,CN=Sites,$cnfg"
    # Delete the site object
    Remove-ADObject $sitedn -Recursive -Confirm:$false
}


# Ensure that a site name was passed into the script. If not, show
# an example of how to use the script and then exit. Else, remove
# the site
if ($args.Length -eq 0)
{
    print_usage
    Exit
}
else
{
    # Get the name of the site from the first command line argument
    $sitename = $args[0]
    try
    {
        remove_site($sitename)
        Write-Host "The site $sitename was successfully deleted."
    }
    catch
    {
        Write-Host "The site $sitename could not be deleted:"
        Write-Host "    $_"
    }
}
```

Create a Site

When you create a site in Active Directory, it isn't required to contain a DC; but in most configurations, it's preferred to have one. Therefore, if you're building a new Active Directory infrastructure, you can create your sites in advance before your DCs are added.

To create a new site, you'll need to create two other objects to go along with it. We'll walk you through this process step by step using ADSI first, and then we'll give you an ADSI-based PowerShell script that you can use to create `site` objects. Feel free to open PowerShell in your lab environment and follow along.

First, you need to connect to the configuration partition's container in the forest. As stated earlier, this is where your site topology information is kept. The following command stores the name of the configuration partition container in the variable called `$cnfg`. The configuration partition used is the one associated with the forest that the machine running the command is in:

```
$cnfg = ([ADSI]"LDAP://RootDSE").configurationNamingContext
```

Next, you need to get a copy of the `Sites` container object. Here you'll store it in the `$sites` variable. Notice that for the LDAP path, you append the name of the configuration partition's container to the end of the string `LDAP://cn=sites`. For example, if the forest name is `contoso.com`, the configuration partition's container name is `cn=configuration,dc=contoso,dc=com`. Therefore, the `Sites` container is located at `cn=sites,cn=configuration,dc=contoso,dc=com`.

```
$sites = [ADSI]("LDAP://cn=sites," + $cnfg)
```

You then create the `site` object as a child to the `Sites` container. To do this, call the `Create` function on the `Sites` container, passing in `site` as the object type and a common name. The common name parameter must begin with `cn=`. In the following commands, the newly created `site` object is stored in the `$site` variable. After the object is created, you need to call the `SetInfo` function to make the changes in Active Directory:

```
$site = $sites.Create("site", "cn=Baltimore")
$site.SetInfo()
```

The `site` object represents the actual site, but you must also create some additional child objects. The `site` object itself has two children that need to exist: the `NTDS Site Settings` object and the `Servers` container. The `NTDS Site Settings` object contains directory service configuration settings for DCs in the site. Some examples of information stored here are the replication schedule and a pointer to query policies that apply to the site.

QUERY POLICIES

A *query policy* is an LDAP policy that defines limits on use of LDAP operations on DCs. Query policies can prevent Denial of Service (DoS) attacks on DCs by setting things like IP block lists, the maximum number of LDAP connections, and timeout values. In most cases, the query policy values don't need to be changed.

To create the `NTDS Site Settings` object, you follow a process similar to the one you used to create the `site` object. Call the `Create` function on the `site` object, and pass in `NTDSSiteSettings` as the object type along with the common name `CN=NTDS Site Settings`:

```
$ntdssettings = $site.Create("NTDSSiteSettings", "CN=NTDS Site ↵
Settings")
$ntdssettings.SetInfo()
```

The last child object that you need to create is the `Servers` container. This container is where your `server` objects will be stored. These `server` objects aren't the same as the DC's computer object, which is stored in the directory's domain partition. The `server` objects here are representations of each DC in the site and contain site-specific information for the DCs. Again, you call the `Create` function to create the `Servers` container, but this time you pass in `ServersContainer` as the object type and `cn=Servers` as the common name:

```
$server = $site.Create("serverscontainer", "cn=Servers")
$server.SetInfo()
```

When all of these objects are created, you have a complete site. The PowerShell script in Listing 3.4 puts these commands together and allows you to create a site by passing the name of the site that you want to create.

LISTING 3.4: **CreateSite-ADSI.ps1**

```
## File Name: CreateSite-ADSI.ps1
## Description: Creates a site in Active Directory with the name
##      that is passed in as the first parameter. This version uses
##      ADSI.
## Prints out information for how to use the script
$script_name = $MyInvocation.MyCommand.Name
function print_usage
{
```

(continues)

LISTING 3-4 *(continued)*

```
        Write-Host "You must specify the site name that you would like " +
            "to create."
        Write-Host
        Write-Host "Example:"
        Write-Host "    $script_name Baltimore"
    }
## Creates the site
function create_site($sitename)
{
    # Add cn= to the site name to make it a common name
    $sitename = "cn=$sitename"

    # Get the configuration partition
    $cnfg = ([ADSI]"LDAP://RootDSE").configurationNamingContext
    # Get the sites containers
    $sites = [ADSI]("LDAP://cn=sites,$cnfg")
    # Create the site object
    $site = $sites.Create("site", $sitename)
    $site.SetInfo()
    # Create the NTDS Site Settings object
    $ntdssettings = $site.Create("ntdssitesettings",
        "CN=NTDS Site Settings")
    $ntdssettings.SetInfo()
    # Create the Servers container
    $server = $site.Create("serverscontainer", "cn=Servers")
    $server.SetInfo()
}
# Ensure that a site name was passed into the script. If not, show
# an example of how to use the script and then exit. Else, create
# the site
if ($args.Length -eq 0)
{
    print_usage
    Exit
}
else
{
    # Get the name of the site from the first command line argument
```

```
$sitename = $args[0]

try
{
    create_site($sitename)
    Write-Host "The site $sitename was successfully created."
}
catch
{
    Write-Host "The site $sitename could not be created:"
    Write-Host "    $_"
}
}
```

Creating a site with the Active Directory module is a little easier than using ADSI, but it still follows the same general process. Unfortunately, there isn't a single cmdlet that you can use to create a site. You'll need to create the site by creating the three objects that were discussed previously.

To create the objects, you can use the New-ADObject cmdlet. This is slightly easier than using pure ADSI, because you're using a PowerShell cmdlet rather than calling functions directly. However, it still requires multiple steps and you may want to use a script.

First, retrieve the DN for the configuration partition using the Get-ADRootDSE cmdlet. In this example, the configuration partition DN is stored in the $cnfg variable:

```
$rootdse = Get-ADRootDSE
$cnfg = $rootdse.ConfigurationNamingContext
```

After you have the configuration partition DN, you can derive the DN of the Sites container by adding CN=Sites to the beginning of the configuration partition's DN:

```
$sites = "CN=Sites,$cnfg"
```

The New-ADObject cmdlet requires that you pass in the common name of the new object, the DN of the object's parent, and the object type. The following command passes these parameters into the New-ADObject cmdlet and creates the site:

```
New-ADObject -Name "CN=Baltimore" -Path $sites -Type Site
```

After the site object is created, you need to create the NTDS Site Settings object and the Servers container. You'll use the New-ADObject cmdlet again to create these objects. This time, the site you just created is the parent, so you must pass in the DN of the site. You can create the DN by prepending the site's common name to the front of the Sites container's DN:

```
$sitedn = "CN=Baltimore,$sites"
```

You can then create the two objects:

```
New-ADObject -Name "NTDS Site Settings" -Path $sitedn ↵
    -Type NTDSSiteSettings
New-ADObject -Name "Servers" -Path $sitedn -Type serversContainer
```

To make this process more repeatable, you can place it in a script. Listing 3.5 uses the Active Directory module to create a site. Pass the name of the site in as the first parameter when you call the script. Also, remember that you'll need to ensure that the AD module is imported before this script will run.

LISTING 3.5: CreateSite-ADModule.ps1

```
## File Name: CreateSite-ADModule.ps1
## Description: Creates a site in Active Directory with the name
##      that is passed in as the first parameter. This version uses
##      uses the Active Directory module for PowerShell.
## Prints out information for how to use the script
$script_name = $MyInvocation.MyCommand.Name
function print_usage
{
    Write-Host "You must specify the site name that you would " +
        "like to create."
    Write-Host
    Write-Host "Example:"
    Write-Host "    $script_name Baltimore"
}
## Creates the site
function create_site($sitename)
{
    # Get the DN of the Sites container
    $rootdse = Get-ADRootDSE
    $cnfg = $rootdse.ConfigurationNamingContext
    $sites = "CN=Sites,$cnfg"
    # Create the site object
    New-ADObject -Name $sitename -Path $sites -Type Site
```

```
    # Get the DN of the site that was just created
    $sitedn = "CN=$sitename,$sites"
    # Create the NTDS Site Settings object and the Servers container
    New-ADObject -Name "NTDS Site Settings" -Path $sitedn ↵
        -Type NTDSSiteSettings
    New-ADObject -Name "Servers" -Path $sitedn -Type serversContainer
}
# Ensure that a site name was passed into the script. If not, show
# an example of how to use the script and then exit. Else, create
# the site
if ($args.Length -eq 0)
{
    print_usage
    Exit
}
else
{
    # Get the name of the site from the first command line argument
    $sitename = $args[0]
    try
    {
        create_site($sitename)
        Write-Host "The site $sitename was successfully created."
    }
    catch
    {
        Write-Host "The site $sitename could not be created:"
        Write-Host "    $_"
    }
}
```

Manage Subnets for a Site

Each site has a list of subnets that are associated with it. This subnet list is what tells
Active Directory which networks are associated with a site. For example, when a client logs on to the domain, the client logon process determines which site the client
is in by examining the client's IP address. This IP address is weighed against the list
of known subnets in Active Directory. The client's logon traffic is processed against
a DC in the site associated with the subnet the client is coming from.

In Active Directory, subnets are defined in Classless Inter-Domain Routing (CIDR) notation. CIDR specifies the subnet in terms of the network's IP address, followed by a forward slash, followed by the number of bits in the bitmask. For example, the Class C network 192.168.0.0 with network mask of 255.255.255.0 is referenced as 192.168.0.0/24 in CIDR notation.

Subnet objects are stored in the configuration partition under the container called CN=Subnets, which is a child object of the Sites container. For example, the Subnets container in the contoso.com domain has a DN of CN=Subnets, CN=Sites, CN=Configuration, DC=contoso, DC=com. The common name of the subnet object that represents each network is the CIDR prefixed with CN=. The common name of the network referenced in the example earlier is CN=192.168.0.0/24. If added to the contoso.com domain, the full DN of the subnet object is CN=192.168.0.0/24, CN=Subnets, CN=Sites, CN=Configuration, DC=contoso, DC=com.

View the Subnets Associated with a Site

Subnets are associated with Active Directory sites by their siteObject attribute. This attribute contains the DN of the site that the subnet is a part of. In addition, each site object also contains an attribute called siteObjectBL, which is a back-link of all the DN references by the subnet objects. When a subnet adds a site object's DN to its siteObject attributes, the back-link is automatically created on the site object in the siteObjectBL attribute. This gives you a single place that you can query to get a list of all the subnets in an Active Directory site. Without this back-link, you would have to enumerate every subnet object and examine the siteObject on each one.

You can use the following steps to use ADSI in PowerShell to view the list of subnets in a site:

1. Connect to the site object in PowerShell. In the following example, you store the site object in the $site variable. To do this, you need to use the site's DN:

   ```
   $site = [ADSI]"LDAP://CN=Baltimore,CN=Sites,CN=Configuration,
   DC=contoso,DC=com"
   ```

2. From here, you can reference the siteObjectBL attribute, which is displayed in the console:

   ```
   $site.siteObjectBL
   ```

If you don't want to use the DN of the site, you can use the script in Listing 3.6 to display the list of subnets in a site. If you specify the name of the site as an input parameter into the script, that particular site's subnets will be displayed. If you don't use any input parameters, the script will enumerate every site in the forest and display the subnets associated with each one.

LISTING 3.6: ListSubnets-ADSI.ps1

```
## File Name: ListSubnets-ADSI.ps1
## Description: Uses ADSI to list the subnets in an Active
##      Directory site.
## Lists the subnets for one site
function list_one($sitename)
{
    # Add cn= to the site name to make it a common name
    $sitename = "cn=$sitename"
    # Get the configuration partition
    $cnfg = ([ADSI]"LDAP://RootDSE").configurationNamingContext
    # Get the site
    $site = [ADSI]("LDAP://$sitename,cn=sites,$cnfg")
    if ($site.distinguishedName -eq $null) { Throw }
    # Display the Site Name and its subnets
    Write-Host $site.Name
    Write-Host "-------------------------------"
    if ($site.siteObjectBL.Count -eq 0)
    {
        Write-Host "No subnets found for this site"
    }
    else
    {
        $site.siteObjectBL
    }
}


# If a site name was not passed into the script, enumerate every site.
# Otherwise, use the site that was passed in.
if ($args.Length -eq 0)
```

(continues)

LISTING 3-6 *(continued)*

```
    {
        # Get the DN of the configuration partition in the current forest
        $cnfg = ([ADSI]"LDAP://RootDSE").configurationNamingContext
        # Get the DN of the Sites container
        $sites = [ADSI]"LDAP://CN=Sites,$cnfg"
        # Loop through each object in the Sites container
        foreach ($site in $sites.children)
        {
            # If the object is a site object, display its subnet list
            if ($site.objectcategory -like "CN=Site*")
            {
                list_one($site.Name)
                Write-Host
            }
        }
    }
    else
    {
        # Get the name of the site from the first command line argument
        $sitename = $args[0]
        try
        {
            list_one($sitename)
        }
        catch
        {
            Write-Host "Could not retrieve the subnets for " +
                "site $sitename:"
            Write-Host "     $_"
        }
    }
```

If you're using the Active Directory module and know the DN of the site, you can retrieve a list of subnets in the site with a one-liner. The following one-liner lists the subnets in the Baltimore site in the contoso.com forest:

```
Get-ADObject 'CN=Baltimore,CN=Sites,CN=Configuration,DC=contoso, ↵
DC=com' -Properties siteObjectBL | foreach { $_.siteObjectBL }
```

If you want to retrieve a list of all subnets in the forest and you don't care which site they're associated with, you can search the directory for all objects that have the type Subnet and list them. The following one-liner does this for the contoso.com forest:

```
Get-ADObject -Filter 'objectclass -eq "subnet"' -SearchBase ↵
"CN=Configuration,DC=contoso,DC=com"
```

The script in Listing 3.7 is similar to the ListSubnets-ADSI.ps1 script, but instead it uses the Active Directory module. Make sure you have the Active Directory module imported before running this script.

LISTING 3.7: ListSubnets-ADModule.ps1

```
## File Name: ListSubnets-ADModule.ps1
## Description: Uses the Active Directory Module to list the subnets
##     in an Active Directory site.
## Lists the subnets for one site
function list_one($sitename)
{
    # Get the DN of the Site object
    $rootdse = Get-ADRootDSE
    $cnfg = $rootdse.ConfigurationNamingContext
    $sitedn = "CN=$sitename,CN=Sites,$cnfg"
    # Get the site
    $site = Get-ADObject $sitedn -properties siteObjectBL
    # Throw an error if the site doesn't exist
    if ($site.distinguishedName -eq $null) { Throw }
    # Display the Site Name and its subnets
    Write-Host $site.Name
    Write-Host "-------------------------------"
    if ($site.siteObjectBL.Count -eq 0)
    {
        Write-Host "No subnets found for this site"
    }
    else
    {
        $site.siteObjectBL
    }
}
```

(continues)

LISTING 3-7 *(continued)*

```
# If a site name was not passed into the script, enumerate every site.
# Otherwise, use the site that was passed in.
if ($args.Length -eq 0)
{
    # Get a collection of sites in the forest
    $rootdse = Get-ADRootDSE
    $cnfg = $rootdse.ConfigurationNamingContext
    $sites = Get-ADObject -Filter 'objectclass -eq "site"' ↵
        -SearchBase $cnfg
    # Loop through each site in the forest and display the
    # list of subnets
    foreach ($site in $sites)
    {
        list_one($site.Name)
        Write-Host
    }
}
else
{
    # Get the name of the site from the first command line argument
    $sitename = $args[0]

    try
    {
        list_one($sitename)
    }
    catch
    {
        Write-Host "Could not retrieve the subnets for " +
            "site $sitename:"
        Write-Host "    $_"
    }
}
```

Create a Subnet

When creating a subnet, you'll need to give Active Directory two pieces of information. The first is the CIDR notation of the subnet. As mentioned earlier in this section, the CIDR is a way of expressing the network segment in terms of an IP address range and a subnet bitmask. The second piece of information you'll need to pass in is the name of the site that the subnet is associated with.

The subnet is created as the object type `Subnet` in the `Subnets` container in the configuration partition. This `subnet` object contains an attribute called the `siteObject` attribute, which specifies which site the subnet belongs to. Therefore, when creating the `subnet` object, you need to set the `siteObject` attribute to be the DN of the site that the subnet is associated with. You can use the following steps to create a `subnet` object with ADSI:

1. Connect to the `Subnets` container in the configuration partition. The `Subnets` container always resides under the `Sites` container; therefore, you can build the DN as a string variable when you have the DN of the configuration partition. The following commands store the DN of the `Subnets` container in the variable $subnets_cn and then connect to the container with the $subnets_obj variable:

   ```
   $cnfg = ([ADSI]"LDAP://RootDSE").configurationNamingContext
   $subnets_cn = "cn=Subnets,cn=Sites,$($cnfg)"
   $subnets_obj = [ADSI]("LDAP://$($subnets_cn)")
   ```

2. Create the `subnet` object as a child object to the `Subnets` container. You should pass in `subnet` as the object type, as demonstrated in the following command. Also, ensure that you use the cn= convention on the subnet's CIDR when passing it into the `Create` method:

   ```
   $new_subnet = $subnets_obj.Create("subnet", ↵
   "cn=192.168.0.0/24")
   ```

3. Before running `SetInfo()` to make the change in Active Directory, put the site's DN into to the `siteObject` attribute on the new `subnet` object. As mentioned earlier, doing so associates the subnet with the Active Directory site. In this example, you associate the subnet with the site named `Seattle`:

   ```
   $new_subnet.Put("siteObject", "cn=Seattle,cn=Sites,$($cnfg)")
   ```

4. Run `SetInfo()` to make the change to Active Directory. It's important to note here that if the CIDR notation of the subnet is invalid, the `SetInfo()` method will throw an error. Therefore, if you're using a script, you may want to embed some logic to verify that the CIDR is valid before attempting to create the subnet in Active Directory:

   ```
   $new_subnet.SetInfo()
   ```

The script in Listing 3.8 uses the steps just discussed to provide an easier approach to creating subnets. When you run this script, pass in the subnet's CIDR as the

Administering
Service Delivery

PART I

-Subnet parameter and the name of the site as the -SiteName parameter, as in the following example:

```
CreateSubnet-ADSI.ps1 -Subnet 192.168.0.0/24 -SiteName Seattle
```

LISTING 3.8: CreateSubnet-ADSI.ps1

```
## File Name: CreateSubnet-ADSI.ps1
## Description:
##      Uses ADSI to create a subnet in an Active Directory site.
Param($Subnet, $SiteName)
## Create the subnet for the specified site
function create_subnet($_subnet, $_sitename)
{
    # Get the DN of the configuration partition
    $cnfg = ([ADSI]"LDAP://RootDSE").configurationNamingContext
    # Build the DN of the site that was passed in
    $site_dn = "cn=$($_sitename),cn=Sites,$($cnfg)"
    # Get the Subnets container
    $subnetcontainer = [ADSI]("LDAP://cn=Subnets,cn=Sites,$($cnfg)")
    # Create the subnet object in the Subnets container
    $subnetobj = $subnetcontainer.Create("subnet", "cn=$($_subnet)")
    $subnetobj.Put("siteObject", $site_dn)
    $subnetobj.SetInfo()
}
# Check to ensure that the correct parameters were specified for
# the script
if ($Subnet -eq $null -or $SiteName -eq $null)
{
    $script_name = $MyInvocation.MyCommand.Name

    Write-Host "`nMissing or invalid parameters. Please ensure" +
        "that you include both a subnet using CIDR notation and" +
        "the name of the site that you want to add the subnet to."
    Write-Host "`nExample:"
    Write-Host "`t$($script_name) -Subnet 192.168.0.0/24 -SiteName" +
        "Baltimore"
    Exit
}
```

```
# Attempt to create the subnet in the specified site
try
{
    create_subnet $Subnet $SiteName
    Write-Host "`nSubnet $($Subnet) successfully created and added" +
        " to the $($SiteName) site."
}
catch
{
    Write-Host "`nCould not create the subnet for site $($SiteName):"
    Write-Host "`t$_"
}
```

You can also use the `New-ADObject` cmdlet in the Active Directory module to create the subnet object. The process is still the same: create the object as a child of the `Subnets` container, and then point the `siteObject` attribute to the site's DN. The following commands demonstrate how to do this with the `New-ADObject` cmdlet:

```
$site_dn = "cn=Seattle,cn=Sites,cn=Configuration,dc=contoso, ↵
dc=com"
$subnets_dn = "cn=Subnets,cn=Sites,cn=Configuration,dc=contoso, ↵
dc=com"
New-ADObject -Name "192.168.0.0/24" -Path $subnets_dn -Type ↵
Subnet -OtherAttributes @{siteObject=$site_dn}
```

The script in Listing 3.9 uses the AD module to create the subnet rather than ADSI. The syntax of the script is the same as the ADSI script used earlier.

LISTING 3.9: CreateSubnet-ADModule.ps1

```
## File Name: CreateSubnet-ADModule.ps1
## Description:
##      Uses the AD Module to create a subnet in an Active Directory
##      site.
Param($Subnet, $SiteName)
## Create the subnet for the specified site
function create_subnet($_subnet, $_sitename)
{
    # Get the DN of the configuration partition
    $cnfg = (Get-ADRootDSE).ConfigurationNamingContext
```

(continues)

LISTING 3-9 *(continued)*

```
    # Build the DN of the site that was passed in
    $site_dn = "cn=$($_sitename),cn=Sites,$($cnfg)"
    # Build the DN of the Subnets container
    $subnets_dn = "cn=Subnets,cn=Sites,$($cnfg)"
    # Create the subnet object in the Subnets container
    New-ADObject -Name $_subnet -Path $subnets_dn -Type Subnet ↵
        -OtherAttributes @{siteObject=$site_dn}
}
# Check to ensure that the correct parameters were specified for
# the script
if ($Subnet -eq $null -or $SiteName -eq $null)
{
    $script_name = $MyInvocation.MyCommand.Name
    Write-Host "`nMissing or invalid parameters. Please ensure " +
        "that you include both a subnet using CIDR notation and" +
        " the name of the site that you want to add the subnet to."
    Write-Host "`nExample:"
    Write-Host "`t$($script_name) -Subnet 192.168.0.0/24 -SiteName" +
        " Baltimore"
    Exit
}
# Attempt to create the subnet in the specified site
try
{
    create_subnet $Subnet $SiteName
    Write-Host "`nSubnet $($Subnet) successfully created and added" +
        " to the $($SiteName) site."
}
catch
{
    Write-Host "`nCould not create the subnet for site $($SiteName):"
    Write-Host "`t$_"
}
```

Remove a Subnet

Subnet objects are associated with sites based on their `siteObject` attribute. Therefore, the only thing required to remove a subnet is to delete its object. No additional cleanup is needed on any of the existing `site` objects in the forest. To remove a subnet with ADSI, use the following process:

1. Retrieve the DN of the forest's configuration partition. The following command stores the configuration partition DN for the current forest in the `$cnfg` variable:

   ```
   $cnfg = ([ADSI]"LDAP://RootDSE").configurationNamingContext
   ```

2. Build out the DN of the subnet that you want to delete. Because all subnet objects are stored in the `Subnets` container, you only need the CIDR name of the subnet to build out the DN:

   ```
   $subnet_dn = "cn=192.168.0.0/24,cn=Subnets,cn=Sites,$cnfg"
   ```

3. Connect to the `subnet` object, and call the `DeleteTree` method. Doing so deletes the `subnet` object from the container. There is no need to call the `SetInfo()` method in this case:

   ```
   $subnet_obj = [ADSI]"LDAP://$($subnet_dn)"
   $subnet_obj.DeleteTree
   ```

To remove a `subnet` object with the AD module, you can run the `Remove-ADObject` cmdlet and specify the subnet's DN. The following example demonstrates this by removing the 192.168.0.0/24 subnet from the `contoso.com` forest:

```
Remove-ADObject "cn=192.168.0.0/24,cn=Subnets,cn=Sites, ↵
cn=Configuration,dc=contoso,dc=com"
```

Associate Existing Subnets with Sites

It's important to ensure that each network subnet in your environment is mapped against an Active Directory site. If not, your clients may use a DC in another site, potentially across the wide area network (WAN) or maybe even on the other side of the world. If you have an existing subnet object that isn't associated with a site, you can make the association by setting the `siteObject` attribute on the subnet. When using ADSI, you can use the following steps to associate a subnet with a site:

1. Retrieve the DN of the forest's configuration partition. The following command stores the configuration partition DN for the current forest in the `$cnfg` variable:

   ```
   $cnfg = ([ADSI]"LDAP://RootDSE").configurationNamingContext
   ```

2. Get the DN of the site to which you want to associate the subnet. Because all `site` objects reside in the `Sites` container, you can build this string out as a variable if you know the site name:

```
$site_dn = "cn=Seattle,cn=Sites,$($cnfg)"
```

3. Build out the DN of the subnet that you want to associate with a new site. Because all `subnet` objects are stored in the `Subnets` container, you only need the CIDR name of the subnet to build out the DN:

```
$subnet_dn = "cn=192.168.0.0/24,cn=Subnets,cn=Sites,$($cnfg)"
```

4. Connect to the subnet object, and call the `Put` method. Put the DN of the site in the subnet's `siteObject` attribute:

```
$subnet_obj = [ADSI]"LDAP://$($subnet_dn)"
$subnet_obj.Put("siteObject", $site_dn)
```

5. Call the `SetInfo()` method to make the change in Active Directory:

```
$subnet_obj.SetInfo()
```

To associate a subnet with a site using the Active Directory module, you can use the `Set-ADObject` cmdlet. You'll need the DN of the subnet that you're associating with the site in addition to the DN of the site. The following series of commands retrieves these DNs using the `Get-ADObject` cmdlet and then associates the subnet with the site:

```
$cnfg = (Get-ADRootDSE).ConfigurationNamingContext
$site = Get-ADObject -Filter 'objectclass -eq "site" -and name ↵
-eq "Baltimore"' -SearchBase $cnfg
$subnet = Get-ADObject -Filter 'objectclass -eq "subnet" -and ↵
name -eq "192.168.0.4/32"' -SearchBase $cnfg
Set-ADObject $subnet.DistinguishedName -Replace ↵
@{siteObject=$site.DistinguishedName}
```

Work With Site Links

Site links are an important piece of your site topology. A site link represents a connection between Active Directory sites. In most cases, a site link should represent a connection between two sites. Sometimes more than two sites in a site link can be appropriate, but this is typically the case when you're using sites directly connected to an Asynchronous Transfer Mode (ATM) backbone. For site links that represent typical point-to-point WAN connections, you should have only two sites in the site link.

Site links specify a couple of different settings as well. The most important settings are outlined in Table 3.1.

TABLE 3.1   Site Link Settings

Setting	Description	Attribute
Site-link cost	The cost determines how expensive it is for Active Directory to communicate with DCs across the site. This is an arbitrary number that is weighted relative to other site links. The higher the number, the more expensive the connection. For example, if there are two site links that AD can choose from, one with a cost of 50 and another with a cost of 100, AD will choose to contact the DC in the site associated with the site link that costs 50.	cost
Replication interval	The replication interval specifies how many minutes must pass before inter-site replication occurs. The lowest value for this setting is 15 minutes. If it's set to 15 minutes, then Active Directory replication occurs between sites in this site link at 15-minute intervals.	replInterval
Schedule	This is the schedule that shows when the site is available for replication. For example, if you don't want replication to occur during certain hours of the day because of WAN bandwidth concerns, you can black-out replication for that time period in the schedule.	schedule
Site list	This specifies the sites that are associated with the site link.	siteList

Create a Site Link

When you create a site link, you're required to give Active Directory some of the aforementioned information about the site link. In particular, the one attribute that is required is siteList, which contains the DN of each site associated with the site link.

Another important attribute that you should pass in is the site-link cost. As mentioned in Table 3.1, the cost determines how likely it is that Active Directory will use one site link over another. This number is completely arbitrary and left up to you to decide. Whether you use a cost of 100 for one site and 50 for another has no significance over using costs of 10 and 5. If you expect to expand to other sites in the future or anticipate network-connection upgrades, you should use a system for site-link costs that gives you some flexibility. When determining the cost of your site links, you should keep three things in mind: bandwidth, saturation, and latency. All three of these items affect Active Directory's performance across sites. Most people make the mistake of basing their site-link costs purely on bandwidth. However, in most cases, replication uses remote procedure calls (RPCs), which are synchronous. This means the DC waits for a response before proceeding with the next RPC call. If there is high latency in the network, replication over that site link will be very slow, because the latency for each RPC call adds up. In this case, you may want to opt to use a lower-bandwidth connection with lower latency instead of a higher-bandwidth connection with lots of latency. In this case, the lower-bandwidth connection has a smaller cost than the higher-bandwidth connection.

The other important attribute you'll give to the site link is the replication interval. This is expressed in minutes and determines how often replication occurs over the site link. By default, this number is 180 minutes, although you can lower it to as little as 15 minutes. This number affects replication convergence, so you should ensure that you factor in how fast you want replication to converge when you determine the replication interval.

To create a site link in Active Directory, you need to create a `siteLink` object under the site-link container that corresponds to the protocol you want to use. If you want to use the Internet Protocol, then the container is `cn=IP, cn=Inter-Site Transports, cn=Sites, <configuration partition DN>`. For the Simple Mail Transfer Protocol, it's `cn=SMTP, cn=Inter-Site Transports, cn=Sites, <configuration partition DN>`. The difference is that SMTP is asynchronous and not RPC-based. Therefore, using SMTP is ideal for site links that have high network latency. However, SMTP replication is limited to replicating data between DCs in different domains. SMTP can replicate the configuration partition, the schema partition, and the read-only global catalog partitions, but not writable domain partitions. Because of this, you'll probably use IP-based site links in most situations. The PowerShell script in Listing 3.10 can be used to create site links in your forest.

LISTING: 3.10: CreateSiteLink-ADSI.ps1

```
## File Name: CreateSiteLink-ADSI.ps1
## Description: Creates a site link in Active Directory with the
##       information passed into the script.
param([string]$Name, [string]$Type="IP", [string]$Site,
    [int]$Cost=100, [int]$Interval=60)


## Creates a site link in the current forest
function create_sitelink($sitelinkname, $sitelinktype, $sitename,
    $cost, $interval)
```

```
{
    # Get the configuration partition
    $cnfg = ([ADSI]"LDAP://RootDSE").configurationNamingContext
    # Determine whether to use an IP or SMTP based site link
    $type = "CN=IP"
    if ($sitelinktype -like "smtp") { $type = "CN=SMTP" }
    # Get the site link container
    $sitelinkcn = [ADSI]("LDAP://$type,cn=Inter-Site Transports,↵
        cn=Sites,$cnfg")
    # Get the DN of the site added to the link
    $sitedn = get_sitedn $sitename
    # Create the site link
    $sitelink = $sitelinkcn.Create("siteLink", "cn=$sitelinkname")
    $sitelink.Put("cost", $cost)
    $sitelink.Put("replInterval", $interval)
    $sitelink.PutEx(2, "siteList", @("$sitedn"))
    $sitelink.SetInfo()
}
## Takes in the friendly name of a site and returns the DN
function get_sitedn($sitename)
{
    # Get the configuration partition
    $cnfg = ([ADSI]"LDAP://RootDSE").configurationNamingContext

    # Build the site's DN
    $sitedn = "CN=" + $sitename + ",CN=Sites," + $cnfg
    # Test the site DN by attempting to connect to the object
    $siteobj = [ADSI]("LDAP://" + $sitedn)
    # If we could not connect to the object, throw an error
    if ($siteobj.distinguishedName -eq $null) { Throw }
    # Return the site's DN
    return $sitedn
}
## Prints out information for how to use the script
$script_name = $MyInvocation.MyCommand.Name
function print_usage
{
    Write-Host "One or more parameters are missing."
    Write-Host
```

(continues)

LISTING 3-10 *(continued)*

```
        Write-Host "Required Parameters:"
        Write-Host "    -Name <string>"
        Write-Host "    -Site <string>"
        Write-Host
        Write-Host "Optional Parameters:"
        Write-Host "    -Type <string> (IP or SMTP)"
        Write-Host "    -Cost <int>"
        Write-Host "    -Interval <int>"
        Write-Host
        Write-Host "Example:"
        Write-Host "    $script_name -Name USSiteLink -Site Baltimore"
}
# If the Name and Site parameter are present, add the site. Otherwise,
# print out the usage information.
if ($Name -and $Site)
{
    create_sitelink $Name $Type $Site $Cost $Interval
}
else
{
    print_usage
}
```

Add a Site to a Site Link

After a site link is created, you'll likely to need to add sites to the link. You can add sites to the link by appending the DNs of the sites to the siteList attribute on the site link's object. The PowerShell script in Listing 3.11 allows you to add a site to an existing site link.

LISTING: 3.11: AddSiteToSiteLink-ADSI.ps1

```
## File Name: AddSiteToSiteLink-ADSI.ps1
## Description: Uses ADSI to add a site to a site link.
param([string]$Name, [string]$Site, [string]$Type="IP")
## Adds a site to an existing site link
function add_site_to_sitelink($sitename, $sitelinkname, $sitetype)
{
```

```
    # Get the site link DN
    $sitelinkdn = get_sitelinkdn $sitelinkname $sitetype

    # Get the site DN
    $sitedn = get_sitedn $sitename

    $sitelink = [ADSI]"LDAP://$sitelinkdn"
    $sitelink.PutEx(3, "siteList", @("$sitedn"))
    $sitelink.SetInfo()
}
## Takes in the friendly name of a site link and its type and returns
## the DN
function get_sitelinkdn($sitelink, $type)
{
    # Get the configuration partition
    $cnfg = ([ADSI]"LDAP://RootDSE").configurationNamingContext

    # Build the site link's DN
    $type = "CN=IP"
    if ($sitelinktype -like "smtp") { $type = "CN=SMTP" }

    # Get the site link dn
    $sitelinkdn = "cn=$sitelink,$type,cn=Inter-Site Transports, ↵
cn=Sites,$cnfg"
    # Test the site link DN by attempting to connect to the object
    $sitelinkobj = [ADSI]("LDAP://" + $sitelinkdn)
    # If we could not connect to the object, throw an error
    if (!$sitelinkobj.distinguishedName) { Throw }
    # Return the site's DN
    return $sitelinkdn
}
## Takes in the friendly name of a site and returns the DN
function get_sitedn($sitename)
{
    # Get the configuration partition
    $cnfg = ([ADSI]"LDAP://RootDSE").configurationNamingContext
    # Build the site's DN
    $sitedn = "CN=" + $sitename + ",CN=Sites," + $cnfg
```

(continues)

LISTING 3-11 *(continued)*

```
    # Test the site DN by attempting to connect to the object
    $siteobj = [ADSI]("LDAP://" + $sitedn)
    # If we could not connect to the object, throw an error
    if (!$siteobj.distinguishedName) { Throw }

    # Return the site's DN
    return $sitedn
}
## Prints out information for how to use the script
$script_name = $MyInvocation.MyCommand.Name
function print_usage
{
    Write-Host "One or more parameters are missing."
    Write-Host
    Write-Host "Required Parameters:"
    Write-Host "    -Name <string>"
    Write-Host "    -Site <string>"
    Write-Host
    Write-Host "Optional Parameters:"
    Write-Host "    -Type <string> (IP or SMTP)"
    Write-Host
    Write-Host "Example:"
    Write-Host "    $script_name -Name USSiteLink -Site Seattle"
}
# If the Name and Site parameter are present, add the site. Otherwise,
# print out the usage information.
if ($Name -and $Site)
{
    add_site_to_sitelink $Site $Name $Type
    Write-Host "Site $Site successfully added to the site link ↵
    $Name"
}
else
{
    print_usage
}
```

Manage Site Settings

Earlier in this chapter, we looked at how to build a site topology using PowerShell. However, there are settings outside of the site topology design that also affect the behavior of Active Directory and how it interacts with end users. In this section, you'll learn about global catalog servers, Universal Group Caching (UGC), domain controller (DC) coverage, and other site settings that are crucial to a good and consistent experience for your end users.

Determine Which Sites Don't Have Global Catalog Servers

In a forest with multiple domains, each domain is only aware of its own data. To find objects in other domains in the forest, you would have to connect to each domain and search them independently. To solve this problem, Active Directory provides the global catalog so you can search in one place for objects across the forest. The global catalog is a special responsibility. DCs that are designated as global catalog servers contain additional read-only partitions in their directory database. These partitions each represent a subset of objects in another domain in the forest. When a search is performed against the global catalog, the DC returns not only the results from its typical partitions, but also the results from the global catalog partitions. For more information on the global catalog, see the section "Manage the Global Catalog Settings" in Chapter 4, "Managing Domain Controllers."

In most cases, you'll want to ensure that at least one DC in every site can serve a global catalog server. Not having a global catalog can impact the site's logon speed, and a global catalog is often required by forest-wide applications such as Microsoft Exchange Server. To determine which sites don't contain global catalog servers, you can enumerate the sites in Active Directory and evaluate each of the DCs in the site. The object that represents the DC in the configuration partition has an attribute called msDS-isGC, which determines whether a DC contains the global catalog.

If you're using ADSI, you can use the following steps to determine whether a site has a global catalog server:

1. Connect to the Sites container in the forest's configuration partition, and get a collection of every site. The following commands store this data in the $sites variable:

```
$cnfg = ([ADSI]"LDAP://RootDSE").configurationNamingContext
$sitescn = [ADSI]"LDAP://CN=Sites,$cnfg"
$sites = $sitescn.Children
```

2. The child objects in the `Sites` container contain `site` objects and also other object types. Use a `foreach` statement to loop through each of the objects. Inside the `foreach` statement, use an `if` statement to ensure that you only work with the `site` objects. To do this, you can examine the `objectCategory` attribute and determine whether it starts with `CN=Site,`. Doing so helps you determine whether the object is a `site` object. The resulting code block resembles the following:

```
# Loop through each object in the Sites container
foreach ($site in $sites.children)
{
    # We only care about the Site objects, so filter out
    # everything else by using an if statement
    if ($site.objectCategory -like "CN=Site,*")
    {
        . . .
    }
}
```

3. Each `site` object will have a `Servers` container that holds the `Server` objects. Each `Server` object is represents a DC in the site. Connect to the `Servers` container so you can read the `Server` objects from it. The following commands store the DN of the `Sites` container in the `$sitedn` variable. Then, a connection is made to the `Servers` container and stored in the `$servers` variable:

```
$sitedn = $site.distinguishedName
$servers = [ADSI]"LDAP://cn=Servers,$sitedn"
```

4. To determine whether the DC is a global catalog server, you examine an attribute on each of the `server` objects. Therefore, the next step is to use another `foreach` loop on the `Servers` container to examine the `server` objects. Each `server` object has a child object with the type `nTDSDSA` and the common name `CN=NTDS Settings`. This is the object you examine for the global catalog setting:

```
# Loop through each of the Server objects in the Servers
# container
foreach ($server in $servers.children)
{
```

```
# Get the DN of the server
$serverdn = $server.distinguishedName

# Connect to the nTDSDSA object for the server
$ntdsobj = [ADSI]"LDAP://cn=NTDS Settings,$serverdn"
...
}
```

5. To determine whether the DC is a global catalog server, ADSI provides the
Options property on the server object. If this property is equal to 1, then
the DC is also a global catalog server. Otherwise, if Options is equal to 0, the
DC isn't a global catalog server:

```
$isgc = $ntdsobj.Options
if ($isgc -eq 1)
{
    Write-Host "Global Catalog server found: ↵
$($server.name)"
}
```

The script in Listing 3.12 puts these steps together and prints out a list of sites that
don't have a global catalog server.

LISTING 3.12: GetSitesWithoutGCs-ADSI.ps1

```
## File Name: GetSitesWithoutGCs-ADSI.ps1
## Description: Uses ADSI to print a list of sites that don't have
##    Global Catalog servers in them.
# Get the DN of the configuration partition in the current forest
$cnfg = ([ADSI]"LDAP://RootDSE").configurationNamingContext
# Get the DN of the Sites container
$sites = [ADSI]"LDAP://CN=Sites,$cnfg"
# Print script banner
Write-Host
Write-Host "Sites without Global Catalog Servers"
Write-Host "===================================="
# Loop through each object in the Sites container
foreach ($site in $sites.children)
{
    # Ensure that we only work with Site objects
```

(continues)

LISTING 3-12 *(continued)*

```
if ($site.objectcategory -like "CN=Site*")
{
    # Connect to the Servers container
    $sitedn = $site.distinguishedName
    $servers = [ADSI]"LDAP://cn=Servers,$sitedn"
    # Reset variables used for storing DC information
    $hasgc = $false
    # Loop through each Server object
    foreach ($server in $servers.children)
    {
        # Connect to the nTDSDSA object for the server
        $serverdn = $server.distinguishedName
        $ntdsobj = [ADSI]"LDAP://cn=NTDS Settings,$serverdn"
        # Determine if the server is a GC. If so, set the $hasgc
        # variable to true
        if ($ntdsobj.Options -eq 1)
        {
            $hasgc = $true
        }
    }
    # If the site has no GCs, then display the site's name
    if (!$hasgc)
    {
        Write-Host " $($site.name)"
    }
}
}
```

When you're using the Active Directory module, the process for determining whether a DC is a global catalog is slightly different. The primary difference is that you can use the Get-ADObject cmdlet, which allows the use of filters. For example, the following command uses Get-ADObject to get all the site objects from the Sites container.

```
$sites = Get-ADObject -Filter 'objectclass -eq "site"' ↵
    -SearchBase $sitesdn
```

When you use the Get-ADObject cmdlet, you don't need to run if statements to filter out the objects you don't want. After you obtain the list of sites, you can use a `foreach` loop to enumerate the sites and obtain a list of the nTDSDSA objects in the site without having to enumerate the servers:

```
foreach ($site in $sites)
{
    # Get the nTDSDSA objects in the site
$ntdsobjs = Get-ADObject -Filter 'objectclass -eq ↵
"nTDSDSA"'-SearchBase $site.DistinguishedName -Properties ↵
Options
    ...
}
```

The script in Listing 3.13 uses the Active Directory module to get a list of sites without global catalog servers. This script is functionally equivalent to the previous ADSI-based script.

LISTING 3.13: GetSitesWithoutGCs-ADModule.ps1

```
## File Name: GetSitesWithoutGCs-ADModule.ps1
## Description: Uses the Active Directory Module to print a list
of sites
##      that don't have Global Catalog servers in them.
# Get the DN of the Sites container
$rootdse = Get-ADRootDSE
$cnfg = $rootdse.ConfigurationNamingContext
$sitesdn = "CN=Sites,$cnfg"
# Get the Site objects
$sites = Get-ADObject -Filter 'objectclass -eq "site"' ↵
    -SearchBase $sitesdn
# Print script banner
Write-Host
Write-Host "Sites without Global Catalog Servers"
Write-Host "===================================="
# Loop through each object in the Sites container
foreach ($site in $sites)
{
    # Get the nTDSDSA objects in the site
    $ntdsobjs = Get-ADObject -Filter 'objectclass -eq "nTDSDSA"' ↵
    -SearchBase $site.DistinguishedName -Properties Options
```

(continues)

LISTING 3-13 *(continued)*

```
# Reset variables used for storing DC information
$hasgc = $false
# Loop through each nTDSDSA object
if ($ntdsobjs)
{
    foreach ($ntdsobj in $ntdsobjs)
    {
        # Determine if the server is a GC. If so, set the
        # $hasgc variable to true
        if ($ntdsobj.Options -eq 1)
        {
            $hasgc = $true
        }
    }
}


# If the site has no GCs, then display the site's name
if (!$hasgc)
{
    Write-Host " $($site.name)"
}
}
```

Enable Universal Group Caching on All Sites

When a user logs on to the domain, the user could potentially be a member of a universal group. It's important to ensure that universal group memberships are included in a user's token, because if a "deny" permission is associated with the group's membership, you need to ensure that the user isn't granted access to a resource they shouldn't have access to. Universal group memberships can occur across domains in a forest. Therefore, a global catalog server must be contacted when a user logs in to determine which universal groups the user is a member of. If no global catalog server is available in the site, you need to contact a global catalog server in another site. To reduce the network traffic associated with this process, Windows Server 2003 introduced the ability to cache universal group memberships.

How Universal Group Caching Works

When Universal Group Caching (UGC) is enabled for an Active Directory site, the DC in the site that authenticates the user obtains universal group memberships from a global catalog server in another site. By default, the site is determined by site-link cost, although you can override this value and set a preferred site.

The UGC setting for each site is configured on the site's NTDS Site Settings object under the Options attribute. The Options attribute is a bit field, meaning that each bit in the attribute corresponds to a unique setting. The bit 100000 (or hexadecimal 0x20) represents the UGC setting. When this bit is set to 1, UGC is enabled for the site. If it's set to 0, then UGC is disabled for the site.

Preserve the Existing Bits

In order to preserve the existing value of the Options attribute, you have to use a bitwise OR operation in PowerShell. The bitwise OR operation looks at two binary values. If either one of the values is equal to 1, then the output is 1. For example, consider the binary number 0001 0100. If you were to OR this value with 0000 0010, the result would be 0001 0110. You can almost think of this like a math formula, similar to how 20 + 2 = 22,

```
   20
+   2
====
   22
```

00010100 + 00000010 = 00010110:

```
   0001 0100
OR 0000 0010
============
   0001 0110
```

To use the bitwise OR operator in PowerShell, you can use -bor. The previous example can be stated as follows:

```
PS C:\> $answer = 00010100 -bor 00000010
PS C:\> $answer
10110
```

In this case, the leading 0s (the 0s on the left side) are trimmed by default. However, this doesn't change the answer. This is similar to writing the number 50,000 instead of 050,000.

Use ADSI to Enable UGC

To use ADSI to enable UGC, you need to first get a copy of the Options attribute for the site's NTDS Site Settings object:

```
$sitentds = [ADSI]("LDAP://CN=NTDS Site Settings,CN=Seattle, ↵
CN=Sites,CN=Configuration, DC=contoso,DC=com")
$options = #sitentds.Get("Options")
```

Then, perform the OR operation against your copy of the Options attribute:

```
$options = $options -bor 0x20
```

Finally, set the new value of the Options attribute on the NTDS Site Settings attribute:

```
$sitentds.Put("Options", $options)
$sitentds.SetInfo()
```

The script in Listing 3.14 uses these techniques to enable UGC for every site in the forest.

LISTING: 3.14: **EnableUGC-ADSI.ps1**

```
## File Name: EnableUGC-ADSI.ps1
## Description: Uses ADSI to enable Universal Group Caching
##       in all sites in the forest
# Get the configuration partition
$cnfg = ([ADSI]"LDAP://RootDSE").configurationNamingContext
# Get the DN of the Sites container
$sites = [ADSI]"LDAP://CN=Sites,$cnfg"
# Loop through each object in the Sites container
foreach ($site in $sites.children)
{
    # Filter out everything except Site objects
    if ($site.objectcategory -like "CN=Site*")
    {
        # Build the DN for the NTDS Site Settings container
        $sitentds = [ADSI]("LDAP://CN=NTDS Site Settings,
            $($site.DistinguishedName)")
        # Set the UGC flag in the Options attribute. If the first
        # attempt fails then the Options attribute doesn't have a
        # value yet. Therefore, write the UGC directly to the
```

```
# attribute instead of trying to perform a bit-wise OR
try {
    $sitentds.Put("Options", $sitentds.Get("Options") ↵
        -bor 0x20)
}
catch {
    try {
        $sitentds.Put("Options", 0x20)
    } catch { }
}
# Update the copy of the NTDS Site Settings object in
# Active Directory
try {
    $sitentds.SetInfo()
    Write-Host "UGC enabled: $($site.name)"
}
catch {
    Write-Host "Error: $($site.name)"
}
}
}
```

Use the Active Directory Module to Enable UGC

The process of enabling UGC in the Active Directory module is similar, in that you still have to perform the OR operation against the Options attribute. However, this process is made easier with the Get-ADObject and Set-ADObject cmdlets. First, obtain the existing value of the Options attribute:

```
$ntdssite = Get-ADObject "cn=NTDS Site Settings, ↵
cn=Seattle,cn=Sites,cn=Configuration,DC=contoso,DC=com" ↵
-properties Options
$options = $ntdssite.Options
```

Next, perform the OR operation with 0x20 on the Options attribute:

```
$options = $options -bor 0x20
```

Then use the Set-ADObject cmdlet to write the value back to Active Directory:

```
Set-ADObject "cn=NTDS Site Settings,cn=Seattle,cn=Sites, ↵
cn=Configuration, ↵
DC=contoso,DC=com" -Replace @{Options=$options}
```

The script in Listing 3.15 puts these concepts together and enables UGC on every site in the forest.

LISTING 3.15: EnableUGC-ADModule.ps1

```
## File Name: EnableUGC-ADModule.ps1
## Description: Uses the Active Directory Module to enable Universal
##      Group Caching on all sites in the forest.

# Get the DN of the Sites container
$rootdse = Get-ADRootDSE
$cnfg = $rootdse.ConfigurationNamingContext
$sitesdn = "CN=Sites,$cnfg"

# Get the Site objects
$sitesettings = Get-ADObject -Filter 'objectclass -eq ↵
    "nTDSSiteSettings"' -SearchBase $sitesdn -Properties Options
# Loop through each NTDS Site Settings object and enable UGC
foreach ($sitesettingobj in $sitesettings)
{
    $options = $sitesettingobj.Options -bor 0x20
    Set-ADObject $sitesettingobj.DistinguishedName -Replace @
{Options=$options}
}
```

DISABLING UGC

If you want to disable UGC, you can use the same process that you used to enable it. However, you'll also have to use the binary XOR operator (-bxor). When you XOR a bit with 1, it toggles the bit to its opposite value. It's almost like flipping a light switch on or off. XOR always ensures that the light switch is in the opposite position that it's currently in. To disable UGC, you first ensure that the bit is flipped to 1 by performing an OR, and then perform an XOR to turn it to 0.

Manual Site-Link Bridging

Site-link bridges are logical groupings of site links that may not have direct routes between each other. By default in Active Directory, all site links are bridged, making them transitive. For example, suppose you have two sites, Site A and Site B, with a site link called LinkAB. Now imagine that you add an additional site, Site C, and link Site B and Site C with a new site link, LinkBC. Your site topology looks like the example in Figure 3.2.

FIGURE 3.2   Example site topology for site-link bridging

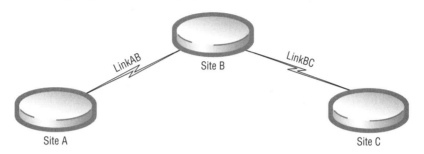

By default, AD will bridge site links LinkAB and LinkBC, making them transitive. This means that a DC in Site A could potentially replicate data directly with a DC in Site C. If this is a single-domain environment and there is a DC in each of the three sites, this topology doesn't make much sense, because it will always be a lower cost for the DC in Site A to talk to the DC in Site B instead of talking to the DC in Site C. However, imagine if there was no DC in Site B. In that case, site-link bridging would allow the DC in Site A to talk directly with the DC in Site C. If you were to remove the site-link bridge for LinkAB and LinkBC, then the DC in Site A wouldn't establish a replication connection with the DC in Site C.

Therefore, it's typically a good idea to leave on automatic site-link bridging. The only appropriate time to turn it off is if for some reason you really don't want replication to occur over a specific route.

Disable Automatic Site-Link Bridging

You can disable automatic site-link bridging on each of the inter-site transport protocols. To do so, set the 0x02 bit on the Options attribute. When the value is set to 0, site-link bridging is on. When it's set to 1, site-link bridging is off. The script in Listing 3.16 uses ADSI to enable or disable automatic site-link bridging in Active Directory. For more information on how to set bits on an attribute value, see the earlier section "Enable Universal Group Caching on All Sites."

LISTING 3.16: BASL-ADSI.ps1

```
## File Name: BASL-ADSI.ps1
## Description: Uses ADSI to enable the "bridge all site links"
##      setting
# Get the configuration partition
$cnfg = ([ADSI]"LDAP://RootDSE").configurationNamingContext
# Connect to the IP and SMTP transport containers
$iplinks = [ADSI]"LDAP://CN=IP,CN=Inter-Site Transports,↵
    CN=Sites,$cnfg"
$smtplinks = [ADSI]"LDAP://CN=SMTP,CN=Inter-Site Transports,↵
    CN=Sites,$cnfg"
# Set the BASL flag in the Options attribute. If the first attempt
# fails then the Options attribute doesn't have a value yet. Therefore,
# write the BASL value directly to the attribute instead of trying to
# perform a binary OR
try {
    if ($args[0] -like "enable") {
        $options = $iplinks.Get("Options") -bor 0x02
        $iplinks.Put("Options", $options -bxor 0x02)
        $options = $smtplinks.Get("Options") -bor 0x02
        $smtplinks.Put("Options", $options -bxor 0x02)
    }
    elseif ($args[0] -like "disable") {
        $iplinks.Put("Options", $iplinks.Get("Options") -bor 0x02)
        $smtplinks.Put("Options", $smtplinks.Get("Options") -bor 0x02)
    }
    else {
        $script_name = $MyInvocation.MyCommand.Name
        Write-Host "Missing or invalid script parameter."
        Write-Host
        Write-Host "To enable Bridge All Site Links, run:"
        Write-Host "    $script_name Enable"
        Write-Host
        Write-Host "To disable Bridge All Site Links, run:"
        Write-Host "    $script_name Disable"
    }
}
```

```
catch {
    try {
        if ($args[0] -like "disable") {
            $iplinks.Put("Options", 0x02)
            $smtplinks.Put("Options", 0x02)
        }
    } catch { }
}
# Update the copy of the IP and SMTP transport containers in Active
# Directory
try {
    $iplinks.SetInfo()
    $smtplinks.SetInfo()
    if ($args[0] -like "disable") {
        Write-Host "Bridge All Site Links Disabled"
    }
    elseif ($args[0] -like "enable") {
        Write-Host "Bridge All Site Links Enabled"
    }
}
catch {
    Write-Host "Error"
}
```

You can also enable or disable site-link bridging using the Active Directory module. To do so, you still need to flip the 0x02 bit in the Options attribute, but you can use the Get-ADObject and Set-ADObject cmdlets to do so. The script in Listing 3.17 uses the Active Directory module to enable or disable site-link bridging.

LISTING 3.17: BASL-ADModule.ps1

```
## File Name: BASL-ADModule.ps1
## Description: Uses the Active Directory Module to enable the
##      "bridge all site links" setting.
# Get the DN of the Sites container
$rootdse = Get-ADRootDSE
$cnfg = $rootdse.ConfigurationNamingContext
$sitesdn = "CN=Sites,$cnfg"
```

(continues)

LISTING 3-17 *(continued)*

```
# Connect to the IP and SMTP transport containers
$links = Get-ADObject -Filter 'objectclass -eq "interSiteTransport"' ↵
    -SearchBase $sitesdn -Properties Options
# Loop through each NTDS Site Settings object and enable UGC
foreach ($link in $links)
{
    if ($args[0] -like "enable") {
        $options = $link.Options -bor 0x02
        $options = $Options -bxor 0x02
        Set-ADObject $link.DistinguishedName -Replace ↵
            @{Options=$options}
    }
    elseif ($args[0] -like "disable") {
        $options = $link.Options -bor 0x02
        Set-ADObject $link.DistinguishedName -Replace ↵
            @{Options=$options}
    }
    else {
        $script_name = $MyInvocation.MyCommand.Name
        Write-Host "Missing or invalid script parameter."
        Write-Host
        Write-Host "To enable Bridge All Site Links, run:"
        Write-Host "    $script_name Enable"
        Write-Host
        Write-Host "To disable Bridge All Site Links, run:"
        Write-Host "    $script_name Disable"
        Exit
    }
}
if ($args[0] -like "enable") {
    Write-Host "Bridge All Site Links Enabled"
}
elseif ($args[0] -like "disable") {
    Write-Host "Bridge All Site Links Disabled"
}
```

Configure Which Sites a Domain Controller Covers

When a site doesn't contain a DC, clients in that site may use a DC in a poorly connected site for authentication. To help prevent this, Active Directory uses a feature called *automatic site coverage*. When a site doesn't have a DC, a DC in a connected site will register its DNS service locator records for the site. The DC that registers itself is a DC in the connected site with the lowest cost. This ensures that clients logging in to a site without DCs will always use the next-closest DC for authentication.

Typically, this is a preferred configuration. However, when using read-only domain controllers (RODCs), Windows Server 2003 DCs don't detect the RODCs in a site as valid. Therefore, Windows Server 2003 DCs will register their DNS service records for a site, even if there are RODCs. Because of this, you'll generally disable automatic site coverage on your Windows Server 2003 DCs when you have RODCs in your domain.

To disable automatic site coverage, you have to modify a Registry key on each DC. You can use the Registry in PowerShell through the Registry provider. Use the following steps to disable automatic site coverage on the DC to which you're currently logged in:

1. In PowerShell, change to the HKEY_LOCAL_MACHINE hive in the Registry:

   ```
   cd HKLM:
   ```

2. Change to the path SYSTEM\CurrentControlSet\Services\Netlogon\ Parameters:

   ```
   cd system\currentcontrolset\services\netlogon\parameters
   ```

3. Create a new DWORD value called AutoSiteCoverage, and set it to 0. To do this, use the New-ItemProperty cmdlet and specify AutoSiteCoverage as the Name parameter. Use 0 for the Value parameter and DWORD for the PropertyType parameter:

   ```
   New-ItemProperty -Path . -Name AutoSiteCoverage -Value 0 ↵
       -PropertyType DWORD
   ```

Move a Domain Controller to a Different Site

When you add a DC to a domain, by default it will join the site that its IP address is in. However, you can move the DC to another site. To do this, you simply have to move the Server object in the site's Servers container to the Servers container of the target site.

Use ADSI to Move a DC to Another Site

You can use the following steps to move the DC to a different site with ADSI:

1. Connect to the Servers container in the site to which you want to move the DC. In the following example, you move the DC named SEA-DC01 from the Default-First-Site-Name site to the Seattle site.

   ```
   $target_site = [ADSI]"LDAP://cn=Servers,cn=Default-First-↵
   Site-Name,cn=Sites,cn=Configuration,dc=contoso,dc=com"
   ```

2. You need the full LDAP path and the relative distinguished name (RDN) of the DC's Server object:

   ```
   $dc_path = "LDAP://
   cn=SEA-DC01,cn=Servers,cn=Default-First-↵
   Site-Name,cn=Sites,cn=Configuration,dc=contoso,dc=com"
   $dc_rdn = "cn=SEA-DC01"
   ```

3. Call the MoveHere function on the target site's object, and pass in the path and RDN of the DC:

   ```
   $target_site.MoveHere($dc_path, $dc_rdn)
   ```

The script in Listing 3.18 takes the DC's name and target site as input and moves the DC to the target site.

LISTING 3.18: MoveDC-ADSI.ps1

```
## File Name: MoveDC-ADSI.ps1
## Description: Moves a Domain Controller to another site
param([string]$DC, [string]$TargetSite)
## Takes in the friendly name of a DC and returns the DN of the
## server object.
function get_dcpath($dc_name)
{
    # Get the configuration partition
    $cnfg = ([ADSI]"LDAP://RootDSE").configurationNamingContext
    # Look for the Server object
    $site_cn = [ADSI]("LDAP://cn=Sites,$cnfg")
    foreach ($site in $site_cn.Children) {
        $servers_cn = [ADSI]"LDAP://cn=Servers,↵
            $($site.DistinguishedName)"
```

```
        foreach ($server in $servers_cn.Children) {
            # Found the server object. Return the DN.
            if ($server.name -like $dc_name) {
                return $server.DistinguishedName
            }
        }
    }
}
# Ensure that valid parameters were passed to the script
if (($DC.Length -eq 0) -or ($TargetSite.Length -eq 0)) {
    $script_name = $MyInvocation.MyCommand.Name
    Write-Host
    Write-Host "Missing or invalid parameters"
    Write-Host
    Write-Host "Example:"
    Write-Host "  $script_name -DC SEA-DC01 -TargetSite Seattle"
    Write-Host
    Exit
}
$dc_rdn = "cn=$DC"
$site_rdn = "cn=$TargetSite"
$cnfg = ([ADSI]"LDAP://RootDSE").configurationNamingContext
$dc_path = get_dcpath($DC)
$site_path = "LDAP://cn=Servers,$site_rdn,cn=Sites,$cnfg"
$target_site = [ADSI]$site_path
try {
    $new_server = $target_site.MoveHere("LDAP://$dc_path", $dc_rdn)
    Write-Host
    Write-Host "Server moved successfully"
} catch {
    Write-Host
    Write-Host "An error was encountered when attempting to move ↵
      the server"
}
```

Use the AD Module to Move a DC to Another Site

When you're using the Active Directory module for PowerShell, you can take advantage of the Move-ADObject cmdlet to move the server. The two things you need to move the server are the DN of the server you're moving and the DN of the location you're moving it to. In this case, you're moving the `server` object to the `Servers` container in another site. To get the DN, you need to run two `Get-ADObject` commands:

```
$new_site = Get-ADObject -Filter 'objectclass -eq "site" -and ↵
cn -eq "Seattle"'-SearchBase "cn=Sites,cn=Configuration, ↵
dc=contoso,dc=com"
$servers_cn = Get-ADObject -Filter 'objectclass -eq ↵
"serversContainer"'-SearchBase $new_site.DistinguishedName
```

After you have the DN of the `Servers` container in the target site, you need the DN of the `Server` object for the DC you're moving:

```
$dc_obj = Get-ADObject -Filter 'objectclass -eq "server" -and ↵
cn -eq"SEA-DC01"' -SearchBase "cn=Sites,cn=Configuration, ↵
dc=contoso,dc=com"
```

The final step is to call the `Move-ADObject` cmdlet to perform the move. Pass in the DN of the `server` object you're moving. For the `TargetPath` parameter, pass in the DN of the target `Servers` container:

```
Move-ADObject $dc_obj.DistinguishedName -TargetPath ↵
    $servers_cn.DistinguishedName
```

The script in Listing 3.19 uses the AD module to move a DC to another site. This follows the same syntax as the previous script: Pass in the name of the DC and the name of the site to which you're moving it.

LISTING 3.19: MoveDC-ADModule.ps1

```
## File Name: MoveDC-ADModule.ps1
## Description: Moves a domain controller to another site using the
##     AD Module for PowerShell
param([string]$DC, [string]$TargetSite)
# Ensure that valid parameters were passed to the script
if (($DC.Length -eq 0) -or ($TargetSite.Length -eq 0)) {
    $script_name = $MyInvocation.MyCommand.Name
    Write-Host
    Write-Host "Missing or invalid parameters"
    Write-Host
```

```
    Write-Host "Example:"
    Write-Host "  $script_name -DC SEA-DC01 -TargetSite Seattle"
    Write-Host
    Exit
}
# Get the DN of the Sites container
$rootdse = Get-ADRootDSE
$cnfg = $rootdse.ConfigurationNamingContext
$sitesdn = "CN=Sites,$cnfg"
# Get the site object for the target site
$target_site = Get-ADObject -Filter 'objectclass -eq "site" -and ↵
    cn -eq $TargetSite' -SearchBase $sitesdn
# Get the servers container object (where the server is actually
# moving to)
$servers_cn = Get-ADObject -Filter 'objectclass -eq ↵
    "serversContainer"' -SearchBase $target_site.DistinguishedName
# Get the existing server object
$dc_obj = Get-ADObject -Filter 'objectclass -eq "server" -and cn ↵
    -eq $DC' -SearchBase $sitesdn
# Move the server to another site
try {
    Move-ADObject $dc_obj.DistinguishedName -TargetPath ↵
        $servers_cn.DistinguishedName
    Write-Host
    Write-Host "Server moved successfully"
} catch {
    Write-Host
    Write-Host "An error was encountered when attempting to " +
        "move the server"
}
```

Manage Replication

Active Directory is a multimaster directory, meaning that more than one Domain Controller (DC) can make changes to the data in the directory at the same time. Active Directory's replication engine is one of the best replication engines found anywhere in any product on the market. Not only can the architecture have multiple servers that perform write operations, but the replication of data occurs on an attribute level. This means that if you change an attribute in an object (for example, a user's last name), only the changed attribute is replicated to other DCs.

To accomplish this, Active Directory uses the concept of *update sequence numbers* (USNs). USNs are unique 64-bit numbers maintained by each DC. Every time an update is made to the database on that DC, the USN is incremented. In this way, the update operation is tied to a unique number. Each DC maintains what it believes to be the current USN of each of its replication partners; this is referred to as the *high watermark value*. When a change is made on a DC, its USN is incremented, and the DC notifies its replication partners of the new USN value. The replication partners compare the new USN to their high watermark value for the DC. From that information, the replication partner knows what changes to request from the DC.

USNs assist in the replication process, but they also play a vital role in ensuring that a DC doesn't get updated with the same data multiple times. Consider the case where one DC is updated by one of its replication partners, and then another replication partner tries to update it again. In this case, the DC needs to be able to tell the second replication partner that it already has the updates so they aren't transferred over the network again. This process is called *propagation dampening*, and it's accomplished using a table stored on each DC called the up-to-dateness vector (UTDV) table. This table contains the USN of every DC where the last write operation occurred. When the DC is notified by its second replication partner that there's a pending change (the watermark it sends is higher than the DC's copy), the DC responds by sending the replication partner a copy of its UTDV table. The replication partner compares the table to its own copy of the UTDV table (which is the same on every DC after full replication convergence). If they match, then the replication partner knows the DC already received the updates from another replication partner. The target DC simply updates its high watermark value with the current USN of the replication partner rather than polling it for all of the changes. Because Active Directory replication happens at the attribute level, this process occurs for every attribute that is changed on any DC in the forest.

View the State of Replication

When DCs have multiple replication partners, the replication process outlined previously can get rather complicated. Fortunately, you don't have to do anything to ensure that replication functions; Active Directory takes care of this on its own. However, things will go wrong from time to time, and you may not notice. Therefore, it's important to keep an eye on replication and make sure it's healthy.

A DC determines who it replicates with by defining a *connection object* with each of its partners. These connection objects are created automatically based on the site topology you've defined. The process that creates the connection objects is called the Knowledge Consistency Checker (KCC). The KCC runs periodically and ensures that any changes to the site topology are reflected in the connection objects for each DC. For example, if a site-link cost changes and makes replication with a particular DC more expensive than it was previously, the KCC may have to generate a new connection object to a less expensive DC to replicate with. The KCC is really the brains behind how DCs determine who to replicate with.

There are two types of replication to consider in Active Directory: intra-site and inter-site. *Intra-site replication* occurs between DCs that are in the same site. This replication happens very quickly, within seconds, over Remote Procedure Calls (RPCs) and therefore assumes that the connectivity between the DCs in the site is fast and reliable. This is why you generally want LAN speeds between each of the IP subnets in an Active Directory site. *Inter-site replication* occurs between two different sites. This replication can be based on RPC as well, but there is also the option to use SMTP messages for inter-site replication. The reason for using SMTP over RPC is primarily concerned with network latency. RPC is a synchronous protocol, meaning that it sends a packet command and waits for a response before sending another command. If you have a network with high latency, your DC may be waiting a while before it sends the next command. On the other hand, SMTP is asynchronous, meaning that it can issue a series of commands one after the other without needing a response in between. The latency doesn't change; but rather than incurring the response latency after each issued command, SMTP incurs it much less frequently and therefore is better for high-latency networks. The most common use case for SMTP is for replicating Active Directory data over sites connected by satellite communication links.

List the Bridgehead Servers in a Site

When replicating data across sites, the KCC process assigns one DC in the site the role of the *inter-site topology generator* (ISTG). This job of this DC is to determine which DCs in the site will act as bridgeheads. *Bridgeheads* are the DCs that replicate data between sites. Inter-site replication traffic only occurs from the bridgehead server in one site to the bridgehead server in another site.

Back in Windows 2000, you could have only one bridgehead per site for each directory partition. This was particularly problematic in hub-and-spoke site topology architectures, because a single DC in a hub site could easily be overburdened when faced with dozens of replication partners. In Windows 2003, however, Microsoft added the ability to have multiple bridgehead servers for each site. By using multiple bridgehead servers, you can spread the inter-site replication load across multiple DCs.

To determine whether a server is a bridgehead server, you can examine the connection objects that the KCC created for the server. If there is a connection object with a server in another site, then the server is considered a bridgehead server. The script in Listing 3.20 enumerates each server in each site in the forest and examines the connection objects to determine which servers are bridgehead servers. The list of bridgehead servers for each site is displayed.

LISTING 3.20: ListBH-ADSI.ps1

```
## File Name: ListBH-ADSI.ps1
## Description:
##      Uses the ADSI to enumerate all of the connection in the
##      forest and determine which servers are bridgehead servers. The
##      list of bridgehead servers for each site is displayed.
##
# Get the configuration partition
$cnfg = ([ADSI]"LDAP://RootDSE").configurationNamingContext
# Get the Sites container
$site_cn = [ADSI]("LDAP://cn=Sites,$cnfg")
# Loop through each child object in the Sites container
foreach ($site in $site_cn.Children)
{
    # Filter out everything except for Site objects
    if ($site.objectcategory -like "cn=site,*")
    {
        # Print the header for the list of BH Servers for the site
        Write-Host
        Write-Host "BH Servers for Site: $($site.name)"
        Write-Host "=================================="
        # Get the site's Servers container
        $servers_cn = [ADSI]"LDAP://cn=Servers,↵
            $($site.DistinguishedName)"
        # Loop through each Server object in the Servers container
        foreach ($server in $servers_cn.Children)
        {
```

```
# Set an internal flag that indicates if we found
# a BH server
$isBH = $false

# Get the NTDS Settings object for the server
$ntdssettingsobj = [ADSI]"LDAP://cn=NTDS Settings,↵
    $($server.DistinguishedName)"

# Loop through each child object under the NTDS Settings
# object
foreach ($conobj in $ntdssettingsobj.Children)
{
    # Filter out everything that's not a connection object
    if ($conobj.objectcategory -like ↵
        "cn=nTDS-Connection,*")
    {
        # Get a copy of the DN of the source DC and
        # manipulate the string to remove everything
        # except for the site name
        [string]$fromServer = $conobj.fromServer
        $fromServer = $fromServer.Replace(",↵
            $($site_cn.DistinguishedName)", "")
        $fromServer = $fromServer.Substring(↵
            $fromServer.LastIndexOf("=")+1)
        # Format the name of the site that the server is
        # in. We're going to compare this with the
        # connection object's site to determine whether
        # or not the connection object is with a DC in a
        #different site. This will tell us that this is
        # a bridgehead server
        [string]$sitename = $site.cn
        # Compare the server's site with the connection
        # object's site. If they are different, set the
        # $isBH flag to true
        if ($fromServer.ToUpper() -ne ↵
            $sitename.ToUpper()) {
            $isBH = $true
        }
    }
```

(continues)

LISTING 3-20 *(continued)*

```
            }


            # If we've found that the server is a bridgehead,
            # display its name
            if ($isBH -eq $true)
            {
                Write-Host " $($server.name)"
            }
        }
    }
}
```

List a Domain Controller's Replication Partners

As mentioned previously, each DC has a list of connection objects that are automatically created by the KCC. These connection objects each represent a replication
partner to the DC. The script in Listing 3.21 enumerates all the connection objects
for each DC and displays a list of replication partners.

LISTING 3.21: GetPartners-ADSI.ps1

```
## File Name: GetPartners-ADSI.ps1
## Description:
##     Uses the ADSI to enumerate all of the connection objects for
##     each DC in the forest and display the DC's replication
##     partners.
##
# Get the configuration partition
$cnfg = ([ADSI]"LDAP://RootDSE").configurationNamingContext
# Get the Sites container
$site_cn = [ADSI]("LDAP://cn=Sites,$cnfg")
# Loop through each child object in the Sites container
foreach ($site in $site_cn.Children)
{
    # Filter out everything except for Site objects
    if ($site.objectcategory -like "cn=site,*")
    {
```

```
# Get the site's Servers container
$servers_cn = [ADSI]"LDAP://cn=Servers,↵
    $($site.DistinguishedName)"

# Loop through each Server object in the Servers container
foreach ($server in $servers_cn.Children)
{
    # Filter out everything except for Server objects
    if ($server.objectcategory -like "cn=server,*")
    {
        # Display header for replication partner list
        Write-Host "`nReplication partners for ↵
            $($server.name) in Site $($site.name):"
        # Get the NTDS Settings object for the server
        $ntdssettingsobj = [ADSI]"LDAP://cn=NTDS Settings,↵
            $($server.DistinguishedName)"
        # Loop through each child object under the NTDS
        # Settings object
        foreach ($conobj in $ntdssettingsobj.Children)
        {
            # Filter out everything that's not a connection
            # object
            if ($conobj.objectcategory -like ↵
               "cn=nTDS-Connection,*")
            {
                # Get the site that the replication partner
                # is in and compare it to the server's site
                # to determine if it's an internal or
                # external partner
                $from_ntds = [ADSI]"LDAP://↵
                    $($conobj.fromServer)"
                $parent = [ADSI]"$($from_ntds.parent)"
                $serverscn = [ADSI]"$($parent.parent)"
                $sitecn = [ADSI]"$($serverscn.parent)"
                $type = "Internal"

                [string]$replsite = $sitecn.name
                [string]$thissite = $site.name
```

(continues)

LISTING 3-21 *(continued)*

```
                                   # If the sites are different, then it's an
                                   # external partner
                                   if ($replsite.ToUpper() -ne ↵
                                       $thissite.ToUpper())
                                   {
                                       $type = "External"
                                   }

                                   # Display the replication partner information
                                   Write-Host "  $type`t`t$($parent.Name)"
                               }
                           }
                       }
                   }
               }
           }
```

Tune Replication Settings

In addition to monitoring your replication status, you'll need to tune some settings every now and then. Replication settings that you may need to adjust are related to how often replication occurs and with whom. In this section, we'll explore some things you can do to tune your replication settings.

Configure a Preferred Bridgehead Server

The ISTG automatically manages which DCs in each site serve as bridgehead servers for replicating data with other connected sites. However, you have the option of overriding this and setting a bridgehead manually if you want to use one or more specific DCs.

You assign this manual bridgehead preference using the `bridgeheadTransportList` attribute on the `server` object. To configure the server as a preferred bridgehead, add the DN of the transport protocol that you want to use (either IP or SMTP).

Use ADSI to Configure a Preferred Bridgehead

If you want to use ADSI to configure the preferred bridgehead, the first step is to connect to the `server` object:

```
$server = [ADSI]("LDAP://cn=SEA-DC01,cn=Servers,cn=Seattle, ↵
cn=Sites,cn=Configuration,dc=contoso,dc=com")
```

Next, you need the DN of the transport. This example uses the IP transport:

```
$iptrans = "CN=IP,CN=Inter-Site Transports,CN=Sites, ↵
CN=Configuration,DC=contoso,DC=com"
```

The final step is to add the transport DN to the `bridgeheadTransportList` attribute on the `server` object:

```
$server.PutEx(3, "bridgeheadTransportList", @("$iptrans"))
$server.SetInfo()
```

Use the AD Module to Configure a Preferred Bridgehead

When using the AD module, you can use the `Set-ADObject` cmdlet to configure the preferred bridgehead setting on your DC's `server` object. Start by using the `Get-ADObject` cmdlet to connect to the DC's `server` object:

```
$server = Get-ADObject "cn=SEA-DC01,cn=Servers,cn=Seattle, ↵
cn=Sites,cn=Configuration,dc=contoso,dc=com"
```

Next, ensure that you have the DN of the inter-site transport for which you'll configure this server as the preferred bridgehead. This example uses the IP transport:

```
$link = "CN=IP,CN=Inter-Site Transports,CN=Sites, ↵
CN=Configuration,DC=contoso,DC=com"
```

Finally, call the `Set-ADObject` cmdlet, and pass in the DN of the server and the DN of the inter-site transport you're using. Add the inter-site transport DN to the multivalued attribute `bridgeheadTransportList`:

```
Set-ADObject $server.DistinguishedName -Add ↵
@{bridgeheadTransportList=$link}
```

Change the Frequency with Which the Automatic Replication Topology Is Built

The KCC periodically builds the replication topology automatically. The frequency at which this occurs out of the box is every 15 minutes. However, you can change this. When you do, the setting affects only the DC on which you change the interval. To change the frequency, add the Registry value `Repl topology update period (secs)` to the following Registry key:

```
HKLM\System\CurrentControlSet\Services\NTDS\Parameters
```

This setting is specified in seconds. If you wanted to change the frequency to every 30 minutes, for example, you would set the value to 1800. You can use the Registry in PowerShell through the Registry provider. Use the following steps to change the KCC replication topology update period on the DC at which you're currently logged in:

1. In PowerShell, change to the HKEY_LOCAL_MACHINE hive in the Registry:

   ```
   cd HKLM:
   ```

2. Change to the path SYSTEM\CurrentControlSet\Services\NTDS\ Parameters:

   ```
   cd system\currentcontrolset\services\ntds\parameters
   ```

3. Create a new DWORD value called Repl topology update period (secs), and set it to the number of seconds you want. In this example, set it to run every 60 minutes, or 3600 seconds. Use the New-ItemProperty cmdlet to create the Registry value. Use 3600 for the Value parameter and DWORD for the PropertyType parameter:

   ```
   New-ItemProperty -Path . -Name "Repl topology update ↵
   period (secs)"-Value 3600 -PropertyType DWORD
   ```

Changing this setting to a longer period was sometimes necessary in the past. In older versions of Windows, the KCC was less efficient, so when complex architectures were involved, it was less likely that the KCC would finish the process of automatically generating the replication topology. Therefore, the period was often increased to give the KCC the additional time it needed.

Replicate After Lingering Object Issues

When an object is deleted in Active Directory, it's not immediately removed from the database. Rather, it's put into a special state and becomes *tombstoned*. When tombstoned, the object's isDeleted attribute is set to True and some of its attributes are removed, leaving only a subset of them in the directory. For all intents and purposes, this object is considered removed because it can no longer be used.

The purpose of the tombstone is to ensure that every DC knows that the object was deleted and can process it accordingly. If the object was deleted from the database immediately without being tombstoned first, then the deletion couldn't be replicated because the object wouldn't exist. The interim tombstone state is important because it ensures that each DC knows about the deletion.

The amount of time that an object resides in the tombstone state before it's permanently removed is referred to as the *tombstone lifetime*. The number of days configured for your tombstone lifetime is determined by the first DC that was promoted in the forest root domain. This may vary depending on the evolution of your Active Directory environment. For example, if your forest started out as a Windows 2000 domain, then the tombstone lifetime will be 60 days. Windows 2003 and later forests default to 180 days.

AD RECYCLE BIN

When you're using a Windows Server 2008 R2 forest, you have the ability to enable the Active Directory Recycle Bin. The AD Recycle Bin modifies the behavior that we just discussed. When the AD Recycle Bin is enabled, objects aren't tombstoned immediately; rather, they reside in the AD Recycle Bin for a period of time before the tombstone process occurs. We'll discuss the AD Recycle Bin in more detail in Chapter 10, "Backing Up Data and Recovering from Disasters."

To understand this better, suppose an object is deleted on a DC named DC01. DC02 is a replication partner to DC01. Ordinarily, DC02 would be notified when the USN change occurs on DC01. This indicates that updates were made to Active Directory that needed to be replicated to DC02. If DC02 was online and functioning properly, it would poll DC01 for the changes and replicate the tombstoning of the deleted object into its own copy of the database.

However, if DC02 was offline or not functioning properly, the tombstone wouldn't replicate to DC02. To make matters worse, if DC02 was offline for more than the tombstone lifetime, then the object might have already been removed from DC01's database. Therefore, when DC02 came back online, the object would be gone from the domain, along with the change that was associated with the deletion's USN. In this case, DC02 wouldn't be aware that the object was deleted and therefore wouldn't remove it from its own database.

When one DC has an object that other DCs don't have, it's called a *lingering object*. You always want your DCs to be in a completely consistent state, so lingering objects represent a big problem. For example, if the lingering object is a user account that was deleted from the forest, the user may still be able to log on with the account if they happen to authenticate against the DC that contains the lingering object. If an attribute on the lingering object is updated, it could replicate back out to the other DCs that it was deleted from, causing the previously deleted object to be reanimated.

Divergent and Corrupt Replication Partners

One way that Active Directory prevents lingering objects from being reanimated into the environment is to cut off replication with DCs that haven't replicated within the tombstone lifetime. If the DC hasn't replicated within the tombstone lifetime, it's considered divergent because it could potentially have lingering objects; an error event with an ID number of 2042 appears in the event logs of its replication partners. But note that when this happens, it doesn't mean lingering object *do* exist; it only means that they *could* exist. If you're certain that your divergent DC doesn't have any lingering objects (or if it does, that you've removed them—see Chapter 7, "Managing Computer Accounts, Objects, and Organizational Units"), then you can force the DC to replicate even though the tombstone lifetime has been exceeded.

To allow replication with a divergent DC, you must set the following Registry key on the DCs that receiving replication from the divergent DC:

```
HKLM\SYSTEM\CurrentControlSet\Services\NTDS\Parameters\Allow
Replication With Divergent and Corrupt Partner = 1
```

After you set this key, you can restart replication on the DC and allow it to replicate with the divergent DC. After successful replication, you should go back and reset the Registry key to 0. Doing so will prevent future divergent DCs from replicating with this partner. Whenever you see a divergent DC, follow this process:

1. Fix the problem that caused the DC to not replicate for longer than the tombstone lifetime.

2. Clean up any lingering objects on the divergent DC.

3. Enable the setting to allow replication with divergent and corrupt partners on the divergent DC's replication partners.

4. Ensure that replication occurs successfully with the divergent DC.

5. Disable the setting to allow replication with divergent and corrupt partners on the divergent DC's replication partners.

You can use the PowerShell Registry provider to allow replication with divergent DCs:

1. In PowerShell, change to the HKEY_LOCAL_MACHINE hive in the Registry:

   ```
   cd HKLM:
   ```

2. Change to the path SYSTEM\CurrentControlSet\Services\NTDS\Parameters:

   ```
   cd system\currentcontrolset\services\ntds\parameters
   ```

3. Edit the value `Allow Replication with Divergent and Corrupt Partner`, and set it to 1. Use the `Set-ItemProperty` cmdlet to change the Registry value. Use 1 for the `Value` parameter. This Registry value name is rather long, so be sure you spell it correctly:

```
Set-ItemProperty -Path . -Name "Allow Replication with ↵
Divergent and Corrupt Partner" -Value 1 -PropertyType DWORD
```

You can also use the script in Listing 3.22 to enable or disable replication with a divergent DC. When you run this script, pass in either `Enable` or `Disable` as a script parameter.

LISTING 3.22: **AllowDivergentReplication.ps1**

```
## File Name: AllowDivergentReplication.ps1
## Description:
##      Enables or disables the ability for a Domain Controller to
##      replicate with a DC that has not replicated a partition for
##      longer than the tombstone lifetime of the forest
$key_path = "HKLM:\system\CurrentControlSet\services\NTDS\Parameters"
$key_name = "Allow Replication with Divergent and Corrupt Partner"
if ($args[0] -like "enable") {
    Set-ItemProperty -Path $key_path -Name $key_name -Value 1
    Write-Host "Replication with divergent DC ENABLED successfully"
}
elseif ($args[0] -like "disable") {
    Set-ItemProperty -Path $key_path -Name $key_name -Value 0
    Write-Host "Replication with divergent DC DISABLED successfully"
}
else {
    $script_name = $MyInvocation.MyCommand.Name
    Write-Host "Missing or invalid script parameter."
    Write-Host
    Write-Host "To enable replication with a divergent DC, run:"
    Write-Host "    $script_name Enable"
    Write-Host
    Write-Host "To disable replication with a divergent DC, run:"
    Write-Host "    $script_name Disable"
}
```

Strict Replication Consistency

You can also prevent the spread of reanimated lingering objects by using the strict replication consistency setting. When strict replication consistency is enabled, the DC doesn't receive replicated updates for objects that it doesn't have a copy of. If a lingering object is updated on a DC, the replication partner cuts off replication to the entire partition from the DC with the lingering object. When this happens, errors with event ID 1988 are shown in the target DC's (the DC that doesn't have the lingering objects) event logs.

It's important to enable strict replication consistency to prevent a lingering object from being reanimated. But keep in mind that if strict replication consistency isn't enabled and then you enable it, you may potentially stop replication for partitions that contain lingering objects. Therefore, take care when enabling strict replication consistency.

Depending on the configuration of your domain, you may already have strict replication consistency turned on by default. The strict replication consistency setting was introduced in Windows Server 2003; in a forest that started out as a Windows Server 2003 forest, the DCs will enable strict replication consistency by default. However, if the forest started out as a Windows 2000 forest and was upgraded to Windows 2003, strict replication consistency won't be turned on by default in newly promoted DCs. Windows Server 2003 and newer DCs will check for the existence of the following object during the promotion process:

```
CN=94fdebc6-8eeb-4640-80de-ec52b9ca17fa,CN=Operations,
CN=ForestUpdates,CN=Configuration,DC=domain,DC=com
```

If the object exists in the configuration partition, then the DC being promoted will enable strict replication consistency. You can create this object in a forest using the script in Listing 3.23.

LISTING 3.23: CreateSRConsistencyObject.ps1

```
## File Name: CreateSRConsistencyObject.ps1
## Description:
##      Creates the object used for automatic enablement of strict
##      replication consistency in the forest.
# Get the DN of the configuration partition
$cnfg = ([ADSI]"LDAP://RootDSE").configurationNamingContext
```

```
# Connect to the Operations container
$ops_dn = "CN=Operations,CN=ForestUpdates,$cnfg"
$ops_obj = [ADSI]"LDAP://$ops_dn"
# Connect to the Strict Replication Consistency container object
$sr_cn = "CN=94fdebc6-8eeb-4640-80de-ec52b9ca17fa"
$sr_dn = "$sr_cn,CN=Operations,CN=ForestUpdates,$cnfg"
$sr_obj = [ADSI]"LDAP://$sr_dn"
# If the object already exists, say so
if ($sr_obj.DistinguishedName)
{
    Write-Host "SR Consistency object already exists"
}
else
{
    # Create the object
    try
    {
        $sr_obj = $ops_obj.Create("container", $sr_cn)
        $sr_obj.Put("showInAdvancedViewOnly", $true)
        $sr_obj.SetInfo()
        Write-Host "The SR Consistency object was successfully ↵
            created"
    }
    catch
    {
        Write-Host "There was an error creating the object"
    }
}
```

Creating this object doesn't automatically enable strict replication consistency; it only ensures that new DCs enable it during the promotion process. Existing DCs must have strict replication consistency enabled manually. This requires a Registry change on the DCs, so you can use the PowerShell Registry provider.

To enable strict replication consistency on a DC, first create a DWORD value called Strict Replication Consistency in the following Registry key:

```
HKLM\System\CurrentControlSet\Services\NTDS\Parameters
```

Set this value 1. If you set it 0, strict replication consistency will be disabled. Use the following steps to enable strict replication consistency on the DC at which you're currently logged in:

1. In PowerShell, change to the HKEY_LOCAL_MACHINE hive in the Registry:

   ```
   cd HKLM:
   ```

2. Change to the path SYSTEM\CurrentControlSet\Services\NTDS\ Parameters:

   ```
   cd system\currentcontrolset\services\ntds\parameters
   ```

3. Create a new DWORD value called Strict Replication Consistency, and set it to 1. Use the New-ItemProperty cmdlet to create the Registry value. Use 1 for the Value parameter and DWORD for the PropertyType parameter:

   ```
   New-ItemProperty -Path . -Name "Strict Replication ↵
   Consistency" -Value 1 -PropertyType DWORD
   ```

CHAPTER 4

Managing Domain Controllers

IN THIS CHAPTER, YOU WILL LEARN TO:

I n this chapter, you'll automate the installation and configuration of domain controllers, the individual servers that authenticate users and other security principals to your Active Directory domain. Each AD domain requires a minimum of one DC to function, though even the smallest environments should have a minimum of two installed in order to provide availability in case one fails.

In the first section, we'll examine the steps needed to install DCs in and remove them from an AD domain, both writeable DCs as well as read-only DCs (RODCs). We'll also cover the steps needed to manage the Flexible Single Master of Operation (FSMO) roles within a domain and a forest, as well as configure the role of the AD global catalog (GC) server.

Once you've deployed a number of DCs in your environment, the next section explores the tasks needed to manage server-specific settings on individual DCs. This includes tasks such as renaming a DC and managing the AD service and where AD files are stored on an individual DC, as well as performing maintenance tasks such as offline defragmentation operations and moving files from one location to another.

Manage How the Active Directory Service Is Provided

In this section, we'll discuss the steps needed to deploy and configure the AD service on your network. Providing this service consists of deploying at least one DC in each domain, or more to provide high availability and better performance for geographically dispersed users.

We'll begin by describing the steps needed to deploy individual AD DCs, both writeable DCs and read-only DCs. This includes installing DCs using the dcpromo process, which may be customized depending on the installations scenario: creating a new domain, adding an additional DC to an existing domain, or customizing other parameters of the DC installation. We'll also describe how to remove a DC from an AD domain.

After covering the DC installation process, we'll examine how to manage the FSMO role holders in a forest and a domain, as well as the AD GC role that may be added to one or more DCs in each domain.

Install Active Directory on the Domain Controller

In a large or complex environment, one of the more common tasks you may perform is installing AD onto one or more new DCs. You'll need to plan your DC placement strategy to accommodate the size of your environment, how many AD sites you've configured, the number of users and devices in those sites, and the speed of the network links between sites. You can find detailed guidance about making these determinations, based on the specific speed of your WAN links and the number of users in each location, by referencing the Infrastructure Planning and Design guide for Active Directory Domain Services, available as a free download here:

```
www.microsoft.com/downloads/en/details.aspx?FamilyID=
ad3921fb-8224-4681-9064-075fdf042b0c&displaylang=en
```

Depending on the specific requirements for the location where you're installing the DC, you may wish to install a writeable DC, or you may wish to install an RODC. As the name implies, an RODC hosts a read-only copy of the AD database that allows users to authenticate to a local DC without the risk that any malicious or inadvertent changes made to that DC will replicate to the rest of the domain or forest. Because of this, RODCs may be a better choice than writeable DCs for locations where you can't necessarily guarantee the physical security of the DC hardware. You may also control which users' and computers' passwords are cached locally on the RODC, which is another significant difference from a writeable DC. By default, no user or computer passwords are cached on an RODC; you need to indicate the specific users and computers whose password information may be cached locally on the RODC. All other authentication requests are proxied back to a writeable DC. In the AD Users & Computers MMC, this is indicated as the list of "Accounts that have been authenticated to this Read-only Domain Controller," as shown in Figure 4.1.

In addition to using the security controls offered by the RODC, you may need to promote a DC residing in a remote location that is separated from your main data center by a slow or heavily utilized WAN link. Beginning in Windows Server 2003, you can speed this process by using the Install From Media (IFM) feature, which allows you to source your new DC from a recent system-state backup of another DC within the domain. In this way, only information that has changed since the time of the source backup needs to be replicated over the network, rather than the entire AD database.

FIGURE 4.1   List of users who have authenticated

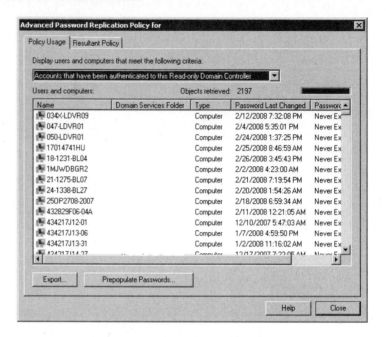

Promote a Server to a Writeable Domain Controller

Dcpromo.exe possesses a significant number of command-line options that allow you to customize the behavior of the DC promotion process to fit your needs. You can either enter the necessary parameters on the same command line as dcpromo or record the parameters into a separate text file for reuse in subsequent domain promotions.

Listing 4.1 shows the command-line switches necessary to add a new writeable DC into the contoso.com AD domain. You can see that the AD database, log files, and SYSVOL directories have been separated onto three separate drives: the AD database stored at d:\ntds, the AD logs stored at e:\ntdslogs, and SYSVOL stored at f:\ sysvol. Also note that the DNS Server service will be installed on this DC during the dcpromo process.

LISTING 4.1: **Creating a Writeable Domain Controller**

```
dcpromo /unattend /replicaOrNewDomain:replica /InstallDns:yes
/databasePath:"d:\ntds" /logPath:"e:\ntdslogs" /
sysvolpath:"f:\sysvol" /safeModeAdminPassword:DS%sdr5!@V8d3 /
rebootOnCompletion:yes
```

Promote a Server to a Read-Only Domain Controller

When you're adding an RODC to an AD domain, there are a number of prerequisite steps that need to be accomplished first. The forest in question must be running at the Windows Server 2003 forest functional level. At least one Windows Server 2008–writeable DC must be deployed within the domain in which you want to deploy an RODC, and you must have run `adprep /domainprep /rodcprep` in that domain. The `dcpromo.exe` command-line tool may also be customized to decommission an existing AD domain. In order to decommission an AD, you must first demote any other DCs in the domain.

You can configure a number of additional parameters when deploying an RODC, most notably around the Password Replication Policy (PRP) on the RODC. The PRP consists of attributes on the RODC's AD computer account that denote the following:

► A list of users, groups, and computers whose password secrets may be cached on this RODC

► A list of users, groups, and computers whose password secrets may not be cached on this RODC

You can see an example of the PRP in Figure 4.2.

FIGURE 4.2   Viewing a PRP

Administering
Service Delivery

PART I

Note that this list designates the list of accounts whose passwords *are permitted* to be cached; it doesn't mean these accounts' passwords have been cached there. A password will only be cached to a particular RODC if that user (or computer) account has actually authenticated to the RODC in question, at which point the accounts are added to the so-called Revealed list (indicating that the password has actually been *revealed* to the RODC). When this has happened, you'll see the account listed in the Active Directory Users & Computers MMC, as shown in Figure 4.3.

FIGURE 4.3   Viewing the Revealed list

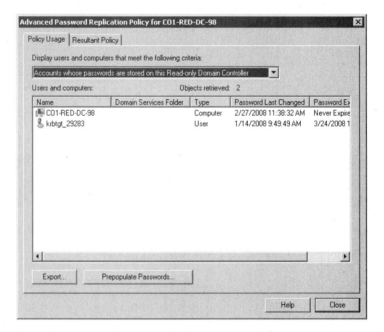

You can also specify the delegated administrator of a particular RODC, which denotes a user or group that can [1] locally administer the RODC without conferring any domain administration permissions to them, and [2] complete the two-stage dcpromo process.

SPECIFYING THE DESTINATION SITE

You can see the `SiteName=` switch listed in the answer file in Listing 4.2. If you wish to specify the AD site name in this manner, the site in question must already be configured within AD; the use of this switch in the answer file won't create the site for you.

Listing 4.2 includes the contents of an answer.txt file that promotes an RODC in the east.contoso.com domain.

LISTING 4.2: **Creating a Read-Only Domain Controller**

```
dcpromo /unattend:answer.txt

[DCINSTALL]
UserName=dcadmin
UserDomain=east.contoso.com
ReplicaDomainDNSName=east.contoso.com
PasswordReplicationDenied=EAST\Domain Admins,EAST\Server
Operators,EAST\Account Operators,CONTOSO\Domain Admins,CONTOSO\
Schema Admins,CONTOSO\Enterprise Admins
PasswordReplicationAllowed=EAST\Branch1Users,EAST\Branch1Computers
DelegatedAdmin=EAST\Branch1Admins
SiteName=Branch1
Password=<The password for the UserName account>
ReplicaOrNewDomain=ReadOnlyReplica
DatabasePath=d:\ntds
LogPath=e:\ntds\logs
SYSVOLPath=f:\sysvol
InstallDNS=yes
ConfirmGC=yes
SafeModeAdminPassword=AD%#Rffvdr523
RebootOnCompletion=yes
```

Promoting a Domain Controller from Backup

Beginning in Windows Server 2003, AD administrators have the ability to promote a DC using a backup of the AD database from an existing DC on the network. Particularly in sites that have a low-bandwidth connection to other DCs, this can significantly speed the process of DC promotion by allowing much of the data to be sourced from the local backup file, rather than requiring all data to be copied over the network. As mentioned, you can use this IFM feature to create an additional DC in an existing domain, either a writeable DC or an RODC.

Listing 4.3 includes an answer file that includes the ReplicationSourcePath switch to indicate the location of the IFM backup file. Notice that this answer file also uses the `ReplicationDC` switch, which lets you configure the specific DC from which changes should be replicated; you can use the `ReplicationDC` switch during any `dcpromo` operation, not just one that uses the `ReplicationSourcePath` switch to promote a DC from an IFM backup.

LISTING 4.3: Promoting a Domain Controller From Backup

```
dcpromo /unattend:answer.txt
[DCINSTALL]
UserName=dcadmin
Password=ADCV#$Rcfw3er4
UserDomain=east.contoso.com
DatabasePath=d:\ntds
LogPath=e:\ntds\logs
SYSVOLPath=f:\sysvol
SafeModeAdminPassword=#$VT$RF#vg434
CriticalReplicationOnly=no
SiteName=Philadelphia
ReplicaOrNewDomain=replica
ReplicaDomainDNSName=east.contoso.com
ReplicationSourceDC=dc1.east.contoso.com
ReplicationSourcePath=e:\backups\
RebootOnCompletion=yes
```

Removing a Domain Controller Gracefully

You've already seen the process of demoting DCs in the "Decommissioning a Domain" section of Chapter 2, "Managing Domains and Forests," because decommissioning a domain is done by demoting the last DC in that domain. If your aim is to decommission a single DC without decommissioning the entire domain, you can use a much simpler syntax for `dcpromo`, as shown in the following example. The most interesting syntax here is the `/DemoteFSMO` switch, which lets a DC be automatically demoted without prompting the administrator, even if that DC holds one or more FSMO roles for the domain or forest:

```
dcpromo /unattend /UserName:contosoadmin /UserDomain:contoso
.com /Password:#$%CVSER$% /AdministratorPassword:%#Q@
DCed23 /AdministratorPassword:%#Q@DCed23 /DemoteFSMO:Yes /
RebootOnCompletion:Yes
```

Removing a Domain Controller Forcibly

The syntax in the previous section assumes that the DC you're demoting is functioning correctly and able to communicate with the existing AD domain. During troubleshooting or disaster recovery, for example, you may encounter a scenario in which you need to remove AD from a DC that isn't being nearly so cooperative. If you need to uninstall AD from a DC that can no longer communicate with the domain, use the syntax shown here:

```
dcpromo /forceremoval
```

After you've forcibly demoted the DC, you need to remove references to it from the AD database—you'll also need to do this if you're removing references to a DC that has failed without first being demoted.

SPECIFYING THE DESTINATION SITE

In order to forcibly remove a DC from an existing domain, you need to connect to an accessible DC in the domain.

Work with the FSMO Roles

AD is a multimaster directory service, which means changes may be made to the directory from any DC (except RODCs!) and those changes will replicate throughout the entire AD domain or forest. Because certain AD operations are extremely sensitive, AD specifies five *operations masters* that must be fixed on the network, so that the tasks they govern may only be performed by targeting the specific DC that holds the relevant operations master role. However, these operations master-role holders are also *flexible*, which means you can transfer ownership of one of these FSMO roles to another DC on the network if required.

There are two forest-wide FSMOs within each AD forest, and three domain-wide FSMO roles within each AD domain. The two forest-wide FSMO role holders reside in the forest root domain by default and perform the following tasks:

- ► *Schema Master FSMO:* Any operation that updates the AD schema must target the Schema Master FSMO. There is one and only one Schema Master in every AD forest.

- ► *Domain Naming Master FSMO:* In order to ensure the integrity of the forest naming structure—that is, to prevent two child domains from being created with the same fully qualified domain name (FQDN)—any operation that attempts to add a new child domain, domain tree, or application partition must target the Domain Naming Master FSMO. There is one and only one Domain Naming Master in every AD forest.

There are three domain-wide FSMOs within each AD domain:

► *PDC Emulator FSMO:* Controls a number of domain-specific critical operations, including acting as the authoritative source for any user who has recently changed their password. If a user changes their password on a DC other than the PDC Emulator, the new password is sent out-of-band to the PDC Emulator so it will always have the most up-to-date password information. That way, if the user attempts to authenticate to a different DC that has not yet received the new password through the normal replication schedule, the other DC will send the authentication request to the PDC Emulator before rejecting it entirely. The PDC Emulator also acts as the authoritative time source for other DCs within the domain, as well as being the default target for any changes to Group Policy Objects (GPOs.) There is one and only one PDC Emulator in each AD domain.

► *RID Master:* Responsible for assigning blocks of relative identifiers (RIDs) to each DC within the domain, in blocks of 500 at a time. Each AD object possesses a security identifier (SID) comprising the domain SID, which is common across all users in the domain, and the RID, which is unique for each object. Because the RID Master is a single DC, this ensures that each RID in the domain is unique, because only one DC will ever be handing out RIDs at a time.

► *Infrastructure Master (IM):* Responsible for updating object references (a user in DomainA is a member of a group in DomainB) in a multidomain environment for DCs that aren't GC servers. If you're operating in a single-domain environment, or if all DCs within a single domain are also GC servers, the IM doesn't actually have any work to do. In any other case, it's important that the IM not be placed on a DC that has been configured as a GC server, because this will interfere with the IM's ability to perform its function.

When you're installing the first AD domain in the forest, all five FSMOs reside on the first DC you install, as shown in Figure 4.4.

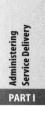

FIGURE 4.4   Default FSMO role placement, single-domain forest

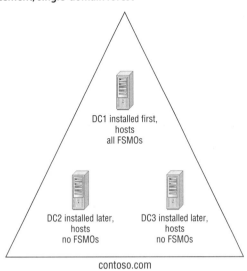

In a multidomain forest, the first DC installed in the forest root domain hosts all five FSMOs by default: the two forest-wide FSMOs, and the three domain-wide FSMOs for the forest root domain. When you install new domains in the forest, the first DC installed in each new domain hosts the three domain-wide FSMOs for that domain; the two forest-wide FSMOs remain where they are. You can see an example of this in Figure 4.5.

Listing the FSMO Role Holders

When you're performing AD monitoring, reporting, or auditing, or for a myriad of other reasons, you'll often need to enumerate the FSMO role holders within a forest or a domain. The first two examples in this section include the `Get-ADForest` and `Get-ADDomain` PowerShell cmdlets, which you can use to easily retrieve this information from the user's currently logged-on domain.

Because the PDC Emulator FSMO role holder registers a specific SRV record in DNS, you can also retrieve the identity of the PDC Emulator role holder by querying DNS. In Windows Server 2008 R2 PowerShell, you can achieve this by using the `Get-ADDomainController` cmdlet, as shown in the third example:

```
Get-ADForest Fabrikam.com | FT SchemaMaster,DomainNamingMaster
Get-ADDomain Fabrikam.com | FT PDCEmulator,RIDMaster,
   InfrastructureMaster
Get-ADDomainController -Discover -Service PrimaryDC
```

FIGURE 4.5   Default FSMO placement, forest root plus child domain

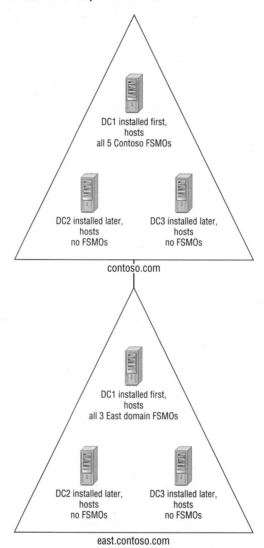

contoso.com

east.contoso.com

Transferring FSMO Roles

When you're managing AD over time, you may need to transfer a FSMO role from one DC to another. PowerShell allows you to do this easily using the `Move-ADDirectoryServerOperationsMasterRole` PowerShell cmdlet. Transferring a FSMO role from one DC to another assumes that both the source and the target

DC are online and functioning correctly; if you need to forcibly move a FSMO role from a failed DC to a new one, use the steps described in the next section.

Figure 4.6 shows how a multidomain forest might be configured after specific FSMO role holders have been transferred from their default locations to other DCs in each domain.

FIGURE 4.6   Customizing FSMO role placement

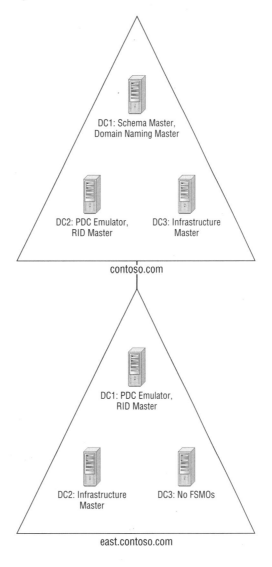

When you're planning for FSMO role-holder placement, keep the following best practices in mind:

► Place the Schema Master and the Domain Naming Master on the same DC.

► Place the PDC Emulator on a highly available DC that has been configured with the processor and memory capacity needed to respond to the additional requests that this DC will receive.

► Place the PDC Emulator and the RID Master on the same DC.

Additionally, the Infrastructure Master FSMO requires special handling in any domain that meets the following criteria:

► You've configured a multidomain forest, and…

► You have a domain within the forest in which *at least one DC* hasn't been configured as a GC server.

In this scenario, you *must* place the Infrastructure Master on a DC that is *not* configured as a GC server. You can see an example of this in Figure 4.7; both the `contoso.com` and `east.contoso.com` domains have been configured correctly to allow the GC server and the Infrastructure Master to interact correctly.

Compare this with the example in Figure 4.8; the `east.contoso.com` domain has been configured incorrectly for Infrastructure Master FSMO placement.

If, on the other hand, an AD domain meets any of the following criteria, then the Infrastructure Master may be placed without worrying about any adverse interactions with the GC:

► The domain is the only domain in the forest, or

► The domain only contains a single DC, or

► Each DC in this domain has been configured as a GC server.

You can see this illustrated in Figure 4.9: In this case, the `east.contoso.com` domain has the Infrastructure Master configured as a GC server, but because all three DCs in the domain are GCs, this interaction doesn't matter. (This does, however, require that any additional DCs added to the domain also be configured as GC servers, or the Infrastructure Master FSMO will need to be moved.)

FIGURE 4.7   Correct GC/infrastructure master interaction

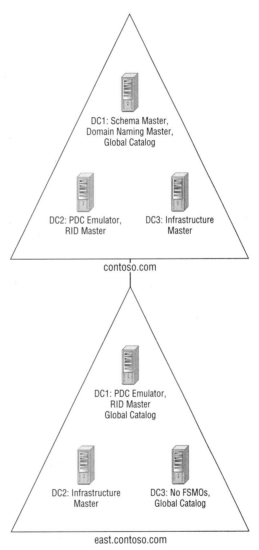

contoso.com

east.contoso.com

FIGURE 4.8   Incorrect GC/infrastructure master interaction

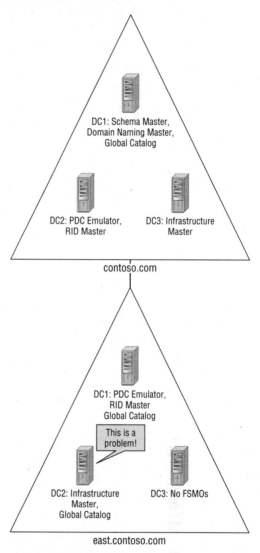

Similar to other cmdlets we have already covered in this book, the -Identity switch can specify the target DC using a number of formats. For this cmdlet, you may specify any of the following as the value of the -Identity argument:

► Name of the server object (name)

► Distinguished name (DN) of the NTDS Settings object

▶ Distinguished Name (DN) of the server object that represents the directory server

▶ GUID (`objectGUID`) of the server object under the configuration partition

▶ GUID (`objectGUID`) of the NTDS Settings object under the configuration partition

FIGURE 4.9   All DCs in the child domain are GCs.

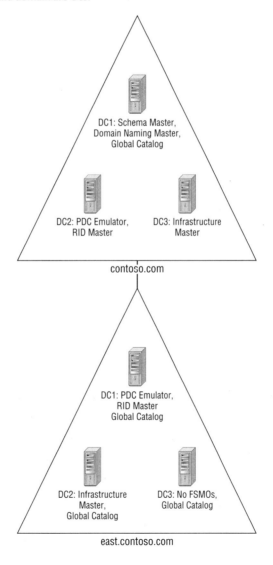

THE INFRASTRUCTURE MASTER AND THE ACTIVE DIRECTORY RECYCLE BIN

In addition to the three scenarios listed previously, placement of the Infrastructure Master FSMO is a non-issue in any forest where you've enabled the Active Directory Recycle Bin feature. The Recycle Bin requires your forest to be at the Windows Server 2008 Forest Functional level.

You'll use the same PowerShell cmdlet regardless of which FSMO role you wish to transfer. The -OperationMasterRole cmdlet takes one of the following arguments:

- ► PDCEmulator
- ► RIDMaster
- ► InfrastructureMaster
- ► SchemaMaster
- ► DomainNamingMaster

The following example demonstrates the syntax to transfer the PDC Emulator FSMO to a DC named CONTOSO-DC1:

```
Move-ADDirectoryServerOperationMasterRole -Identity CONTOSO-DC1
-OperationMasterRole PDCEmulator
```

Seizing FSMO Roles

If the DC that holds a FSMO role fails, you can forcibly seize that role to another DC within the domain or within the forest. The decision to seize a FSMO role should be based on which role has failed and whether you believe the original role-holder may eventually be returned to the network. In the case of the PDC Emulator, for example, an outage of this FSMO role would be noticed by clients and users in relatively short order; therefore, you might be inclined to seize the PDC Emulator FSMO to another DC quickly. By contrast, the Schema Master FSMO only needs to be contacted when the AD schema is being updated, an operation that doesn't occur often in most environments. If the DC holding the Schema Master role fails, but you expect it to be brought back online within a reasonable amount of time (for example, if you're waiting for a replacement part from the hardware vendor), you can feel more comfortable leaving the Schema Master FSMO in place on the failed DC until it's returned to service.

SEIZING FSMO ROLE HOLDERS

Because of the sensitive nature of the operations that each FSMO performs, you need to take care if you must seize a FSMO role holder to a new DC before returning the original role holder to the network. In the case of the RID Master and Schema Master FSMO role holders, Microsoft recommends that you reformat and reinstall the operating system of the original role holder before returning the server to the network, if you find it necessary to seize either of these FSMOs to another DC.

Seizing the PDC Emulator, by contrast, is a low-friction operation that shouldn't pose significant risk to your environment if you need to seize this role to another DC. You can return the original role holder to the network without worry.

The following example shows you the PowerShell syntax used to seize a FSMO role. It's nearly identical to the syntax used to gracefully transfer a FSMO role from one DC to another, with the addition of the –Force switch:

```
Move-ADDirectoryServerOperationMasterRole -Identity FABRIKAM-DC1
-OperationMasterRole SchemaMaster -Force
```

Manage the Global Catalog Settings

For replication purposes, the AD database is divided into multiple *naming contexts (NC)*. Each DC will replicate a minimum of three separate naming contexts:

- ► *Schema NC:* Contains all information within the AD schema. A copy of the Schema NC is held by every DC in the AD forest.

- ► *Configuration NC:* Contains AD configuration information such as AD site and subnet information. A copy of the Configuration NC is held by every DC in the forest.

- ► *Domain NC:* Contains a writeable copy of all information within a single domain, including all user, group, and computer objects; organizational units; and so on. Each DC within a domain replicates a copy of that domain's Domain NC.

To allow easier searches for information contained in other domains, AD also maintains the notion of the GC server. The GC naming context contains a partial attribute set (PAS) for each object in a domain and is a read-only copy of the data. A DC that is designated as a GC will hold a copy of the three default naming contexts, as well as the GC NC for every other domain in the forest. (A GC doesn't need to maintain a GC partition for its own domain, because it already houses its own domain NC.)

In a multidomain forest, you should plan for additional disk space requirements for all DCs that you designate as GC servers. Each GC requires the disk space normally associated with a DC, plus 50 percent of the size of each remote domain's database file (a good estimate for the size of each remote domain's PAS).

Installing the Global Catalog on a Domain Controller

You have the option to configure a DC as a GC server either during the promotion process or after the DC is up and running. In a multidomain environment, promoting a DC as a GC server will take additional time as the read-only GC partitions are copied to the new DCs. Similarly, if you add the GC server role to an existing DC, the DC won't advertise itself to client computers as a GC until the necessary read-only partitions have finished replicating to the new GC.

The following example shows how to promote a new DC as a GC using the /ConfirmGC switch within dcpromo:

```
dcpromo /unattend /replicaOrNewDomain:replica /InstallDns:yes /
databasePath:"d:\ntds" /logPath:"e:\ntdslogs" /sysvolpath:"f:\
sysvol" /safeModeAdminPassword:DS%sdr5!@V8d3 /ConfirmGC:yes /
rebootOnCompletion:yes
```

The next example in this section demonstrates how to add the GC server role to an existing DC by using the Set-ADObject cmdlet. This cmdlet modifies the options attribute of the DC's NTDS Settings object using the bitwise AND or OR operations. ORing a value of 1 adds the GC role; ANDing a value of 0 removes that role. This cmdlet takes the place of selecting or deselecting the Global Catalog check box in the AD Sites & Services MMC shown in Figure 4.10.

(For purposes of error-handling, the example includes a command to check for a value of <not set> when you obtain the current value of the options attribute, because AD won't store a value of 0. In this case, if options is <not set>, you replace it with a value of 0 so the rest of the script can function appropriately.)

```
$obj = Get-ADObject "CN=NTDS Settings,CN=Contoso-
DC1,CN=Servers,CN=Default-First-Site-Name,CN=Sites,CN=
Configuration,DC=Contoso,DC=COM"
$currentVal = $obj.options
```

```
if (! $currentVal) { $currentVal = 0}
$valToOR = 1
$newVal = $currentVal -bor $valToOR
Set-ADObject "CN=NTDS Settings,CN=Contoso-DC1,CN=Servers,
CN=Default-First-Site-Name,CN=Sites,CN=Configuration,DC=Contoso,
DC=COM" -Replace @{options='$newVal'}
```

Administering
Service Delivery

PART I

FIGURE 4.10 Enabling the GC server

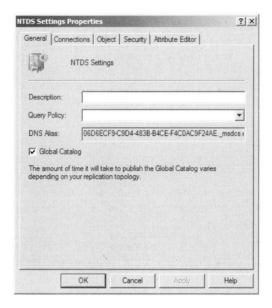

Managing Bitwise Attributes

Certain attributes in AD are *bitwise attributes*, which means they store their information using a specific encoding. A bitwise operator contains a number of digits, each of which may be set to 0 or 1 in binary. Remember that each binary digit represents a power of 2, where $2^0 = 1$, $2^1 = 2$, $2^2 = 4$, $2^3 = 8$, and so on. Each bit in a binary number may be set to 0 or 1; a value of 0 indicates that this bit is *not set*, whereas a value of 1 indicates that this bit is *set*. Take Bit 0 as an example, which is the 2^0 or ones place in a binary number. Bit 0 may be set to one of the following values:

▸ *Bit 0 not set:* $(2^0) \times 0 = 0 \times 1$, for a value of 0

▸ *Bit 0 set:* $(2^0) \times 1 = 1 \times 1$, for a value of 1

The next digit in a binary number, Bit 1, represents the 2^1 or twos place in a binary number. Similar to Bit 0, Bit 1 may be set to one of the following values:

- *Bit 1 not set:* $(2^1) \times 0 = 2 \times 0$, for a value of 0

- *Bit 1 set:* $(2^1) \times 1 = 2 \times 1$, for a value of 2

Each bit in a binary number is evaluated individually and then added to each other bit in the number. So, the binary number 10 is evaluated as follows:

- Bit 0 is *not set*, for a value of 0.

- Bit 1 is *set*, for a value of 2.

- Combining these bits gives a total value of 2.

Similarly, the binary number 1101 is evaluated as follows:

- Bit 0 (the rightmost digit) is *set*, or $(2^0) \times 1$, for a value of 1.

- Bit 1 (the second digit from the right) is *not set*, or $(2^1) \times 0$, for a value of 0.

- Bit 2 (the third digit from the right) is set, or $(2^2) \times 1$, for a value of 4.

- Bit 3 (the left-most digit) is set, or $(2^3) \times 1$, for a value of 8.

- The total value of this number is $8 + 4 + 0 + 1$, or 13.

Bit 0 of the `options` attribute on the DC's NTDS Settings object indicates whether the DC in question is advertising as a GC server. If Bit 0 is set, 1 is added to any other bits that have been set. If Bit 0 isn't set, 0 is added to any other bits that have been set.

In the case of a DC that is configured as a GC server only, the value of the `options` attribute is 1. If, however, that DC were configured as a GC as well as having Universal Group Caching enabled, the value of the `options` attribute would be 33, or $32 + 1$. To remove the GC server option, you would need to configure Bit 0 as not set, which in this case would set the `options` attribute with a value of 32.

Because of this behavior, it's important not to blindly overwrite the value of a bitwise attribute when making a change: If you took the previous example and set the `options` attribute to 0, you would not only be removing the GC server option, but also removing the Universal Group Caching option, which might not be what you had intended to do.

In order to safely *set* a bit in a bitwise operator, you use the PowerShell `-BOR` (bitwise OR) operator. It performs a binary operation that sets the value of one or more specific bits without affecting any other bits that have been configured.

The OR operation takes two binary numbers and evaluates each bit to determine whether that bit is set in one or both of the numbers being evaluated. If the relevant bit is set in either of the two numbers, the OR operation evaluates to 1. If the relevant bit is set in neither of the numbers, the OR operation evaluates to 0.

For example, if you take a value of 16 (binary: 10000) and then OR the value of 1 (binary: 0001), it's evaluated as follows:

Bit 0 is *not set* in 16. Bit 0 is *set* in 1. Bit 0 evaluates to 1.

Bit 1 is *not set* in 16. Bit 1 is *not set* in 1. Bit 1 evaluates to 0.

Bit 2 is *not set* in 16. Bit 2 is *not set* in 1. Bit 2 evaluates to 0.

Bit 3 is *not set* in 16. Bit 3 is *not set* in 1. Bit 3 evaluates to 0.

Bit 4 is *set* in 16. Bit 4 is *not set* in 1. Bit 4 evaluates to 1.

$(2^4) * 1 + (2^3) \times 0 + (2^2) \times 0 + (2^1) \times 0 + (2^0) \times 1 =$

$16 + 0 + 0 + 0 + 1 =$

17

Now let's take the reverse example: you have an `options` attribute of 17, and you want to *clear* Bit 0. The outcome you're looking for is to have the `options` attribute set to $2^3 + 0 + 0 + 0 + 0$, or 16. This requires the use of two additional bitwise operators: AND and NOT. In order to clear Bit 0 from a particular value, you need to create a result that consists of all the bits that are set in the current value, *and not* the bit that you need to clear. You do this as follows:

1. Specify the bit value that you need to clear—1, 2, 4, and so on—such as `$a = 1`.

2. Use the PowerShell –bnot operator to get ready to clear the value, such as `$bitToClear = -bnot $a`.

3. Use the PowerShell –band operator to AND the current value against the bit you need to clear, such as `$newVal = $currentOptions -band $bitToClear`.

You'll see an example of the AND NOT logic in the "Managing Bitwise Attributes" section.

Finally, this example demonstrates how to determine whether a particular DC is currently advertising itself as a GC on the network:

```
Get-ADRootDSE -Server Contoso-DC1 | FT GlobalCatalogReady
```

Removing the Global Catalog on a Domain Controller

If you determine for whatever reason that you don't want a particular DC to function as a GC server, you may remove the GC role by using the `Set-ADObject` cmdlet to modify the `options` attribute of the DC's NTDS Settings object, similar to what you saw in the "Installing the Global Catalog on a Domain Controller" section. In the case of removing the GC server role, you change the value of Bit 0 of the `options` attribute from 1 (indicating that the DC is currently a GC) to 0 (indicating that it isn't a GC). Notice again that the example includes some error-handling to set the value of `options` to 0 if it's currently <not set> in the directory.

You can see this demonstrated as follows:

```
$obj = Get-ADObject "CN=NTDS Settings,CN=Contoso-
DC1,CN=Servers,CN=Default-First-Site-Name,CN=Sites,CN=
Configuration,DC=Contoso,DC=COM"
$currentVal = $obj.options
if (! $currentVal) { $currentVal = 0}
$bitToClear = -bnot 1
$newVal = $currentVal -band $bitToClear
Set-ADObject "CN=NTDS Settings,CN=Contoso-
DC1,CN=Servers,CN=Default-First-Site-Name,CN=Sites,CN=
Configuration,DC=Contoso,DC=COM" -Replace @{options='$newVal'}
```

Obtaining a List of Global Catalogs

In the following example, you first see the PowerShell syntax used to obtain the list of GC servers throughout an AD forest. The second command restricts the results returned to those GCs within a single AD site, `Default-First-Site-Name` in this case:

```
Get-ADForest Fabrikam.com | Format-List GlobalCatalogs
Get-ADDomainController -Filter {Site -eq 'Default-First-Site-
Name'} | Format-Table Name,IsGlobalCatalog
```

Manage Server-Specific Settings

In this section, we'll look at how to customize the configuration of individual DCs in an AD domain. This begins with the steps needed to rename a DC, as well as stopping and restarting the AD service. You'll also learn how to turn AD replication on and off for a particular DC, as well as how to force an individual DC to replicate one or more AD partitions.

We'll close the chapter with various tasks needed to manage the physical files and folders on each DC that make up the AD database and log files. As you administer DCs over time, you may need to perform various maintenance tasks on these files, including performing defragmentation operations and moving the files from one location on disk to another.

Manage Domain Controller Settings

In this section, we'll discuss configuring some additional settings on AD DCs, including modifying the name of the DC, determining which site it's in, and enabling or disabling replication on the DC.

Changing the Name of a Domain Controller

Because DCs need to be accessible by name to client computers within the domain, you must take special precautions when renaming a DC. These are above and beyond the simple steps you might follow to rename an end user's client computer, including updating the necessary DNS records and service principal names (SPNs). By using the netdom.exe commands shown in the next example, you can ensure that the DC is renamed in a graceful manner that doesn't create outages for clients on your network. Unsurprisingly, you'll need Domain Admin privileges to rename a DC within an AD domain. This example renames the DC1.contoso.com DC to a new name of branchdc.contoso.com:

```
NETDOM computername dc1.contoso.com /add:branchdc.contoso.com
NETDOM computername dc1.contoso.com /makeprimary:branchdc
.contoso.com
NETDOM computername branchdc.contoso.com /remove:dc1.contoso.com
```

RENAMING A DOMAIN CONTROLLER USING NETDOM

Prior to running **NETDOM** with the **/makeprimary** switch, you need to ensure that the new DNS name and SPNs have replicated throughout your forest. Otherwise, your clients may experience issues in accessing the DC.

After you've issued the **/makeprimary** command, you'll need to restart the DC.

Determining What Site a Domain Controller Is In

As part of troubleshooting an AD connectivity issue or inventorying an existing environment, you may need a quick way to determine which AD site a particular DC resides in. This can be accomplished easily by using the `Get-ADDomainController` cmdlet; the output of this cmdlet returns a property called `Site` that contains the DC's site membership as its value. As you've seen in previous sections and chapters, the `-Identity` switch of `Get-ADDomainController` can take a number of arguments, including the short name, FQDN, DN, and GUID of the DC.

In the following example, you can see this cmdlet in action, using the `Format-Table` cmdlet to output the DC's name and site into an easily readable format:

```
Get-ADDomainController -Identity CONTOSO-DC1.contoso.com |
Format-Table Name,Site
```

Restarting AD Without Rebooting the Server

Beginning with Windows Server 2008, the AD service can be stopped and started without rebooting the server. (The Active Directory Domain Services service now even appears in the Services MMC, as you can see in Figure 4.11.) This allows you to stop the AD service and take the AD database offline in order to perform a task such as applying updates or performing an offline defragmentation of the AD database without taking the extra time to reboot the DC into Directory Services Restore mode. While the AD is in a stopped state, no new client requests are processed; however, other services running on the server that don't rely on the AD service being started, such as DHCP, continue to function and service client requests normally.

You can start, stop, and restart the AD service on a Windows Server 2008 or 2008 R2 DC using the same `Start-Service`, `Stop-Service`, and `Restart-Service` cmdlets that you'd use for any other service running on a Windows server. The following example shows the syntax for all three of these options:

```
Stop-Service "Active Directory Domain Services"
Start-Service "Active Directory Domain Services"
Restart-Service "Active Directory Domain Services"
```

The next example shows how to obtain the current status of the restartable AD service. By default, this cmdlet returns a table containing the status, name, and display name of the service as it appears in the Services MMC:

```
Get-Service "Active Directory Domain Services"
```

FIGURE 4.11 Managing the AD service in the Services MMC

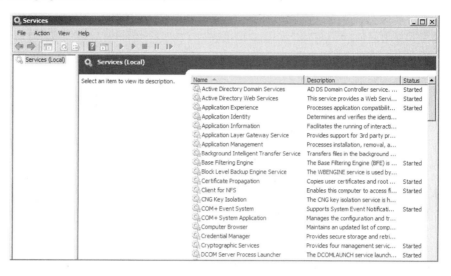

Forcing a Domain Controller to Replicate

At various points during troubleshooting—or if you've created one or more objects on a particular DC and need to quickly make the rest of the environment aware of them—you may need to force a DC to replicate with a specific replication partner or with all of its replication partners for one or more AD partitions.

You force replication using the repadmin.exe tool, specifying the DC that is requesting the changes as well as (if replicating from a specific partner) the DC from which changes are being requested. Remember that all AD replication is pull-based, which means DC2 requests change from DC1 before DC1 sends any changes over the network. In this simple example, DC2 is considered the *destination DC*, and DC1 is considered the *source DC*.

The following example shows how to force DC2.contoso.com to request all replication changes from DC1.contoso.com for the dc=contoso,dc=com naming context. Notice that you specify the name of the destination DC, dc2 .contoso.com, whereas you specify the GUID of the source DC, DC1:

```
repadmin /sync dc=contoso,dc=com dc2.contoso.com 8e90169a-dbf4-
461b-97f5-1535085b9c04 /force
```

Next, you can use a slightly different syntax to force dc2.contoso.com to request replication from all of its replication partners for the Configuration naming context:

```
repadmin /syncall dc2.contoso.com dc=configuration,dc=contoso,
dc=com /force
```

USING REPADMIN /SYNCALL

If you omit the name of the partition in the previous example, `repadmin` will request all replication changes for the `Configuration` and `Schema` partitions only.

Preventing a Domain Controller from Replicating

In addition to numerous other features, the `repadmin.exe` tool has the ability to stop inbound and/or outbound replication entirely for a particular DC. When replication is disabled using this method, normal AD replication doesn't occur, and `repadmin` commands using the `/replicate`, `/sync`, and `/syncall` commands fail. However, you should exercise caution in disabling replication without also taking additional steps such as removing network connectivity, because an administrator can override the steps described here by using the `/force` switch in `repadmin`, or by using other replication commands that may not honor the `repadmin` used to disable inbound and outbound replication. The following example shows how to enable and disable outbound as well as inbound replication:

```
repadmin /options +DISABLE_OUTBOUND_REPL
repadmin /options -DISABLE_OUTBOUND_REPL
repadmin /options +DISABLE_INBOUND_REPL
repadmin /options -DISABLE_INBOUND_REPL
```

Manage the Active Directory Database

The AD database is based on the Extensible Storage Engine (ESE) format, similar to the database used by Microsoft Exchange. Like any database, the AD ESE database consists of a number of different tables with a row for each value in each table. When an object is deleted from AD, one or more rows are deleted from multiple tables in the underlying database. Each DC runs an internal defragmentation process every 12 hours by default to optimize the internal structure of the database; or you can manually compact the database to reclaim free space. You can also move the database, log files, or `SYSVOL` directory from one disk drive to another if a particular DC is low on disk space.

Viewing the Amount of Whitespace in the Directory Database

Because AD information is stored in a database format, deleting objects creates whitespace in the database that may need to be optimized over time. By default, each DC performs an online defragmentation of the AD database every 12 hours. However, this process doesn't reduce the size of the database file; rather, the online defragmentation optimizes data storage in the database and reclaims space in the directory for new objects. To view the amount of whitespace in the AD database, you can turn on additional levels of diagnostics that cause an event to be written to the Event Viewer recording this information. The following example demonstrates how to modify the Registry of an AD DC to enable the necessary logging level to capture this information:

```
Set-ItemProperty -Path hklm:\SYSTEM\CurrentControlSet\Services\
NTDS\Diagnostics -Name "Garbage Collection" -value 1 -type Decimal
```

When the necessary Garbage Collection logging level has been configured, Event ID 1646 is logged to the Directory Services Event Viewer, indicating the amount of disk space that may be reclaimed by running an offline defragmentation of the AD database. The following example shows how to use PowerShell to retrieve the contents of the specific Event ID from the Directory Services Event Viewer:

```
Get-EventLog -LogName "Directory Services" | where { $_.eventID
-eq 1646}
```

Performing an Offline Database Defragmentation

The online defragmentation that is performed every 12 hours by default doesn't reduce the overall size of the AD database file. By performing an offline defragmentation of the database, you create a new, compacted version of the ntds.dit file. If your AD database is significantly fragmented, the new compacted file may end up being considerably smaller than it was before the defragmentation. You should consider performing an offline defragmentation if you need to delete a significant number of records from your AD database, such as after you've migrated a large portion of your AD users to a remote AD forest as part of a company merger or divestiture.

Offline defragmentations are performed using the ntdsutil.exe utility and may be performed in Directory Services Restore Mode or by stopping the AD service. As part of this process, you need to have a separate location on disk that can temporarily store the compacted AD database until the defragmentation is complete. As a precaution, Microsoft recommends that you make a full backup of your AD prior to performing these steps.

The following example lists the sequence of `ntdsutil` commands you enter to perform this task. Here you use `d:\temp` as the location to temporarily store the AD database during the defragmentation:

```
ntdsutil
files
info
compact to d:\temp
quit
quit
```

USING THE INFO COMMAND

The `info` command displays the current information about the location and size of the AD database and log files before continuing.

When the defragmentation has completed, delete all log files in the AD log file directory, and then copy the compacted DIT file (in `d:\temp`, in this example) back to the original database location, overwriting the original file.

Moving the Active Directory Database

As you manage your DCs over time, you may need to move the AD database or log files to another drive letter. It may be the case that your database file has grown and needs to be moved to a larger drive, or you may wish to move the database and the log files to separate hard drives in order to improve disk performance. This process is similar to performing an offline defragmentation; and just like that process, Microsoft recommends that you perform a backup of your AD prior to moving any files. This task must be performed either in Directory Services Restore Mode or with the Active Directory Domain Services service stopped. As a part of moving the AD database to a new location, `ntdsutil` also performs an offline defragmentation of the database.

You move the AD database using the `ntdsutil.exe` command-line tool. The following example lists the `ntdsutil` commands used to perform this task. This example moves the AD database to `d:\ntds` and the AD log files to `e:\ntds\logs`:

```
ntdsutil
files
move db to d:\ntds
move logs to e:\ntds\logs
quit
quit
```

After you've moved these files, you need to restart the DC or restart the AD service. As a final step, you should make a new backup of the DC with the files in their new location.

Moving SYSVOL to Another Location

In addition to moving the AD database and log files to alternate locations, you may also need to move the SYSVOL shared directory to a new location, particularly if the drive containing SYSVOL is running low on space.

Especially for environments that are using the File Replication System (FRS) for SYSVOL replication, the safest and most efficient way to relocate SYSVOL on a DC is to demote the DC and then re-promote the DC, specifying the new SYSVOL location. The "Removing a Domain Controller Gracefully" section demonstrates the syntax needed to demote a DC. The "Install Active Directory on the Domain Controller" section demonstrates how to promote the DC in order to specify the new SYSVOL location. Particularly if your AD database is large in size, you can shorten the time required to re-promote the DC by using the IFM option demonstrated in Listing 4.3.

MOVING SYSVOL MANUALLY

If this is the only DC in your environment, you can move the SYSVOL directory manually using the steps listed in the following Microsoft Knowledge Base article: `http://support.microsoft.com/kb/842162`.

Reapplying the Default Security Permissions to SYSVOL

If you've manually moved the SYSVOL directory to a new location, one step in the process is to apply a set of default permissions to the SYSVOL directory. You may also need to reapply this default set of permissions if they're accidentally or maliciously altered, resulting in errors in the application of GPOs, login scripts, or access to other data that is stored in SYSVOL.

To apply or reapply these permissions, you must first create a file containing the text shown in Listing 4.4, and save it to `%systemroot%\security\templates\sysvol.inf`.

LISTING 4.4: **Creating the `sysvol.inf` File**

```
[Unicode]
Unicode=yes
[Version]
signature="$CHICAGO$"
Revision=1
[Profile Description]
Description=default perms for sysvol
[File Security]
"%Sysvol%",2,"D:P(A;CIOI;GRGX;;;AU)(A;CIOI;GRGX;;;SO)
(A;CIOI;GA;;;BA)(A;CIOI;GA;;;SY)(A;C
     IOI;GA;;;CO)"
"%Sysvol%\domain\policies",2,"D:P(A;CIOI;GRGX;;;AU)
(A;CIOI;GRGX;;;SO)(A;CIOI;GA;;;BA)(A;C
        IOI;GA;;;SY)(A;CIOI;GA;;;CO)(A;CIOI;GRGWGXSD;;;PA)"
```

After you've created this file, you apply the permissions it specifies to the SYSVOL folder using the secedit command, as shown here:

```
secedit /configure /cfg %systemroot%\security\templates\sysvol
.inf /db %systemroot%\security\templates\sysvol.db /overwrite
```

Changing the Directory Services Restore Mode Password

When you promote a new DC, you're prompted to create a separate administrator password to be used when you boot the server into Directory Services Restore Mode. This password is unique to each DC and may be used to authenticate to the DC when the AD database is unavailable, such as when the DC is booted into Directory Services Restore Mode.

If you forget the Restore Mode password for a particular DC, any Domain Admin can change the password using the `ntdsutil.exe` utility. You must change the password when the DC is *not* in Directory Services Restore Mode; that is, you must change the restore mode password while the AD database is online. The following example shows the commands you enter to change the DSRM password for the DC that you're currently logged on to. (If you want to change the Restore Mode password for a remote DC, substitute the name of the DC for `null`.)

```
ntdsutil
set dsrm password
reset password on server null
<Enter the new password>
<Re-Enter the new password>
quit
quit
```

You can see what this command output looks like in Figure 4.12.

FIGURE 4.12 Changing the Directory Services Restore Mode password

PART II

Managing Active Directory Data

CHAPTER 5

Configuring Active Directory Dependencies

IN THIS CHAPTER, YOU WILL LEARN TO:

When you're designing and implementing an Active Directory infrastructure, there are some dependencies that you need to take into account. Active Directory is dependent on multiple technical and nontechnical factors. For example, in order for just authentication to work when a user logs in to a domain-joined client workstation, there are dependencies on the network configuration, name resolution, system time, Dynamic Host Configuration Protocol (DHCP), system policies, security policies, and a slew of other environmental dependencies. We've covered many of these dependencies in other chapters of this book, but we'll examine two in particular in this chapter: the Domain Name System (DNS) and the time service.

Both of these elements are absolutely necessary in order for your Active Directory environment to even function. Name resolution is one of the more obvious dependencies, because without it, domain controllers (DCs) can't be found. But the dependency of an accurate time-service infrastructure is often overlooked. In this chapter, we'll explore how both of these dependencies work and how you can automate their management via PowerShell.

Configure DNS

The Domain Name System (DNS) is nothing more than a way to represent IP addresses as friendly names that humans can remember. However, its usage is essential to Active Directory (AD). AD uses DNS to publish service information, locate other DCs, and locate other systems on the network. Client computers, in turn, use DNS to find DCs to use.

The process that a client computer uses to find a DC is referred to as the DC Locator process. This process is performed by the netlogon service on client computers that are joined to a domain. One of the key pieces of this discovery process involves the client performing a DNS query to its configured domain in order to determine which DCs to talk to. These records that the client queries for are called *service locator (SRV) records*, which are used to identify servers that host services for the network. SRV records in DNS contain the following information:

- ► The name of the service being hosted (such as LDAP)

- ► The protocol used to talk to the server (such as TCP)

- ► A weight and priority setting that determines which server to use if there is more than one registered for a particular service

- ► The port number on which the service is hosted

- ► The name of the server that is hosting the service

DCs use SRV records to publish service information for LDAP connections, global catalog connections, Kerberos logons, and Kerberos password changes. If a client computer doesn't know what site it's in, it performs a DNS query to obtain a list of DCs for the domain. The query is performed for the following DNS name:

```
_ldap._tcp.dc._msdcs.<DomainFQDN>
```

For example, if the client is in the domain contoso.com, the client's netlogon service queries for

```
_ldap._tcp.dc._msdcs.child.contoso.com
```

From the list of DNS records returned, the client performs another DNS query to resolve the DC's IP address. The client then uses this IP address to establish a UDP connection to the LDAP service on the DC and query for the NETLOGON attribute in RootDSE. This attribute doesn't actually exist in the directory; rather, it's used to perform an LDAP ping. When the DC receives a query for this attribute, it checks to ensure that the query string contains the other elements that it expects and then returns a success response that contains some additional information:

► The DNS name of the forest (such as contoso.com)

► The DNS name of the domain (such as child.contoso.com)

► The DC's fully qualified host name (such as dc1.child.contoso.com)

► The NetBIOS name of the domain (such as CHILD)

► The DC's NetBIOS name (such as DC1)

► The site that the DC is in (such as BALTIMORE)

► The site that the client is in (such as SEATTLE)

Two of the key elements in the LDAP response are the site the DC is in and the site the client is in. The DC is able to determine the client's site by performing a directory lookup using the IP address of the client. The DC maps this IP address to a subnet object in the directory (covered in Chapter 3, "Managing Sites and Replication"). The DC can extrapolate which site the subnet is associated with by reading the siteObject attribute on the subnet object.

This information is returned to the client so the client can make a decision as to whether it should use the DC. If the DC is in the same site as the client, the client uses the DC. Otherwise, it tries to find a DC that is in the same site by performing another SRV record query. This time, however, the client knows what site it's in, so it queries for the following record:

```
_ldap._tcp.<sitename>._sites.dc._msdcs.<DomainFQDN>
```

Using the previous example, the next query would resemble the following:

```
_ldap._tcp.SEATTLE._sites.dc._msdcs.child.contoso.com
```

The same LDAP query process is repeated. If no DCs are found in the same site as the client, the client uses the DC that the first LDAP query was performed against. Because of this, it's important to ensure that your client's subnets are registered to a site in AD. If they are not, a random DC could be used.

Configure DNS Server Settings

In addition to using DNS for locating DCs, the DC can also double as a DNS server. In fact, this is a fairly common configuration, because using AD DCs for your DNS servers has some advantages. When you're working with DNS servers via PowerShell, the best method is to use the Windows Management Instrumentation (WMI) provider. Windows DNS servers have the option of storing their data in AD (which we'll discuss in depth in this chapter), but they can also store data in DNS zone files. Therefore, you can't write PowerShell scripts with the assumption that the DNS data exists as AD objects. Because of this, WMI gives you the most flexibility with DNS scripts.

Understanding How DNS Works

In general, DNS servers listen for DNS requests and respond to them appropriately. For example, a client may want to resolve the name `contoso-dc1.contoso.com` to an IP address. The client performs a query by asking the DNS server to give it the IP address for `contoso-dc1.contoso.com`. When the DNS server receives the query, it looks up the information in its internal database and then returns it to the client. The process is simple enough, but designing what the DNS infrastructure looks like can become complex because there are many things to take into consideration.

DNS Zones

Domain names in DNS are represented by zones. A domain that contains multiple names stores these name-to-IP address mappings in the zone for that domain. For example, consider the DNS domain named `contoso.com`. The DNS records for `www.contoso.com` and `mail.contoso.com` both fall under the `contoso.com` domain name. As such, the `contoso.com` zone on the DNS server would contain both of the DNS records and the IP addresses they resolve to.

Any given DNS server can contain multiple zones. For example, a DNS server can host both the `contoso.com` zone and the `fabrikam.com` zone. In traditional DNS implementations, the data for each of these zones is kept in a *zone file*. The zone file is essentially the database that maps the naming information and the IP informa-tion for each zone. To be considered RFC compliant, zone files must adhere to the format imposed in RFC 1035, which describes how a zone file is to be structured. Most of the time, the files aren't edited manually. Instead, there is typically a more user-friendly interface that administrators interact with, and the zone file is updated by the administration application.

Recursion

DNS clients can make two types of queries:

► Recursive query

► Iterative query

PART II

To understand the difference between the two, consider a situation where a client tries to browse to www.contoso.com. The network settings on each client include the IP address of the client's DNS server. Any time a client computer needs to resolve a DNS name to an IP address, this is the DNS server that it goes to first. If the client doesn't already have the IP address for www.contoso.com in its cache, it queries its DNS server and asks for it.

The DNS server first determines if it owns the record for www.contoso.com. If not, it begins looking for another DNS server to ask. This process starts at the root of the DNS name (.com in this case) and performs the query there. An Internet root DNS server for the .com name checks to see if it has the answer; if not, it issues a refer-ral for the requesting DNS server and gives it another server to check with. In this case, it's referred to the server that owns the contoso.com domain. The requesting DNS server then sends the query to the server it was referred to. This same process is followed again for the contoso.com DNS server. This time, however, the server does own the record for www.contoso.com, so it resolves the query and sends the answer back to the requesting DNS server. That DNS server then sends the answer back to the client that requested it. This process that we just described is called a *recursive query* and is demonstrated in Figure 5.1.

When the client requested the IP address for www.contoso.com from its config-ured DNS server, it told the server that the query is recursive. This means it's up to the DNS server to find the IP address and give it back to the client. If the DNS server can't find it, then the client believes the address doesn't exist and doesn't bother querying other servers. After the client requested the recursive query, the DNS server went through the process of finding the IP address, looking in one server after another. In this example, we illustrated recursion by having the client's DNS server query only two servers. However, in reality it could take more or even less.

Managing Active Directory Data

For example, if the DNS server for the .com domain already had the address for www.contoso.com in its cache, it would have returned the answer back to the client's DNS server rather than returning a referral.

FIGURE 5.1   **How a recursive query works**

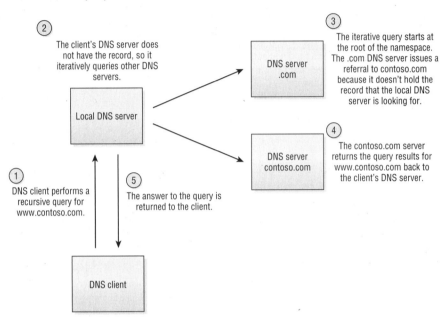

② The client's DNS server does not have the record, so it iteratively queries other DNS servers.

Local DNS server

③ The iterative query starts at the root of the namespace. The .com DNS server issues a referral to contoso.com because it doesn't hold the record that the local DNS server is looking for.

DNS server .com

DNS server contoso.com

④ The contoso.com server returns the query results for www.contoso.com back to the client's DNS server.

① DNS client performs a recursive query for www.contoso.com.

⑤ The answer to the query is returned to the client.

DNS client

If the client performed an iterative query, the client's DNS server wouldn't go out and look for the IP address. Instead, it would examine its own database or cache and return the best information it had. For example, if it knew the IP of www.contoso.com, it would return it; but if not, it might return a referral to the client to the contoso .com DNS server. It would then be the client's responsibility to go out and query the DNS server that it was referred to. This is the process that was followed in our illustration when the client's DNS server queried the .com DNS server for the IP address of www.contoso.com. The client's DNS server issued an iterative query; it wasn't expecting the .com server to go out and find the name for it. Instead, the client's DNS server would follow the referral chain and find the address on its own.

Forwarders

A DNS server can also be configured to forward queries to a separate DNS server. This may be useful if you have all your clients pointing to an internal DNS server and want a separate DNS server to resolve queries over the Internet. When the client queries the configured DNS server, the DNS server checks its local zone information and cache. If it doesn't know the answer to the client's query, it forwards the query to the DNS server that is configured as its forwarder. This causes the client's DNS server to behave differently than we previously described. Typically, the client's DNS server uses recursion to find the IP address and return it to the client. However, when forwarders are used, the client's DNS server sends the query to the forwarders (one at a time) and waits for a response. When the client's DNS server gets the IP address from the forwarder, it sends the IP address back to the client. If the forwarders don't respond, the client's DNS server falls back to using recursive queries, although the fallback to recursion can be disabled.

In Windows Server 2003, Microsoft introduced a new type of forwarder called a *conditional forwarder*. With regular forwarders, every DNS query to which the server doesn't know the answer is forwarded to the forwarder. With conditional forwarders, the server forwards the query only for the domain specified. For example, if you set up a conditional forwarder for the domain contoso.com, then the DNS server would use recursion to answer DNS queries for other domain names. But when a DNS query comes in for a contoso.com domain name, the DNS server would forward the query to the server specified as the conditional forwarder. This comes in handy in a couple different cases:

Unpublished Domain Names   If you need to resolve queries to another domain name that is unpublished (has an irregular name), such as root.admin, you can use a conditional forwarder can. I (Ken) have personally had cases in the past when I had to put a forest-level trust in place between two forests with unpublished names. The DNS domain name root.admin isn't an official DNS name hosted by the root DNS servers on the Internet, so recursion can't be used to resolve the names in this case. Instead, you can set up a conditional forwarder so that any query to root.admin gets sent to the IP address of the server that hosts that zone.

Lab Scenarios   Another case where I frequently use conditional forwarders is when I'm working in my lab. This is especially the case when I'm working with two separate forests, such as contoso.com and fabrikam.com. I'll configure each forest with a conditional forwarder to the other forest so DNS queries can be resolved properly.

High Availability

Client computers are configured to talk to a specific DNS server by IP address. This is typically configured either through DHCP or manually. When using DHCP, the client receives its network configuration automatically from the DHCP server, and part of this configuration is one or more DNS servers that it needs to talk to. When configuring the DNS servers on a client computer manually, you type in the IP address of the server the client should use. In most cases, manual configuration isn't preferable. Not only can it be cumbersome and error prone, but if your DNS server's IP address changes, you have to go back and reconfigure all those manual clients. Scripting this change can make this task much easier for you, so later in this section we'll give you a script for changing the DNS configuration on multiple client computers on your network. In most cases, however, DHCP is used because no one wants to manually configure the network settings on more than just a few computers. The exception is on your server workloads. Most organizations tend to configure the network settings on servers manually.

Because clients point to the DNS server's IP address directly, if the DNS server goes offline, the client can't use DNS. As we discussed earlier in this chapter, DNS is critical when clients use AD, because it's how they find DCs. Therefore, if a client can't reach the DNS server, the user can't log in to the domain. Because of this, there are usually multiple DNS servers in the environment. Client computers are configured to use more than one DNS server, although one is configured as primary and the others as secondary, tertiary, and so on. If the client can't contact the primary DNS server by its IP address, it walks down the list of alternate DNS servers.

For this to work, each DNS server needs to retain a copy of the DNS data. In traditional DNS implementations, a single master architecture is used to accomplish this. This means one DNS server is designated as the primary holder of the DNS information for a zone. Updates can only occur on the primary server. The other DNS servers are consider secondary holders of the DNS information, and they have read-only copies of the zone. DNS data is copied from a primary server to a secondary server or from one secondary server to another secondary server. This direct exchange of DNS data between two DNS servers is called a *zone transfer*. In a zone transfer, the server that is sending the data is referred to as the *master*, and the server receiving the data is referred to as the *slave*. In the past, masters were required to send the entire zone to slaves when any data in the zone changed, even if only one record changed. Now, however, we have incremental zone transfers. These allow the master to send only the DNS data that has changed since the last transfer. Figure 5.2 illustrates the concept of zone transfers.

When you encounter DNS architectures that were built on a single master DNS technology, you'll usually find that the design of the DNS architecture was built around this limitation. We've seen designs in the past where organizations broke DNS architectures into dozens of zones in order to have primary zone servers local to different sites. Architectures like this tend to cause problems when clients are joined to AD domains, because the DNS host names of the client computers may be different than the DNS name of the domain. You can work around these issues, but not without some administrative pain.

FIGURE 5.2   Zone-transfer concepts

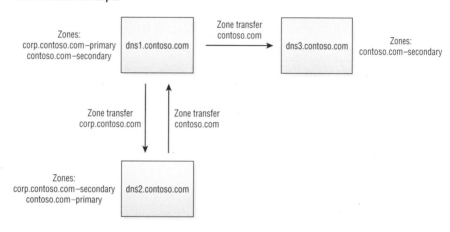

Creating a DNS Zone

Microsoft DNS servers can host multiple zones. In fact, after a default installation of AD, you'll find that there are two zones created that represent the forest or domain. To create a new DNS zone, you can use the CreateZone method in WMI. You need to specify a couple of settings when doing so. Here is what the method looks like:

```
CreateZone(ZoneName, ZoneType, IsADIntegrated, ZoneFileName, ↵
    PrimaryIPAddress, AdminEmail)
```

ZoneName   The name of the zone; for example, corp.contoso.com.

ZoneType   The type of zone that you're creating (0 = primary, 1 = secondary, 2 = stub zone, 3 = forwarder).

IsADIntegrated   Whether the zone is AD-integrated. This value is $true or $false.

ZoneFileName   If you choose to not use an AD-integrated zone, you can optionally specify the zone file that is used. If this is omitted, the name of the zone file is the DNS name of the zone followed by .dns. For example, the zone file for the corp.contoso.com zone is corp.contoso.com.dns.

PrimaryIPAddress   When you're creating a secondary zone, this parameter provides the IP address for the primary zone holder. The zone is transferred to the secondary from this server.

AdminEmail   The email address of the zone's administrator. This parameter is optional.

You'll find the `CreateZone` WMI method in the `MicrosoftDNS_Zone` class in WMI. The easiest way to invoke this method is to use the `WMICLASS` type accelerator. The `WMICLASS` type accelerator is an alias to the `System.Management.ManagementClass` object type. When you use this type accelerator, you pass it the path to the WMI class that you want to use, and then you can call the methods directly. The following example creates a `System.Management.ManagementClass` object in PowerShell that points to the `MicrosoftDNS_Zone` class, which is where the `CreateZone` method is kept. This object is being stored in the variable named `$objWMIClass`:

```
$objWMIClass = [WMICLASS]"root\MicrosoftDNS:MicrosoftDNS_Zone"
```

From here, you can call the `CreateZone` method straight from the `$objWMIClass` object. This example creates an AD-integrated zone called `corp.contoso.com`. Because all AD-integrated zones are considered primary zones (because they can all write DNS data), you can mark the zone type as primary:

```
$objWMIClass.CreateZone("corp.contoso.com", 0, $true)
```

To create the same zone as a standard primary zone that isn't AD-integrated, you can use the following command:

```
$objWMIClass.CreateZone("corp.contoso.com", 0, $false)
```

By default, when you create an AD-integrated zone using the `CreateZone` method, it's stored in the domain naming context and replicated to all DCs in the same domain as the DNS server. You can (and probably should) modify the replication scope after the zone is created. We'll show you how to do this later on in this chapter.

Creating a Reverse Lookup Zone

In DNS, a standard zone is also known as a *forward lookup zone*. A forward lookup zone is used to resolve a DNS name to an IP address. There is also the concept of a *reverse lookup zone*. A reverse lookup zone has the opposite effect; it resolves an IP address to a DNS name. Reverse lookup zones operate similarly to forward lookup zones. Rather than using host records, a reverse lookup zone uses *pointer (PTR) records*. The PTR record stores the IP address and the host name and provides the reverse lookup information to DNS clients.

To create a reverse lookup zone, you can use the same method as creating a forward lookup zone. The difference, however, is in what you name the zone. Reverse lookup zones require a specific name. The first part of the DNS name of a reverse lookup zone is the masked part of the subnet's IP address in reverse order. So if the subnet is 192.168.0.0 with a subnet mask of 255.255.255.0, then you specify 0.168.192 as the first part of the zone name. The second part of the name for a reverse lookup zone is always in-addr.arpa. The complete name of the reverse lookup zone for the 192.168.0.0/24 subnet is 0.168.192.in-addr.arpa.

To create a reverse lookup zone, you should use the same CreateZone WMI method that you use when creating a regular forward lookup zone. The only difference in the code is the name of the zone. The following commands create the reverse lookup zone for the 192.168.0.0/24 subnet:

```
$objWMIClass = [WMICLASS]"root\MicrosoftDNS:MicrosoftDNS_Zone"
$objWMIClass.CreateZone("0.168.192.in-addr.arpa", 0, $true)
```

In the previous command, the reverse lookup zone is being created as a primary zone that is AD-integrated. Everything else about using this method for reverse lookup zones is exactly the same as when creating forward lookup zones. For more information about using the CreateZone method, see the previous section, "Creating a DNS Zone."

Determining Which Zones a DNS Server Has

It isn't required that every DNS server host the same zones. Each DNS server in your environment can contain a different set of zones and a unique configuration; this is entirely dependent on your DNS design. You can use WMI to target a specific DNS server and determine which zones that server hosts. To do this, you can connect to the MicrosoftDNS WMI namespace on the DNS server and view all the instances of the MicrosoftDNS_Zone class. The following PowerShell command uses the Get-WMIObject cmdlet to connect to the local server and display a list of the zones that it currently has:

```
gwmi -Namespace root\MicrosoftDNS -Class MicrosoftDNS_Zone | ↵
    ft Name
```

To target a different DNS server, you can specify the `ComputerName` parameter onto the `Get-WMIObject` cmdlet. The following example lists the DNS zones on the DNS server named BAL-DC01:

```
gwmi -Namespace root\MicrosoftDNS -Class MicrosoftDNS_Zone ↵
    -ComputerName BAL-DC01 | ft Name
```

Converting a Zone to AD-Integrated

As mentioned throughout this chapter, a Microsoft DNS server can host a DNS zone as a standard zone in a zone file or as an AD-integrated zone. When you integrate your zones with AD, a couple of things happen. First, the data for the zone is stored in AD rather than in a zone file. Prior to Windows Server 2003, the DNS data could only be stored in the domain partition of AD. This meant only DNS servers inside the same domain could host an AD-integrated DNS zone. Other DNS servers could receive a copy of the zone, but they acted as secondary DNS servers, and their copy was read-only. When you think about it, this makes sense, because DCs can only write to the domain partition for the domain they're in. So a DC in a different domain (even in the same forest) can't update DNS objects for a different AD domain. This sometimes posed a problem in AD architectures with multiple domains. If you wanted a local primary DNS server for a site that had multiple domains, you had to ensure that a DC for that domain was in the site. This changed in Windows Server 2003 with the introduction of application partitions. Application partitions allow other applications to create a partition in AD for storing its data. The DCs that get a replica of this partition can span any domain in the forest. AD-integrated DNS zones can be stored in an application partition instead of the domain partition, enabling the zone to be replicated to any DNS server in the forest.

The second thing that happens when you make a zone AD-integrated is that the server hosting the zone becomes a primary zone holder. This means updates to the DNS information can be written by this server. This happens because AD is a multimaster system, so DNS is using the platform that already exists to update data on any of the DNS servers.

The last thing worth mentioning is that because the DNS data is stored as objects in the directory, each record has an Access Control List (ACL) tied to it. Therefore, you can enforce a setting called Secure Updates. When this setting is enabled on the zone, only the computer account that created the DNS record can update it. This enforces the domain's permission model onto DNS and ensures that DNS records don't succumb to traditional record-hijacking techniques. It's rare that we would recommend turning off Secure Updates on an AD-integrated DNS zone. In the past, we've only had to do this for compatibility issues with some non-Microsoft technologies that absolutely require dynamic updates.

To convert a zone from a standard zone to an AD-integrated zone, you need to modify the Type setting on the zone. You can do this by calling the `ChangeZoneType` WMI method. When you do, the method converts the zone to a primary zone and specifies that it should be AD-integrated. Calling the method with the following syntax accomplishes this:

```
ChangeZoneType(0, $true)
```

Before you can change the zone type, however, you need to get an object that references the zone you want to convert. To do this, you use the `Get-WMIObject` cmdlet in PowerShell. In the following command, the `Get-WMIObject` cmdlet (or `gwmi` for short) is used to get a WMI object of the class `MicrosoftDNS_Zone` whose name is `corp.contoso.com`. The object is stored in the `$objDNSZone` variable.

```
$objDNSZone = gwmi -Namespace "root\MicrosoftDNS" -Class ↵
"MicrosoftDNS_Zone" -Filter "ContainerName='corp.contoso.com'"
```

From there, you can call the `ChangeZoneType` method, telling WMI to convert the zone to AD-integrated:

```
$objDNSZone.ChangeZoneType(0, $true)
```

Enabling the GlobalNames DNS Zone

The GlobalNames zone was added in Windows Server 2008 as a means of performing name resolution for single-label names. By single-label names, we mean names that aren't fully qualified. For example, if you had a server named `print server.contoso.com`, its single-label name would be `printserver`. Single-label names are usually resolved via NetBIOS methods using one of the following three approaches:

DNS Name Suffixes   When a client attempts to resolve a single-label name, it appends the domain name to the single-label name and uses DNS to perform the query. Clients can have name suffix lists that contain other names to append to a single-label name in case it isn't resolved from an earlier name.

Windows Internet Name Service (WINS)   WINS is similar to DNS but is focused solely on resolving single-label names rather than fully qualified names. If a client has a WINS server configured in the network settings, that client contacts the WINS server to attempt to resolve the single-label name.

Network Broadcast   When all else fails, a broadcast packet is sent across the network segment to determine if anyone hosts the requested single-label name. This technique offers limitations, such as resolution across network routers.

One of the methods that we just outlined will typically work for most people. However, there are limitations and system designs that can make these options less appealing. For example, consider the situation where an environment includes multiple domains or multiple forests. When using the DNS suffix search order, you have to configure multiple DNS suffixes to search through on each and every client. You can make this somewhat easier by using Group Policy, but even so, the client has to enumerate that list of suffixes, which takes time. Also consider the situation where you're transitioning to IPv6. WINS doesn't support IPv6 and therefore can't be used to resolve single-label names to IPv6 addresses.

How the GNZ Works

To help with single-label name resolution, Microsoft introduced the GlobalNames zone (GNZ) in Windows Server 2008. The GNZ is basically a typical forward lookup zone with a special name (GlobalNames) that the DNS servers are aware of. When the GNZ is deployed in your environment, the name-resolution process on your Windows Server 2008 DNS servers is modified. When a query is received, the single-label portion of the name is first queried in the GNZ. If the record exists, then the query completes and the result is returned. If the record doesn't exist in the GNZ, then the DNS server runs through its typical name-resolution process. Because of this modified behavior, it's important to ensure that all the single-label names in the GNZ are unique across your forest. If they aren't, names won't resolve correctly. As a byproduct, you're required to update the GNZ with static records.

The single-label records in the GNZ are just CNAME records: aliases pointing to the real fully qualified name of the server. For example, the `printserver` record in the GNZ resolves to `printserver.contoso.com`.

Enabling the GNZ

To enable the GNZ, you must do two things:

1. Create the `EnableGlobalNamesSupport` Registry key, and set it to 1 in the following Registry path: `HKLM\System\CurrentControlSet\Services\DNS\Parameters`. Do this on every DNS server.

2. Create the GNZ, and add your records to it.

Before you can do this, there are a couple of things you should keep in mind. First, ensure that all your DNS servers are at least Windows Server 2008 servers. If not, you'll get mixed results because some clients may be pointing to DNS servers that don't support the GNZ and thus single-label resolution won't work as expected for those clients. Second, ensure that you replicate the GNZ across the whole forest. And third, if you're using multiple forests, you can configure an SRV record in the _msdcs DNS domains of the domains in your other forests. These records point to the servers that host the authoritative copies of the GNZ. In this case, you need to ensure that these servers are also configured for the GNZ (using the Registry key discussed earlier) and that the names in the GNZ are unique across all of the forests.

You can use the PowerShell script in Listing 5.1 to enable the GNZ in your forest. This script can't search your entire environment for DNS servers, so you must manually edit the variables at the beginning of the script to include all the DNS servers in your environment. The script performs the following steps:

1. Ensure that each DNS server is running a minimum version of Windows Server 2008.

2. Set the GlobalNames Registry key on each DNS server.

3. Create the GNZ on the DNS server that you specify. This zone is set to an AD-integrated zone.

One other thing to mention is that this script only enables the GNZ in one forest. If you have multiple forests, you can create the _globalzones._mcdcs.*<DomainName>* SRV records in those other forests by hand. You should create multiple SRV records, each pointing to a DNS server that hosts a copy of the GNZ.

LISTING 5.1: EnableGNZ.ps1

```
## File Name: EnableGNZ.ps1
## Description:
##   Enables the GlobalNames zone on the DCs
##   that you specify in this script.
##
## Edit this list of DNS servers to identify which DNS servers
## will be enabled for the GlobalNames zone.
$colDNSServers = @("SEA-DC01", "BAL-DC01")
```

(continues)

LISTING 5-1 *(continued)*

```
## Enumerate the list of DNS servers
foreach ($DNS in $colDNSServers)
{
    ## Check to ensure that the DNS server is running Windows
    ## Server 2008 or R2
    $objOSInfo = gwmi Win32_OperatingSystem -Computer $DNS
    if ($objOSInfo.Version.StartsWith(6))
    {
        # Set the registry key that enables the GlobalNames zone
        $objReg = [WMICLASS]"\\$($DNS)\root\cimv2:StdRegProv"
        $objReg.SetDWordValue(2147483650,
            "SYSTEM\CurrentControlSet\Services\DNS\Parameters",
            "EnableGlobalNamesSupport", 1)
    }
}
## The zone is created on the first server in the list of
## servers specified in the $colDNSServers array
$objWMIClass = [WMICLASS]"\\$($colDNSServers[0])\root\" +
    "MicrosoftDNS:MicrosoftDNS_Zone"
$objWMIClass.CreateZone("GlobalNames", 0, $true)
```

Forwarding Unresolved DNS Queries to Another Server

Earlier in this chapter, we discussed how a server resolves a DNS query by using recursion. Rather than going through the process of recursively looking for an answer to a client's query, a DNS server can be configured with a forwarder, another concept that we discussed earlier in this chapter. The forwarder then takes on the responsibility of answering the query.

Forwarders can take two forms: either a standard forwarder, which forwards all queries to other DNS servers, or a conditional forwarder, which only forwards queries about a certain namespace. Standard forwarders are configured on a server-by-server basis. Conditional forwarders, however, can be stored in AD and replicated to multiple DNS servers.

Setting Up a Forwarder

Forwarders are configured independently for each DNS server in your environment. In some DNS architectures, an organization may use a different DNS infrastructure for external name resolution. In this case, a standard DNS configuration item on the network may be to forward queries to a specific set of DNS servers. One of the things you can do is script the configuration of the DNS forwarder and add it to the installation process you use for standing up new DNS servers. The following script (Listing 5.2) will configure the DNS forwarder settings on the server that you specify.

LISTING 5.2: ConfigDNSForwarders.ps1

```
## File Name: ConfigDNSForwarders.ps1
## Description:
##   Configures the DNS forwarders on the DNS server that you
##   specify when you run this script. If there is no DNS
##   server specified, the local machine is used.
##
param([string]$ServerName = ".")
## Before running this script, add your forwarders into this
## array variable.
$arrForwarders = @("192.168.0.100","192.168.0.110")

## Get the WMI object for the DNS server. This object contains
## the DNS settings and is where we will update the forwarder
## list.
$objDNSServer = gwmi -Namespace "root\MicrosoftDNS" `
  -Class MicrosoftDNS_Server -ComputerName $ServerName
## Set and commit the forwarders to the DNS servers that we
## specified in the $arrForwarders variable.
$objDNSServer.Forwarders = $arrForwarders
$output = $objDNSServer.Put()
Write-Host "Configuration complete."
```

Setting Up a Conditional Forwarder

You can configure conditional forwarders on a DNS server by using the CreateZone method that we discussed earlier in this chapter in the section "Creating a DNS Zone." When you execute this method, you need to pass in the name of the DNS domain that the conditional forwarder is for and a list of IP addresses for the servers that are the domain's forwarders.

The following command creates a conditional forwarder for the contoso.com domain to the DNS server at 192.168.0.10:

```
$objWMIClass = [WMICLASS]"root\MicrosoftDNS:MicrosoftDNS_Zone"
$objWMIClass.CreateZone("contoso.com", 3, $true, "", ↵
  @("192.168.0.10"))
```

Managing Active
Directory Data

PART II

Manage the DNS Server

In addition to configuring DNS, you can use PowerShell for managing certain aspects of the DNS server itself. There are times when you'll have to perform administrative tasks on the server, such as restarting the DNS service, keeping an eye on its configuration, or viewing some of the server's statistics.

Restarting the DNS Service

Sometimes you may have to restart the DNS service. Maybe you've made a change that will need a restart to take effect, or you're having a problem with the service itself. There are a couple of different ways to restart services with PowerShell, such as by using the PowerShell `Restart-Service` cmdlet. However, the `Restart-Service` cmdlet only affects services on the local machine, so you would need to use a remote PowerShell connection to restart services on other computers. Because of this, it makes more sense to the use the WMI methods for restarting the DNS services. If you're making a DNS configuration change on a remote computer using WMI, you can call the following methods to restart the service on that computer remotely:

- `StopService`
- `StartService`

You can call these methods by using the `Invoke-WMIMethod` cmdlet or by using its alias, `iwmi`. The following command stops the DNS service on the computer SEA-DC01:

```
iwmi StopService -Namespace root\MicrosoftDNS -Path ↵
   "MicrosoftDNS_Server.Name='.'" -ComputerName SEA-DC01
```

You can also shorten the command by specifying the full path to the class:

```
iwmi StopService -Path ↵
   "root\MicrosoftDNS:MicrosoftDNS_Server.Name='.'" ↵
-ComputerName SEA-DC01
```

Viewing the DNS Server Configuration

Having the properties and methods of a DNS server exposed through WMI makes gathering information on the DNS server very convenient. In fact, you can use this methodology to regularly check up on your DNS servers and verify that the config-uration is correct. To view the configuration of a DNS server, you simply need to use WMI to connect to that server and view the `MicrosoftDNS_Server` class. This

WMI class contains all the configuration items for the DNS server itself. Anything specific to the configuration of the DNS zones, on the other hand, is found in the `MicrosoftDNS_Zone` class. You can connect to the class through the server you're examining by using the `Get-WMIObject` cmdlet. The following example gets the DNS server settings for the local computer. If you want to get the settings for a different computer remotely, use the `-ComputerName` parameter and specify the DNS server's name:

```
gwmi -Namespace "root\MicrosoftDNS" -Class MicrosoftDNS_Server
```

When you run this command, you'll see several DNS settings output to the screen. Now that this information is available to you, you can put it into a script so you can format it, narrow it down, or perform other operations with it. When you're creating a PowerShell script for viewing the DNS server configuration, you may ask yourself what properties of a DNS server are important to you. For the example script in Listing 5.3, we chose the following properties:

▸ The name and type of each zone that the DNS server holds a copy of

▸ Configuration of the DNS scavenging settings

▸ A list of configured forwarders, both standard and conditional

Unfortunately, there is no reliable method available for getting a list of all the DNS servers in your environment. Therefore, this script won't go out and discover DNS servers on which to view the information. Instead, we've provided a way for you to specify your DNS servers in a variable at the beginning of the script, and the script will enumerate each one. The script uses WMI to read DNS configuration settings and creates an HTML report for you.

LISTING 5.3: ViewDNSConfig.ps1

```
## File Name: ViewDNSConfig.ps1
## Description:
##    Outputs the DNS configuration of one or more servers. You
##    specify the list of servers by modifying the arrDNSServers
##    variable near the beginning of the script.
##
## Modify this variable to specify your DNS servers.
$arrDNSServers = @("SEA-DC01","BAL-DC01")
$output_file = "c:\dns_config.html"
## Defines the style of the HTML output
```

(continues)

LISTING 5-3 *(continued)*

```
$style = "<style>"
$style += "H1{font: bold 20px 'Trebuchet MS';"
$style += " color: #000000;"
$style += " letter-spacing: 2px;"
$style += " text-transform: uppercase;"
$style += " text-align: left;}"
$style += "TABLE{border-style: solid;"
$style += " border-width: 1px;}"
$style += "TD{border-right: 1px solid #C1DAD7;"
$style += " border-bottom: 1px solid #C1DAD7;"
$style += " background: #fff;"
$style += " padding: 6px 6px 6px 12px;"
$style += " color: #6D929B;}"
$style += "TH{font: bold 11px 'Trebuchet MS';"
$style += " color: #6D929B;"
$style += " border-right: 1px solid #C1DAD7;"
$style += " border-bottom: 1px solid #C1DAD7;"
$style += " border-top: 1px solid #C1DAD7;"
$style += " letter-spacing: 2px;"
$style += " text-transform: uppercase;"
$style += " text-align: left;"
$style += " padding: 6px 6px 6px 12px;"
$style += " background: #CAE8EA;}"
$style += "</style>"
## Define the HTML heading and table rows
$html = "<H1>DNS Configuration</H1>"
$html += "<table cellpadding=2 cellspacing=0><tr>"
$html += "  <th>Server Name</th>"
$html += "  <th>Zones</th>"
$html += "  <th>Scavenging</th>"
$html += "  <th>Forwarders</th>"
$html += "  <th>Conditional Forwarders</th>"
$html += "</tr>"
## Add the DNS Configuration details as separate rows
foreach ($DNSServer in $arrDNSServers)
{
```

```
## Get the DNS Server's properties
$dns_properties = gwmi -Namespace "root\MicrosoftDNS" `
  -ComputerName $DNSServer -Class MicrosoftDNS_Server
## Get the zones and their properties
$dns_zones = gwmi -Namespace "root\MicrosoftDNS" `
  -ComputerName $DNSServer -Class MicrosoftDNS_Zone
## Output the name of the server
$html += "<tr><td>$($dns_properties.name)</td>"

## Output each zone and its type
$html += "<td>"
foreach ($zone in $dns_zones)
{
  $ztype = "Primary"
  if ($zone.ZoneType -eq "2") { $ztype = "Secondary" }
  elseif ($zone.ZoneType -eq "3") { $ztype = "Stub" }

  if ($zone.ZoneType -ne "4") {
    $html += $zone.name + ": " + $ztype + "<br>"
  }
}
$html += "</td>"

## Output the Scavenging Interval
$html += "<td>$($dns_properties.ScavengingInterval) Days</td>"

## Output the forwarders
$html += "<td>"
foreach ($fwd in $dns_properties.Forwarders)
{
  $html += $fwd + "<br>"
}
$html += "</td>"

## Output the Conditional Forwarders
$html += "<td>"
foreach ($zone in $dns_zones)
```

Managing Active Directory Data

PART II

(continues)

LISTING 5-3 *(continued)*

```
  {
    if ($zone.ZoneType -eq "4") {
      $html += $zone.name + "<br>"
    }
  }
  $html += „</td></tr>"
}
$html += „</table>"
# Write the HTML file
ConvertTo-Html -PostContent $html -Head $style | `
  Out-File $output_file
# Display the HTML report
Invoke-Expression $output_file
```

This information alone can be very valuable. However, it's even more valuable when
you combine it with the information from other parts of AD that we show you how
to script throughout this book. You might even consider reporting this information alongside the information in the next section in order to really get a handle on
what's happening on your DNS servers.

Gathering DNS Server Statistics

The Microsoft DNS server maintains a wide range of statistical data that can be
viewed and used for monitoring and reporting. This data includes things like the
number of queries (broken up by record type), responses, memory usage, cache
statistics, and much more. Almost 700 pieces of statistical data are readily available, and you can view them by enumerating the instances of the MicrosoftDNS_
Statistic class. The easiest way to do this is to use the Get-WMIObject cmdlet.
The following command dumps all this information out to a CSV file that you can
use in reports or additional scripts:

```
Get-WMIObject -Namespace "root\MicrosoftDNS" -Class ↵
  "MicrosoftDNS_Statistic" | Export-CSV c:\DNSStats.csv
```

You can use this command in the script that we provided in the previous section
to give your administrators a good amount of information about how DNS is configured and how it's performing. You might even consider adding in some of the
performance characteristics of the DNS server, as we'll demonstrate in Chapter 11,
"Monitoring Health and Performance."

Configure Active Directory DNS Records

AD uses a few different types of records in DNS. First, there are the standard computer host records, which resolve the host name of the DC to its IP address. An example of this is shown in Figure 5.3.

FIGURE 5.3 DC host records

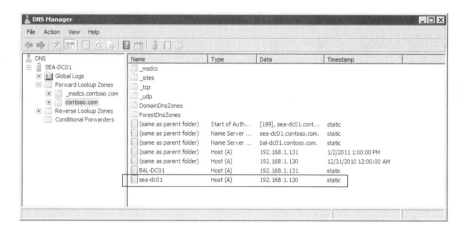

Second, each DC uses a CNAME record in the _msdcs.<DomainName> DNS zone to make the Globally Unique Identifier (GUID) resolvable to the DC's host record. This record is shown in Figure 5.4.

FIGURE 5.4 DC CNAME records

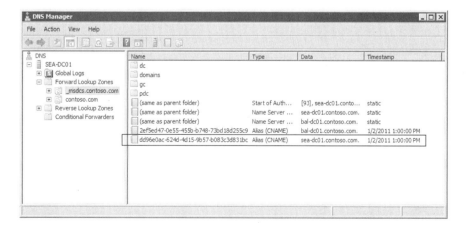

And finally, a series of SRV locator records are used throughout the _msdcs zone that identify the various services that the DC hosts. These service locator records were discussed earlier in this chapter.

Manually Registering a DC's DNS Records

DCs use multiple services to automatically register their DNS records. The netlogon service is responsible for registering the DC's CNAME and SRV locator records. In Windows Server 2008 and Windows Server 2008 R2, the DNS client service is responsible for registering the DC's host record. If your DCs are running on Windows 2000 Server or Windows Server 2003, the DHCP client service is used to register the host record instead. DCs use dynamic updates in DNS, so they register these records themselves when they're able to. Sometimes you may need to register these records manually. Perhaps the DNS server that you're using doesn't support dynamic DNS, or maybe there's a problem with the DC and the records aren't registering.

In either case, it's not fun to manually type in server GUIDs, and it can generally be an error-prone process. So for Microsoft DNS servers, you can use the DNS WMI interface to manually register the records. To do this, you first need to understand how to register DNS records in PowerShell.

Using the MicrosoftDNS_ResourceRecord Class

There are a couple of different ways to register DNS records with PowerShell. The first way that we'll examine uses the `MicrosoftDNS_ResourceRecord` class in WMI. This class contains a method called `CreateInstanceFromTextRepresentation`, which allows you to create a resource record from its standard DNS text string. This is the text of the record as it would exist in the DNS zone file. A typical resource record's text representation looks like the following:

```
sea-dc01.contoso.com.   IN   A   192.168.1.130
```

This representation is broken into multiple fields. Each field is separated by one or more spaces. The first is the name of the record. In the previous example, this is the DNS record for our DC, which is named `sea-dc01.contoso.com`. Notice that this name ends with a dot. In a typical DNS zone file, a resource record entry can either end in a dot or not. If it doesn't end in a dot, the name of the domain is appended to the end of the record. On the other hand, the dot at the end signifies that this is the complete name of the record.

The second field (IN) is the class of the record. IN signifies that the class is an Internet record; that will be the case for the records you'll typically be working with.

The third field represents the type of record. In this case, a host record (which maps a DNS name to an IP address) is represented by A. Often you'll hear people refer to *host record* and *A record* interchangeably. This field is followed by a field that contains the record's data.

The fourth field is also referred to as the *RDATA field*. This is the actual data of the resource record. In this case, because we're looking at an A record, this data is the IP address that the DNS name resolves to. This will be different for different types of DNS records.

To create the host record, you call the `CreateInstanceFromText Representation` method and pass in the name of the DNS server on which you're creating the record, the name of the zone in which you're creating the record, and the text representation we just described. The following PowerShell commands demonstrate this by creating a host record for `printserver .contoso.com`, resolving to the IP address 192.168.0.10 in the `contoso.com` DNS zone:

```
$strDNSServer = "sea-dc01.contoso.com"
$strDNSDomain = "contoso.com"
$strRR = "printserver.contoso.com. IN A 192.168.0.10"
$objRRClass = [WMICLASS]"root\MicrosoftDNS:↵
  MicrosoftDNS_ResourceRecord"
$objRR.CreateInstanceFromTextRepresentation($strDNSServer, ↵
  $strDNSDomain, $strRR)
```

In addition to host records, you also need to register *alias records* in the DNS. These alias (or CNAME) records are DNS records that point one DNS name to another DNS name. DCs use alias records to map a DNS name containing the DC's GUID to its host record.

You can use the same process for creating alias records that you use when creating host records. The difference is in the text representation that you pass to the `CreateInstanceFromTextRepresentation` method. For alias records, you need to specify CNAME as the type of the record and include the DNS name that the record is an alias for in the RDATA field. The following example is a text representation of an alias record:

```
www.contoso.com.   IN  CNAME  contoso-web.contoso.com.
```

Managing Active Directory Data

PART II

In this example, the record is an alias for `contoso-web.contoso.com` called `www.contoso.com`. For DCs, however, the alias record might resemble the following:

```
dd96e0ac-624d-4d15-9b57-b083c3d831bc._msdcs.contoso.com. IN
CNAME sea-dc01.contoso.com.
```

One thing that you may notice is that the record's name in the RDATA ends in a dot, similar to how the first field in the text representation looks. You must include that dot, or the WMI method will fail. The following example demonstrates how to create the GUID CNAME record. You'll notice how similar this is to the previous commands for registering the host records. The difference between the two is the DNS domain in which the record is registered and the text representation of the record itself:

```
$strDNSServer = "sea-dc01.contoso.com"
$strDNSDomain = "_msdcs.contoso.com"
$strRR = "dd96e0ac-624d-4d15-9b57-b083c3d831bc._msdcs.contoso ↵
  .com. IN CNAME sea-dc01.contoso.com."
$objRRClass = ↵
  [WMICLASS]"root\MicrosoftDNS:MicrosoftDNS_ResourceRecord"
$objRR.CreateInstanceFromTextRepresentation($strDNSServer, ↵
  $strDNSDomain, $strRR)
```

The last record type that you need to register is the service locator records. A DC needs to create multiple SRV records in order for AD to function correctly. Also, the SRV records that need to be registered depend not only on what site the DC is in, but also on what services the DC is advertising. For example, the DC that is acting as the PDC emulator for the domain registers an SRV record in DNS that indicates this. One way to approach this is to run a tool to determine which records are missing. The tool for this job is called `DCDIAG.EXE`. When you run the tool, use the following command:

```
dcdiag /test:DNS /DnsRecordRegistration
```

The results of this command tell you what records are missing. An example of the output is shown in Figure 5.5. Notice here that a site-specific LDAP record for this DC is missing.

After you know which SRV record needs to be registered, you can use the `CreateInstanceFromTextRepresentation` WMI method to register the record. For SRV locator records, the text representation string is slightly different. An SRV representation resembles the following:

```
_ldap._tcp.Seattle._sites.contoso.com. IN SRV 0 100 389 ↵
  SEA-DC01.contoso.com.
```

FIGURE 5.5   DCDIAG identifies a missing LDAP SRV record.

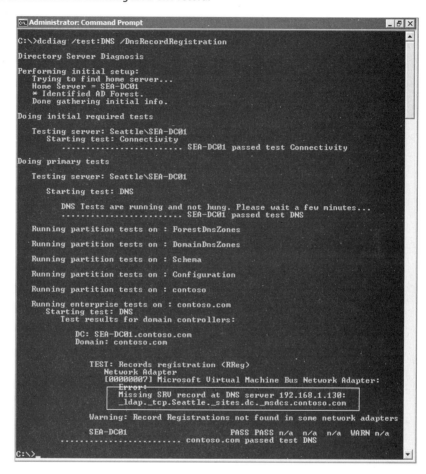

The difference here is in the RDATA field, which includes a few different items that pertain to the SRV record. These items (in order) are

- ▶ The record's priority (0)

- ▶ The record's weight (100)

- ▶ The port that the service is listening on (389)

- ▶ The server that the service is running on (SEA-DC01.contoso.com)

A Better Way

If you had to use this process every time you wanted to manually register the DC's DNS records, it would be somewhat labor-intensive. And after all, the purpose of scripting and PowerShell is to make our lives easier. Fortunately, there's another way to manually register a DC's records.

On each DC, there is a file called `netlogon.dns`. This file exists in the system folder under the `System32\Config` directory. For a default install of Windows, this file is found at

```
C:\Windows\System32\Config\netlogon.dns
```

The `netlogon.dns` file is the text representation of every DNS resource record that the DC registers dynamically through the netlogon service. If the DC can't dynamically register these records, you can use this file to register them manually.

Forcing a DC to Register Its Service Records

If you have a DNS server that supports dynamic updates, but the DC's records aren't up to date, you can attempt to force this update. There are a couple of ways to accomplish this:

- ► Restart the netlogon service on the DC that needs to refresh its records.

- ► Run `NLTEST /DSREGDNS` from a command prompt.

When you restart the netlogon service, the service attempts to register the SRV records during its startup process. In PowerShell, you can force the DC to attempt this registration by calling the `Restart-Service` cmdlet:

```
Restart-Service netlogon
```

`NLTEST.EXE` is a tool that allows you to perform some network-related tasks. A lot of the functionality of `NLTEST` can be performed using PowerShell directly. However, `NLTEST` does some things that are more difficult to reproduce in a PowerShell. `NLTEST` is included in Windows Server, so in the case of forcing DNS record registration, it makes sense to call `NLTEST` directly from your PowerShell scripts. The difference between using `NLTEST` and restarting the netlogon service is that there is no downtime during the record registration. To use `NLTEST` to force DCs to register their DNS SRV locator records, you use the following command, either in PowerShell or in a Windows command prompt:

```
nltest /dsregdns
```

Adjusting the Weight and Priority of Active Directory Service Records

Each service record that is registered by a DC has a weight and priority associated with it. This weight and priority are used together to determine how frequently a particular DC is used for the services it provides. When multiple SRV records are registered for the same service, DNS uses a round-robin technique to resolve the name.

For example, consider the case where there are two DCs, SEA-DC01 and SEA-DC02. In this case, both DCs register an SRV record for the LDAP service. When a client performs a DNS query to determine which DC is advertising the LDAP service, DNS chooses one of these two DCs. To make this choice, DNS sees that there are two records, so in each DNS response, the DNS server alternates which record is first in the list. This helps to ensure that the load for these services is distributed among multiple DCs. The weight and priority setting affects how often a particular DC is used, if at all.

Adjusting the Weight

The weight setting is used relative to other records. By default, the weight used for all DC SRV records is 100. If two DCs have SRV records with the weight of 100, then they're both used equally. This means that out of 200 queries, each DC will be returned as the first entry in the response list 100 times. If you change the weight for one of those DCs, however, this affects how frequently it's first in the list. Let's assume that you change the weight of one SEA-DC01 to 50 and leave the SEA-DC02 at 100. That means that for every 150 queries, SEA-DC01 will be returned first in the list 50 times and SEA-DC02 will be first 100 times. In this case, SEA-DC02 is used 66 percent of the time. By doing this, SEA-DC02 incurs twice the load of SEA-DC01.

Not all organizations should adjust the weight of DC SRV records, although sometimes this is appropriate. One instance is if the hardware of a particular DC is older than other DCs. You'll probably want the DC with the older hardware to be used less frequently. Another case where it may be acceptable to adjust the weight is when a particular DC hosts services other than AD. Those other services may be using DC resources, so you might not want to tax the server with the additional load of a full-time DC.

To adjust the weight, however, you don't simply want to modify the weight setting on the SRV record. This approach will make the change in DNS, but it also has an adverse effect. When the DC's netlogon service restarts (at the next reboot, for example), it will see that the SRV record on which you adjusted the weight isn't the same record that is recorded in its `netlogon.dns` file. Then, the netlogon service will proceed to create a new SRV record that does match what it thinks should be there. However, when it does, the record that you manually adjusted isn't removed. The end result is that there are two SRV records for that service pointing to the same DC. This has the opposite effect that you intended.

Imagine that you manually changed the weight on SEA-DC01 to 50, and then SEA-DC01 rebooted. When the netlogon service starts, it will register a new record with a weight of 100. So now you have the following SRV records registered for that service:

- ► SEA-DC01 with a weight of 50

- ► SEA-DC01 with a weight of 100

- ► SEA-DC02 with a weight of 100

Now, out of every 250 queries, SEA-DC01 will be selected 150 times, meaning that it incurs 60 percent of the load. To properly set the weight of the DCs' records, you need to make the change in such a way that netlogon can recognize the change and know that the adjusted weight is the correct one. To do this, you can adjust the weight by adding a Registry key called `LdapSrvWeight` to the following Registry location:

```
HKLM\System\CurrentControlSet\Services\Netlogon\Parameters
```

Set this key to a DWORD type, and give it the weight of the record as the value. To make a proper weight change for the scenario that was just described, set `LdapSrvWeight` to be a value of **50**. You can do this in PowerShell using the following steps:

1. In PowerShell, change to the HKEY_LOCAL_MACHINE hive in the Registry:

   ```
   cd HKLM:
   ```

2. Change to the path SYSTEM\CurrentControlSet\Services\Netlogon\ Parameters:

   ```
   cd system\currentcontrolset\services\netlogon\parameters
   ```

3. Create a new DWORD value called `LdapSrvWeight`, and set it to the desired weight of the DC's SRV records. To do this, use the `New-ItemProperty` cmdlet, and specify `LdapSrvWeight` as the `Name` parameter. Use the weight for the `Value` parameter and `DWORD` for the `PropertyType` parameter:

   ```
   New-ItemProperty -Path . -Name LdapSrvWeight -Value 50 ↵
   -PropertyType DWORD
   ```

If you want to make this change as part of a script, you can use the following one-liner:

```
New-ItemProperty -Path "HKLM:\System\CurrentControlSet\Services\↵
    Netlogon\Parameters" -Name LdapSrvWeight -Value 50 ↵
    -PropertyType DWORD
```

Adjusting the Priority

When you adjust the priority setting of an SRV record, it has a different effect than the weight. The weight determines how frequently a DC is used, but the priority determines whether the DC is used in the first place. If you have two DCs (for example, SEA-DC01 and SEA-DC02) with the same priority, then both of those DCs can be returned in the query for that SRV record. However, if they have different priorities, the DC with the lower priority value is used. The significance of the values for the priority is the opposite of the weight setting. With the weight, the higher values get used more frequently. With priority, the lower value means that the DC is used.

Like the weight setting, the priority setting can't be adjusted by manually editing the DNS record. There is a Registry key for the priority that you must set on the DC whose priority you want to change. To change the priority, create a new DWORD Registry value called `LdapSrvPriority` in the following Registry location:

```
HKLM\SYSTEM\CurrentControlSet\Services\Netlogon\Parameters
```

Set the value of the `LdapSrvPriority` key to be the priority setting that you want this DC's SRV records to have. You can do this using the following steps:

1. In PowerShell, change to the HKEY_LOCAL_MACHINE hive in the Registry:

   ```
   cd HKLM:
   ```

2. Change to the path SYSTEM\CurrentControlSet\Services\Netlogon\Parameters:

   ```
   cd SYSTEM\CurrentControlSet\Services\Netlogon\Parameters
   ```

3. Create a new DWORD value called `LdapSrvPriority`, and set it to the desired priority of the DC's SRV records. To do this, use the `New-ItemProperty` cmdlet, and specify `LdapSrvPriority` as the `Name` parameter. Use the priority for the `Value` parameter and `DWORD` for the `PropertyType` parameter:

   ```
   New-ItemProperty -Path . -Name LdapSrvPriority -Value 10 ↵
       -PropertyType DWORD
   ```

If you want to make this change as part of a script, you can use the following one-liner:

```
New-ItemProperty -Path "HKLM:\System\CurrentControlSet\Services\↵
    Netlogon\Parameters" -Name LdapSrvPriority -Value 10 ↵
    -PropertyType DWORD
```

By default, all SRV records for the DC have a priority of 0. Therefore, by changing the priority to any value greater than 0, you ensure that the DC isn't used unless all the other lower-priority DCs are offline.

Manage Domain Time

Another important dependency that AD has is the accuracy of the time on the systems in the forest. The Kerberos authentication protocol used by AD uses the time values on the systems during the authentication sequence to ensure that network credentials aren't reused in replay attacks. By default, the time is allowed to be skewed by 5 minutes in either direction—5 minutes early or 5 minutes late. The time comparison occurs with Universal Time Coordinates, so the time zone of the clients and servers don't affect the authentication sequence if the time is set correctly.

To aid in keeping the time close in computers across the forest, Windows offers a time-synchronization system. This system is based on the Network Time Protocol (NTP), which is defined in RFC 1305 to standardize how time synchronization occurs across the network. The W32Time service in Windows is responsible for synchronizing the system's clock against its configured NTP time source.

AD defines what this time-synchronization hierarchy looks like inside a forest. The DC that holds the PDC emulator Flexible Single Master of Operation (FSMO) role for the forest's root domain is the authoritative time source for the forest. Even if this server's time is wrong, authentication within a forest will still work successfully because all the machines will be wrong by the same amount of time. The PDC emulators in the next level of child domains (the ones whose parent is the forest's root domain) synchronize their time from the root forest's PDC emulator. The time-synchronization hierarchy continues in like fashion throughout the remainder of the domain, where the PDC emulator in each child domain synchronizes its time from the PDC emulator in its parent domain.

Inside each domain, the DCs that don't hold the PDC emulator FSMO role synchronize their clocks with the PDC emulator inside the same domain. From there, the clients and servers in a domain synchronize their time with the DCs that they authenticated with. Figure 5.6 illustrates this time-synchronization hierarchy.

FIGURE 5.6   Time synchronization inside the forest

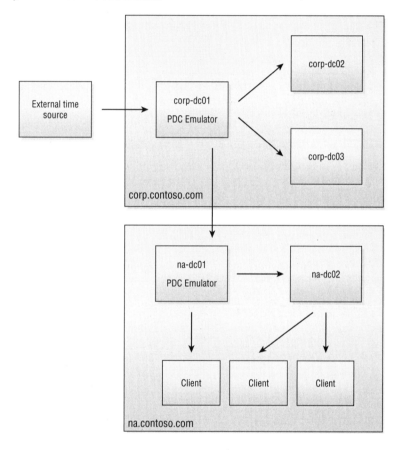

View Time Service Information

The time service can be manually changed on each client and server, and it can be configured to point to an alternate time source. Therefore, you'll want to understand how the time is currently being synchronized in your environment and be able to enable some advanced logging functionality to help with troubleshooting issues that you may encounter.

Determining How Time Is Synchronized in the Forest

To determine how time is synchronized in the forest, you need to look at what each server is synchronizing its time with. You can find this out by looking at the Registry key called `Type` under the following Registry location:

```
HKLM\System\CurrentControlSet\Services\W32Time\Parameters
```

Table 5.1 describes the potential values that the `Type` key can have.

TABLE 5.1   Possible Type Values for Synchronizing Time

Value	Description
NT5DS	When configured, this computer will synchronize its time with the domain time hierarchy. Any time server entry specified in the `NtpServer` key is ignored.
NTP	The computer is configured to the manually configured time servers for synchronizing time. The servers used are listed in the `NtpServer` key.
NoSync	No time synchronization is occurring on this computer.

To determine how time is synchronized in the forest, we'll enumerate the domains in the forest and examine this Registry key on each DC. Only the DC that holds the PDC emulator role in the forest root domain should have an external time source set. Every other DC should be using the domain time hierarchy.

It's important to note that some organizations designate certain DCs as backup FSMO role holders. If you do this, you should ensure that the DC that is the backup for the PDC emulator in the root domain is also configured to point to the same external time source as your PDC emulator. In the event of an emergency where you have to transfer or seize the PDC emulator role, you may forget to configure this external time server, so it's a good idea to do it ahead of time.

You can use the Registry provider to determine whether a computer is using the domain time hierarchy. The following command returns the value of the `Type` key for the computer you're currently logged in at:

```
Get-ItemProperty -Path "HKLM:\System\CurrentControlSet\Services\↵
    W32Time\Parameters" -Name Type
```

The problem with this command is that it only works on the local machine. If you want to query the time source for each DC, you'll need to execute this command remotely. For remote Registry access, we typically default to using the `StdRegProv` class in WMI. The following commands get the `Type` key from the Registry on the DC named SEA-DC01:

```
$objReg = [WMICLASS]"\\SEA-DC01\root\cimv2:StdRegProv"
$objReg.GetStringValue(2147483650, "SYSTEM\CurrentControlSet\
Services\W32Time\Parameters", "Type")
```

The script in Listing 5.4 uses this technique to query all the DCs in the forest and report back on the ones that aren't synchronizing their clocks according to the domain time hierarchy.

LISTING 5.4: CheckDCTimeSync.ps1

```
## File Name: CheckDCTimeSync.ps1
## Description:
##    Examines every Domain Controller in the forest and reports
##    on which DCs aren't using the domain time hierarchy for
##    clock sync.
##
## Import the Active Directory Module
Import-Module ActiveDirectory
## Get the list of domains
$objForest = Get-ADForest
$colDomains = $objForest.Domains
## Enumerate the Domain Controllers in each domain
foreach ($strDomain in $colDomains)
{
  $objDomain = Get-ADDomain $strDomain
  $DCCN = $objDomain.DomainControllersContainer
  $colDCs = Get-ADComputer -SearchBase $DCCN -Filter *

  Write-Host
  Write-Host "Domain Controllers that are not synchronizing" +
    " time with the domain time hierarchy"

  foreach ($objDC in $colDCs)
  {
    ## Look up the Type key in the registry on each DC
```

(continues)

LISTING 5-4 *(continued)*

```
        $strDCName = $objDC.DNSHostName
        $objReg = [WMICLASS]"\\$($strDCName)\root\cimv2:StdRegProv"
        $objType = $objReg.GetStringValue(2147483650, "SYSTEM\" +
          "CurrentControlSet\Services\W32Time\Parameters", "Type")
        ## If the Type indicates something other than NT5DS, display
        ## this DC in the list
        if ($objType.sValue.CompareTo("NT5DS") -ne 0)
        {
            Write-Host "- " $strDCName
        }
    }    Write-Host
}
```

The previous script was written to use the AD module for discovering the DCs in the forest. The script in Listing 5.5 provides the same functionality with Active Directory Services Interface (ADSI), in the event that you can't use the AD module.

LISTING 5.5: CheckDCTimeSync-ADSI.ps1

```
## File Name: CheckDCTimeSync-ADSI.ps1
## Description:
##    Examines every Domain Controller in the forest and reports
##    on which DCs aren't using the domain time hierarchy for
##    clock sync. This script uses ADSI to enumerate the Domain
##    Controllers in the forest.
##
Write-Host "`nDomain Controllers that are not synchronizing" `
    "time with the domain time hierarchy"
## Get the forest object
$objForest = [DirectoryServices.ActiveDirectory.Forest]::`
  GetCurrentForest()
## Enumerate the Domains the forest
foreach ($objDomain in $objForest.Domains)
{
  ## Enumerate the DCs in each Domain
  foreach ($objDC in $objDomain.DomainControllers)
  {
    ## Look up the Type key in the registry on each DC
```

```
$strDCName = $objDC.Name
$objReg = [WMICLASS]"\\$($strDCName)\root\cimv2:StdRegProv"
$objType = $objReg.GetStringValue(2147483650, "SYSTEM\" +
  "CurrentControlSet\Services\W32Time\Parameters", "Type")

## If the Type indicates something other than NT5DS, display
## this DC in the list
if ($objType.sValue.CompareTo("NT5DS") -gt 0)
{
    Write-Host "- " $strDCName
}
}    Write-Host
}
```

Enabling the Debug Log for the Time Service

Sometimes you may need more information when debugging issues with time synchronization. The time-synchronization service in Windows allows you to enable debug logging, which provides verbose information about what the time service is doing. Often, when you're troubleshooting time-synchronization issues on a computer, the debug log can be very handy.

Enabling the logs is a two-step process:

1. Configure the debug log settings in the Registry.

2. Restart the Windows Time service in order for the new settings to take effect.

The debug log settings are found in the Registry under the following location:

```
HKLM\System\CurrentControlSet\Services\W32Time\Config
```

Three Registry keys in this location control the behavior of the debug log:

- FileLogName: The full path to where you want the log file to be written.

- FileLogSize: How big the log should get, specified in bytes.

- FileLogEntries: The amount of information you want in your log entries. We recommend turning on all the possible logging entries by setting this key to a string value of "0-300".

To enable the log, you simply need to add these Registry keys. On the other hand, if you want to turn off the time debug log, you can delete these keys. The PowerShell script in Listing 5.6 will either enable or disable the time debug log. When it enables the log, it sets the appropriate Registry keys and reloads the Windows Time service configuration in order for the debug log change to take effect.

Managing Active Directory Data

PART II

LISTING 5.6: SetTimeDebugLog.ps1

```
## File Name: SetTimeDebugLog.ps1
## Description:
##   Enables or disables the debug log for the Windows Time
##   service on the current computer
##

param([switch]$Enable, [switch]$Disable)

# Set the debug log registry keys
$reg_path = "HKLM:\System\CurrentControlSet\Services" +
  "\W32Time\Config"

function EnableTimeDebugLog()
{
  $r = New-ItemProperty -Path $reg_path -Name "FileLogName" `
    -Value "C:\w32time_debug.log" -PropertyType String `
    -ErrorAction silentlyContinue

  $r = New-ItemProperty -Path $reg_path -Name "FileLogSize" `
    -Value 10485760 -PropertyType DWORD `
    -ErrorAction silentlyContinue

  $r = New-ItemProperty -Path $reg_path -Name "FileLogEntries" `
    -Value "0-300" -PropertyType String `
    -ErrorAction silentlyContinue

  Write-Host "Time Debug Log Enabled"
}

function DisableTimeDebugLog()
{
  Remove-ItemProperty -Path $reg_path -Name "FileLogName" `
    -ErrorAction silentlyContinue

  Remove-ItemProperty -Path $reg_path -Name "FileLogSize" `
    -ErrorAction silentlyContinue
```

```
Remove-ItemProperty -Path $reg_path -Name "FileLogEntries" `
  -ErrorAction silentlyContinue

Write-Host "Time Debug Log Disabled"
}


if ($Enable)
{
  EnableTimeDebugLog
}
else
{
  DisableTimeDebugLog
}


# Reload the configuration of the Windows Time service
w32tm /config /update
```

Configure the Time Service

Understanding how your time-synchronization strategy is laid out is just one aspect of administering time synchronization for the domain. You also have to know how to make the necessary configuration changes. Some of these changes may be time settings that you want to target at a specific computer in your domain. Others may be time-configuration settings that you want to ensure are consistently applied to your DCs. In this section, we'll look at a few of the items you need to configure for time synchronization and provide some ways to automate it via PowerShell.

Configuring a Forest Time Source

Because the time-synchronization hierarchy for a forest chains back to the DC in the forest root domain that holds the PDC emulator FSMO role, the only thing you need to configure to use an external time source is the NTP server that this DC synchronizes its time with. This setting is controlled via a couple of Registry keys on this DC.

The first key is one that we've already talked about: the Type key. It's located in the following Registry location:

```
HKLM\System\CurrentControlSet\Services\W32Time\Parameters
```

The Type key indicates whether the computer is synchronizing time from an external NTP provider, the internal domain hierarchy, or not at all. To configure the DC to synchronize its time from an external NTP provider, you'll want to set the value of the Type key to NTP. The following commands make this configuration change. Make sure that you substitute **<DCName>** for the name of the PDC emulator role holder for the forest root domain:

```
$objReg = [WMICLASS]"\\<DCName>\root\cimv2:StdRegProv"
$objReg.SetStringValue(2147483650, ↵
    "SYSTEM\CurrentControlSet\Services\W32Time\Parameters", ↵
    "Type", "NTP")
```

The next key is NtpServer, which is a string value that is stored in

```
HKLM\System\CurrentControlSet\Services\W32Time\Parameters
```

The NtpServer key is used to specify the name or IP address of the server from which you're synchronizing the time. By default, this is set to time.windows.com, but many organizations set it to a government-run NTP service, such as one hosted by the National Institute of Standards and Technology (NIST). You can find the list of NTP servers hosted by NIST at http://tf.nist.gov/tf-cgi/servers.cgi.

You can use the following commands to set the NTP server in this key. If you want to configure more than one NTP server, separate the entries with a space:

```
$objReg = [WMICLASS]"\\<DCName>\root\cimv2:StdRegProv"
$objReg.SetStringValue(2147483650, ↵
    "SYSTEM\CurrentControlSet\Services\W32Time\Parameters", ↵
    "NtpServer", "time.nist.gov")
```

The PowerShell script in Listing 5.7 allows you to set the external time server for the forest. You can pass in the list of time servers separated by spaces, and the script will find the PDC emulator role holder for the forest root domain and set the time source on it. This is a handy script to use if you manually fail over the PDC emulator role due to a downed DC. You can also set the default NTP server list manually in a script so you don't need to specify a script parameter to set it.

LISTING 5.7: SetForestTimeSource.ps1

```
## File Name: SetForestTimeSource.ps1
## Description:
##    Discovers which Domain Controller is the PDC Emulator in the
```

```powershell
##    forest's root domain and configures it to use an external
##    NTP time source.
##

param($NTPSource)

## Import the Active Directory module
Import-Module ActiveDirectory

## Default time source. Use this time service if the NTPSource
## parameter isn't specified when the script is run.
$time_source = "time.nist.gov"

if ($NTPSource -ne $null)
{
    $time_source = $NTPSource
}

# Obtain the name of the PDC Emulator in the root domain
$objForest = Get-ADForest
$objRootDomain = Get-ADDomain $objForest.RootDomain
$strPDCE = $objRootDomain.PDCEmulator

# Set the NTP registry keys on the PDCE
$objReg = [WMICLASS]"\\$($strPDCE)\root\cimv2:StdRegProv"
$r = $objReg.SetStringValue(2147483650,
  "SYSTEM\CurrentControlSet\Services\W32Time\Parameters",
  "Type", "NTP")
$r = $objReg.SetStringValue(2147483650,
  "SYSTEM\CurrentControlSet\Services\W32Time\Parameters",
  "NtpServer", $time_source)

# Restart the time service
$objTimeSvc = gwmi Win32_Service -Computer $strPDCE `
  -Filter "name='W32Time'"
$r = $objTimeSvc.StopService()
$r = $objTimeSvc.StartService()

Write-Host "Forest time source set to $($time_source)"
```

The previous script uses the AD module for discovering the PDC emulator in the forest root domain. If you aren't able to use the AD module, you can use the alternative script in Listing 5.8, which uses ADSI instead.

LISTING 5.8: SetForestTimeSource-ADSI.ps1

```
## File Name: SetForestTimeSource-ADSI.ps1
## Description:
##    Discovers which Domain Controller is the PDC Emulator in
##    forest's root domain and configures it to use an external
##    NTP time source. This version of the script uses ADSI to
##    discover the PDC Emulator in the forest root domain.
##

param($NTPSource)

## Default time source. Use this time service if the NTPSource
## parameter isn't specified when the script is run.
$time_source = "time.nist.gov"

if ($NTPSource -ne $null)
{
    $time_source = $NTPSource
}


# Obtain the name of the PDC Emulator in the root domain
$objForest = [DirectoryServices.ActiveDirectory.Forest]::`
  GetCurrentForest()
$objContext = New-Object `
  DirectoryServices.ActiveDirectory.DirectoryContext('domain',
  $objForest.RootDomain)
$objRootDomain = [DirectoryServices.ActiveDirectory.Domain]::`
  GetDomain($objContext)
$strPDCE = $objRootDomain.PdcRoleOwner

# Set the NTP registry keys on the PDCE
$objReg = [WMICLASS]"\\$($strPDCE)\root\cimv2:StdRegProv"
```

```
$r = $objReg.SetStringValue(2147483650,
  "SYSTEM\CurrentControlSet\Services\W32Time\Parameters",
  "Type", "NTP")
$r = $objReg.SetStringValue(2147483650,
  "SYSTEM\CurrentControlSet\Services\W32Time\Parameters",
  "NtpServer", $time_source)

# Restart the time service
$objTimeSvc = gwmi Win32_Service -Computer $strPDCE `
  -Filter "name='W32Time'"
$r = $objTimeSvc.StopService()
$r = $objTimeSvc.StartService()

Write-Host "Forest time source set to $($time_source)"
```

Removing Custom Time Settings

You may be in a situation where you have a manual time synchronization configured on computers in your forest. One way to convert them over to the domain time hierarchy is to use a PowerShell script to change their time source. To convert the time-synchronization method to the domain time hierarchy, you only need to change the Registry value called Type in the following location:

```
HKLM\System\CurrentControlSet\Services\W32Time\Parameters
```

The Type value determines how the computer is configured to synchronize its time. If you recall from Table 5.1 earlier in this chapter, the possible options for this value are NT5DS, NTP, or NoSync.

In this case, you need to determine if the Type value is already configured to NT5DS. If so, then this computer is already synchronizing its time with the domain. If not, then you must set it to the value of NT5DS to tell it to synchronize its time with the domain hierarchy. Listing 5.9 performs this action on the computer that you specify when you run the script. To execute this script and remove the custom time-synchronization settings from a computer, run the following command:

```
RemoveCustomTime.ps1 -ComputerName "[ComputerName]"
```

Managing Active Directory Data

PART II

LISTING 5.9: RemoveCustomTime.ps1

```
## File Name: RemoveCustomTime.ps1
## Description:
##  Removes the custom time setting from the computer specified.
##  Forces the specified computer to synchronize time according
##  to the domain time hierarchy.
##
param([string]$ComputerName="")
if ($ComputerName -eq "") { $ComputerName = "." }
## Open the HKLM registry key on the computer
$reg = [Microsoft.Win32.RegistryKey]::OpenRemoteBaseKey(
  "LocalMachine", $ComputerName)
## Open the Parameters sub key
$key = $reg.OpenSubKey("System\CurrentControlSet\Services\" +
  "W32Time\Parameters", $true)
## Set the Type value to NT5DS to indicate that the time is
## synchronized via the domain hierarchy
$key.SetValue("Type", "NT5DS", "String")
# Restart the time service
$objTimeSvc = gwmi Win32_Service -Computer $ComputerName `
  -Filter "name='W32Time'"
$ret = $objTimeSvc.StopService()
$ret = $objTimeSvc.StartService()
Write-Host "$($ComputerName) updated"
```

Ensuring That Domain Controllers Synchronize Their Clocks

If your AD domain has been around for a while, it's very possible that you may have moved FSMO roles around and changed time sources on various DCs. For example, let's assume that you configure the PDC emulator in your forest root domain with an external time source that is supplied to your forest through the domain time hierarchy. At some point in the future, you may have to move that PDC emulator role to another DC, either temporarily or permanently. What happens to that time source? Chances are, you probably didn't think to reset that DC's time source back to the domain time hierarchy. Also, you may have not remembered to configure the new PDC emulator role holder to use the external time source. If this is the case, you could potentially have problems with the DC that is now pointing to a different time source than the rest of your domain.

Fortunately, you can use PowerShell to help write a script that ensures you'll never encounter this problem. The script in Listing 5.10 does two things:

▶ It finds the PDC emulator in the root domain and determines whether its time source is pointing to an external clock.

▶ It examines every other DC and, if the DC is configured to point to another time server, reconfigures the DC to use the domain time hierarchy.

This is one script that you may want to run periodically without having to think about the configuration parameters. Therefore, you can configure your domain's external time source under the $external_clock variable at the beginning of the script. When this script is run, it always ensures that the DC holding the PDC emulator FSMO role in your forest root domain is using this external time source. Every other DC is configured to use the domain time hierarchy.

Managing Active Directory Data

PART II

LISTING 5.10: SetDCTimeSource.ps1

```
## File Name: SetDCTimeSource.ps1
## Description:
##    Ensures that the PDCE in the forest root domain is
##    synchronizing with the external clock and that every other
##    DC in the forest is using the domain time hierarchy.
##
# Configure the external clock that you want to synchronize with
$external_clock = "nist1.aol-va.symmetricom.com"
# Import the Active Directory Module
Import-Module ActiveDirectory
##
## Part 1 - Configure the PDCE in the root domain to sync with
## the external time source
##
# Get the name of the PDC Emulator in the root domain
$objForest = Get-ADForest
$objRootDomain = Get-ADDomain $objForest.RootDomain
$strPDCE = $objRootDomain.PDCEmulator
$objReg = [WMICLASS]"\\$($strPDCE)\root\cimv2:StdRegProv"
$objType = $objReg.GetStringValue(2147483650,
  "SYSTEM\CurrentControlSet\Services\W32Time\Parameters",
  "Type")
```

(continues)

LISTING 5-10 *(continued)*

```
# If the server is configured for NTP
if ($objType.sValue.CompareTo("NTP") -eq 0)
{
  # Get the name of the external clock that the PDCE is
  # synchronizing with
  $curServer = $objReg.GetStringValue(2147483650,
    "SYSTEM\CurrentControlSet\Services\W32Time\Parameters",
    "NtpServer")
  # If the external clock is not the clock that you want
  # the server to sync with, then change it
  if ($curServer.sValue.CompareTo($external_clock) -ne 0)
  {
    $ret = $objReg.SetStringValue(2147483650,
      "SYSTEM\CurrentControlSet\Services\W32Time\Parameters",
      "NtpServer", $external_clock)
    # Restart the time service
    $objTimeSvc = gwmi Win32_Service -Computer $strPDCE `
      -Filter "name='W32Time'"
    $ret = $objTimeSvc.StopService()
    $ret = $objTimeSvc.StartService()
    Write-Host "PDCE ($($strPDCE)) is already configured to" `
      "use an external time source, but it's pointing to the" `
      "wrong server. Updated PDCE time source to" `
      "$($external_clock)"
  }
}
else
{
  # The PDCE is not set for NTP, so set it
  $ret = $objReg.SetStringValue(2147483650,
    "SYSTEM\CurrentControlSet\Services\W32Time\Parameters",
    "Type", "NTP")
  $ret = $objReg.SetStringValue(2147483650,
    "SYSTEM\CurrentControlSet\Services\W32Time\Parameters",
    "NtpServer", $external_clock)
  # Restart the time service
```

```
  $objTimeSvc = gwmi Win32_Service -Computer $strPDCE `
    -Filter "name='W32Time'"
  $ret = $objTimeSvc.StopService()
  $ret = $objTimeSvc.StartService()
  Write-Host "PDCE ($($strPDCE)) is now configured to use" `
    "$($external_clock) as its time source."
}
##
## Part 2 - Configure every other DC to sync with the domain
## time hierarchy
##
# Get a list of domains in the forest
$colDomains = $objForest.Domains
# Enumerate each domain name
foreach ($strDomain in $colDomains)
{
  # Get the domain object based on its name
  $objDomain = Get-ADDomain $strDomain
  # If this is the root domain
  if ($objDomain.DnsRoot.ToLower() -eq
    $objRootDomain.DnsRoot.ToLower())
  {
    foreach ($strDC in $objDomain.ReplicaDirectoryServers)
    {
      if ($strDC.ToLower() -ne $strPDCE.ToLower())
      {
        $objReg = [WMICLASS]"\\$($strDC)\root\cimv2:StdRegProv"
        $objType = $objReg.GetStringValue(2147483650, "SYSTEM" +
          "\CurrentControlSet\Services\W32Time\Parameters",
          "Type")
        # If the DC is not synchronizing with the domain time
        if ($objType.sValue.ToLower() -ne "nt5ds")
        {
          $ret = $objReg.SetStringValue(2147483650, "SYSTEM" +
            "\CurrentControlSet\Services\W32Time\Parameters",
            "Type", "NTP")
          Write-Host "Updated $($strDC) to use the domain" `
```

(continues)

Managing Active Directory Data

PART II

LISTING 5-10 *(continued)*

```
                    "time hierarchy."
              # Restart the time service
              $objTimeSvc = gwmi Win32_Service `
                 -Computer $strDC -Filter "name='W32Time'"
              $ret = $objTimeSvc.StopService()
              $ret = $objTimeSvc.StartService()
         }
       }
     }
   }
 }
```

The previous script uses the AD module for locating the PDC emulator for the forest root domain and for enumerating the DCs in the forest. If you can't use the AD module, you can use the script in Listing 5.11 instead, which uses ADSI to perform the same tasks.

LISTING 5.11: **SetDCTimeSource-ADSI.ps1**

```
## File Name: SetDCTimeSource-ADSI.ps1
## Description:
##    Ensures that the PDCE in the forest root domain is
##    synchronizing with the external clock and that every other
##    DC in the forest is using the domain time hierarchy. This
##    version of the script leverages ADSI for discovering the
##    PDC Emulator in the forest root domain and for enumerating
##    the Domain Controllers in the forest.
##
# Configure the external clock that you want to synchronize with
$external_clock = "nist1.aol-va.symmetricom.com"
##
## Part 1 - Configure the PDCE in the root domain to sync with
## the external time source
##
# Obtain the name of the PDC Emulator in the root domain
$objForest = [DirectoryServices.ActiveDirectory.Forest]::`
  GetCurrentForest()
```

```
$objContext = New-Object `
  DirectoryServices.ActiveDirectory.DirectoryContext('domain',
  $objForest.RootDomain)
$objRootDomain = [DirectoryServices.ActiveDirectory.Domain]::`
  GetDomain($objContext)
$strPDCE = $objRootDomain.PdcRoleOwner.Name
$objReg = [WMICLASS]"\\$($strPDCE)\root\cimv2:StdRegProv"
$objType = $objReg.GetStringValue(2147483650,
  "SYSTEM\CurrentControlSet\Services\W32Time\Parameters",
  "Type")
# If the server is configured for NTP
if ($objType.sValue.CompareTo("NTP") -eq 0)
{
  # Get the name of the external clock that the PDCE is
  # synchronizing with
  $curServer = $objReg.GetStringValue(2147483650,
    "SYSTEM\CurrentControlSet\Services\W32Time\Parameters",
    "NtpServer")
  # If the external clock is not the clock that you want
  # the server to sync with, then change it
  if ($curServer.sValue.CompareTo($external_clock) -ne 0)
  {
    $ret = $objReg.SetStringValue(2147483650,
      "SYSTEM\CurrentControlSet\Services\W32Time\Parameters",
      "NtpServer", $external_clock)
    # Restart the time service
    $objTimeSvc = gwmi Win32_Service -Computer $strPDCE `
      -Filter "name='W32Time'"
    $ret = $objTimeSvc.StopService()
    $ret = $objTimeSvc.StartService()
    Write-Host "PDCE ($($strPDCE)) is already configured to" `
      "use an external time source, but it's pointing to the" `
      "wrong server. Updated PDCE time source to" `
      "$($external_clock)"
  }
}
else
{
```

(continues)

LISTING 5-11 *(continued)*

```
        # The PDCE is not set for NTP, so set it
        $ret = $objReg.SetStringValue(2147483650,
          "SYSTEM\CurrentControlSet\Services\W32Time\Parameters",
          "Type", "NTP")
        $ret = $objReg.SetStringValue(2147483650,
          "SYSTEM\CurrentControlSet\Services\W32Time\Parameters",
          "NtpServer", $external_clock)
        # Restart the time service
        $objTimeSvc = gwmi Win32_Service -Computer $strPDCE `
          -Filter "name='W32Time'"
        $ret = $objTimeSvc.StopService()
        $ret = $objTimeSvc.StartService()
        Write-Host "PDCE ($($strPDCE)) is now configured to use" `
          "$($external_clock) as its time source."
    }

##
## Part 2 - Configure every other DC to sync with the domain
## time hierarchy
##
## Enumerate the Domains in the forest
foreach ($objDomain in $objForest.Domains)
{
  # If this is the root domain
  if ($objDomain.Name.ToLower() -eq
    $objRootDomain.Name.ToLower())
  {
    foreach ($objDC in $objDomain.DomainControllers)
    {
      $strDC = $objDC.Name
      if ($strDC.ToLower() -ne $strPDCE.ToLower())
      {
        $objReg = [WMICLASS]"\\$($strDC)\root\cimv2:StdRegProv"
        $objType = $objReg.GetStringValue(2147483650, "SYSTEM" +
            "\CurrentControlSet\Services\W32Time\Parameters",
            "Type")
        # If the DC is not synchronizing with the domain time
```

```
      if ($objType.sValue.ToLower() -ne "nt5ds")
      {
        $ret = $objReg.SetStringValue(2147483650, "SYSTEM" +
          "\CurrentControlSet\Services\W32Time\Parameters",
          "Type", "NTP")
        Write-Host "Updated $($strDC) to use the domain" `
          "time hierarchy."
        # Restart the time service
        $objTimeSvc = gwmi Win32_Service `
          -Computer $strDC -Filter "name='W32Time'"
        $ret = $objTimeSvc.StopService()
        $ret = $objTimeSvc.StartService()
      }
    }
  }
}
}
```

CHAPTER 6

Administering User and Group Accounts

IN THIS CHAPTER, YOU WILL LEARN TO:

Because managing user and group accounts involves frequent and often repetitive tasks for any Active Directory (AD) administrator, the tasks described in this chapter are extremely suited for automation using a tool such as Windows PowerShell. The AD PowerShell module introduced in Windows Server 2008 R2 includes a number of cmdlets that simplify the process of user and group management; these cmdlets are all created using the familiar Add-, Get-, Move-, Set-, and Remove- verb-noun format. For example, you can use Get-ADUser to retrieve information about one or more AD user accounts, whereas New-ADGroup, predictably, creates a new group object in AD. Each cmdlet includes a number of parameters that you can use to refer to common attributes of user and group objects, such as -Description to refer to the description LDAP attribute, as well as more advanced syntax to allow you to access and manipulate any additional attributes that don't have a parameter associated with them. By using the examples included in this chapter, you'll be able to automate the critical tasks associated with managing user and group objects on your AD network.

Manage User Accounts

Even in small AD domains consisting of a single forest, a single domain, and even a single site, managing user accounts will be a significant part of your life as an AD administrator. Without a user account and a password, no one in your organization will be able to access any network resources such as file servers or email. It's important to be able to quickly and efficiently create new user accounts when necessary, to manage passwords for users who have forgotten theirs or need passwords changed, and to manage other aspects of information configured on AD user accounts in any environment that you oversee.

Add and Remove Users

Before a new user in your organization can access any network resources, such as a file share, email account, or SharePoint document library, an administrator must create a user account that allows this user to access these resources. Each user account in AD has a number of attributes associated with it, the most important of which is probably the security identifier (SID) used by Windows to assign permissions to this user object. The SID is a long numeric value that is assigned "under the covers" when you create a user with a friendly name like *Andy Ruth*; the SID doesn't change if you change the user's friendly name. In most cases, end users aren't aware of the existence of their SID—only their username and password—but understanding the function of the SID is important in order for an AD administrator to administer and troubleshoot user-account access in an AD environment.

AD user objects also possess numerous additional attributes, such as those corresponding to personal information about the user (first name, last name, telephone) and attributes that control how the user's password is configured and whether the account is enabled or disabled.

In this section, you'll learn how to create one or multiple user accounts within an AD domain, as well as how to configure certain attributes such as an expiration date for a temporary user account. You'll also learn about managed service accounts, a feature introduced in Windows Server 2008, and how to use and manage this new feature.

Creating and Deleting a User Account

Creating and deleting user accounts is one of the most common tasks you'll perform as an AD administrator, and thus it's suitable for automation. The PowerShell cmdlet you use to create a user is New-ADUser; this cmdlet has numerous switches that allow you to configure many well-known parameters of AD user objects. Here's some example syntax for the New-ADUser cmdlet:

```
New-ADUser -SamAccountName "arose" -GivenName "Andy"
-Surname "Rose" -DisplayName "Andy Rose" -Path
'CN=Users,DC=contoso,DC=com'
```

The full list of parameters that you can specify in the New-ADUser cmdlet is as follows:

Name	City	EmployeeID
AccountExpirationDate	Company	EmployeeNumber
AccountNotDelegated	Country	Enabled
AccountPassword	Department	Fax
AllowReversible PasswordEncryption	Description	GivenName
CannotChangePassword	DisplayName	HomeDirectory
Certificates	Division	HomeDrive
ChangePasswordAtLogon	EmailAddress	HomePage

HomePhone	PasswordNever Expires	SmartcardLogon Required
Initials	PasswordNot Required	State
Instance	Path	StreetAddress
LogonWorkstations	POBox	Surname
Manager	PostalCode	Title
MobilePhone	ProfilePath	TrustedFor Delegation
Office	sAMAccountName	Type
OfficePhone	ScriptPath	UserPrincipalName
Organization	Server	
OtherName	ServicePrincipal Names	

If you wish to specify any attributes that aren't available via a defined switch, you can use the -OtherAttributes switch, which takes a multivalued argument that allows you to specify multiple attributes (using their LDAP display name) and their values. Here are some examples of how the -OtherAttributes switch can specify one or more LDAP values, including the necessary syntax when one of the attributes is itself multivalued:

```
-OtherAttributes @{'shoeSize'="8.5"}
-OtherAttributes @{'openProjects'="ProjectX","ProjectY"}
-OtherAttributes @{'shoeSize'="8.5"; 'dateOfBirth'="
12/10/1973";'openProject'="ProjectX","ProjectY"}
```

NOTE Even if an attribute may be specified using an individual switch, you can still populate its value using the **-OtherAttributes** switch. This may come in handy if you're populating information from an import file or database. (The **sAMAccountName** switch is mandatory for all user objects created with **New-ADUser**.)

Listing 6.1 shows a few different combinations of syntaxes.

LISTING 6.1: **Creating New Active Directory User Accounts**

```
New-ADUser -sAMAccountName "arose" -GivenName "Andy" -Surname
"Rose" -DisplayName "Andy Rose" -Path 'CN=Users,DC=contoso,DC=com'
-AccountExpirationDate "10/25/2012"

New-ADUser -SamAccountName "arose" -GivenName "Andy" -Surname
"Rose" -DisplayName "Andy Rose" -Path 'CN=Users,DC=contoso,DC=com'
-AccountExpirationDate "10/25/2012" -EmployeeNumber "225373"
-Enabled $false

New-ADUser -SamAccountName "arose" -GivenName "Andy" -Surname
"Rose" -DisplayName "Andy Rose" -Path 'CN=Users,DC=contoso,DC=com'
-AccountExpirationDate "10/25/2012" -EmployeeNumber "225373"
-Enabled $false

New-ADUser -Name arose -Path 'CN=Users,DC=contoso,DC=com'
-OtherAttributes @{givenName="Andy";surName="Rose";employeeNumber=
"225373";title="Director"}
```

Just as you use `New-ADUser` to create AD user objects, you use `Remove-ADUser` to delete them. You can specify an individual user to delete by using the `-Identity` switch, which may take any of the following values as a way to identify the user in question:

- ► Distinguished Name (DN)
- ► sAMAccountName
- ► Globally Unique Identifier (GUID)
- ► SID

You can also perform a search of AD for user objects that meet certain criteria, and then pipe the results of the search to `Remove-ADUser` in order to remove all users in the result set. The following is an example of both of these syntaxes: (Notice that the second command uses the `-Confirm` switch to prompt the user before each deletion.)

```
Remove-ADUser -Identity "CN=Andy Ruth,OU=Marketing,DC=Contoso,DC=COM"
Search-ADAccount -AccountDisabled | where {$_.ObjectClass -eq
'user'} | Remove-ADUser -Confirm
```

Managing Active Directory Data

PART II

Creating Several Users from a CSV File

Another common task is creating a large number of users based on information in an input file such as a comma-separated values (CSV) file. In this case, the `Import-CSV` cmdlet makes the process relatively straightforward. With `Import-CSV`, you can assign a name to each field in the CSV file on the basis of the header row in the file and then pipe that information, using `ForEach-Object` to invoke `New-ADUser` for each entry in the CSV file.

The following example shows a CSV file you can use to create a large number of users and the PowerShell cmdlet that reads the input file and creates the corresponding user objects:

```
sAMAccountName,Path,GivenName,Surname,DisplayName,EmployeeNumber
arose,"CN=Users,DC=Contoso,DC=Com,",Andy,Ruth,"Andy Ruth",123456
mabx,"OU=Marketing,DC=Contoso,DC=Com",Max,Benson,"Max
Benson",234567
Import-CSV "users.csv" | Foreach-Object {New-ADUser -Name
$_.sAMAccountNAme -Path $_.Path -GivenName $_.GivenName -SurName
$_.SurName -DisplayName $_.DisplayName -OtherAttributes @
{employeeNumber=$_.EmployeeNumber}
```

Changing the Default Location for User Accounts

To maintain backward compatibility with pre–Windows 2000 environments, each AD domain is installed containing two container objects called `CN=Users, <domain DN>` and `CN=Computers, <domain DN>`. By default, all user objects that are created are placed in the `Users` container, and all computer objects are placed in the `Computers` container. Within AD, the container object class is a parent of the organizational unit (OU) object class—container objects may contain other objects similar to OUs; but unlike OUs, you can't link Group Policy Objects (GPOs) to containers.

To ensure that all newly created user objects receive the correct security and GPO settings from the moment they're created, you can redirect the default location where new user objects are created. This change requires that the domain in question be operating at the Windows Server 2003 domain functional level or higher. The simplest way to make this change is to use the built-in `redirusr.exe` utility.

NOTE The `Users` and `Computers` containers may be renamed by an AD administrator, but they may not be deleted.

The following example shows the syntax required to redirect the default location for newly created user objects to the `DefaultUsers` organizational unit:

```
Redirusr.exe OU=DefaultUsers,DC=Contoso,DC=Com
```

Creating a Managed Service Account

One of the largest challenges of managing AD-aware applications is the need to create and manage application service accounts over time—in particular, the difficulty of configuring and updating the passwords for these service accounts over time. Administrators are often forced to configure service accounts with non-expiring passwords to avoid application outages. Doing so can create significant security exposure on a network, because service accounts often have highly elevated permissions; but the alternative is to incur application outages resulting from service-account passwords expiring without warning.

To help address this issue, Windows Server 2008 R2 introduces the concept of the *managed service account (MSA)*, a new object class that inherits from both the computer and user object classes. Unlike traditional service accounts, for which account passwords must be set and managed manually, MSAs have a 240-character random password that is automatically created by AD and that changes every 30 days by default. By default, all MSAs in the `contoso.com` domain would be created in the following container: `CN=Managed Service Accounts,DC=contoso,DC=com`.

WARNING   An MSA may be used on only one computer object at a time. And if you're running at the Windows Server 2008 R2 domain functional level, MSAs can automatically maintain any service principal names (SPNs) that are associated with the MSA if the MSA is renamed at any point. (The downside to the fact that you can associate an MSA with only a single computer object is that MSAs may not be used to run applications in clustered environments.) MSAs can only be configured on computers that are running Windows Server 2008 R2 or Windows 7.

Deploying a new MSA involves four steps:

1. Create the MSA.

2. Associate the MSA with a computer account.

3. Install the MSA on the computer that was associated.

4. Configure the service(s) to use the MSA.

Managing Active Directory Data   PART II

The following demonstrates how to perform the first two of these steps, from a domain controller (DC) or a client computer:

```
New-ADServiceAccount -Name SAPServiceAccount
Add-ADComputerServiceAccount -Identity CN=SAPServer,OU=Servers,
CN=Contoso,CN=COM -ServiceAccount SAPServiceAccount
```

After you've created the MSA and associated it with the computer account you want, you're left with installing it on the computer, as shown in the following example. In order to perform this portion of the process, you must be a local administrator on the computer and you need the ability to modify the properties of the MSA object:

```
Install-ADServiceAccount -Identity SAPServiceAccount
```

Finally, you need to change the properties of the service to log on as the MSA. You can see the syntax required for this in the following code (notice that it sets the password to $null):

```
$account="Contoso\SAPServiceAccount"
$password=$null
$svc=gwmi win32_service -filter "name='SAP Service'"
$inParams = $svc.psbase.getMethodParameters("Change")
$inParams["StartName"] = $account
$inParams["StartPassword"] = $password
$svc.invokeMethod("Change",$inParams,$null)
```

Finally, this last code example shows the two commands necessary to remove an MSA. You disassociate the MSA from the computer account and remove it from AD.

```
Remove-ADComputerServiceAccount -Identity SAPServer
-ServiceAccount SAPServiceAccount
Remove-ADServiceAccount -Identity SAPServiceAccount
```

Preventing a User from Being Accidentally Deleted

An oft-recurring challenge for AD administrators, particularly when working within GUI tools like Active Directory Users and Computers, is recovering from accidentally deleting one or more objects. This error is often caused by the prover-bial "fat finger," where an administrator is trying to select one object and ends up selecting a different object (or even a different container or OU). To help prevent this, Windows Server 2008 introduced the Protect Object From Accidental Deletion check box in Active Directory Users and Computers. This protection prevents an administrator from deleting an object without first removing this protection; in the UI, you do so by selecting the check box. This protection is enabled by default on all new OUs created in Windows Server 2008 and higher, but it may be configured on any object in the domain—even leaf objects like users and groups. Because this protection simply applies a Deny Delete and Deny Delete Subtree Access Control List (ACL) on the object to the EVERYONE group, applying this protection can also be automated at the command line.

The following shows how to protect an individual user from accidental deletion using the dsacls.exe utility:

```
Dsacls "cn=Andy Ruth,ou=Users,dc=contoso,dc=com" /d EVERYONE:SDDT
```

Setting the Expiration Date of a User Account

In some cases, you may need to configure a user account that has a finite lifetime during which the user is permitted to log in. This is a common scenario for vendor accounts and temporary or contingent staff who are fulfilling the terms of a time-based contract. You can use the Set-ADUser PowerShell cmdlet to set a user's expiration date, as shown in this code:

```
Set-ADUser -Identity "CN=Andy Ruth,OU=Users,DC=Contoso,DC=Com"
-AccountExpirationDate 12/10/2011
```

Maintain User Passwords

In almost every AD domain, each user account that you create will have a password associated with it that the user must enter whenever they wish to log onto their workstation or access a resource from a non-domain-joined machine. (After the user logs onto a domain-joined workstation, they aren't prompted to re-enter their password to access any resource that relies on Integrated Windows Authentication to provide single sign-on.) In this section, you'll learn how to perform a number of common tasks related to managing user passwords, including changing or resetting a user's password, flagging a user to change their password the next time they log onto the network, and notifying users whose passwords are close to their expiration date using a simple email notification.

Determining Which Users' Passwords Have Replicated to an RODC

The computer account of each read-only domain controller (RODC) possesses a number of attributes that control how AD user and computer account passwords are replicated to that RODC. The attributes you'll find on the RODC's computer object are as follows:

msDS-Reveal-OnDemandGroup   This attribute corresponds to the Allowed List option for each RODC. Each member of the allowed list (user, computer, or group) may have their passwords replicated to the RODC. This doesn't necessarily mean that the passwords have already been replicated there, merely that the passwords are permitted to replicate there.

msDS-NeverRevealGroup   This attribute is the converse of msDS-Reveal-On DemandGroup and corresponds to the Denied List option for each RODC. This list corresponds to users, computers, and groups whose passwords will never be replicated to this RODC. (This doesn't impact the ability of these security principals to authenticate using the RODC; it simply means that any requests are forwarded to a writeable DC.) A default list of security principals whose credentials are denied replication to the RODC is configured on each new RODC in a domain and consists of high-security groups such as Domain Admins, Enterprise Admins, and Schema Admins.

msDS-RevealedList   This attribute is a list of user and computer accounts whose current passwords have been replicated to this RODC.

msDS-AuthenticatedToAccountList   This is a list of user and computer accounts that have authenticated to the RODC, although their passwords may or may not be included in the RevealedList. Administrators can use this attribute to help refine the Password Replication Policy for an RODC by determining which users and computers are authenticating frequently to a particular RODC.

The next example shows you how to query for the contents of the RevealedList attribute for a particular RODC, to determine which users and computers are using this RODC to authenticate:

```
Get-ADComputer -Identity "CN=RODC1,OU=Domain
Controllers,DC=Contoso,DC=COM" -Properties msDS-RevealedList
```

And the following code shows you how to query for all RODCs in a domain and obtain this information for each one:

```
Get-ADDomainController -Server "research.fabrikam.com"
-Filter { isReadOnly -eq $true } | Get-ADComputer -Properties
msDS-RevealedList
```

Finding Accounts Whose Passwords Will Expire Soon

A common request for AD administrators is to obtain a list of user accounts whose passwords are about to expire. In Windows PowerShell, you can query this using the Search-ADAccount cmdlet with the –AccountExpiring parameter. The following example uses the DateTime function in PowerShell to obtain a list of users whose passwords will expire within the next 90 days:

```
Search-ADAccount -AccountExpiring -TimeSpan 90.00:00:00
```

Changing the Password of a User Account

Although it seems like a simple matter, changing a user's AD password has a number of subtleties that must be considered before you perform the operation. The first question to ask is whether the user knows their current password, which will allow them to change the password, or if the user has lost or forgotten their current password, which will require an administrator to reset the password. If a user resets their password, it has several implications for their local desktop, including losing access to files that they have encrypted using the Encrypting File System (EFS) unless they previously created a password-reset disk.

The simplest mechanism for changing or resetting a user's password is to use the Set-ADAccountPassword cmdlet and allow it to prompt you to enter the old and/ or new passwords. This code shows the cmdlet in action, followed by the output you see from the cmdlet:

```
Set-ADPassword -Identity "CN=Andy Ruth,OU=Users,DC=Contoso,DC=Com"

Please enter the current password for 'CN=Sara Davis,CN=Users,
DC=Fabrikam,DC=com'
Password:**********
Please enter the desired password for 'CN=Sara Davis,CN=Users,
DC=Fabrikam,DC=com'
Password:**********
Repeat Password:**********
```

If you need to specify the old or new password at the same time you enter the cmdlet, you'll need to use the ConvertTo-SecureString method to convert the

Managing Active
Directory Data

PART II

plain text of the password, because the `Set-ADAccountPassword` cmdlet requires a secure string as input. This code line demonstrates this option:

```
Set-ADAccountPassword -Identity arose -OldPassword (ConvertTo
-SecureString -AsPlainText "p@ssw0rd" -Force) -NewPassword
(ConvertTo-SecureString -AsPlainText "qwert@12345" -Force)
```

Finally, the following example shows how to reset a user's password if the user has forgotten it or if you don't have the user's current password available:

```
Set-ADAccountPassword 'CN=Andy Rose,OU=Users,DC=Fabrikam,DC=
com' -Reset -NewPassword (ConvertTo-SecureString -AsPlainText
"p@ssw0rd" -Force)
```

Forcing a User to Change Their Password at Next Logon

In the next snippet, you can see how to use the `Set-ADUser` cmdlet to force a user to change their password the next time they log onto their workstation. This function assumes that the user knows their current password; if they don't, you'll need to reset their password before setting this option:

```
Set-ADAccountPassword 'CN=Andy Rose,OU=Users,DC=Fabrikam,DC=com'
-ChangePasswordAtLogon $true
```

Emailing Users When Their Passwords Are About to Expire

Automating the process of emailing user notifications has a number of moving parts, as you might imagine. In this code, you can see an example of this functionality in action:

```
Search-ADAccount -AccountExpiring -TimeSpan 7.00:00:00 | foreach
{
  $UserName=$_.GivenName
  $EmailAddress=$_.EmailAddress
  $MyVariable = @"Dear $UserName: Your password will expire in
$display days."@
send-mailmessage -to $EmailAddress -from NoReply@domain.test
-Subject "IT Information: Your password will expire in $display
days" -body $MyVariable -smtpserver smtp.contoso.com
}
```

To send the mail message, this script relies on the `send-mailmessage` PowerShell cmdlet, which lets you specify common parameters associated with sending an email message:

▶ To specifies the email recipient

▶ From specifies the Reply-To address

- ▸ Subject specifies the Subject line of the email

- ▸ Body specifies the body of the email

- ▸ Smtpserver specifies the mail server that will be used to transmit the messages

Manage User Access

Each user account that you create in an AD domain receives certain default privileges to resources on your network: for example, resources that have been secured to the Domain Users and Authenticated Users groups, of which each user is automatically made a member. Because of this, it's important to manage user access to your environment over time as users enter and leave your organization. Using attributes on the user account, you can determine the last time a user account was used to access the network; if it hasn't been used for a significant amount of time, this may indicate that the user has left the organization and the account is no longer required.

In this section, you'll learn how to search for unused accounts and enable or disable them if desired. You'll also learn additional mechanisms for controlling a user's access to an AD environment, such as requiring a user to use a smart card for two-factor authentication in high-security environments, or restricting a user account to only be able to log on from specific workstations that you have identified. Finally, you'll learn how to search for and manage accounts that have been locked out due to repeated failed attempts to enter the correct password associated with the account.

Unlocking a User Account

Many AD environments implement an account-lockout policy, which locks out a user's account if the user enters an incorrect password a certain number of times within a specified time frame—5 bad login attempts within 45 minutes, for example. Depending on how the account-lockout policy is configured, users' accounts may automatically unlock themselves after a specific duration, or users may be required to have an administrator unlock their accounts manually. In either case, administrators can unlock user accounts from the command line using the Unlock-ADAccount PowerShell cmdlet.

As with many AD PowerShell cmdlets, a mandatory parameter of this cmdlet is -Identity, which specifies the user account that should be unlocked. Unlock-ADAccount may consume a user identity presented in any of the following formats:

- ▸ GUID

- ▸ SID

> ▶ DN

> ▶ sAMAccountName

This code demonstrates how to unlock an AD user account:

```
Unlock-ADAccount -Identity "cn=Andy Ruth,ou=Users,dc=contoso,dc=com"
```

Finding User Accounts That Haven't Logged On in 30 Days

A common AD administration task is to identify user accounts that haven't logged onto AD within a specified period of time, in order to disable or delete these users and thus prevent unauthorized use of those accounts by terminated or resigned employees. The AD PowerShell cmdlets in Windows Server 2008 R2 make it easy to search for users in this category with the Search-ADAccount cmdlet using the -AccountInactive switch. You can search for accounts that haven't logged onto AD within the past *X* number of days ("users who haven't logged on in the last 90 days"), or you can specify a particular date to search against ("users who haven't logged on since January 1, 2009.")

This code shows an example of each type of search:

```
Search-ADAccount -AccountInactive -TimeSpan 30.00:00:00 | where
{$_.ObjectClass -eq 'user'}
Search-ADAccount -AccountInactive -DateTime 01/01/2009 | where
{$_.ObjectClass -eq 'user'}
```

NOTE   Because you're specifically searching for user objects, instead of computer objects or inetOrgPerson objects, you use a where clause to filter the output of the Search-ADAccount command.

To provide a common example of piping the output of one cmdlet into another, the following code shows how to search for inactive accounts and then disable them within the same command:

```
Search-ADAccount -AccountInactive -TimeSpan 30.00:00:00 | where
{$_.ObjectClass -eq 'user'} | Disable-ADAccount
```

Enabling and Disabling a User Account

From time to time, you may need to disable an AD user account rather than delete it outright. A user may be taking a temporary but extended leave of absence from the company, or a vendor may have completed work on a specific contract but expects to return on another contract in a few weeks. By disabling an account instead of deleting it, you may reenable the account later and allow it to maintain all of its old attributes, such as security group memberships, without needing to restore the account from a backup.

The following example shows how to disable and enable a specific user account using the `Disable-ADAccount` and `Enable-ADAccount` cmdlets, respectively. Like other cmdlets we've discussed, these two require the `-Identity` parameter to identify the account to be enabled or disabled; this may take the form of a DN, GUID, SID, or sAMAccountName:

```
Enable-ADAccount -Identity "dn=maxb,ou=Users,dc=contoso,dc=com"
Disable-ADAccount -Identity arose
```

Searching for Disabled User Accounts

Similar to other common searches, you can use the `Search-ADAccount` cmdlet to search for a list of disabled user accounts in AD. Because `Search-ADAccount` searches for user, computer, and service accounts, you use a where clause to filter the results of the search operation. You can also use the `-SearchScope` parameter to search only for disabled user accounts within a particular OU in AD:

```
Search-ADAccount -SearchBase "ou=Active Users,dc=contoso,dc=com"
-AccountDisabled | where {$_.ObjectClass -eq 'user'}
```

Determining the Last Time a User Logged On

Because AD is a distributed system, where information may be updated on a number of DCs throughout the environment, determining the last time that a user logged on is a more complicated question than it may appear on the surface. Each user object possesses an attribute called `lastLogon`, which is updated with the current timestamp each time a user authenticates to a writeable DC. This attribute doesn't replicate between DCs, so if a user authenticates against DC1 today and then authenticates against DC2 tomorrow, the `lastLogon` attribute will have a different value depending on which DC you're querying. This created challenges in determining a user's most recent logon time in Windows 2000, because it requires you to query every single DC in a domain and compare the values of this attribute to determine the most recent timestamp.

Beginning in Windows Server 2003, the `lastLogonTimestamp` attribute was introduced. It creates a timestamp that is replicated between DCs; but in order to

PART II

reduce the amount of replication traffic within a domain, this attribute isn't replicated every single time a user logs on—the `lastLogonTimestamp` attribute is accurate within approximately 7 days by default. It creates an easier mechanism for determining a user's last logon time, but at the expense of 100 percent accuracy.

You can query for a user's `lastLogonTimestamp` in PowerShell by using `Get-ADUser` and searching for the `LastLogonDate` property. `LastLogonDate` is calculated from the value of the `lastLogonTimestamp` parameter; the value of `lastLogonTimestamp` is translated into the corresponding date in your local time zone. (If the user doesn't have a value set for `lastLogonTimestamp`, the result of the `-LastLogonDate` property will be blank.)

This line shows you how to determine the last logon date for a specific AD user account:

```
Get-ADUser -Identity arose -Properties "LastLogonDate"
```

Forcing a User to Log Onto Only One Computer at a Time

A common request among AD administrators is for the ability to force users to only log onto a single workstation, or to a group of designated workstations. In AD, the only way to enforce this limitation is to specify a list of computer names (using the short NetBIOS name or the fully qualified DNS domain name [FQDN]) that each user may log onto. You can automate this process by using the `Set-ADUser` cmdlet along with the `-LogonWorkstations` parameter, as shown here:

```
Set-ADUser -Identity arose -LogonWorkstations
"aroseDesktop,aroseLaptop.contoso.com,terminalserver1.contoso.com"
```

Getting a List of All Users Who Are Locked Out

Similar to searching for a list of disabled or inactive users, the `Search-ADAccount` PowerShell cmdlet provides an easy way to search for user accounts in an AD domain that have been locked out due to violations of the domain's account-lockout policy. This code demonstrates how to use the `Search-ADAccount` cmdlet in this manner, using a `where` clause to filter the results of the search to include only user objects:

```
Search-ADAccount -LockedOut | where {$_.ObjectClass -eq 'user'}
```

Requiring a User to Log On With a Smart Card

If you've deployed a Public Key Infrastructure (PKI) on your network, you may choose to deploy smart cards for some or all of your users. Doing so increases the security of users authenticating to your AD domain by enabling the use of two-factor authentication: logging onto AD will require something you have (the smart card inserted into the smart card reader) and something you know (the smart card PIN entered when prompted). In high-security environments, you may require smart-card logons for all user accounts, or you may only require smart-card logon for specific user accounts, such as elevated administrator accounts in the Domain Admins and Enterprise Admins groups.

To further protect the security of a user account, you can configure an account to require smart-card authentication: If a user attempts to log on using a username and password only, the logon will fail. You can configure this at the command line using the Set-ADUser cmdlet, as shown here:

```
Set-ADUser -Identity "cn=arose,ou=Users,dc=contoso,dc=com"
-SmartCardLogonRequired $true
```

Manage Account Information

In our final section on managing user accounts in AD, we'll discuss a number of tasks that haven't been covered in previous lessons. The Set-ADUser cmdlet allows you to modify one or more attributes on a single user or on multiple users simultaneously. You'll also learn how to determine which group objects a particular user belongs to, as well as how to convert the friendly name of an AD user account to and from its corresponding SID.

Modifying Basic Information About a User

You can use the Set-ADUser cmdlet to modify any properties of an AD user account. A number of commonly accessed properties are included as named parameters of the Set-ADUser cmdlet; you can also manually specify any property that doesn't have an explicit parameter associated with it. You have already seen individual examples of parameters used in association with the Set-ADUser cmdlet; here is the full list of available parameters:

AccountExpiration Date	CannotChange Password	City
AccountNotDelegated	Certificates	Company
AllowReversible PasswordEncryption	ChangePassword AtLogon	Country

Department	HomePhone	ProfilePath
Description	Initials	SamAccountName
DisplayName	LogonWorkstations	ScriptPath
Division	Manager	ServicePrincipal Names
EmailAddress	MobilePhone	SmartcardLogon Required
EmployeeID	Office	State
EmployeeNumber	OfficePhone	StreetAddress
Enabled	Organization	Surname
Fax	OtherName	Title
GivenName	PasswordNever Expires	TrustedFor Delegation
HomeDirectory	PasswordNot Required	UserPrincipal Name
HomeDrive	POBox	
HomePage	PostalCode	

Many of these parameters simply take a string as their value: for example, –Title "Manager" or –Surname "Ruth". In some cases, the attribute is a boolean that requires a value of $true or $false: –TrustedForDelegation $true or –Enabled $false. You can specify the user to be modified using the –Identity parameter, providing a GUID, SID, DN or sAMAccountName; or you can use the Get-ADUser cmdlet to search for the required user and then pipe the results into Set-ADUser.

The next block shows a few examples of how to modify user settings with the Set-ADUser cmdlet:

```
Set-ADUser -Identity "cn=arose,ou=Users,dc=contoso,dc=com"
-SmartCardLogonRequired $true
Get-ADUser arose | Set-ADUser -Description "Manager of Training"
Get-ADUser -Identity S-1-5-1234-13454565-2479453 | Set-ADUser
$_ -DisplayName ($_.Surname + ' ' + $_.GivenName)
```

To modify attributes that don't have named parameters associated with them, you can use the –Add, –Clear, –Replace, and –Remove parameters. You can specify multiple properties at a time by separating them by semicolons, and you can separate individual values within a single multivalued attribute by separating them with commas. This code shows some examples of this syntax:

```
Set-ADUser -Identity "cn=arose,ou=Users,dc=contoso,dc=com"
 -Add @{otherTelephone='555-222-1111', '555-222-3333';
otherMobile='555-222-9999'}
Set-ADUser -Identity "cn=arose,ou=Users,dc=contoso,dc=com"
-Clear description
Set-ADUser -Identity arose -Replace @
{otherTelephone='555-222-2222', '555-222-1111'} # This removes
555-222-2222 in the otherTelephone attribute and adds 555-222-
1111 in its place
Set-ADUser arose -Remove @{otherMailbox="andy.rose"}
```

NOTE   The difference between **–Clear** and **–Remove** is that **–Clear** completely removes all data within an attribute. You can use **–Remove** to remove a single value from a multivalued attribute, such as removing a single phone number without affecting other items in the list.

Determining What Groups a User Belongs To

Determining which groups a user belongs to can be a simple or a complex operation, depending on the configuration of your AD environment. This is because AD has three different group scopes:

- ► Global and universal groups are visible from any domain in a multidomain forest.

- ► Domain local groups are only visible from DCs within the domain that contains the group, but the groups may contain users from remote domains.

The Get-ADPrincipalGroupMembership cmdlet obtains the AD group membership for a particular user, computer, or service account, or even the nested group membership of another group. If your environment contains only a single domain, the syntax of this cmdlet is relatively straightforward. If you need to retrieve a user's group memberships in domain local groups in other domains, you must specify a DC in the remote domain using the –ResourceContextServer and –ResourceContextPartition parameters, so these domain local groups may be queried.

N O T E   This cmdlet must target a global catalog server in order to perform the search.

The following code demonstrates the syntax of the `Get-ADPrincipalGroup Membership` cmdlet; you may specify the identity to be queried using a GUID, an SID, a DN, or a sAMAccountName. You can also search for the desired user with the `Get-ADUser` cmdlet and pipe the results of the search to the `Get-ADPrincipalGroupMembership` cmdlet. This example queries for the group memberships of a user in the adatum.com domain, specifying a DC in the emea .adatum.com child domain to check for any group memberships that the user may have within that child domain:

```
Get-ADPrincipalGroupMembership -Identity "cn=arose,ou=Users,
dc=adatum,dc=com" -ResourceContextServer dc1.emea.adatum.com
-ResourceContextPartition "dc=emea,dc=adatum,dc=com"
```

Cleaning Up SIDHistory

As a convenience measure during AD migrations, AD security principals also possess an attribute called `sidHistory`, which allows migrated user objects to retain records of any old SIDs they once possessed. This lets a migrated object continue to access a resource that used its premigration SID in an ACL. If a user attempts to access a resource with their new SID and is denied access, for example, Windows checks the `sidHistory` attribute to determine if any previous SIDs are listed in the ACL that allow or deny access.

When a migration has been completed and the old domain decommissioned, it's a best practice to clear the `sidHistory` attribute of all migrated user accounts. Because `sidHistory` is retained as an attribute of each AD user account, you can use the `Set-ADUser` cmdlet to clear this attribute, as shown here:

```
Set-ADUser arose -Clear @{sidHistory}
```

Limiting How Many Objects a User Can Create

A potential risk of delegating permissions to non-administrators is the possibility that a user may create a large number of objects in AD, potentially creating a denial-of-service attack against a DC by filling up the available space on the disk drive containing the `NTDS.DIT` file. You can help to minimize this risk by establishing one or more quotas in AD. You can establish a default quota for a particular naming context, as well as individual quotas for one or more users or groups.

Quotas are applied on the basis of how many objects a particular user owns: If a user exceeds their quota, you can transfer ownership of one or more objects to another user, such as an administrator, so the user may create more objects. Tombstoned objects apply against a user's quota at a reduced rate—by default, a tombstoned object is given one fourth the weight of a live object. When configuring the default quota for a partition, you must also specify the weight of tombstoned objects.

T I P   Domain Admins and Enterprise Admins aren't subject to AD quotas, and quotas may not be applied to the schema naming context.

The next example demonstrates how to establish quotas for individual users and groups using the dsadd.exe command-line utility, and how to modify the default quota for a particular naming context by using dsmod.exe. This example establishes a default quota limit of 100 users in which each tombstoned object counts as one tenth of a live object, and an individual quota for arose of 1000 users.

```
dsmod.exe partition dc=adatum,dc=com -qdefault 100 -qtmbstnwt 10
dsadd.exe -quota -part dc=adatum,dc=com -acct cn=arose,ou=users,
dc=contoso,dc=com -qlimit 1000
```

Converting an SID to an Account Name

Each AD security principal has a numeric SID associated with it; this SID remains the same even if an object is renamed. Because all Windows permissions (AD, file system, and so on) are based on SIDs, the persistence of the SID allows administrators to rename an object without needing to completely reassign the user's permissions across the environment.

In Windows PowerShell, you can take an object's SID and convert it to the user's sAMAccountName, and vice versa. Because there are no built-in cmdlets that perform this functionality, you use native .NET calls to perform this task, as shown next. Here's how you convert an SID to an account name:

```
$objSID = New-Object System.Security.Principal.SecurityIdentifier
("S-1-5-21-1556476127-1285835555-1973985555-1210")
$objUser = $objSID.Translate([System.Security.Principal
.NTAccount])
$objUser.Value
```

And here's how you convert an account name to an SID:

```
$objUser = New-Object System.Security.Principal
.NTAccount("contoso", "arose")
$strSID = $objUser.Translate([System.Security.Principal
.SecurityIdentifier])
$strSID.Value
```

Changing a Property on Several Users Simultaneously

So far in this chapter, you have seen examples of how to use Set-ADUser to modify a single user at a time, specifying the user to be modified with the –Identity parameter. You can also use PowerShell's piping functionality to modify many objects at once, by searching for those objects with Get-ADUser or Search-ADAccount and then using the | operator to use those search results as the input for Set-ADUser. You can also use PowerShell's native capabilities to read a text file containing a list of users and then take an action based on each line of that file.

This code shows how to modify multiple users on the basis of a Get-ADUser search:

```
Get-ADUser -SearchBase 'OU=Sales,OU=Users,DC=contoso,DC=com' |
foreach {Set-ADUser -description "Sales"}
Get-ADUser -LDAPFilter "(department='Sales')" | foreach
{Set-ADUser -Add @{costCenter='1010'}
```

This code demonstrates how to loop through a text file containing one username per line:

```
Get-Content c:\scripts\usernames.txt | foreach {Set-ADUser
-Enabled $false}
```

Manage Groups

To ease the administrative burden of assigning permissions to resources on a network, an administrator can create group objects that contain one or more AD security principals: users, computers, MSAs, and group objects nested within other groups. In this way, an administrator can assign resource permissions to a group object, and those permissions will be assigned to each security principal in that group, rather than the administrator having to assign permissions to individual security principals one at a time. To provide flexibility across different environments, AD includes a number of different configuration options for group objects, including the type of group (distribution or security) as well as the scope of the group (domain local, global, or universal.)

In this section, you'll see in action the Windows Server 2008 R2 PowerShell cmdlets that let you automate repetitive tasks associated with group objects: creating and deleting groups, managing the configuration of group objects, and managing the membership of a group object within an AD domain.

Add and Remove Groups

This section describes some of the fundamental tasks required to automate the management of group objects in AD. You'll begin by creating and deleting group objects of various scopes and types, and then you'll use the Get-ADGroup cmdlet to obtain a list of all groups within a domain. You'll also learn how to move a group object from one AD OU to another, as well as how to gather the membership of an AD group and record that information in a text file for reporting or troubleshooting purposes.

Creating and Deleting Distribution Groups

AD specifies two different types of group objects: distribution groups and security groups. Distribution groups may be used in conjunction with an AD-integrated email platform, such as Microsoft Exchange, to send email to multiple users at a time. You can also use security groups to send emails to the users belonging to the group, but security groups also let you assign permissions within AD, the Windows file system, and the like.

The New-ADGroup PowerShell cmdlet allows you to easily automate the creation of AD group objects, with named parameters corresponding to common attributes of a group object:

```
Name

GroupScope—DomainLocal or 0, Global or 1, Universal or 2

Description

DisplayName

GroupCategory—Distribution or 0, Security or 1

HomePage

ManagedBy
```

OtherAttributes—Uses the format -OtherAttributes @{"attribute"="value"}. Separate attributes are separated by semicolons. Individual values in a multivalued attribute are separated by commas, such as OtherAttributes @{'projects'="Project1","Project2"; 'dateOfBirth'=" 12/10/1973"}.

Path—OU in which the group will be created

samAccountName

The next code block demonstrates how to create a distribution group using New-ADGroup and then delete that group using Remove-ADGroup. When you're deleting a group using Remove-ADGroup, you must specify the identity of the group to be removed; you can do so using a DN, a GUID, an SID, or sAMAccountName:

```
New-ADGroup -Path "ou=Sales,dc=contoso,dc=com" -name "Sales
Users" -GroupScope Universal -GroupCategory Distribution
-DisplayName "Sales Users" -ManagedBy "cn=Andy Ruth,ou=Users,
dc=contoso,dc=com"
Remove-ADGroup -Identity "cn=Sales Users,ou=Sales,dc=contoso,dc=com"
```

Creating and Deleting Security Groups

You can use the New-ADGroup cmdlet to create an AD security group as well as a distribution group. Security groups may be used as a single point of administration to assign permissions to all users who are members of that group. Security groups may also be used for purposes of sending email, whereas a distribution group can't be used to assign permissions.

In this code, you see how to create and delete a security group using PowerShell:

```
New-ADGroup -Path "ou=Sales,dc=contoso,dc=com" -name "Sales
Users" -GroupScope Global -GroupCategory Security -DisplayName
"Sales Users" -ManagedBy "cn=Andy Ruth,ou=Users,dc=contoso,
dc=com" -samAccountName SalesUsers
Remove-ADGroup -Identity SalesUsers
```

Gathering a List of All Groups and Their Designated Managers

Similar to using Get-ADUser to search for AD users who meet certain criteria, you can use Get-ADGroup to search for group objects, and to return the group and one or more properties of the group object. One such property is the managedBy attribute, which specifies the DN of the user who is responsible for administration of the group. The following code retrieves all group objects in the current domain and outputs the name of the group along with the DN contained in its `managedBy` attribute:

```
Get-ADGroup -Filter * -Properties Name, ManagedBy | Format-Table
Name, ManagedBy
```

The next code line restricts the output of the `Get-ADGroup` search operation to include only universal security groups:

```
Get-ADGroup -Filter 'GroupCategory -eq "Security" -and
GroupScope -eq "Universal"' -Properties Name, ManagedBy |
Format-Table Name, ManagedBy
```

Moving a Group to Another Organizational Unit

You can use OUs in AD to group objects together for the purpose of delegating administration and applying GPOs to users and computers. As you administer an AD environment over time, you'll probably find it necessary to move objects from one OU into another. When you do so, the objects automatically inherit all the security and GPO settings of the new OU, such as one or more delegated administrators who have permissions over objects within only one specific OU or another.

You use the `Move-ADObject` cmdlet to move a group object from one OU to another within a single domain; but you can use this cmdlet to move almost any other object type in AD, including user objects, computer objects, and contact objects. (If you wish to move a DC into another OU, use the `Move-ADDirectoryServer` cmdlet instead.) You can specify the identity of the object to be moved as either the object's DN or its GUID:

```
Move-ADObject -Identity "CN=SalesAdmins,OU=Sales,DC=Contoso
,DC=Com" -TargetPath "OU=Groups,DC=Contoso,DC=Com" -server
"FABRIKAM-SRV1:60000"
```

N O T E   If you wish to delegate the ability to move an object in AD, you must delegate the ability to delete objects on the source OU and the ability to create objects in the destination OU. (You can further restrict this permission by object type if desired, delegating the ability to create and delete only group objects or only user objects, for example.)

Dumping Every Group and Its Membership to a File

Whether for reporting or troubleshooting purposes, it's often useful to be able to record the membership of an AD group object into a text file for later viewing or analysis. The next code example uses the `Get-ADGroup` cmdlet to retrieve every group object within the domain and then pipe the output of that cmdlet to the `Get-ADGroupMember` cmdlet for processing. (When you specify the –`Recursive` switch for `Get-ADGroupMember`, PowerShell also records the membership of any nested groups within the specified group; if you omit –`Recursive`, you'll only see the direct members of the group as output.)

```
Get-ADGroup -Filter * | Foreach { Get-ADGroupMember -Recursive |
Out-File -FilePath c:\groupmembers.txt -Append }
```

In a more advanced example of the PowerShell pipeline, you can then take *that* result and pipe it one more time to the `Out-File` cmdlet to record the group membership information to a text file. (If your AD environment is very large, this sequence of cmdlets may take a very long time to run. You may wish to restrict the output of the `Get-ADGroup` cmdlet to a specific OU or to a specific scope or type of group, for example.)

Manage Group Settings

This section will demonstrate how to perform and automate a number of tasks relating to AD group objects. As you do with user objects, you may use the `dsacls.exe` command to protect one or more group objects from accidental deletion. You can also use Windows Server 2008 R2 cmdlets to designate a manager of a group, change the scope or type of the group, and view all configured information about one or more group objects.

Preventing a Group from Being Deleted Accidentally

Similar to user objects, as an AD administrator you may wish to protect certain group objects from being accidentally deleted by yourself or by other administrators. To help prevent this, Windows Server 2008 introduced the Protect Object From Accidental Deletion check box in AD Users and Computers, as shown in Figure 6.1.

This protection prevents an administrator from deleting an object without first removing the protection; in the UI, this is done by deselecting this check box.

NOTE   Protect Object From Accidental Deletion is enabled by default on all new OUs created in Windows Server 2008 and higher, but you can configure it on any object in the domain—even leaf objects like users or groups.

FIGURE 6.1   Protecting objects from accidental deletion

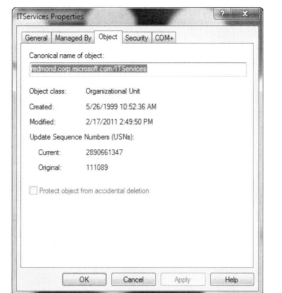

Because this protection simply applies a Deny Delete and Deny Delete Subtree ACL on the object to the EVERYONE group, applying this protection may also be automated at the command line.

This code shows how to protect an individual group object from accidental deletion using the dsacls.exe utility:

```
Dsacls "cn=SalesUsers,ou=Groups,dc=contoso,dc=com" /d
Everyone:SDDT
```

Designating Someone to Manage a Group

In a large or distributed AD environment, you may wish to delegate the ability to perform certain tasks within the domain. One common task is delegating the ability to manage the membership of a security or distribution group. You can perform this task in a number of different ways, one of which is to manipulate the managedBy attribute on the group object. When you add a security principal to the managedBy attribute, AD adds an access control entry (ACE) with the Allow - Write Members permission on the group to the managedBy account.

You can use the `Set-ADGroup` attribute to modify the `managedBy` attribute on a group object, as shown next. You can specify the identity of the security principal in the `managedBy` field by its DN, GUID, SID, or `sAMAccountName`:

```
Set-ADGroup DN=SalesAdmin,OU=Groups,DC=Contoso,DC=Com -ManagedBy
"CN=Andy Ruth,OU=SalesUsers,DC=Contoso,DC=Com"
```

Changing the Scope and Type of a Group

After you've created a group object with a particular type (security or distribution) and scope (domain local, global, or universal), you may later determine that you need to modify one or both of these configured choices. For example, you may have created a group as a distribution group solely for the purpose of sending email messages, but later determine that you also need to use this group to assign permissions to a file share. As another example, you may have accidentally created a group with a global scope only to realize that it should have been a universal group instead. You can use the `Set-ADGroup` cmdlet to modify either of these configuration items as shown:

```
Set-ADGroup -Identity SalesAdmins -GroupCategory Distribution
Set-ADGroup -Identity SalesAdmin -GroupScope Global
```

N O T E   Each AD group scope has certain restrictions on how its scope may be changed. A universal group may be converted to a domain local group, or to a global group if it doesn't contain any universal groups as members. A global group may only be converted to a universal group, and then only if it isn't a member of any other global groups. A domain local group may only be converted to a universal group, and then only if it doesn't include any members that are domain local groups. If you attempt to modify the scope of a group in an unsupported manner, PowerShell will return an error.

Viewing All Information About a Group

Similar to the `Get-ADUser` cmdlet that you saw in the first half of this chapter, you can use `Get-ADGroup` to obtain all configured information about an AD group object. This code demonstrates the syntax of the `Get-ADGroup` cmdlet that performs this task, including piping the output using the `Format-Table` command to present the information in an easily-readable format:

```
Get-ADGroup -Identity CN=SalesAdmin,OU=Groups,DC=Contoso,DC=Com
-Properties * | Get-Member
```

Manage Group Membership

For the final section in this chapter, we'll discuss how to manage the security principals that are configured as members of one or more AD group objects. The most common task you'll need to perform in this vein is adding and removing users from one or more groups, but you'll also find it useful to be able to view the membership of one or more groups, export that information to a file, and even to compare the membership of one group to the membership of another.

Documenting the Membership of Privileged Groups

As a security best practice in any AD domain, you should regularly audit the membership in highly privileged security groups from time to time to ensure that they only contain authorized and intended members. For example, a common security misconfiguration occurs when a user account is "temporarily" added to an administrative group by a technician in order to troubleshoot an issue, but then the technician forgets to remove the user from the group when troubleshooting is completed.

The following code demonstrates how to copy the membership of the Administrators, Schema Admins, Domain Admins, Enterprise Admins, Server Operators, and Account Operators security groups to a text file, with each group's information appending to the end of the file in turn:

```
Get-ADGroupMember Administrators -Recursive | Out-File c:\
admingroups.txt -append
Get-ADGroupMember "Schema Admins" -Recursive | Out-File c:\
admingroups.txt -append
Get-ADGroupMember "Enterprise Admins" -Recursive | Out-File c:\
admingroups.txt -append
Get-ADGroupMember "Server Operators" -Recursive | Out-File c:\
admingroups.txt -append
Get-ADGroupMember "Account Operators" -Recursive | Out-File c:\
admingroups.txt -append
```

NOTE   As a challenge, see if you can use cmdlets that you have learned about elsewhere in this book to read in a list of group names from a text file instead.

Viewing the Membership of a Group

The next code example demonstrates how to use the Get-ADGroupMember cmdlet to retrieve the membership of an AD group. Similar to other examples of managing users and groups that you've seen in this chapter, you can specify the group object that Get-ADGroupMember should target by its GUID, SID, DN, or sAMAccountName:

```
Get-ADGroupMember -Identity "CN=Marketing Project,OU=Groups,
    DC=Contoso,DC=Com"
```

Adding Users to and Removing Users from a Group

The AD PowerShell module in Windows Server 2008 R2 introduces the Add-ADGroupMember and Remove-ADGroupMember cmdlets to easily add a security principal (user, computer, MSA, or another group) to and remove a security principal from an AD group object. You can specify the members to be added or removed as GUIDs, SIDs, DNs, or sAMAccountNames; you can specify multiple individual members by separating the values with commas. You can also use another cmdlet like Get-ADUser to locate several accounts that meet a particular search criterion and pipe the results to either the Add- or Remove- cmdlet.

Because group memberships are determined when a user first logs onto AD and receives their ticket-granting ticket (TGT), changes in group membership aren't reflected until the user logs out of their workstation and logs back in, or uses a tool like klist.ee to destroy their Kerberos tickets. In order for a computer account to reflect a change in group membership, the computer must be rebooted.

This code block shows several examples of how to add users to and remove them from an AD group using PowerShell:

```
Add-ADGroupMember -Identity "CN=SalesUsers,OU=Groups,DC=Contoso,
DC=Com" -Members Arose, Maxb, JSmith
Remove-ADGroupMember -Identity "CN=SalesUsers,OU=Groups,DC=Contoso,
DC=Com" -Members "CN=Andy Ruth,OU=Users,DC=Contoso,DC=Com", Maxb
```

Copying the Membership of One Group to Another

In the following code, you can see how to use a combination of the Get-ADGroup Member and Add-ADGroupMember cmdlets to retrieve the membership of one group (SalesGroup1, in this example) and pipe the output of Get-ADGroupMember as input to `Add-ADGroupMember`, to add each of those security principals to another group (SalesGroup2, in this case):

```
Get-ADGroupMember -Identity SalesUsers -Recursive | Foreach {
Add-ADGroupMember -Identity ProjectUsers -Member $_
```

Exporting Group Membership to a File

Whether for reporting or troubleshooting purposes, it's often useful to be able to record the membership of an AD group object into a text file for later viewing or analysis. The following code uses the `Get-ADGroupMember` cmdlet to retrieve the membership of a single AD group. When you specify the `-Recursive` switch for `Get-ADGroupMember`, PowerShell also records the membership of any nested groups within the specified group; if you omit `-Recursive`, you only see the direct members of the group as output:

```
Get-ADGroupMember -Identity SalesUsers -Recursive
```

Comparing the Membership of Two Groups

Using a combination of the `Get-ADGroupMember` cmdlet and the `Compare-Object` cmdlet, you can compare the membership of two different AD security groups. When you use `Compare-Object` to compare two sets of objects—in this case, two different group memberships—you specify one set of objects as the *reference set* and the other as the *difference set*. An object that only appears in (is only a member of) the reference set is indicated by the <= symbol in the cmdlet output. An object that only appears in the difference set is indicated by =>. If you include the `-IncludeEqual` parameter, objects that appear in both sets are indicated by the == symbol:

```
$salesUsersMembers = Get-ADGroupMember -Identity SalesUsers
$marketingUsersMembers = Ge-tADGroupMember -Identity
MarketingUsers
Compare-Object -ReferenceObject $salesUsersMembers
-DifferenceObject $marketingUsersMembers
```

Managing Computer Accounts, Objects, and Organizational Units

IN THIS CHAPTER, YOU WILL LEARN TO:

n the last chapter, you learned about automating some of the most visible pieces of AD: users and groups. We're going to expand on that topic in this chapter and discuss the automation of any type of object, with a focus on computer objects and organizational units. If you're a day-to-day administrator of an AD environment, then Chapters 6, "Administering User and Group Accounts," and this chapter will probably be the two that you refer to most in this book.

When talking about directory services, such as AD, there are really two parts that can be administered. The first part is the directory service. When administering the directory service, you're administering the way the directory is provided to clients. Some examples include ensuring that replication is healthy or the domain controller (DC) remains running. The second part is to administer the data. This involves keeping the data updated and backed up, and day-to-day administration of data such as adding users and groups. When you put together service administration and data administration, you have the complete picture of what needs to be administered in AD.

Manage Objects

Objects are very generic. The term *object* describes a grouping of attributes or properties that have some structure around them. Users or groups, for example, are just objects with different sets of attributes. The schema is the thing that defines what the object is. If you look at the user object class in the AD schema, you'll see the attributes that user objects can contain. Figure 7.1 shows the attribute definitions for the user object class.

You'll notice that two fields define attributes: Mandatory and Optional. The Optional field is full of different attributes a user can have, but the Mandatory field is empty! Does this mean the user object isn't required to have any attributes? On the contrary, user objects are required to have some attributes, but in order to understand which ones, you have to look at the inheritance of the object. Object classes in AD inherit from other object classes in a type of hierarchy. If you look at the Relationship tab in the user object class, you can see the user object's parent (see Figure 7.2). In this case, it's another object class called organizationalPerson.

FIGURE 7.1   Attributes on the user object class in AD

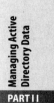

FIGURE 7.2   Showing the parent of the user object class

Now, if you looked at the Relationship tab for the `organizationalPerson` object class, you would see that it inherits from the `person` object class. And if you looked at the `person` object class, you'd see two other things. First, there is a mandatory attribute on the class called `cn`. So, the type of object that inherits from the `person` class must have the `cn` attribute defined. Second, the `person` class also has a parent class, and its name is `top`. The `top` class is a special object class because every object in the directory inherits from it in one way or another. This is essentially the root of the object structure in AD. If you were to examine the `top` class, you'd see a few more mandatory attributes defined. The attributes that an object requires to exist are a combination of the mandatory attributes for each object class in its inheritance hierarchy.

However, parent classes aren't the only objects in a class's inheritance hierarchy. If you look back at Figure 7.2, you'll see an Auxiliary Classes field. An *auxiliary class* is an abstract class, meaning you can't actually create an object from the class. For example, the `mailRecipient` class is an auxiliary class, so you can't create a `mailRecipient` object. Instead, auxiliary classes must be attached to other object classes. In doing so, the other object classes inherit the mandatory and optional attributes from the auxiliary class. This way, you can apply a set of attributes to a specific object class without affecting the other objects in its inheritance chain. A good example is the `securityPrincipal` class. It's an auxiliary class that turns the object it attaches to into a security principal. In doing so, it adds the `objectSID` and `samAccountName` attributes as mandatory attributes on the object. You could add these attributes directly to objects themselves, but using the auxiliary class provides a sort of template, which makes the process easier.

The last thing we want to point out in Figure 7.2 is the Possible Superior field. When you're administering objects, the data in this field is useful because it may prevent some frustration when you write AD scripts. Possible Superior defines the types of objects in which the object class can be created. The most common is the `organizationalUnit` class. If you look back at Figure 7.2, you'll see that it's saying that `user` objects can exist in a `builtinDomain` object, a `domainDNS` object, or an `organizationalUnit` object.

Now that you understand what objects are made of, let's look at how to manage them.

Create and Edit Objects

Creating and editing objects in AD are the fundamental characteristics of most of the PowerShell scripts you'll write to automate tasks. This applies not only to the management of data in AD, but also to many of the service-management aspects of AD, which involve modifying objects as well. Because these skills are core to AD administration with PowerShell, it's important to fully understand them and be able to use these skills efficiently. Also, as you work through this chapter, you'll see several examples involving different objects types. Keep in mind that these techniques apply to all objects in AD, including users, groups, computers, printers, and so on.

The AD PowerShell modules provide several cmdlets for working with objects. In this section, you'll be working primarily with these cmdlets. We'll discuss objects in light of using Active Directory Services Interface (ADSI) as well, but for Windows Server 2008 R2 environments, it's much easier to use the cmdlets in AD PowerShell. You can retrieve a list of these object cmdlets by running the following command in PowerShell after you've imported the AD module:

```
Get-Command -Module ActiveDirectory *object*
```

Table 7.1 lists these cmdlets and explains what each does. You'll be using most of these cmdlets in this section, but a couple of others (such as `Restore-ADObject`) will be discussed in later chapters.

TABLE 7.1   PowerShell Cmdlets Used for Working With AD Objects

Cmdlet	Description
Get-ADObject	Retrieves an object from AD.
Move-ADObject	Moves an object to a different location in AD.
New-ADObject	Creates a new object in AD.
Remove-ADObject	Deletes an object in AD.
Rename-ADObject	Changes the name (and Common Name) of an object in AD. This cmdlet can't be used to change the samAccountName, UPN, or any other attribute that may be used for identifying the object—only the name and CN attributes.
Restore-ADObject	Restores a deleted object from the AD Recycle Bin or from its tombstoned state. This cmdlet does not restore data from backups of AD.
Set-ADObject	Configures attributes on objects. Unlike the Rename-ADObject cmdlet, Set-ADObject can be used to change the samAccountName and various other attributes on an object.

Creating and Removing Objects

When creating AD objects in PowerShell, you need to specify a few different items:

▶ A name for the object

▶ The type of object you're creating

▶ Any mandatory attributes for the object

To create objects, you can use the `New-ADObject` cmdlet. Creating an object can be as simple as providing its name and type. The following example creates a `Contact` object for Lincoln Alexander:

```
New-ADObject "Lincoln Alexander" -Type Contact
```

The value specified in the `Type` parameter is the LDAP display name of the object's definition in the schema. To determine what this value is, you can use the AD Schema tool to find the display name:

1. From a DC (or a workstation with the AD management tools installed), open a command prompt and type the following command:

   ```
   regsvr32 schmmgmt.dll
   ```

   You should see a dialog that says the DLL was registered successfully. This DLL is used for managing the schema and isn't registered by default.

2. Open the Microsoft Management Console by typing **mmc** at the command prompt.

3. In the MMC dialog, click File ➢ Add/Remove Snap-In.

4. In the Add Or Remove Snap-ins dialog, select AD Schema from the list on the left, and click the Add button. Then, click OK.

5. When the AD Schema snap-in has loaded, expand the Classes folder in the browser tree in the left pane. This folder lists all the object classes that AD can create.

6. Double-click a class to bring up its Properties dialog.

7. In the General tab of the dialog, you note the Common Name field. This is the property you'll use when creating an instance of this object, as shown in Figure 7.3.

FIGURE 7.3   Viewing the name of the object class for the object you're creating

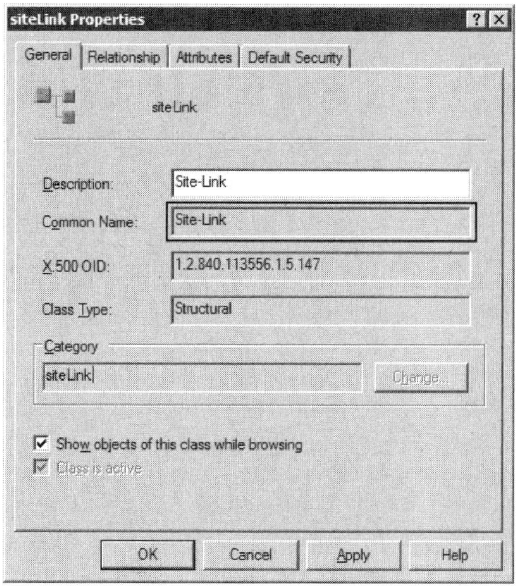

You can also indicate the attributes to set during the creation of the object by specifying the `OtherAttributes` parameter and listing the attributes and values in an array. This form looks like the following. Notice that each attribute and value are separated by a semicolon:

```
@{Attribute1="Value1"; Attribute2="Value2"; Attribute3="Value3"}
```

For example, if you want to add a phone number to the `contact` object you create, you can add the `telephoneNumber` attribute:

```
New-ADObject "Jenny Jones" -Type Contact -OtherAttributes ↵
    @{telephoneNumber="867-5309"}
```

Finding an Object

Searching for objects is one of the most common operations that AD performs. Directory-search algorithms are optimized, so whether you need a single object or an array of objects, AD can return those objects quickly. There is more than one way to search for objects in the directory, but we'll start by examining how to do this with the AD module. The cmdlet you use is `Get-ADObject`. The

Get-ADObject cmdlet can retrieve any object type that exists in AD. If you want to specifically focus on users, computers, or groups, there are special cmdlets for those object types that are a little easier to use. Those cmdlets are discussed in other chapters throughout this book. But to find one or more generic objects, you use the Get-ADObject cmdlet.

To use the Get-ADObject cmdlet, the only thing you need to pass in is a filter. This filter defines what objects are returned in the query. These objects can be captured in an object variable in PowerShell and used however you'd like. The filter you specify defines the attribute on which you're matching, the value you want to match, and the comparison operator you're using. For example, to find all users whose last name is Smith, you can use the following filter:

```
{sn -eq "Smith"}
```

In this example, the sn attribute represents the surname (last name) of the user. -eq is the comparison operator and states that the last name must be equal to the value you specify. We discussed comparison operators in Chapter 1 ("Using PowerShell with Active Directory"), so we recommend going back and looking at Table 1.6 for a refresher. And finally, "Smith" is the value of the last name you're matching on. Because you're comparing string values in this case, the comparison isn't case-sensitive.

You can also use more than one filter statement in the command. For example, suppose you want to return all objects whose last name is Smith or Jones. That filter looks like this:

```
{sn -eq "Smith" -or sn -eq "Jones"}
```

After you've constructed your filter, you just need to call the Get-ADObject cmdlet and pass your filter in with the -Filter parameter:

```
Get-ADObject -Filter {sn -eq "Smith"}
```

Following this example will output the Smiths to the screen in a list. The more likely case is that you'll want to capture the Smiths into a variable that you can use later:

```
$smiths = Get-ADObject -Filter {sn -eq "Smith"}
```

By default, only a few LDAP properties are returned with the object. You can get additional properties by specifying the -Properties parameter on the Get-ADObject cmdlet. If you need additional properties, you can list them in the -Properties parameter and separate them with commas. For example, to get the department name and telephone number for each of the Smiths, you can use the following command:

```
$smiths = Get-ADObject -Filter {sn -eq "Smith"} -Properties ↵
   department, telephoneNumber
```

Enumerating the Properties of an Object

Often you just want to grab an object and view its properties. Because PowerShell is an object-based command environment, you can place a copy of the AD object into a variable in PowerShell and work with that copy in your script. If you're using the object multiple times in a script, this approach makes the most sense because you're working with a cache of the object.

First you need to retrieve a copy of the AD object. You can do this by using the Get-ADObject cmdlet as described in the previous section, "Finding an Object." When you have the object in a variable, you can list its properties by typing in the variable name. For example, the following commands retrieve the object whose name is Lincoln Alexander and display its properties in a list:

```
PS C:\> $obj = Get-ADObject -Filter {cn -eq "Lincoln Alexander"}
PS C:\> $obj | fl
DistinguishedName : CN=Lincoln Alexander,OU=Contacts,DC=contoso
                    ,DC=com
Name              : Lincoln Alexander
ObjectClass       : contact
ObjectGUID        : 7a8f353f-029c-498f-92f8-a24d0a775f2c
```

As you can see, this doesn't provide much information about the object. A default set of properties is returned. Therefore, you need to specify the additional properties that you want when you search for the object. We showed you how to do this using the -Properties parameter in the previous section. But when enumerating the properties of an object, you may not know which properties exist or which ones you want to view. Therefore, you can use a wildcard in this command to return every property that has a value. This command resembles the following:

```
PS C:\> $obj = Get-ADObject -Filter {cn -eq "Lincoln ↵
   Alexander"} -Properties *
PS C:\> $obj | fl
c                             : US
CanonicalName                 : contoso.com/Contacts/Lincoln
```

```
                                          Alexander
        CN                              : Lincoln Alexander
        co                              : United States
        company                         : Contoso
        countryCode                     : 840
        Created                         : 3/24/2011 9:29:51 PM
        createTimeStamp                 : 3/24/2011 9:29:51 PM
        Deleted                         :
        department                      : Human Resources
        Description                     :
        DisplayName                     : Lincoln Alexander
        DistinguishedName               : CN=Lincoln Alexander,OU=Conta
                                          cts,DC=contoso,DC=com
        dSCorePropagationData           : {12/31/1600 7:00:00 PM}
        givenName                       : Lincoln
        instanceType                    : 4
        isDeleted                       :
        l                               : Anytown
        LastKnownParent                 :
        mail                            : lincoln@contoso.com
        Modified                        : 3/24/2011 9:35:06 PM
        modifyTimeStamp                 : 3/24/2011 9:35:06 PM
        Name                            : Lincoln Alexander
        nTSecurityDescriptor            : System.DirectoryServices.Acti
                                          veDirectorySecurity
        ObjectCategory                  : CN=Person,CN=Schema,CN=Config
                                          uration,DC=contoso,DC=com
        ObjectClass                     : contact
        ObjectGUID                      : 7a8f353f-029c-498f-92f8-a24d0
                                          a775f2c
        postalCode                      : 73841
        ProtectedFromAccidentalDeletion : False
        sDRightsEffective               : 15
        sn                              : Alexander
        st                              : NT
        streetAddress                   : 123 Oak Street
        telephoneNumber                 : 555-123-4567
        title                           : Analyst
        uSNChanged                      : 20578
```

```
uSNCreated                    : 20572
whenChanged                   : 3/24/2011 9:35:06 PM
whenCreated                   : 3/24/2011 9:29:51 PM
```

Moving an Object to Another OU

Moving an object to another OU is an easy task when you're working in the Active Directory Users and Computers tool. There, you can drag and drop the object wherever you'd like. However, in a command line or script, you're changing the Distinguished Name (DN) attribute of the object. When you do this, you change the logical hierarchy that the object falls under. At its deepest levels, AD doesn't have a hierarchy. When objects are stored in the AD database, each object is stored in the table in a separate row. In this database, there is no sense of hierarchy; every object is just a record. This hierarchy is built out according to the DN of each object when the directory is accessed by an application. Building out the application's view of this hierarchy is performed by NTDSA.DLL.

One impact you need to keep in mind is that when you move an object, the object's parent changes. Often, an object will receive a set of permissions or Group Policies based on its parent container or a grandparent container. By moving the object, you'll likely affect these permissions or Group Policies. Consider the following example. Suppose that you have a Group Policy applied to a user object in the Sales OU. If you move that user to the Accounting OU, that Group Policy will no longer be applied to that user. The same is true for permissions on the object. Suppose an administrator has permissions to change the telephone number attribute on the users in the Sales OU. The users in that OU get this permission applied through an access control entry (ACE) on the object. The user object has inheritable permissions enabled on it and therefore receives the permissions applied at its parent (the Sales OU) or grandparent object. When you move that user from the Sales OU to the Accounting OU, the set of inherited permissions changes as well. This isn't irreversible, however: You can move the object back or apply the Group Policy or permissions to the new OU.

First, let's look at what it takes to move an object using the AD module. To move an object, you use the Move-ADObject cmdlet. This cmdlet is easy to use; you only need to pass in two parameters. The first parameter (-Identity) is the DN of the object you're moving. The second parameter (-TargetPath) is the DN of the target location for the object. This location doesn't have to be an OU—it can be a container or any other location that can act as a parent to the object type you're moving. Both parameters are positional, so you can run the cmdlet without having to specify the parameter name as long as you put them in the correct order. For example, the following cmdlet moves Nora Shea's contact object from the Sales OU to the Accounting OU:

```
Move-ADObject "cn=Nora Shea,ou=Sales,dc=contoso,dc=com" ↵
   "ou=Accounting,dc=contoso,dc=com"
```

This command is functionally equivalent to the following command, with the difference being that you're specifying the parameter name rather than depending on the position of the parameter:

```
Move-ADObject -Identity "cn=Nora Shea,ou=Sales,dc=contoso,↵
   dc=com" -TargetPath "ou=Accounting,dc=contoso,dc=com"
```

To use ADSI to move an object, you use the `MoveTo` method. The parameter you pass in to the method is the LDAP of the target location. For example, the following commands move Nora Shea's contact object to the Accounting OU, just as the AD module example did:

```
PS C:\> $nora = [ADSI]"LDAP://cn=Nora Shea,ou=Sales,↵
   dc=contoso,dc=com"
PS C:\> $nora.MoveTo("LDAP://ou=Accounting,dc=contoso,dc=com")
```

One important thing to keep in mind when using ADSI to move objects is that you're required to specify the target location as an LDAP path, meaning that you must prefix the DN with `LDAP://`. Also, in the `LDAP://` prefix, `LDAP` must be all capital letters. If you use lowercase letters (`ldap`), ADSI will throw an error. This is generally how all LDAP paths are processed in ADSI.

Determining When an Object Was Created or Last Changed

When an object in AD is created or modified, metadata is stored about that object. Much of this metadata is used during the replication process to help determine whether an object or attribute was updated and whether it needs to be replicated to another DC. There is also some timestamp information stored with each object. In particular, each object stores two attributes that can be used to determine when it was created or last modified, `whenCreated` and `whenChanged`.

Getting the Creation Date

To determine when an object was created, you can use the `whenCreated` attribute. This attribute is included in the abstract class `top`, from which every object is derived. Because of this abstract class, the `whenCreated` attribute exists on all objects in the directory. Therefore, you can use this attribute to determine when any object was created, including the domain object at the root of the directory. As a side note, if you examine the whenCreated attribute of the domain object, you can see when the domain was created.

The only thing you need to do to read this data is grab the object in PowerShell and display the whenCreated property. First, use the Get-ADObject cmdlet to get the object you want to examine, as shown in the section "Finding an Object." From there, you can simply display the whenCreated attribute. The following example looks at the domain object for the contoso.com domain and displays its creation date:

Managing Active Directory Data

PART II

```
PS C:\> $domain = Get-ADObject "dc=contoso,dc=com" ↵
  -Properties whenCreated
PS C:\> $domain.whenCreated


Saturday, December 11, 2010 3:36:01 PM
```

If you leave off the -Properties parameter, the whenCreated attribute won't be available. By default, this attribute isn't included in the set of attributes that are available in the Get-ADObject cmdlet.

Getting the Modified Date

The process of learning when an object was modified is very similar to the process for getting its creation date. This information is kept in the attribute whenChanged. Therefore, in order to get the information, you only need to display this attribute. The following example displays the date and time when Nora Shea's contact object was last updated:

```
PS C:\> $user = Get-ADObject "cn=Nora Shea,ou=contacts, ↵
  dc=contoso,dc=com" -Properties whenChanged
PS C:\> $user.whenChanged


Friday, January 28, 2011 9:50:18 AM
```

Searching for Recently Created Objects

Knowing the creation date and modified data by itself may not be all that useful. However, when used in the appropriate script, it can provide some very useful information about your directory. As an example, the script in Listing 7.1 uses this technique to display all objects created in the past seven days.

LISTING 7.1: *GetRecentObjects.ps1*

```
## File Name: GetRecentObjects.ps1
## Description:
## Retrieves a list of the recently created objects from Active
## Directory. Modify the $num_days and $output_file variables
##  to change the number of days back that we are looking for
##  new objects and the HTML file that the report is written to.
##
# Set the HTML file that you want to write the report to
$output_file = "c:\recent_objects.html"
# Set the number of days that we are searching for objects
$num_days = 7
# Header displayed on the HTML report
$header = "Objects Created Within the Past $num_days Day(s)"
# Defines the style of the HTML output
$style = "<style>BODY{background-color:lightgrey;}"
$style += "TABLE{border-width: 1px;border-style: solid;"
$style += "border-color: black;border-collapse: collapse;}"
$style += "TH{border-width: 1px;padding: 0px;"
$style += "border-style: solid;border-color: black;"
$style += "background-color:#333; color: white}"
$style += "TD{border-width: 1px;padding: 0px;"
$style += "border-style: solid;border-color: black;"
$style += "background-color:#EFF4FB}</style>"
# Gets the current date minus 7 days for the search filter
$current_date = Get-Date
$past_days = New-Timespan -Days $num_days
$start_date = $current_date.Subtract($past_days)

# Retrieve all objects created within the past 7 days
$objects = Get-ADObject -Filter {whenCreated -gt $start_date} `
  -Properties whenCreated
# Write the objects out to the HTML file
$formatted_obj = $objects | Select-Object distinguishedName,
  whenCreated, objectClass
$html_out = $formatted_obj | ConvertTo-HTML -head $style `
  -body "<H2>$header<H2>"
```

```
$html_out | Out-File $output_file
# Display the HTML report
Invoke-Expression $output_file
```

Clearing an Object's Attribute

Sometimes, when you're working with objects, you may need to clear the contents of an attribute. This may not be as easy as it sounds. Depending on the type of attribute, simply setting the attribute to a null string may not work. Fortunately, this is simple when you're working with the AD module in PowerShell. You can call the `Set-ADObject` cmdlet and set its `-Clear` parameter to the attribute you want to clear out. The following example clears the `manager` attribute in Nora Shea's contact object:

```
Set-ADObject "cn=Nora Shea,ou=contacts,dc=contoso,dc=com" ↵
  -Clear manager
```

Using ADSI, on the other hand, is a bit trickier. ADSI contains a flag called `ADS_PROPERTY_CLEAR`. Instead of setting an attribute to null or an empty string, you pass in the `ADS_PROPERTY_CLEAR` flag. To use this flag, you call the `PutEx` method on the ADSI object and pass in the `ADS_PROPERTY_CLEAR` flag as the first parameter. This flag has a value of 1, so you can also pass in 1 as the first parameter. The following example clears out the `manager` attribute on Nora Shea's contact object:

```
PS C:\> $nora = [ADSI]"LDAP://cn=Nora Shea,ou=contacts,↵
  dc=contoso,dc=com"
PS C:\> $nora.PutEx(1, "manager", 0)
PS C:\> $nora.SetInfo()
```

Exporting Objects to a File

So far in this chapter, we've given you some methods you can use to search for objects, report on them, and manipulate them. Often, you'll want to not only view this information, but also extract some of it from AD so you can generate reports outside of PowerShell. For example, you may want to dump objects into a comma-separated values (CSV) file so you can import them into a lab environment or a build a spreadsheet from them.

PowerShell has built-in cmdlets for handling this functionality. In order to export objects from AD, you need to pass the objects into one of the following cmdlets:

► `Export-CSV`: Exports data to a comma-separated file

► `Export-CliXML`: Exports data to an XML file

Dumping Objects to a CSV File

First we're going to look at how to export objects to a CSV file. CSV files can be useful because they can be easily imported into Microsoft Excel and used to generate reports or perform mass manipulation of the data. To export AD objects to a CSV file, you pass the objects into the `Export-CSV` cmdlet. The following example uses the AD module to export a list of `contact` objects and their properties:

```
$contacts = Get-ADObject -Filter {objectClass -eq "contact"} ↵
  -Properties *
$contacts | Export-Csv c:\contacts.csv
```

The CSV file has a header row that contains the name of the attribute in each of the fields. When you import the CSV file into Excel or a similar spreadsheet application, the fields in the CSV are parsed into cells.

Exporting Objects to an XML File

You can also export the objects into an XML file. Doing so can be useful if you have another script or application that can consume this data in the XML format. To export the data to XML, use the `Export-CliXML` cmdlet. The process is similar to the CSV file export; just pipeline the objects into the `Export-CliXML` cmdlet, and specify the name of the output file:

```
$contacts = Get-ADObject -Filter {objectClass -eq "contact"} ↵
  -Properties *
$contacts | Export-CliXML c:\contacts.xml
```

Work with Service Principal Names

Service principal names (SPNs) are often misunderstood. Usually, when they're needed, they're created either by the application or by the administrator without a second thought. However, they're also a major source of frustration when they don't work right. Before we dive into how to work with SPNs, we'll first spend some time explaining how they work.

Registering a Service Principal Name

Perhaps the best way to understand SPNs is to take a look at how clients authenticate to services. The primary authentication protocol used in Windows is the Kerberos protocol. In older versions of Windows, the NT LAN Manager (NTLM) protocol was the primary protocol used, and it still is for non-domain joined machines. Kerberos is a more secure protocol, so when possible, Kerberos is preferred over NTLM. However, NTLM is still used as a fallback in some cases.

When a client accesses a service on a remote server, the client has to be authenticated. For instance, consider the case where a user accesses a file share. The server must know who the user is so it can enforce the appropriate permissions on the file share. If the server uses NTLM to authenticate the user, it generates some random data and gives it to the client. The client uses its password to encrypt this data and sends it back to the server. The server then takes the encrypted data from the client and sends it to a DC along with the client's user name and the random data in unencrypted form. The DC uses the client's password in AD to encrypt the unencrypted data (because this is the same data that the server sent to the client). If the data encrypted by the DC matches the data that the client encrypted, then that is used as proof that the client knew the password.

Kerberos, on the other hand, uses the concept of *tickets*. When Kerberos authentication is used in the same scenario, the file server never challenges the user for authentication. Rather, the user goes to the DC and requests a ticket that it can use to access the server. This ticket is encrypted with a hash of the server's password (also referred to as a *long-term secret*) and given back to the client. Because the server's ticket is encrypted, the client can't view what's inside or modify it. The client sends the ticket to the server, and the server decrypts the ticket with its copy of the long-term secret. When the DC issued the server's ticket to the client, it embedded a session key that the server can use to authenticate the client. After the server decrypts the ticket, it then has this session key and can use it to decrypt the client's authenticator message, which was also passed in the ticket. The bottom line is that the server has everything it needs to authenticate the client without having to mediate the client's communication with the DC.

The process we just described explains the need for an SPN. The SPN creates an identity for a service. When the client requests a ticket for the service, the client sends the SPN to the DC. The DC then determines which account holds the SPN (an SPN can only be associated with one account, but one account can have multiple SPNs). The DC uses the long-term secret of this account to encrypt the ticket that it sends back to the client. When the client sends this ticket to the service (as in the Kerberos walkthrough we just discussed), the account under which the service is running uses its long-term secret to decrypt the ticket. The result is that the service now has a shared secret with the client that it can use for secure communications and to verify the client's identity.

HOST SPNs

In working with AD, you may come across a particular SPN known as a HOST SPN. The HOST SPN is a generic SPN that applies to many services. The account under which these services run is the server's computer account, such as Local System. Therefore, when an SPN is used to acquire a Kerberos ticket for these HOST services, AD maps the HOST SPN to the server's computer object in AD and uses its long-term secret to encrypt the ticket.

One other common point of confusion with SPNs is how many different SPNs should be registered for a service. The answer is, as many as are needed. When the client requests a Kerberos ticket for a service, it doesn't have any way of finding the service's SPN. Instead, the client constructs what it thinks the SPN is from the information it has. For example, it may use a configuration setting in the client application or the name of the server that you tell the client to use. It doesn't really matter what this name is. If the client could potentially use it to build the SPN, an SPN needs to be created for that name and associated with the account under which the service is running. That's why you'll often see SPNs registered as both fully qualified names and NetBIOS names. For that particular application, there's a chance that the client could use either the fully qualified name or the host name to build the SPN, so the DC needs to be able to resolve that SPN to an account for creating the Kerberos ticket.

SPNs are stored on the account they're associated with in the `servicePrincipalName` attribute. This attribute is multivalued, because multiple SPNs can be associated with a single account. When it comes down to it, an SPN is just an attribute on a user or computer account in AD. To create an SPN, you need to set this attribute. But before you can do that, you need to know how the attribute is formatted. The format of the `servicePrincipalName` attribute is as follows.

```
ServiceClass/HostName:Port AccountName
```

There are generally four parts to an SPN. Table 7.2 explains what each of the components does.

TABLE 7.2   Components of an SPN

Name	Requirement	Description
ServiceClass	Mandatory	Identifies an instance of the service that the SPN is for.
HostName	Mandatory	Identifies the host name on which the service is running.
Port	Optional	Identifies the port on which the service is listening. There may be more than one instance running on the host. If so, the port component distinguishes one instance from another.
AccountName	Optional	Allows you to associate an additional account identifier with the SPN.

More often than not, when you're dealing with SPNs, you'll only use the ServiceClass/HostName format. You may use the port every now and then, but as shown in Table 7.2, the port isn't a required component. One question that often comes up is, "What should you use for the HostName component?" Generally speaking, you want an SPN registered for each alias the host goes by. For instance, if you're registering an SPN for a web service running on the computer contoso-web.contoso.com to use Kerberos authentication, you might register the following SPNs:

- ► http/contoso-web.contoso.com
- ► http/contoso-web
- ► http/www.contoso.com

The key thing to remember is that the client that requests the service ticket for the contoso-web.contoso.com server needs to build the SPN and send it to the DC. If the client accesses the server with the name contoso-web.contoso.com, then that's likely to be what the client builds the SPN on. The DC then needs to be able to associate the SPN http/contoso-web.contoso.com with the account under which the web service is running, which is the account on which you create the SPN.

To create an SPN in PowerShell, you first need to get an instance of the account the SPN will be associated with. Then, you need to set the servicePrincipalName attribute. With the AD module in PowerShell, you can do this with a single command. The following command sets an SPN called `http/contoso-web` `.contoso.com` on the account `svc_http`. To add additional SPNs, you can run this command as many times as needed. Each time, the SPN will be added to the multivalued attribute:

```
Set-ADObject "cn=svc_http,ou=Accounts,dc=contoso,dc=com" -Add ↵
@{servicePrincipalName="http/contoso-web.contoso.com"}
```

Finding Duplicate Service Principal Names

As discussed in the previous section, SPNs play a vital role in the Kerberos authentication process. In the past, SPNs have caused a lot of problems because they're often misunderstood. It's understandable why that's the case, because you need a lot of background knowledge about authentication protocols if you really want to understand what the SPN is for.

One aspect of SPNs that has plagued administrators for years is the issue of duplication. If you think back to the previous section, we discussed the fact that an account can have multiple SPNs associated with it. This makes sense, because a single service account could be used for multiple services on many different servers. However, we also stated that you can only associate an SPN with one account. The reason is that the DC needs to be able to tie an SPN to a single account in AD. Because the SPN represents the identity of the service, that identity must be unique. So although you can have one account with multiple SPNs, you can only use an SPN on one account.

If you're experiencing a problem and think a duplicate SPN may be the culprit, there are a couple of different ways to tell. The quickest is to look in your DC's event logs for an error event whose source is the Kerberos Key Distribution Center (KDC) with event ID 11. If you find this event-log entry, it will specifically tell you that there are duplicate SPNs and will even tell you which SPNs are duplicates. At that point, you need to determine which account the SPN really needs to be associated with and then remove the SPN from the accounts it doesn't belong to.

If you don't want to wait for an error event in your DC, you can use PowerShell to find duplicate SPNs as well. This technique can be useful if you're scripting the installing of a network service, such as SQL or Forefront Identity Manager. Before creating your SPN via PowerShell, it's a good idea to check for duplicates first.

Checking for duplicate SPNs is as simple as retrieving all the SPNs in the domain and performing a query against each one to see if it exists anywhere else. The

PowerShell script in Listing 7.2 uses the AD module to find and report on each duplicate SPN in the current domain. This script prints out the list of duplicates to the PowerShell console, but you can use the function in your own scripts to make decisions about whether you should continue with creating an SPN or not.

LISTING 7.2: *GetDuplicateSPNs.ps1*

```
## File Name: GetDuplicateSPNs.ps1
## Description:
## Uses a function called FindDupSPNs to report on duplicate
## SPNs found in the current domain.
##
Function FindDupSPNs
{
    $objects = Get-ADObject -Filter {servicePrincipalName
        -like "*"} -Properties ServicePrincipalName
    foreach ($col_SPN in $objects)
    {
        foreach ($SPN in $col_SPN.servicePrincipalName)
        {
            $all += @($SPN)
        }
    }
    $unique_SPNs = $all | Sort-Object | Get-Unique
    foreach ($SPN in $unique_SPNs)
    {
        $dup_search = Get-ADObject -Filter {servicePrincipalName
            -eq $SPN}
        if ($dup_search.Count -gt 1)
        {
            Write-Host "Duplicate SPN found: $SPN"
            Write-Host "-" -NoNewLine
            $dup_search | ft distinguishedName -HideTableHeaders
        }
    }
}


FindDupSPNs
```

Manage Computer Accounts

The AD module in PowerShell gives you the ability to handle generic objects through the *ADObject cmdlets. Realistically, you can likely handle any situation on any object type you're working on using these cmdlets. However, the module also provides some cmdlets that are focused on working with computer objects specifically. Although at the end of the day, computer objects are really just another object type, sometimes some administrative tasks require more handling than just modifying an attribute. In this section, we'll focus on computer objects and explain how to use PowerShell to manipulate them.

Create and Modify Computer Accounts

When you're working with computer objects in the directory, the AD module provides several cmdlets that you can use. You can view this list of cmdlets by running the following command:

```
Get-Command *computer -Module ActiveDirectory
```

Table 7.3 describes each of these cmdlets and how they're used to work with computer objects.

TABLE 7.3   AD Module Computer Cmdlets

Cmdlet	Description
New-ADComputer	Creates a new computer object in the domain
Remove-ADComputer	Removes an existing computer object from the domain
Get-ADComputer	Retrieves one or more computer objects based on the criteria that you specify when running the cmdlet
Set-ADComputer	Can be used to change the properties of a computer object

Pre-creating Computer Accounts

Computer accounts don't always have to be created ahead of time in AD. However, there are some cases when doing so is necessary or beneficial. For instance, you may have a group of administrators or users adding computers to the domain in a remote location. By creating the computer accounts in the domain for them, the users don't need permissions in the directory to create these accounts themselves. Rather, their accounts just need permissions to use the existing computer account.

Pre-created computer accounts are also necessary when you're performing an offline domain join or joining a computer to a domain via a read-only DC (RODC; both scenarios are covered later in this chapter).

Creating a computer account in AD is relatively straightforward. You use the `New-ADComputer` cmdlet to create a computer object and set its properties at the time it's created. After the account is created, anyone with adequate permissions can add a computer to the domain that uses that account. When the account is created, a random 240-character password is set; this password is used to authenticate the computer to the domain. In order for a secure session to be established by a computer and a DC, this password must be known by both parties. This can happen in one of two ways:

- ▶ The password for the computer account can be set to the name of the computer in lowercase characters. This is what happens when you reset the password for the computer object in Active Directory Users and Computers.

- ▶ The password can be randomly generated. When the computer joins the domain, you're prompted for account credentials, which are used for authentication instead of a prenegotiated password.

The `New-ADComputer` cmdlet generates a random password by default, but you can choose to specify your own using the `AccountPassword` parameter. If you specify the name of the computer object in lowercase letters as the password, then this is functionally equivalent to assigning the computer object as a pre-Windows 2000 computer when creating the computer account in the Active Directory Users and Computers tool.

The following command creates a computer account in the domain at which you logged in:

```
New-ADComputer <computername>
```

Modifying a Computer Account's Properties

To modify the properties of a computer account, you can use the `Set-ADComputer` cmdlet. The only thing you have to do is specify the name of the computer and the attributes you want to change. The convenient thing about using this cmdlet instead of the `Set-ADObject` cmdlet is that you don't have to know the DN of the computer object. Because of this, it's not necessary to know where the computer resides in the OU structure; nor do you have to perform an additional query to obtain this information before running the cmdlet.

Managing Active
Directory Data

PART II

The following example changes the description of the computer account called tom-laptop:

```
Set-ADComputer tom-laptop -Description "Tom's Windows 7 Laptop"
```

There are several named parameters included with this cmdlet that you can use to change the properties directly. In the previous example, Description is one such named parameter. However, there won't be a parameter for every attribute that you want to modify. If you encounter an attribute that doesn't have a parameter, you can use the Replace parameter to replace an attribute's value by name. For example, the following command updates the Department attribute, which isn't exposed as a named parameter in the Set-ADComputer cmdlet:

```
Set-ADComputer tom-laptop -Replace @{department="Sales"}
```

When specifying the values to replace, use the format @{*attribute*="*value*"}. If you need to replace additional attributes, you can separate them with semicolons inside the curly brackets.

Deleting a Computer Account

To delete a computer account from your domain, you can use the Remove-ADComputer cmdlet. It's important to note that deleting the account doesn't mean the computer is properly unjoined from the domain. If you don't unjoin the computer from the domain first, the computer will still think it's a valid computer on the domain. If you're allowing cached credentials on the computer, a user who has previously logged in can unplug the network connection and log in with those cached credentials. Therefore, it's important to keep in mind that deleting a computer account isn't an adequate procedure to control data leakage during a security breach.

The following example removes the computer account for the computer named tom-laptop from the domain. The presence of the Confirm parameter at the end of the command ensures that you're not prompted with an "Are you sure that you want to continue?" message:

```
Remove-ADComputer tom-laptop -Confirm:$false
```

In removing computer accounts, you may run into a situation where you receive the following error message:

```
Remove-ADComputer : The directory service can perform the requested
operation only on a leaf object
At line:1 char:18
+ Remove-ADComputer <<<<  tom-laptop -Confirm:$false
```

```
    + CategoryInfo          : NotSpecified: (tom-laptop:ADComp
 uter) [Remove-ADComputer], ADException
    + FullyQualifiedErrorId : The directory service can
 perform the requested operation only on a leaf object,
 Microsoft.ActiveDirectory.Management.Commands.RemoveADComputer
```

This error message means child objects were attached to the computer object. The Remove-ADComputer cmdlet can't delete those child objects, so you must remove them manually before using the Remove-ADComputer cmdlet to delete the computer account. An easier approach may be to use the Remove-ADObject cmdlet instead and specify the -Recursive parameter. The difference is that when you use the Remove-ADObject cmdlet, you need to know the DN of the computer account, so this technique requires some additional work. The following commands remove the computer account using this approach:

```
PS C:\> $comp = Get-ADComputer tom-laptop
PS C:\> Remove-ADObject $comp.DistinguishedName -Recursive ↵
  -Confirm:$false
```

Changing the Default Location for Computer Accounts

The default location for computer accounts in the domain is known as a *well-known container*. This means a globally unique identifier (GUID) that never changes is associated with this location. DCs are hard-coded with this GUID and maintain a mapping of the GUID and the location in the directory. For the Computers well-known container, this GUID is AA312825768811D1ADED00C04FD8D5CD. To see a list of well-known containers, you can run the following commands:

```
PS C:\> $rootDSE = Get-ADRootDSE
PS C:\> $wko = Get-ADObject $rootDSE.DefaultNamingContext ↵
  -Properties wellKnownObjects
PS C:\> $wko.wellKnownObjects


B:32:6227F0AF1FC2410D8E3BB10615BB5B0F:CN=NTDS Quotas,DC=contoso,
DC=com
B:32:F4BE92A4C777485E878E9421D53087DB:CN=Microsoft,CN=Program
Data,DC=contoso,DC=com
B:32:09460C08AE1E4A4EA0F64AEE7DAA1E5A:CN=Program Data,DC=contoso,
DC=com
B:32:22B70C67D56E4EFB91E9300FCA3DC1AA:CN=ForeignSecurityPrincipals,
DC=contoso,DC=com
```

```
B:32:18E2EA80684F11D2B9AA00C04F79F805:CN=Deleted Objects,DC=contoso,
DC=com
B:32:2FBAC1870ADE11D297C400C04FD8D5CD:CN=Infrastructure,DC=contoso,
DC=com
B:32:AB8153B7768811D1ADED00C04FD8D5CD:CN=LostAndFound,DC=contoso,
DC=com
B:32:AB1D30F3768811D1ADED00C04FD8D5CD:CN=System,DC=contoso,DC=com
B:32:A361B2FFFFD211D1AA4B00C04FD7D83A:OU=Domain Controllers,
DC=contoso,DC=com
B:32:AA312825768811D1ADED00C04FD8D5CD:CN=Computers,DC=contoso,
DC=com
B:32:A9D1CA15768811D1ADED00C04FD8D5CD:CN=Users,DC=contoso,DC=com
```

You can see from this list that the GUID AA312825768811D1ADED00C04FD8D5CD maps to the location CN=Computers,DC=contoso,DC=com. So, to modify the default location for computer accounts, you need to modify that location. The next example makes the new default location OU=Workstations,OU=Accounts, DC=contoso,DC=com. To make this change, you simply need to call the Set-ADObject cmdlet and replace the value in the multivalued string attribute. Assuming that you haven't changed this default location in the past, you can use the following commands:

```
PS C:\> $rootDSE = Get-ADRootDSE


PS C:\> Set-ADObject $rootDSE.DefaultNamingContext -Add ↵
   @{wellKnownObjects="B:32:AA312825768811D1ADED00C04FD8D5CD:↵
   OU=Workstations,OU=Accounts,DC=contoso,DC=com"} -Remove ↵
   @{wellKnownObjects=" B:32:AA312825768811D1ADED00C04FD8D5CD:↵
   CN=Computers,DC=contoso,DC=com"}
```

If you've already changed the location of the Computers container in the past, you'll need to read the existing values and parse the strings before setting the new location.

Manage Computers

When we think of managing computers in AD, other things come to mind aside from modifying the computer objects. PowerShell can help you manage other aspects of domain-joined computers as well. In this section, we'll show you how to perform an offline domain join, how to find and filter out certain computers in your domain that meet criteria such as operating system version, and how to allow your users to join more than 10 computers to the domain. At the end of the section, we'll even provide you with a script you can use to detect, disable, move, or delete stale computer accounts.

Performing an Offline Domain Join

One of the more interesting new features in Windows Server 2008 R2 and Windows 7 is the ability to join a computer to the AD domain while the network is offline. This feature, called Offline Domain Join (ODJ), was created with image deployment in mind. Although the computer gets joined to the domain, the user can't log in until a DC is reachable. In more active deployment scenarios, the ODJ feature may not be as important. However, there is a place for ODJ when you're deploying many domain-joined virtual machines. This feature allows you to deploy these domain-joined computers without requiring network credentials.

ODJ can only be used for Windows Server 2008 R2 and Windows 7 computers. But these computers can be joined to any version of AD and the ability to perform the ODJ doesn't require a Windows Server 2008 R2 DC.

Joining a computer to the domain offline is a two-part process. In the first part, you use a tool supplied with Windows called `djoin.exe`. When run with the `/provision` switch, this tool pre-creates a computer object and sets some metadata on it. As a result, a file is output from the command.

In the second part of the process, the file that was output from the first part is given to the offline computer, and `djoin.exe` is run on the client. This time, the client uses the `/requestodj` switch, which indicates that this computer will be joining the domain. The computer will be joined to the domain upon the next reboot, without ever having to contact a DC.

Staging the Computer Account

We're going to cheat here. The `djoin.exe` tool is a utility supplied with the operating system and not a PowerShell cmdlet or script. Because this tool does more than just pre-create a computer account, you still use the tool in PowerShell. However, PowerShell brings value to the table when you want to join multiple computers to the domain, which is usually the case. When you call this command from PowerShell, you can have PowerShell read a list of computers from a CSV file and perform an ODJ for those computers. There's a lot of value in wrapping some automation around this process.

Managing Active
Directory Data

PART II

When calling the `djoin.exe` command to stage the computer object, you use the following syntax:

```
djoin /provision /domain <DomainName> /machine <ClientName> ↵
  /savefile <FileLocation>
```

You take the output of the command, specified in the `/savefile` parameter, and copy it to the client you're joining to the domain.

Joining the Client to the Domain

After you've copied the output file to the Windows 7 or Windows Server 2008 R2 client computer, log onto that computer with your local administrator credentials and run the `djoin.exe` tool again. This time, specify the `/requestodj` switch, which tells the computer to join the domain on the next reboot. The command to run on the client has the following syntax:

```
djoin /requestodj /loadfile <FileLocation> /windowspath ↵
  <WindowsPath> /localos
```

The previous command is used for a client computer that you're currently logged onto. If you have an image instead—a VHD file, for example—then you can mount the VHD file and run the same command without the `/localos` switch. When you do, specify the location of the target computer's Windows path, not the Windows path of the machine you're currently logged onto.

Troubleshooting

If you encounter issues with the offline domain-join process, you can trouble-shoot them by reviewing the `netsetup` log. Because this is a two-part process, two separate logs are kept. When you're troubleshooting errors that occur when attempting to stage the computer account, look at the `netsetup.log` file on the computer from which you're running the `djoin.exe` command. This file is kept in the `%systemroot%\debug` folder. When you're troubleshooting issues that involve the client computer becoming joined to the domain, con-sult the `netsetup.log` file on the client computer. This file is kept in the same place—`%systemroot%\debug`.

One other thing you may want to do when troubleshooting is to ensure that the user has the appropriate permissions to perform an offline domain join. The permis-sions required are the same permissions needed to perform an online domain join. The user must either be granted permission to "Add workstations to the domain" in the User Rights Assignment policy in a Group Policy Object or be able to create computer objects in the target OU for the account.

Finding a Computer Based on the Operating System

There are many ways to try to find computers in your domain. One of the more useful approaches is to search by OS. This method is often employed when filtering Group Policy Objects (GPOs) for different versions of Windows. Four attributes in AD contain OS information about the computer. Table 7.4 describes these attributes.

TABLE 7.4   Operating System Attributes in AD

Attribute	Description
operatingSystem	Specifies the name of the OS, such as "Windows 7 Enterprise"
operatingSystemHotfix	Specifies the hotfix level of the computer
operatingSystemServicePack	Reports the computer's current service-pack level
operatingSystemVersion	Details the current version of the OS, including the build; for example, "6.1 (7600)"

These OS attributes are updated by the client computers and first populated during the domain-join process. Therefore, after a client successfully boots up on the domain, these attributes are available to be used in queries and scripts. The easiest way to filter your search results with these attributes is to use the Get-ADComputer cmdlet in the AD module. You can specify the version you're looking for as part of the Filter parameter. When using this parameter, you'll more than likely prefer to use the -like comparison operator so you can use wildcards in your search. For example, to retrieve a list of all Windows 7 clients in the domain, you can run the following command:

```
Get-ADComputer -Filter {operatingSystem -like "Windows 7*"}
```

In a similar manner, if you want to return all computers that are running Windows 7 or Windows Server 2008 R2 (both use kernel version 6.1), you can run the following command:

```
Get-ADComputer -Filter {operatingSystemVersion -like "6.1*"}
```

From here, you can treat your results list just as you would any other list of objects in PowerShell and wrap some automation around tasks that you may perform on these computers.

Changing the Number of Computers a User Can Join to a Domain

By default, users who are allowed to join computers to the domain are limited in the number of computers they can add. This limit is specified in the `ms-DS-MachineAccountQuota` attribute, which resides on the domain object in AD. You can modify the number of computers that users can join by modifying this attribute.

To determine the current value of the object, you can run the following PowerShell commands:

```
PS C:\> $rootDSE = Get-ADRootDSE
PS C:\> Get-ADObject $rootDSE.defaultNamingContext -Properties ↵
   ms-DS-MachineAccountQuota
```

```
DistinguishedName          : DC=contoso,DC=com
ms-DS-MachineAccountQuota  : 10
Name                       : contoso
ObjectClass                : domainDNS
ObjectGUID                 : 15f1ef14-7d0c-4540-854a-d3ae2a450baa
```

Notice from this output that the default setting is 10. When the user attempts to add the eleventh computer to the domain, they hit their limit and are prevented from adding the computer. Modifying this attribute directly solves the problem. The following command increases the limit to 25:

```
Set-ADObject $rootDSE.defaultNamingContext -Replace ↵
   @{"ms-DS-MachineAccountQuota"=25}
```

Removing Stale Computer Accounts from the Domain

As administrators, we often find that our systems often suffer from years of built-up issues. When it comes to large, enterprise-scale systems like AD, this is especially true, because it's nearly impossible to catch every little thing. One issue that may have been creeping up over the years is computers that were added to your forest and that no longer exist. How do you detect these computers and get rid of them?

There are a few different ways to detect stale computer accounts. Perhaps the most effective way is to look at when the computer object's password was last changed. Unless you explicitly disabled machine account password resets at some point (which is possible if your domain was upgraded from Windows NT), all computers that are joined to the domain will automatically change their own password every

30 days. Because computer accounts are security principals just like user accounts, this is a security feature of AD. Therefore, to determine whether a computer is *stale* (the computer no longer exists, but the object is still there), you can search for computers whose passwords haven't been changed within the past 30 days. This date is stored in the pwdLastSet attribute. The following series of PowerShell commands retrieves all computer objects whose passwords haven't changed in the past 30 days:

```
PS C:\> $current_date = Get-Date
PS C:\> $past_days = New-Timespan -Days 30
PS C:\> $start_date = $current_date.Subtract($past_days)
PS C:\> Get-ADComputer -Filter {pwdLastSet -lt $start_date} ↵
  -Properties pwdLastSet
```

Now that you have a list of computers that you consider stale, the next step is to determine what to do with them. If you're bold, you can go right ahead and delete them. However, if you make a mistake, then you should be ready to rejoin that computers to the domain. A better move is to move the computers to an alternate OU and attempt to contact the owners. Be aware, though, that by moving a computer to another OU, the GPOs applied at its current OU may not apply, and that may impact how the computer functions. If you have executive sponsorship, consider disabling the accounts as well. That way, if a computer is still being used, you can reenable the account and move it back.

The script in Listing 7.3 can help you clean up stale computer accounts. This script includes the following switches:

- -delete: Deletes the computer account
- -move: Moves the computer account to the specified OU
- -disable: Disables the account

If you run the script without any switches, it will display a report of computers that are considered stale but won't do anything with them.

LISTING 7.3: *ManageStaleComputers.ps1*

```
## File Name: ManageStaleComputers.ps1
## Description:
## Enumerates the computers in the domain, searching for
##  computer accounts whose passwords have not been changed
```

(continues)

LISTING 7-3 *(continued)*

```
##   within the past 30 days. This script can delete, disable,
##   and/or move the computer accounts to an alternate OU.
##

param([switch]$Disable, [switch]$Delete, [string]$Move="")

# Gets the current date minus 30 days for the search filter
$current_date = Get-Date
$past_days = New-Timespan -Days 30
$start_date = $current_date.Subtract($past_days)
# Retrieve all computer accounts whose passwords haven't changed
# within the past 30 days
$objects = Get-ADComputer -Filter {pwdLastSet -lt $start_date} `
    -Properties pwdLastSet
# If the -Delete switch was specified, delete the object
if ($Delete)
{
    foreach ($computer in $objects)
    {
        Remove-ADComputer $computer -Confirm:$true
    }
}
else
{
    # If the -Disable switch was specified, disable the object
    if ($Disable)
    {
    foreach ($computer in $objects)
        {
            Set-ADComputer $computer -Enabled $false
        }
    }
    # If the -Move switch was specified, move the computer to
    # the target OU
    if ($Move.Length -gt 0)
    {
        foreach ($computer in $objects)
```

```
        {
            Move-ADObject $computer -TargetPath $Move
        }
    }

    # If no switches were used, print a list of stale computers
    if ($Disable -ne $true -and $Move.Length -eq 0)
    {
        $objects | ft Name, pwdLastSet
    }
}
```

Manage Organizational Units

OUs are cornerstone objects in your AD domain. They provide your directory with some much-needed structure to manage the vast number of objects that it will surely collect over the years. However, another object type provides similar functionality, and because of that there has been some confusion over the years. Container objects can also be used to organization your directory. A few container objects are created by default in an AD domain. In fact, in a default installation, all of the top-level objects are containers. Only one object is an OU, and that's the DC's OU. The primary difference between an OU and a container, however, is subtle. Containers can't have GPOs attached to them. You can attach a GPO at a higher level and have it applied downstream to a container, but you can't attach the GPO directly to the container itself. Because of this, many organizations choose not to use the default locations for the user and computer objects because they're both containers.

But in their truest sense, OUs and containers both are designed to be parent objects. This means they were designed to hold other objects. This doesn't mean that only an OU or a container can have child objects—any object can potentially be a parent for child objects as long as the AD schema specifies that it's okay to do so. But OUs and containers are different from other parent objects, in that their sole purpose is to be parents.

Build Organizational Unit Structures

There are many philosophies regarding how an OU structure should be configured. In working with dozens of clients over the years, I (Ken) think I've seen just about every model in existence. Back in May 2008, I wrote an article for *TechNet*

Magazine called "Designing OU Structures that Work" (`http://technet` `.microsoft.com/en-us/magazine/2008.05.oudesign.aspx`). In this article, I analyzed a few different OU design models and laid out the good and the bad. One of the points that I made up front in the article was that a poorly planned OU structure tends to take on a life of its own. I've seen this truth manifested time and time again. If your OU structure has multiple admins dipping their hands in it, and if it has little actual structure, then it will surely get out of hand. And when it does, that dramatically affects the management of the structure and even the management of the domain. Therefore, the first rule in managing OUs is to make sure your model is planned appropriately for your business.

Creating an Organizational Unit

The AD module provides a series of easy-to-use cmdlets for working with OUs in AD. Similar to other cmdlets in the AD module, the OU cmdlets are scoped to only work with OU objects themselves, so there's no need to specify object types when creating the OU objects. To create OU objects, you can use the `New-ADOrganizationalUnit` cmdlet. You can call this cmdlet with the name of the OU that you want to create, and it will create the OU in the top level of the domain. The following example creates the Sales OU at the root of the current domain:

```
New-ADOrganizationalUnit "Sales"
```

It's a more likely scenario, though, that you'll be creating OUs that reside at places other than the top of the OU structure. To add an OU at a different level of the structure, you can specify the `Path` parameter in the `New-ADOrganizationalUnit` cmdlet. When you use this parameter, enter the DN of the OU's parent object. The following example creates the Sales OU inside the Departments OU in `contoso.com`:

```
New-ADOrganizationalUnit "Sales" -Path ↵
    "ou=Departments,dc=contoso,dc=com"
```

Removing an Organizational Unit

When removing OUs, you can use the `Remove-ADOrganizationalUnit` cmdlet. This cmdlet removes the OU that you specify as its first positional parameter (the `Identity` parameter). If your OU isn't configured for protection from accidental deletion (discussed later in this chapter), the following command will delete the OU that you specify:

```
Remove-ADOrganizationalUnit ↵
    "ou=Sales,ou=departments,dc=contoso,dc=com"
```

If there are child objects in the OU, you'll receive an error when running the previous command. By default, the `Remove-ADOrganizationalUnit` cmdlet isn't recursive, so objects within the OU are left intact. If you want to delete the OU and all of the objects under it, you can specify the `Recursive` switch in the command. The following example demonstrates this:

```
Remove-ADOrganizationalUnit ↵
    "ou=Sales,ou=departments,dc=contoso,dc=com" -Recursive
```

Modify Organizational Unit Objects

After your OU structure is planned and built, the work doesn't stop. As you maintain AD over time, it becomes necessary to revisit the basics and ensure that your OUs are necessary and well maintained. So, you'll want to modify your OUs to keep their properties current and ensure that there is ownership and protection of that OU.

Modifying the Properties of an Organizational Unit

In addition to creating and removing OUs, the AD module provides the `Set-ADOrganizationalUnit` cmdlet for modifying an OU's properties. We always recommend that when you create an OU, you should always fill out two properties: `Description` and `ManagedBy`. These two properties tell you who created the OU and what the OU is for. The following example configures the `Description` attribute for the Departments OU:

```
Set-ADOrganizationalUnit "ou=Departments,dc=contoso,dc=com" ↵
    -Description "Department-level OUs"
```

Assigning Someone as an OU Manager

As mentioned in the previous section, we recommend that you not only add a description to your OUs, but also specify the OU manager. If you do this, then you have a place to direct any questions about the contents or permissions assigned to the OU. Also, this gives you a single touch-point if you find stale accounts in that OU or accounts that are out of compliance with your policies.

Adding a manager to an OU is a two-step process. The first step is to connect to AD and bind to the user object of the person who will be the manager. The next example searches on the `samAccountName` (the NT-style logon name) attribute of the account and places that result in the `$user` variable.

Managing Active
Directory Data

PART II

After you have a representation of the user object, you can call the
`Set-ADOrganizationalUnit` cmdlet for the OU on which you want to set the
manager. To configure the manager, you set the `ManagedBy` attribute to be the user
object gathered in the first step. An example of the commands that perform these
steps is shown here:

```
PS C:\> $user = Get-ADUser -Filter {samAccountName -eq "nora"}
PS C:\> Set-ADOrganizationalUnit ↵
   "ou=Departments,dc=contoso,dc=com" -ManagedBy $user
```

Preventing an OU from Being Deleted Accidently

Have you ever witnessed an AD administrator deleting an OU full of objects and
realizing what they've done after the deletion was underway? I (Ken) had a client a
number of years ago who accidently deleted one of their AD-integrated DNS zones,
which happened to contain thousands of manually registered DNS records for
UNIX servers. When we attempted to recover the data, we found that no one knew
the Directory Services Restore Mode password on the DC's backup image! With
no backups and a zone full of DNS records on the line, we began to panic. As we
walked down to the desk of another AD administrator, we learned that by divine
intervention, the other administrator had left his DNS MMC console open and displaying the data for the zone that was just deleted. Fortunately, he hadn't yet clicked
the Refresh button. There before us were thousands upon thousands of DNS records
that had just been deleted but were cached in the list box control in the MMC. With
great caution, we used the export function in the MMC to export the DNS records
to a text file, all the while praying that the process wouldn't crash. As we opened the
text file and viewed its glorious contents, we all breathed a sigh of relief, knowing
that we got through this one by the skin of our teeth. I spent the rest of the evening
writing a script to parse the exported file and feed the contents into thousands of
`DNSCMD.EXE` commands to re-create the DNS records one by one. That was the day
that I truly fell in love with scripting.

Our job wouldn't have been this nerve-wrecking on that day if the next feature had
been included in AD early on. So, I was very excited to see that Windows Server
2008 introduced the ability to prevent people from deleting objects by accident.
This feature is manifested by a check box in the Object tab of the object's Properties
dialog in the Active Directory Users and Computers tool (see Figure 7.4).

Although it's a new option in the user interface, this check box is nothing more than
a Deny permission on the Delete and Delete Subtree operations for the object (see
Figure 7.5).

FIGURE 7.4   The Protect Object From Accidental Deletion setting

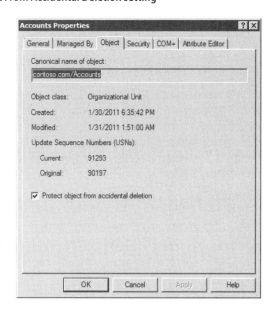

FIGURE 7.5   Preventing accidental deletions involves nothing more than a Deny ACE.

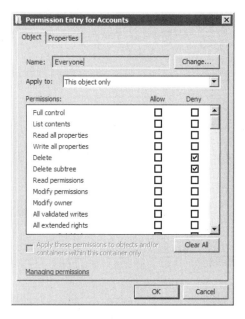

Fortunately, you don't have to edit the ACL for an AD object to turn this setting on or off. Rather, the `Set-ADOrganizationalUnit` cmdlet provides a parameter to control this setting. The parameter is called `ProtectedFromAccidentalDeletion`, and you can toggle it on or off by setting it to `$true` or `$false`. The following example turns off accidental deletion on an OU:

```
Set-ADOrganizationalUnit "ou=Departments,dc=contoso,dc=com" ↵
   -ProtectedFromAccidentalDeletion $false
```

When you turn off this setting, it doesn't affect the child objects in the OU recursively. The result is that if you intend to delete an OU and all of its child objects, you first have to go through each child object and disable accidental-deletion prevention.

Managing Group Policies

IN THIS CHAPTER, YOU WILL LEARN TO:

n Windows Server 2008 R2, you may use PowerShell to perform many of the same tasks that you could previously perform only through the graphical user interface, most commonly using the Group Policy Management Console (GPMC). You can use the Group Policy PowerShell cmdlets to perform the following tasks:

- ► Create, remove, back up, and import Group Policy Objects (GPOs)

- ► Create, update, and remove Group Policy links to any Active Directory container: site, domain, or organizational unit (OU)

- ► Configure permissions and inheritance flags on AD OUs and domains

- ► Update, retrieve, and remove Registry-based policy settings and the Group Policy preferences Registry settings within a GPO

- ► Create and edit starter GPOs

In order to use PowerShell to manage GPOs in your environment, you must be running one of the following:

- ► At least one Windows Server 2008 R2 domain controller

- ► At least one Windows Server 2008 R2 member server (you must manually install the GPMC)

- ► At least one Windows 7 workstation with the Remote Server Administration Tools (RSAT) installed

In addition, you'll need to issue the following command from the PowerShell console prior to running any GPO-related PowerShell cmdlets: `import-module grouppolicy`. After you've imported the Group Policy module into PowerShell, you can obtain a full list of the GPO-related PowerShell cmdlets by running the following command: `get-command -module grouppolicy`.

Manage Group Policy Settings

In this section, we'll discuss various scenarios around managing GPO settings within AD. We'll begin with a discussion of how to create and modify GPOs, including steps needed to automate creating and copying GPOs, working with starter GPOs, and modifying and removing GPOs.

When designing your Group Policy placement strategy, the most important result is that your GPO design meets the business requirements as defined by your organization. To make sure this happens, you need to understand the settings the business requires to be deployed to user and computer objects, as well as any additional requirements the business may have, such as specific settings that should be enforced within a particular scope or for a particular group of computers or users based on location or job role. When you've determined these requirements, you can define one or more GPOs that may be linked at one or more levels within your AD structure.

After we've gone over the steps needed to create and remove GPOs, we'll examine the process of creating Fine-Grained Password Policies (FGPP) in Windows Server 2008 and higher. FGPP was introduced in Windows Server 2008 as a way to apply more than one password policy to user, computer, and group objects within a single AD domain.

Managing Active
Directory Data

PART II

Create and Modify Policies

We'll begin with a discussion of how to create and modify GPOs within an AD domain or forest. Each AD domain ships with two default GPOs: the Default Domain Policy, which is linked at the domain level and contains default settings for password and account-lockout policies; and the Default Domain Controller Policy, which is linked to the Domain Controllers OU within each domain. In order to customize the configuration of user and computer objects, you can modify an existing GPO or create one or more new ones that may be linked at the site, domain, or OU level.

We'll also examine a new Group Policy feature that was introduced in Windows Server 2008: the starter GPO. Starter GPOs provide the ability for administrators to create a collection of administrative template settings within a single GPO. Any new GPOs that are created on the basis of a starter GPO receive all the settings configured in the starter GPO, although these starter settings may be modified or removed after the GPO has been created.

Creating a Group Policy Object

When you've determined your Group Policy placement and settings strategy, you then need to create and link the GPOs for each domain. You can create and link the GPOs in a single operation, or you can create the GPOs first and link them to the appropriate container (site, domain, OU) later on. To create a new GPO, you can use the syntax shown in the following example:

```
New-GPO -Name "Common User Settings" -Comment "Top-level GPO
containing common GPO settings" -Domain contoso.com
```

If you omit the –domain parameter, the GPO is created in the same domain as the user account being used to create the GPO. You can also use the –Server parameter to target a specific server on which the GPO should be created.

The –StarterGPOGuid and –StarterGPOName parameters specify the Globally Unique Identifier (GUID) and name of a starter GPO whose settings are used to initially populate the new GPO. We'll cover the steps needed to create a starter GPO later in the chapter.

Notice that the example in this section will only create the GPO; later in the chapter, you'll see how to create, update, and delete links to GPOs in your environment.

Creating a Copy of a Group Policy Object

You can use the Copy-GPO cmdlet to make a copy of a GPO, either within a single domain or across a domain trust within an AD forest. In the simplest case, you're simply creating a second policy object with a new name containing the same settings as the original. In this case, you use the following syntax:

```
Copy-GPO –SourceName "GPO1" –SourceDomain contoso.com –TargetName
"GPO2" –TargetDomain contoso.com –CopyACL –SourceDomainController
dc1.contoso.com –TargetDomainController dc7.contoso.com
```

As you can see, this cmdlet takes the GPO1 GPO and uses it to create the GPO2 destination GPO containing the same settings. (If a GPO called GPO2 already existed in the target domain, the cmdlet would return an error.) The –CopyACL parameter, as you may imagine, copies the Access Control List (ACL) from the source GPO to the target GPO.

You can use the –SourceDomain and –TargetDomain switches to copy a GPO from one domain to another; if you omit either or both of these switches, they will default to the user's domain membership. Both of these switches require the fully qualified domain name (FQDN) of the source and target domains being specified. Similarly, the –SourceDomainController and –TargetDomainController parameters can be used to specify which DCs should be used as the source and target for the copy operation: if you omit either or both of these, the PDC Emulator of the domain in question is used.

When copying a GPO from one domain to another, you may need to transform the values of certain settings rather than leaving all the original settings intact. For example, you may need to change a file server path from \\SERVER1\HomeDirectories to \\SERVER3\HomeDirectories, or to change one administrative group to another. In order to perform this task, you'll need to create a *migration table*.

A migration table is a file that maps domain-specific references such as users, groups, computers, and UNC paths in a source GPO to new values specified in the destination GPO. A migration table consists of one or more mapping entries that consist of a source reference and its associated destination reference. If you specify a migration table when performing an import or copy, each reference to the source entry in the source GPO is replaced with the destination entry when writing the settings into the destination GPO. These transformations can even apply to entries in the GPO's ACL when copying a GPO with the `-CopyACL` entry; the migration table transforms entries in the Discretionary Access Control List (DACL) on the GPO, as well as the DACLs on any software installation settings within the GPO.

Within a GPO, the following entries may contain DACL settings that can be modified using a migration table:

- ► User rights assignments
- ► Restricted groups
- ► Services
- ► File system
- ► Registry
- ► Advanced folder-redirection policies
- ► DACL entries on the GPO
- ► DACL entries on software installation objects

You can also transform Universal Naming Convention (UNC) paths in any of the following settings:

- ► Folder-redirection policies.
- ► Software installation policies (for software distribution points).
- ► Location of scripts that are stored outside the GPO. (Script themselves aren't copied as part of the GPO copy operation unless the script is stored inside the source GPO.)

Although you can specify a migration table when copying a GPO by using the `-MigrationTable <path to file>` parameter, you must create the migration table itself using the GPMC. You can specify entries in the migration table manually, or you can autopopulate the migration table by scanning a source GPO for DACL and UNC entries.

Managing Active Directory Data

PART II

You can see an example of a partially populated migration table in Figure 8.1:

FIGURE 8.1   GPMC Migration Table

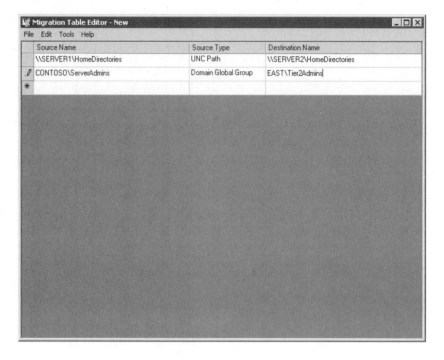

Removing a Group Policy Object

To remove a GPO from an AD domain, you can use the `Remove-GPO` cmdlet as shown in the following example. You can identify the GPO that needs to be removed by specifying its display name or its GUID within the domain. You can optionally specify the domain containing the GPO that needs to be removed; if you don't specify the domain name, PowerShell will use the domain to which the user account running the cmdlet belongs:

```
Remove-GPO -Name TestGPO -Domain east.contoso.com
```

Modifying a Group Policy Object's Settings

Beginning in Windows Server 2008 R2, you can automate the modification of certain settings within a GPO. In previous versions of Windows, even though you had the ability to script the creation, deletion, linking, and unlinking of GPOs, actually modifying the settings of GPOs could only occur using a graphical user interface. With the PowerShell cmdlets in Windows Server 2008 R2 and Windows 7, you can now automate the creation of the following types of Group Policy settings:

▶ Registry preference items, under either the Computer Configuration or User Configuration section of a GPO

▶ Registry-based policy settings, also under either the Computer Configuration or User Configuration section of a GPO

Group Policy Preferences (GPPs) includes a number of advanced Group Policy features for clients that support their use. One of these is the ability to automate the creation of Registry keys and values on client computers whenever the GPO is refreshed; this allows AD administrators to use GPOs to automate aspects of configuration management on large numbers of client computers.

The Set-GPPrefRegistryValue cmdlet lets you manage Registry preference items within an existing AD GPO. For example, you can create a particular Registry key or value on any client that receives a particular GPO, as well as update or delete a Registry key or value on all affected clients. You can see how a Registry preference item is managed in the GPMC in Figure 8.2.

FIGURE 8.2   Managing Registry preference Items

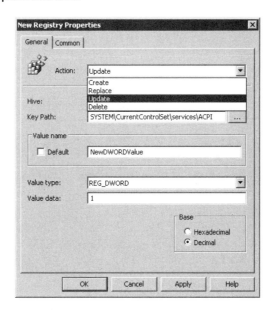

You can use the Set-GPPrefRegistryValue cmdlet to manage Registry preference items in either the Computer Configuration or User Configuration section

of a GPO, and you can configure a Registry preference item to pertain to either a Registry *key* or a Registry *value*.

In order to create a new Registry preference item, you must specify the following parameters:

- ► The GPO to which the Registry preference item should be added. You can specify the GPO by its name or by its GUID.

- ► The -Context parameter, to indicate whether the Registry preference item should be added to the User Configuration or Computer Configuration section of the GPO.

- ► The -Action parameter, to define whether this Registry preference item should create, replace, update, or delete a Registry key or value on the client computers.

The available options for the -Action parameter are as follows:

- ► Create configures a Registry preferences item that creates a new Registry key or value.

- ► Replace configures a Registry preferences item that replaces an existing Registry key or value with a new one.

- ► Update configures a Registry preferences item that updates an existing Registry key or value.

- ► Delete configures a Registry preferences item that deletes an existing Registry key or value.

You can configure a Registry preference item for either a Registry key or a Registry value. To configure a Registry key, you specify the -Key parameter only. To configure a Registry value, you specify the following parameters:

- ► Key. For example: HKEY_CURRENT_USER\Control Panel\Colors. You can specify a Registry key in any of the following hives:

    - ► IIKEY_CLASSES_ROOT (HKCR)

    - ► HKEY_CURRENT_USER (HKCU)

    - ► HKEY_LOCAL_MACHINE (HKLM)

    - ► HKEY_USERS (HKU)

    - ► HKEY_CURRENT_CONFIG (HKCC)

- `ValueName`. For example: `ActiveWindow`.

- `Type` indicates the data type of the Registry value. You can specify any of the following:

  - `String`

  - `ExpandString`

  - `Binary`

  - `DWord`

  - `MultiString`

  - `Qword`

- `Value` indicates the contents of the Registry value.

When you're creating a Registry preference item via PowerShell, you should be aware of two additional parameters:

Disable   If you set this to `$true`, the Registry preference item is created in a disabled state, which means it doesn't modify any client when the GPO containing the item is applied to any client. It's important to note that this doesn't disable any existing Registry preference items within the GPO; rather, it creates a *new* Registry preference item in a disabled state. (If you need to disable an existing Registry preference item, you must do so using the GPMC graphical tool.)

Order   This parameter specifies the order in which the Registry preference item is processed, relative to other Registry preference items configured on the GPO. If you use a parameter of `-Order 1`, for example, this item will be the first item configured.

The following example creates a Registry preference item within an existing GPO that creates a new Registry key on client computers:

```
Set-GPPrefRegistryValue -Name TestGPO -Context computer -Action
Create -Key "HKEY_LOCAL_MACHINE\SOFTWARE\Microsoft\ExampleKey\
ExampleKey2"
```

In addition to Registry preference items, you can also configure Registry-based *policies* using the `Set-GPRegistryValue` cmdlet. You can see the Policies and Preferences nodes visually in the GPMC shown in Figure 8.3.

FIGURE 8.3 Viewing the Group Policy Management Console

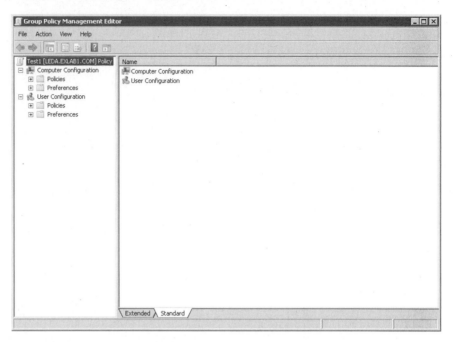

Similar to Registry preference items, Registry-based policies can be configured under either the Computer Configuration or User Configuration node within a GPO. Unlike Registry preference items, Registry-based policy settings can only modify items in the following Registry hives:

- ▶ HKLM for settings in the Computer Configuration node of Group Policy

- ▶ HKCU for settings in the User Configuration node

You can specify the GPO that you wish to modify by its name or GUID, or by using the `Get-GPO` cmdlet and piping the result to the `Set-GPRegistryValue` cmdlet. By default, when a GPO applies a Registry-based policy setting on a client computer, any existing values under that key are deleted before the policy-based setting is applied. You can override this behavior by using the `-Additive` parameter.

Also, unlike Registry preference items, in the case of Registry-based policy settings you can delete Registry values on a client by disabling the policy setting using the `-Disable` parameter. If you specify a Registry key to disable, all values under that key are removed—the key itself isn't removed, and any subkeys (and values within those subkeys) also aren't removed. If you specify a Registry value to disable, only the specific value is removed from the Registry.

N O T E   If you want to remove a Registry-based policy setting from a GPO, but you don't want to affect any existing Registry keys or values that have been configured on the client, you should instead use the `Remove-GPRegistryValue` cmdlet.

You specify the Registry key and value to set using the following parameters:

- ► -Key *HKLM* or -Key *HKCU*. For example: `HKLM\Software\Policies\ Microsoft\Windows NT\NetBIOS`.

- ► `Type` specifies the data type of the Registry key being set; you can specify any one of the following:

  - ► `String`

  - ► `ExpandString`

  - ► `Binary`

  - ► `DWord`

  - ► `MultiString`

  - ► `Qword`

- ► `ValueName` specifies the name of the Registry value.

- ► `Value` specifies the data for the Registry value being set. For `String` and `ExpandString` data types, you can specify multiple values separated by commas; for all other data types, you can only specify a single value.

The following example uses the `Set-GPRegistryValue` cmdlet to set the screen saver timeout in the Computer Configuration node of a GPO:

```
Set-GPRegistryValue -Name "Workstations" -key "HKCU\Software\
Policies\Microsoft\Windows\Control Panel\Desktop" -ValueName
ScreenSaveTimeOut -Type DWORD -value 600
```

Creating a GPO from a Security Template

In Windows Server 2003 and Windows Server 2008, you can use *security templates* to configure one or more GPOs with dozens or even hundreds of security settings in a single operation. You can use one of the preconfigured security templates that ship with Windows, you can take one of the preconfigured templates and tweak it to fit your organization's needs, or even create a brand-new template from scratch using the Security Templates MMC from the Windows administrative tools.

The predefined templates that ship with Windows include the following:

► *Default security (*Setup security.inf*)*—This template is created during the installation of each computer and represents default security settings such as default permissions on the system drive.

► *Domain controller default security (*DC security.inf*)*—This template is created when a server computer is promoted to DC status.

► Compat*.inf *(*compatdc.inf, compatws.inf*)*—This is a basic security template that provides the most open security model, primarily used to supply backward compatibility for legacy software.

► Secure*.inf *(*securedc.inf, securews.inf*)*—This template applies additional security settings beyond the basic template, including locking down LAN Manager and clock-skew settings.

► Hisec*.inf *(*hisecdc.inf, hisecws.inf*)*—This template provides tighter security measures than any others. Microsoft recommends that you test all software and services for any compatibility issues prior to deploying the high-security templates.

You can see an example of a configured security template in Figure 8.4:

FIGURE 8.4   **Managing security templates**

When you've selected and configured the security template that you want to deploy via GPO, you can import it into a GPO by using the Group Policy Editor in the GPMC, as follows:

1. Open the GPO you wish to modify in the Group Policy Editor.

2. Drill down to Computer Configuration ➢ Policies ➢ Windows Settings ➢ Security Settings.

3. Right-click the Security Settings node, and click Import Policy, as shown in Figure 8.5.

FIGURE 8.5   Import Policy

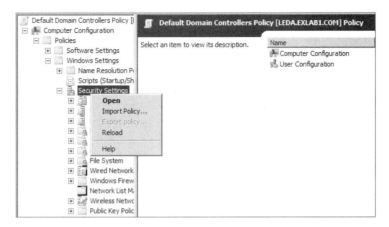

Creating a Starter GPO

Windows Server 2008 R2 introduces a new feature called a *starter GPO*, which is a progression from security templates that allows you to create a GPO template that specifies not only security settings, but also settings within Administrative Templates and other Group Policy nodes.

When you install the first 2008 R2 DC in a domain, you can open the GPMC to create a number of default starter GPOs, as shown in Figure 8.6, or you can use the New-GPStarterGPO PowerShell cmdlet.

You can specify the display name of the starter GPO by using the –Name *<Name>* parameter and the domain that the starter GPO should be created in by using the –Domain *<Domain Name>* parameter. (If you omit the –Domain parameter, the cmdlet uses the domain of the user that's running the PowerShell cmdlet.) You can also enter a description of the starter GPO by using the –Comment parameter.

For example, the following example creates a starter GPO called Default Corporate Settings in the contoso.com domain:

```
New-GPStarterGPO -Name 'Default Corporate Settings' -Domain
contoso.com
```

When you've created the starter GPO and configured the necessary settings in it, any GPO that you create based on the starter GPO will receive all the settings configured in the starter GPO. The New-GPO command includes the –StarterGPOGUID and –StarterGPOName parameters, which allow you to spec-ify the starter GPO on the basis of its GUID or its display name. Figure 8.7 shows a partially configured starter GPO in the GPMC.

FIGURE 8.6   Managing starter GPOs

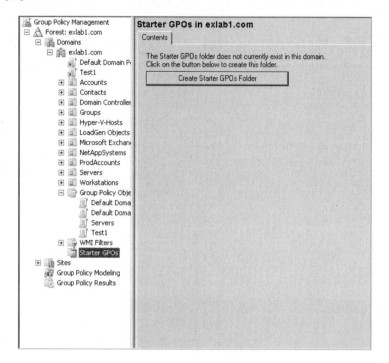

FIGURE 8.7   Starter GPO in the GPMC

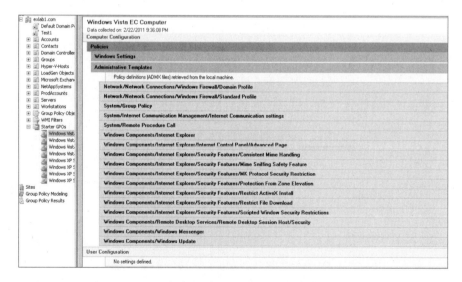

Use Advanced GPO Operations

In this section, we'll discuss additional operations that you'll need to perform when administering GPOs in an AD environment. We'll begin by describing how to move one or more GPOs from a testing environment into a production environment, which allows you to test Group Policy settings in an isolated environment and then transfer them to your production domains after you've ensured that they won't have any adverse effects on your user and computer population.

Next, we'll describe the steps needed to create, configure, and manage FGPPs in order to enable multiple password and account-lockout policies within a single AD domain. This feature, introduced in Windows Server 2008, lets an administrator designate one or more users or groups of users to receive a different password and/or account-lockout policy than are configured as the default domain policies. We'll discuss the steps required to create and configure an FGPP, to link the FGPP to a user or group object, and to determine the effective FGPP that applies to a particular user object within a domain.

Moving Group Policies Between a Lab and a Production Environment

When you're configuring GPOs in your environment, if possible it's recommended that you set up an isolated test environment that mimics the configuration and behavior of your production domains and forests, so you can test new and updated GPOs against unexpected behavior when applied to client computers. After you're satisfied with the behavior of the new or updated GPOs in your test environment, you can then copy them into your production environment.

To ensure that the GPOs deployed in production are identical to those that were deployed in the test environment, you can use the `Backup-GPO` and `Import-GPO` PowerShell cmdlets to automate the process.

The `Backup-GPO` cmdlet can be used to back up a single GPO or all GPOs configured in a domain. To back up a single GPO, you can specify the GPO by name using the `-Name` parameter or by GUID using the `-GUID` parameter. Alternately, you can use the `-All` parameter to back up all GPOs in the domain.

In addition to specifying which GPO or GPOs to back up, the `Backup-GPO` cmdlet also requires you to specify the `-Path` parameter, which indicates the directory that should contain the backups. This can be a local directory such as `C:\Backups` or a network path such as `\\SERVER1\Docs`. (In either case, the destination path must already exist or the `Backup-GPO` cmdlet will throw an error; the cmdlet won't create the path for you if it doesn't exist.)

The following example backs up all GPOs in a domain to the `C:\Backups` directory on the local hard drive:

```
Backup-GPO -All -Path C:\Backups
```

The `Backup-GPO` cmdlet creates a folder with the same name as the GUID of the GPO, as shown in Figure 8.8.

FIGURE 8.8   Managing GPO backups

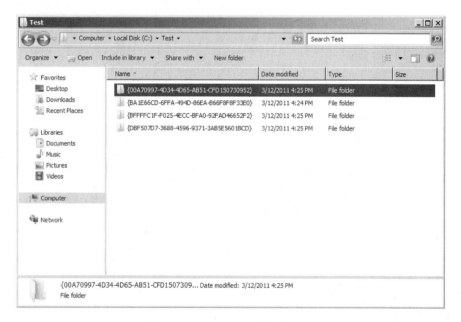

After you've backed up the desired GPOs in the source environment, you use the `Import-GPO` cmdlet in the target environment to import the GPO backups into production. You can tell the `Import-GPO` cmdlet which backup to import using either the `-BackupID` parameter, which specifies the GUID of the desired backup, or the `-BackupGPOName` parameter, which specifies the display name of the desired backup. You also need to specify the `-Path` parameter indicating the folder containing the backup files.

You specify the GPO into which the settings should be imported by specifying the `-TargetName` parameter followed by the display name of the target GPO. If the target GPO doesn't yet exist, you can use the `-CreateIfNeeded` parameter to create a GPO with the same display name as the one specified in the backup.

As in the "Creating a Copy of a Group Policy Object" section, you can specify a migration table when importing a GPO from a backup to translate environment-specific configuration items such as server names, group names, and the like. Just as with the `Copy-GPO` cmdlet, you do so using the `-MigrationTable` parameter followed by the path to the migration table file you wish to use.

The following example imports a GPO using the GUID of the backup, specifying the target name of the GPO into which the settings should be imported:

```
Import-GPO -BackupId B3529175-F5BA-367A-2356-A43CBCA5A421
-TargetName MarketingGPO -path c:\backups
```

Defining a Fine-Grained Password Policy

Prior to Windows Server 2008, AD imposed a limitation that only one password and account-lockout policy could be configured within a single AD domain. If an organization had a business or security requirement to configure more than one password or account-lockout policy, it was forced to deploy a multidomain forest, which resulted in significant administrative overhead to fulfill this requirement.

Beginning in Windows Server 2008, AD introduces the *Fine-Grained Password Policy (FGPP)* feature, which allows you to create multiple password and account-lockout policies within a single domain and apply them to individual users or groups of users in that domain. (There is not, however, a mechanism to link an FGPP to an OU; an FGPP can be linked to user or group objects only.)

FGPPs exist in a special container within each domain located under `CN=Password Settings Container,CN=System` in the domain naming context (`dc=contoso,dc=com`, for example.) You can create each FGPP object in the ADSIEdit MMC console or at the command prompt using Windows PowerShell.

The `New-ADFineGrainedPasswordPolicy` cmdlet accepts the following parameters. Some of these are optional, depending on how the FGPP is to be configured:

► `Name` defines the CN of the policy `DomainUsersPSO`.

► `Precedence` defines the precedence assigned to each FGPP. If multiple FGPPs are applied to a user, the `Precedence` attribute helps to determine which one should apply.

► -ComplexityEnabled accepts a $true or $false value to indicate whether the FGPP should require a complex password. The password-complexity rules for an FGPP are the same as the Windows default, where a complex password must have a minimum of six characters and a mix of uppercase, lowercase, and non-alphanumeric characters.

► -Description denotes the description field for the FGPP.

► -DisplayName defines the display name of the FGPP.

► –LockoutDuration defines how long an account should be locked out when the bad-password threshold has been exceeded. For example, to define a lockout duration of 12 hours, you specify "0.12:00:00".

► –LockoutObservationWindow specifies the duration of time during which exceeding the bad-password threshold will result in locking out the account. For example, a LockoutObservationWindow of 15 minutes means that X number of bad passwords entered within one 15-minute span will result in an account lockout. This attribute accepts the same format as LockoutDuration, where "0.00:15:00" indicates a value of 15 minutes.

► –LockoutThreshold indicates the number of bad password attempts within a given observation window that constitute an account lockout. This parameter takes a simple numeric argument like 10.

► –MaxPasswordAge indicates the maximum age of a password. A value of "60.00:00:00" requires users to change their passwords every 60 days.

► –MinPasswordAge indicates the minimum age of a password before it can be changed again. A value of "1.00:00:00" requires users to wait at least one day after changing their password before they can change it again.

► –MinPasswordLength indicates the minimum password length for this FGPP, such as eight characters.

► –PasswordHistoryCount indicates the number of unique passwords a user must enter when changing their password, before a previous password can be reused.

► –ReversibleEncryptionEnabled takes a value of $true or $false to indicate whether passwords should be stored in the directory using reversible encryption.

The following example demonstrates how to create an FGPP with a number of these settings configured (this is one PowerShell command that should be entered on a single line):

```
New-ADFineGrainedPasswordPolicy -Name "Administrative Users PSO"
-Precedence 1 -ComplexityEnabled $true -Description "Strong
Password Policy for Administrative Accounts"-DisplayName
"Administrative Users PSO" -LockoutDuration "0.15:00:00"
-LockoutObservationWindow "0.00:15:00" -LockoutThreshold
30 -MaxPasswordAge "30.00:00:00" -MinPasswordAge
"5.00:00:00" -MinPasswordLength 12 -PasswordHistoryCount 24
-ReversibleEncryptionEnabled $false
```

When you've created one or more FGPPs, you must link each FGPP to at least one user or group in order for it to take effect. You do so using the `Add-ADFineGrainedPasswordPolicy` PowerShell cmdlet, which uses the `-Subjects` parameter to define one or more users or groups that the FGPP should apply to. The following example applies the FGPP you just created to a specific number of groups and user objects:

```
Add-ADFineGrainedPasswordPolicy "Administrative Users PSO"
-Subjects "Domain Admins", "Enterprise Admins", "Schema Admins",
CONTOSO\arose
```

FGPP Priority and Conflict Resolution

Because of the flexibility available to you when configuring and applying FGPPs, you may wind up in a situation where multiple FGPPs could potentially apply to a single user. A user may belong to multiple security groups, each one of which has an FGPP associated with it, or the user may have multiple FGPPs linked to their account. In a situation like this, which FGPP will take precedence on the user's account?

When you're examining multiple individual FGPPs to determine which one will apply, it's important to remember that FGPPs can be applied in one of two ways:

► Directly to a user object

► To a group object of which one or more users are members

If an FGPP has been assigned directly to a user object, as well as to a group object of which the user is a member, the FGPP that was assigned directly to the user (in other words, the one that was assigned more specifically) takes precedence. So if user aruth is a member of the Sales&Marketing group, and two FGPPs are assigned to the Sales&Marketing group and to aruth's user account directly, the FGPP assigned directly to aruth's account is the one that applies.

Additionally, each FGPP possesses two attributes that are used to determine which one will take precedence in a case where a tie-breaker is required:

Priority   This value is assigned by the administrator when the FGPP is created. It can have a value that is any whole number from 1 to 100. When you're assigning priorities to FGPPs, an FGPP with a lower number takes precedence over an FGPP that is assigned a precedence with a higher number: an FGPP with `Priority` of 1 takes precedence over an FGPP with a `Priority` of 2; an FGPP with `Priority` 10 takes precedence over an FGPP of `Priority` 99, and so on. These numbers are only interesting in relation to each other—it doesn't matter if you use consecutive numbering (1, 2, 3, 4…) or some other scheme (5, 10, 15, 20…), as long as the FGPP that should take precedence is configured with the lower-numbered `Priority`.

GUID   Each AD object is assigned a GUID that is unique to the object across an entire AD forest and doesn't change for the lifetime of the object within the forest. In the extreme case where more than one FGPP applies to the same user *and* has the same priority, the object with the lower GUID takes precedence. (A GUID of 12345 takes precedence over a GUID of 23456.) Because each object within an AD forest possesses a unique GUID, `GUID` creates a final tie-breaker to determine which FGPP should apply to a given user.

You can see this tie-breaker logic illustrated in Figure 8.9—although perhaps the most important lesson to be learned here is that it's usually best to apply the KISS principle to the creation of FGPPs: Keep It Simple, Silly!

Determining Which Password Policy Applies to a User Account

As you saw in the previous section, it's possible for multiple FGPPs to be linked to a given user, either by linking the FGPP directly to the user or by linking an FGPP to one or more groups of which the user is a member.

For troubleshooting purposes, it's helpful to be able to quickly determine which FGPP applies to a particular user in AD. You can easily accomplish this using the `Get-ADUserResultantPasswordPolicy` cmdlet, followed by the `samAccountName` of the user in question. The following example retrieves the effective password policy that applies to the `CONTOSO\arose` user object:

```
Get-ADUserResultantPasswordPolicy arose
```

FIGURE 8.9 Determining FGPP precedence

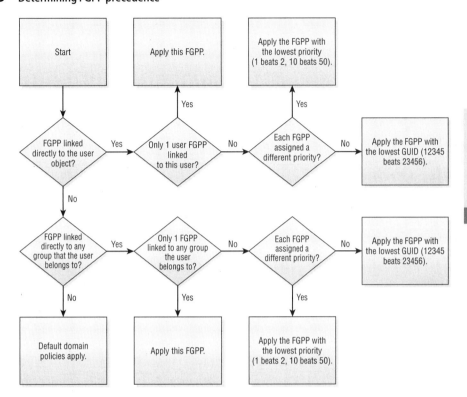

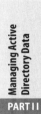

Manage Group Policy Application

Now that you've learned how to create various configurations of GPOs, including GPOs, starter GPOs, security templates, and FGPPs, the next step is to determine how these GPOs will be deployed throughout your organization. A GPO can be linked to one or more AD containers—a site, a domain, or an OU. By default, linking a GPO to one of these containers causes that GPO to apply to all user and computer objects that exist within that container, although you can customize this behavior using WMI filters and/or security group filtering.

In this part of the chapter, we'll examine the steps needed to automate the application of GPOs in an AD environment, including linking GPOs to one or more AD containers, customizing the behavior of Group Policy applications, and viewing and reporting on the configuration of one or more GPOs in the AD environment.

Apply Group Policies

In this section, we'll examine the steps needed to link a GPO to one or more containers in an AD environment. You'll also learn how to customize this behavior so that a particular GPO will only apply to a subset of users or groups within a container, either by virtue of the object's security group membership or on the basis of a WMI filter that tests against operating system, service pack level, available hard drive space, or any number of other characteristics.

Linking a GPO to an OU, a Site, or a Domain

After you've created a GPO, you need to determine where the GPO should apply. You can link a GPO to the following locations in AD:

- ► Domain
- ► Site
- ► OU

You can use the New-GPLink PowerShell cmdlet to specify which container the GPO should be linked to; you use the -Target parameter to specify the link target, followed by the distinguished name (DN) of the container. You can specify the GPO to be linked by using either the -Name or -GUID parameter; the -Name parameter takes the GPO's display name as an argument, whereas the -GUID parameter takes the GUID of the GPO.

When creating the GPO link, you can specify the following optional parameters:

- ► -Enforced ensures that the settings in this GPO won't be overridden by settings configured in a GPO linked to a lower-level container.

- ► -LinkEnabled defaults to Yes, but you have the option to configure a new link as disabled by setting this to No. Setting the link to disabled means the settings configured in the GPO won't apply to users in the container until you enable the GPO link at a later time.

- ► -Order determines what order GPOs will apply in, if more than one GPO is linked to the same container. Because GPOs operate on a last-writer-wins model by default, GPOs that are applied later will override GPOs that are applied earlier. GPOs with a higher (larger) -Order number will be applied before GPOs with a lower (smaller) -Order number, so that a GPO configured with $-Order$ 5 will be applied before a GPO link configured with $-Order$ 1.

The following example demonstrates how to link a GPO to the domain root of the `contoso.com` domain:

```
New-GPLink -Name 'Default Contoso Domain Settings' -LinkEnabled
Yes -Target dc=contoso,dc=com
```

APPLYING MULTIPLE GPOs

In an AD environment, it's common for more than one GPO to apply to a given user/computer combination. In many cases, there will be settings that conflict between these multiple GPOs, and as an administrator you'll need to determine which settings should take precedence. By default, Group Policy operates on a last-writer-wins model, which means the final GPO that applies to a user or computer is the one whose settings will take precedence.

In an AD environment, GPOs are applied in the following order:

1. The local GPO and its settings are applied to the user and the computer.

2. Any GPOs linked to the AD site containing the user and computer (if different) are processed. If multiple GPOs are linked to the AD site, an administrator can specify the order in which these GPOs should apply from first to last.

3. Any GPOs linked to the AD domain containing the user and computer (if different) are processed. If multiple GPOs are linked to the AD domain, an administrator can specify the order in which these GPOs should apply from first to last.

4. Any GPOs linked to the AD OU containing the user and computer (if different) are processed. In an environment where multiple GPOs have been nested, GPOs linked to each OU are processed in order: first all GPOs linked to a grandparent OU, followed by all GPOs linked to a parent OU, followed by all GPOs linked to a child OU, and so on. If multiple GPOs are linked to any level of the AD OU structure, an administrator can specify the order in which these GPOs should apply from first to last.

There are some notable exceptions to this default processing order: specifically, the password (length, complexity, minimum/maximum age) and account-lockout policies that apply to the user are the ones that are linked to the AD domain. (This will be the case unless FGPPs have been configured, as discussed earlier in the chapter.)

(continues)

(continued)

Here's a graphical depiction of the default GPO processing order:

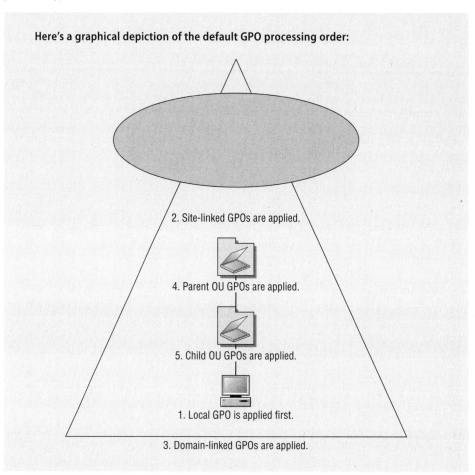

2. Site-linked GPOs are applied.

4. Parent OU GPOs are applied.

5. Child OU GPOs are applied.

1. Local GPO is applied first.

3. Domain-linked GPOs are applied.

Creating a Custom Filter for a GPO

By default, a GPO linked to a container (domain, site, or OU) applies to all objects held within that container. In order to specify at a more granular level which objects the GPO should apply to, you can create a *WMI filter* and apply it to the GPO in question. After you've applied a WMI filter to a particular GPO, only computers that meet the criteria of the filter will have the GPO applied.

For example, you can create a WMI filter that requires that a GPO apply only to computers of a particular operating system, that possess a particular hardware configuration, or that have a specific piece of software installed. The following

WMI filter searches for computers that have at least 100 MB free on their
C: drive:

```
Select * from Win32_LogicalDisk where FreeSpace > 104857600 AND
Caption = "C:"
```

You can see another example here, which searches for computers that are running
Windows Vista Service Pack 1 only:

```
Select * FROM Win32_OperatingSystem WHERE Caption="Microsoft
Windows Vista" AND CSDVersion="Service Pack 1"
```

In order to link a WMI filter to a GPO, you need to use the GPMC; at present, there
is no way to automate linking a WMI filter to a GPO.

First you create the WMI filter in the WMI Filters node, as shown in Figure 8.10.

FIGURE 8.10 Creating a WMI filter

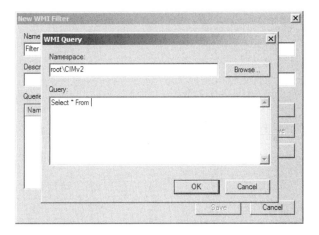

When the WMI filter has been created, you can link it to a GPO by using the WMI
Filtering drop-down box on the GPO's Scope tab, as shown in Figure 8.11.

Because evaluating WMI filters can be a processor-heavy operation, you should
thoroughly test any filters that you intend to deploy and use them only on an
exception basis if you've deployed numerous GPOs in your organization.

Applying a GPO to a Subset of Objects in an OU

In addition to using WMI filters to restrict the application of a GPO, you can also
use *security group filtering* to restrict the objects to which a GPO applies. By default,

the Authenticated Users group in AD is granted the Read and Apply Group Policy on each GPO. You can restrict the security settings on a GPO in one of two ways:

▶ Remove the default Authenticated Users access control entry (ACE) on the GPO, and explicitly grant the Read and Apply Group Policy permissions to only those users and computers that should receive the GPO settings.

▶ Leave the default Authenticated Users ACE in place, and explicitly deny the two required permissions to the specific users or groups that should *not* receive the GPO settings.

FIGURE 8.11 Linking a WMI filter

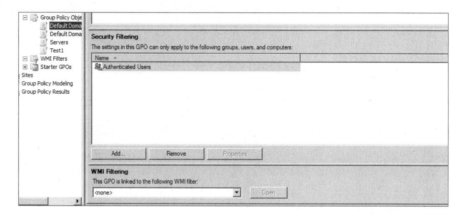

You can modify the security settings on a GPO using the Set-GPPermissions PowerShell cmdlet. You can modify the permissions for a single GPO by specifying the –Name or –GUID parameter. After you've specified the GPO that you want to modify, you use the –PermissionLevel parameter with one of the following values:

▶ GPORead—Read permission on the GPO.

▶ GPOApply—Apply Group Policy permissions on the GPO.

▶ GPOEdit—Edit permission on the GPO.

▶ GPOEditDeleteModifySecurity—Edit, Delete, and Modify Security permissions on the GPO.

▶ None—No permissions on the GPO.

In addition to the –PermissionLevel parameter that specifies the permission you're configuring, you need to use the –TargetName and –TargetType parameters to specify the user, computer, or group that should receive that permission. `-TargetName` can be in any of the following formats:

- `arose`

- `CONTOSO\arose`

- `Domain Admins`

- `CONTOSO\Domain Admins`

- `COMPUTER3`

- `CONTOSO\COMPUTER3`

The `-TargetType` parameter needs to be specified and can be one of the following values:

- `User`

- `Computer`

- `Group`

Finally, you can use the `-Replace` parameter to specify whether any existing permissions for the user, computer, or group should be replaced if that permission already exists. For example, if you add the GpoRead permission to a particular group and do *not* specify the `-Replace` parameter, and the group has already been configured with the GpoEdit permission, no changes will be made because the GpoEdit permission already confers GpoRead. (The reverse doesn't apply, though: if the group has already been assigned GpoRead and you add the GpoEdit permission, GpoEdit *will* overwrite GpoRead because it's a higher permission level than what already exists.) In the case of the `-Replace` switch, if you add the GpoRead permission to a group that already has GpoEdit, *and* you specify the `-Replace` switch, then the GpoEdit permission will be replaced by the GpoRead permission.

The following example adds the GpoEdit permission to a GPO for a specific user in AD:

```
Set-GPPermissions -Name 'Marketing GPO' -PermissionLevel GPOEdit
-TargetName CONTOSO\arose -TargetType USER
```

The next command assigns the GpoRead permission on the same GPO to the same user. Because this command doesn't use the `-Replace` parameter, no changes will actually be made to the GPO, because the GpoEdit permission level already confers Read permission on the GPO:

```
Set-GPPermissions -Name 'Marketing GPO' -PermissionLevel GPORead
-TargetName CONTOSO\arose -TargetType USER
```

Next, you issue the same command using the –Replace parameter. Because the –Replace parameter is specified, the GpoEdit permission will be removed from CONTOSO\arose, and the GpoRead permission will be added in its place:

```
Set-GPPermissions -Name 'Marketing GPO' -PermissionLevel GPOEdit
-Replace -TargetName CONTOSO\arose -TargetType USER
```

Preventing a Down-Level OU from Overriding a GPO

By default, all GPOs use a last-writer-wins model when applying their settings. Consider an example where a user and computer reside in the ou=sales, ou=marketing,dc=contoso,dc=com OU. Let's assume that GPO1 is linked to the ou=marketing,dc=contoso,dc=com OU, and GPO2 is linked to the ou=sales,ou=marketing,dc=contoso,dc=com OU. The user in the Sales OU will receive any settings configured in GPO1 first. If any individual settings are specified in both GPO1 and GPO2, GPO2 will win on any individual settings that conflict, but any settings from GPO1 that don't conflict with GPO2 will still apply.

In order to prevent a lower-level OU from overriding parent OU GPO settings, you can configure the GPO1 link to the Marketing OU with the –Enforced parameter. In this case, the user in the Sales OU will receive settings configured in GPO1 first. If any individual settings are specified in both GPO1 and GPO2, *GPO1* will win on any individual settings that conflict, but any settings from GPO2 that don't conflict with GPO1 will still apply. (Notice that this effectively reverses the default last-writer-wins Group Policy model.)

To create a new GPO link using the –Enforced link, you can use the New-GPLink cmdlet described earlier in this section. If you need to modify an existing Group Policy link, you use the Set-GPLink cmdlet using the following parameters:

 ▶ –Name or –GUID to specify the name or GUID of the GPO

 ▶ –Target to specify the DN of the container to which the GPO is linked

 ▶ –Enforced to configure the existing GPO link as Enforced

The following example modifies an existing Group Policy link to use the Enforced option:

```
Set-GPLink -Name 'Marketing GPO' -Target 'ou=marketing,
dc=contoso,dc=com' -Enforced
```

APPLYING THE ENFORCE SETTING AT MULTIPLE LEVELS

As you've just seen, the use of the Enforce setting can prevent a GPO linked to a lower-level OU from overriding settings that were configured by a GPO linked to a higher-level OU. But what happens if you have a parent OU and a child OU, both of which have GPOs linked to them that use the Enforce option? If you create a grandchild OU and link a GPO to this new OU, which of the Enforced GPOs will prevail in the case of any setting conflicts: the parent OU or the child OU?

You've already seen that normal GPO processing operates on a last-writer-wins model: The settings from the parent OU's GPO will be applied first, then the settings from the child OU's GPO, and then the settings from the grandchild OU's GPO; whichever settings were written *last* are the ones that will take effect. When Enforced is used, though, this model is reversed: whichever Enforced GPO is applied *first* is the one that will prevail. In the example where the parent and child OUs' GPOs are both configured using the Enforced option, any conflicting settings between the parent, child, and grandchild GPOs will be settled in favor of the highest GPO in the OU structure—the parent OU, in this case. You can see the default precedence here:

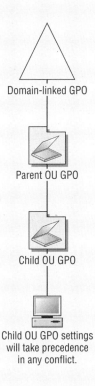

Domain-linked GPO

Parent OU GPO

Child OU GPO

Child OU GPO settings
will take precedence
in any conflict.

(continues)

Managing Active Directory Data

PART II

(continued)

You can see the behavior when multiple Enforced settings are in use here:

As is often the case when designing and applying GPOs, though, it's best not to overuse exception settings like Enforced as described in this example, because doing so creates confusion and difficulty in troubleshooting when clients receive (or don't receive!) the GPO settings they are expecting.

View Existing Policies

In our final section, we'll examine the tasks required to view the settings of GPOs you've configured in your environment. These can include generating a simple report of one or more GPOs or starter GPOs in your domain and generating a report of the effective policy settings that have been applied to a particular user and computer in the environment. The tasks outlined in this section are useful for maintaining documentation of your GPOs, as well as for helping troubleshoot issues surrounding Group Policy application for a particular user or computer that may be having difficulties.

Creating a GPO Settings Report

When you've created and configured one or more GPOs, you can use the Get-GPOReport PowerShell cmdlet to obtain a list of settings that have been configured on those GPOs. You can specify the GPO or GPOs for which you wish to generate a report by using the following parameters:

- Get-GPOReport -Name *<Display Name of the Starter GPO>*

- Get-GPOReport -GUID *<GUID of the Starter GPO>*

- Get-GPOReport -ALL (retrieves a report on all GPOs in the domain)

The Get-GPOReport cmdlet can create output in either XML or HTML format using the -ReportType parameter; you use the -Path parameter to specify the folder and filename that the report should be saved as. You can specify the -Domain parameter to specify the domain containing the GPO that you wish to report on, if it isn't the domain that you're currently logged onto.

Figure 8.12 provides an example of an HTML report generated by Get-GPOReport.

FIGURE 8.12 HTML GPO report

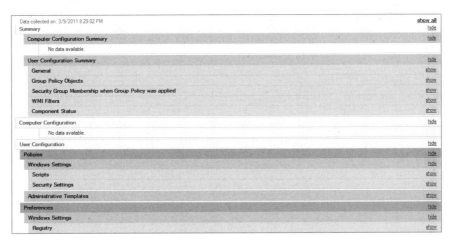

Retrieving a List of All GPOs

In order to retrieve single starter GPO or a list of all starter GPOs within a domain, you use the `Get-StarterGPO` PowerShell cmdlet. When using this cmdlet, you can use one of the following parameters to determine which starter GPO or GPOs to retrieve:

▶ `Get-StarterGPO –Name` *<Display Name of the Starter GPO>*

▶ `Get-StarterGPO –GUID` *<GUID of the Starter GPO>*

▶ `Get-StarterGPO –ALL` (retrieves all GPOs in the domain)

You can use this cmdlet to view the properties of the GPO or GPOs that are retrieved, as shown in Figure 8.13, or you can retrieve an object reference to one or more GPOs and pipe the output of this cmdlet into another cmdlet in order to modify the GPOs you've retrieved.

FIGURE 8.13 Obtaining a list of GPOs

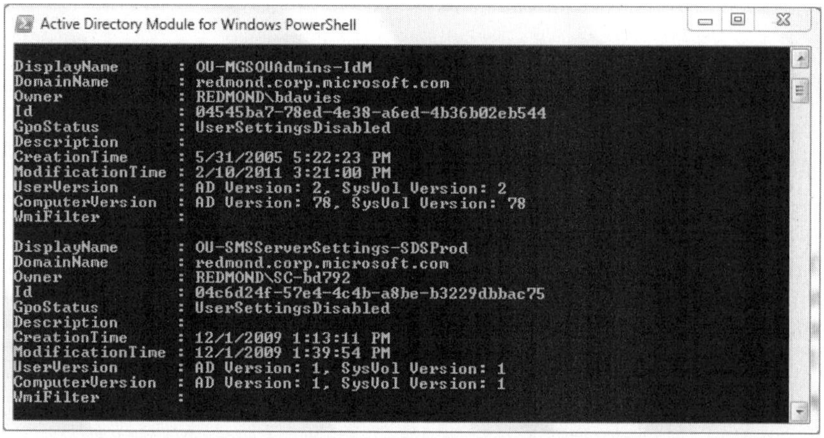

Retrieving a List of Starter GPOs

Similar to the `Get-GPO` cmdlet that we just discussed, to retrieve single starter GPO or a list of all starter GPOs within a domain, you use the `Get-StarterGPO` PowerShell cmdlet. When using this cmdlet, you can use one of the following parameters to determine which starter GPO or GPOs to retrieve:

▶ `Get-StarterGPO –Name` *<Display Name of the Starter GPO>*

▶ `Get-StarterGPO –GUID` *<GUID of the Starter GPO>*

▶ `Get-StarterGPO –ALL` (retrieves all starter GPOs in the domain)

Generating the Resultant Set of Policies Applied

A common requirement when performing troubleshooting of GPOs is having the ability to answer, "What policies are being applied to my computer right now?" In order to meet this requirement, Microsoft Group Policy offers users and administrators the ability to generate a *Resultant Set of Policy (RSoP)* report for a user logged on to a particular computer. The quickest way to return this information is to simply type **rsop** from the Run line or command prompt of the local workstation; doing so returns a graphical report indicating the following:

► Which GPO settings are configured

► Which GPO applied the setting (useful if you're troubleshooting the application of multiple GPOs)

You can see the result of the rsop command in Figure 8.14.

FIGURE 8.14 Resultant Set of Policy output

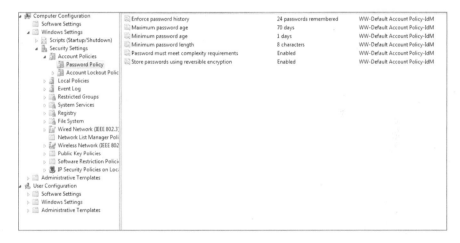

You can also obtain this information using the Get-GPResultantSetOfPolicy PowerShell cmdlet, which returns a more verbose set of information, including which groups the user is a member of. You can customize the behavior of this cmdlet using a number of additional parameters:

► -Path specifies the path to the output file.

► -Computer specifies which computer the RSoP report should be run for, if not the local computer.

▶ -User specifies which user the RSoP report should be run for, if not the
currently logged-on user.

▶ -ReportType [XML | HTML] saves the output in either XML or HTML
format.

Figure 8.15 shows some sample output from the Get-GPResultantSetOfPolicy
tool.

FIGURE 8.15 Sample `Get-GPResultantSetOfPolicy` output

Protecting Your Investment in Active Directory

Automating Active Directory Security

IN THIS CHAPTER, YOU WILL LEARN TO:

n today's enterprise environment, security can no longer be treated as an afterthought. Instead, it's foremost on the minds of everyone involved in managing IT infrastructure. There are a number of reasons for this, from regulatory compliance to protection of resources from insider and outsider cyber threats. Regardless of the requirement or need, it's widely accepted that security must be engineered in from the beginning and not merely bolted on after the fact.

In this chapter, we'll focus on how to use PowerShell to secure the Active Directory environment. There are an extraordinary number of security objects in Windows and AD, many more than can be covered in the scope of a single chapter, so we'll focus on some descriptive examples for essential security components in AD that can be applied widely.

First we'll explore how to secure the forest through the fundamentals of directory permissions, password management, and account management using PowerShell. Then you'll learn how to manage the Windows volume-encryption feature called BitLocker. We'll show you how to use PowerShell to manage BitLocker's configuration and settings as well as how to manage BitLocker recovery in AD.

Secure the Forest

Let's begin by examining how to automate security aspects of AD in order to secure the forest. At the core of AD security is the AD permission model, which is designed to provide secure access for all AD containers and objects. We'll focus on illustrating some of the cmdlets that automate AD security management at the cmdlet level. Keep in mind that to automate large-scale tasks, you can easily combine these cmdlets into PowerShell scripts like those that have been shown throughout the book.

Automate Directory Permissions

In AD, default security permissions are assigned to the administrator of the domain or forest—in other words, the domain administrator or the enterprise administrator. Every container and object in AD has an associated permission model, which we'll discuss in more detail in a moment. Each object has permissions associated with it by default. Understanding what permissions are associated with the objects in the directory is essential for effective AD administration.

If a user or computer has insufficient permissions to certain objects in the directory, then critical operations may fail. On the other hand, if users or computers are
granted excessive permissions, then accidental or deliberate harm may come to the
directory through data alteration or deletion. Let's examine how to delegate permissions to an OU.

Delegating Permissions to an Organizational Unit

To effectively manage AD for the enterprise, as well as reduce the exposure of the
enterprise administrative accounts, a good security practice is to delegate administrative control to certain users or groups in the directory. In this section, we'll
examine how to accomplish this using PowerShell.

You can enable others to administer an OU in AD by delegating the permissions on
a specific OU to a user or group of users. Objects in AD have permissions associated
with them using an Access Control List (ACL). Although it's possible to delegate
control to a single user, it's usually a better strategy to delegate control to a group;
users can be added to or removed from the group without the need to change the
underlying permissions on the AD objects or containers.

Each object in AD has a security descriptor associated with it. The security descriptor is the means by which you can modify access control to the object. A security
descriptor consists of a discretionary ACL (DACL) and a system ACL (SACL). In
this sense, there are two separate ACLs for each object. Each ACL contains one
or more access control entries (ACEs). The ACE is the means to set allow or deny
access to an object.

ACEs support the concept of inheritance. Setting the inheritance behavior of an
ACE enables permissions to propagate down the AD hierarchy. For example, you
can set an ACE to delegate permissions on an OU, and those permissions will propagate to the child objects in the OU, namely the user accounts in the specified OU.

Viewing the ACL on an OU in Active Directory

An OU is a container in AD, and like other objects in AD, an OU has permissions
associated with it as just described. PowerShell provides a straightforward approach
to viewing the ACLs on objects in AD, including an OU.

First, let's say you want to list all the OUs in the domain. As you've seen throughout the course of this book, there is often more than one way to accomplish the
same task using PowerShell, so the techniques presented may not be the only way

to accomplish a specific task. The following cmdlet lists the OUs in the domain by name using one of these methods:

```
Get-ADOrganizationalUnit -Filter {Name -like '*'} | FT Name
```

The expected output looks something like this:

```
Name
----
Domain Controllers
Finance
Sales
Marketing
Managers
Engineering
```

Now that you have the list of names, you can select the OU you want to delegate permissions on or perhaps use as a prototype OU to copy a template ACL to a new OU, as we'll illustrate in the next section. You can use the following cmdlet to view the ACL on an OU.

```
Get-Acl "AD:OU=Engineering,DC=contoso,DC=COM" | Format-List
```

This cmdlet displays the path, owner, group, access, audit, and Security Descriptor Definition Language (SDDL) for the Engineering OU. Armed with this information, an administrator may begin to evaluate the permissions to determine necessary changes to allow or restrict permissions. In this case, your goal is to delegate administrative control of the OU, so let's more closely examine the next steps for that task.

Setting the ACL on an OU in Active Directory

In the previous section, we showed you how to list the OUs that exist in the domain and how to view the ACL for those OUs. It's possible to create specific ACEs that provide rights on an object for delegation using a script, although an easier way is to use the Delegation of Control Wizard in the Microsoft Management Console (MMC) snap-in for Active Directory Users and Groups. Use the Security tab on the property page to view the ACL for the object or container.

Using this approach, you can create a template ACL that can be used as a prototype to apply to other OUs you create. Alternatively, you can use the `dsacls` utility to modify the ACLs on a prototype OU, which can then be applied to new OUs. For this example, let's assume you've created an ACE for a user in the Engineering OU; you've done this so this user can be a delegated administrator for the Engineering

OU and because you want to apply that same permission to a new OU for the Engineering Research department.

To accomplish this, you can create a new OU called Research and then apply the ACL from the Engineering OU. The following script creates the new OU and sets a prototype ACL on an OU from the Engineering OU:

```
#Applies an ACL prototype to a new OU
$ACL=Get-Acl "AD:OU=Engineering,DC=contoso,DC=COM"
$OU=New-ADOrganizationalUnit -Name Research
Set-Acl $OU -AclObject $ACL
```

Viewing the ACL of a User

As described earlier, each object in AD has an ACL associated with it to control access to the object. Manipulation of the ACL will *allow* or *deny* certain rights to the object. To view specific rights for objects in AD, look in the AD Computer and Users snap-in under the Security tab. Let's briefly examine how to modify the ACL directory using PowerShell.

An administrator may want to grant or restrict access to a specific object in AD. We demonstrated earlier how to use Get-Acl and Set-Acl to view and set an ACL on an OU in AD. You can also use these cmdlets to view and set an ACL on other objects in AD, such as users, computers, and groups.

The following script demonstrates how to view the access permissions for the user account for Jane User:

```
(Get-ACL 'AD:\CN=JaneUser,CN=Users,DC=contoso,DC=com').Access
 | FT IdentityReference,AccessControlType -A
```

Assigning an Administrator to a Particular OU

OUs in AD may contain user, group, and computer objects. When administrators create OUs, they may choose to delegate management control of that OU to a specific administrator. This is common for resource OUs, where the domain administrator may want to assign a specific administrator to manage that OU.

The following AD module cmdlet makes it simple to add a manager to an OU. This example sets the manager of the Engineering Servers OU to be Jane User:

```
Set-ADOrganizationalUnit 'OU=Engineering Servers,DC=contoso,
DC=com' -ManagedBy 'CN=Jane User,OU=Engineers,DC=contoso,DC=com'
```

Manage Passwords

Passwords are literally the key to the security of Windows, and as such they're the first line of defense and require extraordinary precautions to ensure the security of the enterprise. Passwords are a necessity when it comes to running an AD enterprise. In some cases, passwords are managed transparently by Windows; but in the majority of cases that administrators worry about, they require manual password administration.

Typically we think of users first when we're concerned with password management, although other types of accounts have passwords that you must also be aware of in AD. As we mentioned, some of these accounts have passwords automatically managed by Windows, whereas others require that the enterprise administrator manage them. The first category of accounts, computer accounts, has passwords automatically managed by Windows. The second category of accounts are managed-service accounts and virtual accounts, which were introduced in Windows Server 2008 and Windows 7.

In this section, we'll describe techniques you can use to manage passwords in AD to help mitigate risks associated with passwords for user and service accounts. The AD module for Windows PowerShell greatly simplifies the work required to manage these passwords in a number of cases by reducing what was formerly complex Active Directory Services Interface (ADSI) script to what in many cases is now a single-line cmdlet of PowerShell—which is great news for administrators.

ACTIVE DIRECTORY MODULE FOR WINDOWS POWERSHELL

Windows 2008 R2 includes a module to simplify administration of AD, the AD module, which consolidates a group of cmdlets for AD administration. This module can only be installed on computers running Windows Server 2008 R2 or Windows 7 with the Windows Server 2008 R2 Remote Server Administration Tools (RSAT). The module is automatically installed on Windows 2008 R2 DC and can be found under Administrative Tools from the Start menu. At least one instance of Windows 2008 R2 AD Web Services must be installed on a DC in order to use this module for administration of the domain.

Changing the Password of a Service Account

In this section, we'll describe how to use PowerShell to change service account passwords. As mentioned earlier, Windows 2008 R2 introduced a new feature for managed-service accounts. Managed-service accounts allow for automatic password management for service accounts when the forest is at the Windows Server 2008 R2 functional level. Windows PowerShell cmdlets are available to add, update, or delete managed-service accounts, because Windows Server 2008 R2 doesn't provide a management user interface to managing these new accounts. The following steps show the cmdlets you can use to create a managed-service account and reset the password of the account.

1. Create a new AD managed-service account using the following PowerShell command. You can set additional optional attributes using this command when creating an account:

   ```
   New-ADServiceAccount [-samAccountName <String>][-Path
   <String>]
   ```

2. Reset the service account into AD DS. The following PowerShell command resets the managed-service account password. (For complete details on the command to reset the managed-service account password, use Get-Help -detailed.)

   ```
   Reset-ADServiceAccountPassword [-samAccountName <String>]
   ```

Enterprises that are unable to operate at the Windows Server 2008 R2 functional level must manually manage service account passwords. In those instances, service accounts that are used to manage services across the forest or domain are AD accounts. The following command is an example of what you can use to reset or change the password of an AD account:

```
Set-ADAccountPassword -Identity MyServiceAccount -Reset
-NewPassword (ConvertTo-SecureString -AsPlainText
"@StrongP@ssw0rd!" -Force)
```

Forcing a Domain-Wide Password Reset

Sometimes you may want to perform a domain-wide password reset. Examples include a domain security breach or something as benign as a central administrator leaving the company. Should the need arise to perform a domain-wide password reset, scripting can help greatly to accomplish this task. Let's look at a simple example of how to approach this task:

1. Obtain a list of all domain users. The following PowerShell command retrieves the list of domain users for the domain specified or, if it's left unspecified, the domain of which the computer is a member. You can limit this to

a specific OU using the -SearchBase parameter or explicitly specify the domain from which you want to retrieve the user list. This example retrieves the list of users from the default domain for the DC:

```
Get-ADUser -Filter 'Name -like "*"'
```

Or even more simply, you can list just the usernames:

```
Get-ADUser -Filter * | FT Name
```

NOTE Many of the tasks demonstrated in this section can be accomplished using an [adsisearcher] if the AD module for PowerShell is not available.

2. Set the user account to require a password change on the next logon:

```
Set-ADUser -Identity [$user] -ChangePasswordAtNextLogon $true
```

Resetting the Passwords of a Compromised RODC

If a read-only domain controller (RODC) is compromised, it's not possible to clear the password cache. Therefore, you must reset the passwords for the users on the RODC. Fortunately, PowerShell provides a relatively straightforward method to accomplish this task.

You can reset the user passwords on the RODC using a script like this:

```
Set-ADAccountPassword -Identity [$user] -Reset -NewPassword
(ConvertTo-SecureString -AsPlainText "Pa$$w()rd1" -Force)
```

Ensuring That No User Has a Blank Password

Next, we'll look at how to ensure that users don't specify blank passwords in AD. You can accomplish this by managing the Fine-Grained Password Policy (FGPP). The AD module provides support to enforce essential password security policies that include password complexity, password lockout duration, password age, password length, and password history.

Although the policy doesn't check for user accounts that already exist before the policy is set, it ensures that subsequent accounts that are created or passwords that are reset meet the policy as specified.

Here's a sample that illustrates how to set the FGPP to ensure that no user has a blank password:

1. Determine the current default domain password policy. This cmdlet returns the policy for reference. Regularly examining the default domain password policy is a good security practice to ensure that changes haven't occurred to the policy that drift away from what's expected:

```
Get-ADDefaultDomainPasswordPolicy
```

2. Set the default FGPP for the domain to ensure that no blank password may be created:

```
Set-ADDefaultDomainPasswordPolicy -Identity companyname.com
-PasswordHistoryCount 10 -MinPasswordLength 16
-MinPasswordAge 1.00:00:00 -MaxPasswordAge 90.00:00:00
-LockoutObservationWindow 0.00:30:00 -LockoutThreshold 3
```

In this example, the policy requires that passwords created on the domain must have a minimum password length of 16 and ensures that the same password isn't used again for at least 10 password resets. Additionally, this policy requires user passwords to be reset every 90 days.

Finding Users Who Have Passwords Set Never to Expire

It's important to domain security for administrators to understand which accounts have passwords that don't conform to your site policy. In some cases you may have legitimate accounts that don't have expiring passwords; but you need to regularly monitor for accounts that don't fit into that category.

This is important because accounts with passwords that don't expire may create a serious security risk on the domain. Should those passwords become compromised, an attacker could go undeterred in their use of those compromised accounts. Routinely changing passwords on accounts that are used by services ensures that this threat is mitigated.

Here's a cmdlet that lets you report which accounts have passwords set to never expire:

```
Search-ADAccount -PasswordNeverExpires
| where {$_.ObjectClass -eq 'user'} | FT Name,ObjectClass -A
```

Dealing with Account Lockouts

During the course of administering an AD enterprise environment, you may have users with locked-out accounts. This can be the result of an individual user's action or of brute-force password attacks against the domain. In either case, you need an efficient method to unlock those accounts to enable users to log onto the domain and get back to work.

When a single user is locked out, an administrator can use the AD Administrative Center or the Active Directory Users and Computers (ADUC) management console to unlock the user account. However, in those cases of widespread account lockouts, a script will prove to be invaluable.

In the following sections, we'll examine scripts that will search for accounts in AD that are locked out and how to unlock those accounts using PowerShell.

Finding Accounts That Are Locked Out

Finding locked-out user accounts is straightforward using the following AD Administration cmdlet:

```
Search-ADAccount -LockedOut | where {$_.ObjectClass -eq 'user'}
 | FT Name
```

This example filters the class of accounts that are searched for to include only user accounts. You could use this same technique to search for other accounts that are locked out by modifying that search condition.

Unlocking User Accounts

Unlocking accounts that have been locked out is a simple operation using the following cmdlet:

```
Unlock-ADAccount -Identity "CN=Joe User,OU=Engineering,
DC=contoso, DC=COM"
```

In instances where a number of user accounts have been locked out and need to be unlocked, using the PowerShell pipeline or creating a short script is appropriate. Combining the two cmdlets to find and unlock accounts can accomplish this task, assuming that every locked-out account in the OU in question is to be unlocked for use (see Listing 9.1).

LISTING 9.1: *Unlock-UserAccounts.ps1*

```
## File Name: Unlock-UserAccounts.ps1
## Description: Unlocks locked-out user accounts in the Contoso
## domain
# Get the user accounts that are locked-out
$accts = Search-ADAccount -LockedOut | where {$_.ObjectClass
 -eq 'user'}
# Loop through each object in $accts
```

```
foreach ($acct in $accts)
{
    Unlock-ADAccount -Identity $acct.samAccountName
}
```

Manage BitLocker

BitLocker was introduced in Windows Vista and Windows Server 2008 and provides Full Volume Encryption (FVE) for Windows client and server computers. For Windows Server, BitLocker is an optional feature that must be installed prior to use. The default behavior of BitLocker is for use with a Trusted Platform Module (TPM). Using BitLocker in conjunction with a TPM provides a secure root of trust (that is, a secure boot) for the FVE solution. Although using a TPM is the default behavior, BitLocker may also be configured on systems without a TPM by using an alternative protection method such as storing a key on the USB drive. In BitLocker terminology, the usage method of BitLocker may be referred to by the *key protector* that is being used. You'll notice that *key protector* is a term we'll use frequently in this discussion. A "*key protector*" is the method by which BitLocker implements cryptography to ensure that a volume's cryptographic key is protected when not in use by the system. Microsoft defines key protector as "a method for accessing the [volume master key]. Examples are PIN, external key, recovery password, and recovery key." We will discuss these examples over the course of this chapter.

It's important to note that BitLocker is volume-based encryption, so rather than encrypting an entire hard-disk drive, BitLocker instead encrypts the volumes on the drive. This is an essential point, because we'll be examining a script to get status and to configure BitLocker, and this will be accomplished per volume. As mentioned, you can configure BitLocker a variety of ways using key protectors.

Manage BitLocker Settings

In this section, you'll develop an understanding of how to manage BitLocker in the enterprise using PowerShell. Although BitLocker doesn't have a PowerShell module that allows direct management, it does have a Windows Management Interface (WMI) management interface that includes methods and properties for essentially every aspect of BitLocker that you'll need to manage that can be accessed using PowerShell. Even though BitLocker doesn't provide a PowerShell module of its own, you can organize the script we'll examine in the following sections into functions to further simplify BitLocker management in your environment.

Table 9.1 summarizes the support key protectors for BitLocker in Windows 7 and Windows Server 2008 R2.

TABLE 9.1   **BitLocker Key Protectors**

Operating System Volume	Data Volumes
TPM	Password
TPM + PIN	Smartcard
TPM + PIN + USB	Automatic unlock
USB (startup key)	Recovery key
Recovery Key	Recovery password
Recovery Password	Data recovery agent (certificate)
Data Recovery Agent (Certificate)	

Before we jump into specific tasks involved in BitLocker management, let's look at the WMI interface you'll be working with. You're interested in two WMI provider classes when managing BitLocker with a TPM:

- `Win32_TPM`
- `Win32_EncryptableVolume`

Each of these classes contains a number of WMI properties and methods that you can access using PowerShell. In the remainder of the chapter, we'll demonstrate how to use the power of the WMI classes with PowerShell to manage BitLocker.

WIN32 API FOR BITLOCKER AND TPM SERVICES

Microsoft has documented the Win32 API for its WMI for BitLocker and TPM services. For more information about the properties and methods available, see `http://msdn.microsoft.com/en-us/library/aa376476(v=VS.85).aspx`.

Determining Whether a Computer Has BitLocker Enabled

The first step in automating any deployment of BitLocker is to determine whether BitLocker is enabled on a system. This process may be as simple as checking the status of BitLocker on the system, referred to as `ProtectionStatus`; the process can be made more comprehensive by evaluating whether the system has a BitLocker-capable TPM.

Let's begin by examining how to verify the BitLocker protection status of a system using the most direct method. This one-liner accomplishes that task for the local system and returns the status of all the volumes attached to the local system:

```
Get-WMIObject -Class Win32_EncryptableVolume -namespace "root\
CIMV2\Security\MicrosoftVolumeEncryption"
```

Similarly, if you want to verify the TPM status of the local system, this one-line script does that:

```
Get-WMIObject -Class Win32_Tpm -namespace
"root\CIMV2\Security\MicrosoftTpm"
```

You can run either of these using the -computername parameter to query the status of BitLocker or the TPM on a remote computer, which lends itself to automating this activity over a group of computers.

You can determine the available properties using the Get-Member or gm option. For example, the following script returns the available properties for BitLocker:

```
$BDE=Get-WMIObject -Class Win32_EncryptableVolume -namespace
"root\CIMV2\Security\MicrosoftVolumeEncryption"
$BDE | Get-Member
```

Displaying the properties you're interested in is easily accomplished using the select option, as shown in the following example, which displays the drive letter and associated BitLocker ProtectionStatus on the local computer:

```
$BDE=Get-WMIObject -Class Win32_EncryptableVolume -namespace
 "root\CIMV2\Security\MicrosoftVolumeEncryption"
$BDE | select DriveLetter,ProtectionStatus
```

Now that you have a sense of the basics required to interface with the BitLocker WMI classes through PowerShell, let's examine how you can use PowerShell to automate some of the configuration management tasks necessary to effectively deploy and manage BitLocker.

Automating the Configuration of BitLocker

Given the concerns around data protection in the enterprise today, which sometimes include the need to adhere to regulatory compliance or corporate governance requirements, it's beneficial to have implementations of data protection that are as automated as possible. Unfortunately, Windows Vista and Windows 7 lack native support to automatically turn on BitLocker. But using PowerShell, you can create a script that can improve certain aspects of automation.

In this section, we'll look at the minimum steps that an enterprise might consider when developing a rudimentary capability to enable BitLocker automatically using PowerShell.

The following list contains the basic steps to enable BitLocker using a TPM for Windows 7 or later versions of Windows:

1. Is the TPM activated and owned?

2. Is the computer running Windows 7 or later?

3. Is there sufficient room on the hard drive to enable BitLocker?

4. If all the conditions are satisfied, turn on BitLocker.

Let's take each of these steps and examine it more closely in the context of the PowerShell script required to accomplish it.

Determining Whether the TPM Is Activated and Owned

To determine whether the TPM on the machine is activated, you can use the following script (we go into details about how to activate and take ownership of a TPM later in this chapter):

```
$TPM=Get-WMIObject -Class Win32_Tpm -namespace
  "root\CIMV2\Security\MicrosoftTpm"
$TPM.IsEnabled()
$TPM.IsActivated()
$TPM.IsOwned()
```

The output variable of each of these methods is a Boolean that, if it evaluates to True, indicates that the TPM is enabled, activated, and owned. Alternatively, the TPM class provides initial property values that you can check, although they don't update after an instance of the class has been instantiated. The properties are as follows:

- ▶ IsActivated_InitialValue

- ▶ IsEnabled_InitialValue

- ▶ IsOwned_InitialValue

The methods provide a more accurate accounting of the current state of the TPM because they query the TPM each time they're invoked.

PREPARING THE TPM FOR USE WITH BITLOCKER

Preparing the TPM for BitLocker is typically a three-step process. The three states are activated, enabled, and owned. The Trusted Computing Group (TCG, `www.trustedcomputinggroup.org/`) requires a physical presence check as part of activating a TPM. See the section "Enabling and Taking Ownership of the TPM" for more information about the PowerShell script necessary to accomplish these steps.

Determining the Version of the Operating System

You can determine the version of the operating system and check to see if it's at least Windows 7 using the following script:

```
$OS=Get-WMIObject -Computername $ComputerName
 Win32_OperatingSystem
$OS
```

Determining the Amount of Free Space on the Disk

BitLocker sets aside around 6 GB of free space for the user to use while it encrypts. For our purposes, let's say you want to have 10 GB of free space on the drive. You can check free space with the following script:

```
$C=Get-WMIObject -Class Win32_Volume -Filter "driveletter =
 'C:'"
$C
```

The `if` statement to verify that the free space is larger than 10 GB is as follows (note that the value is in bytes):

```
if ($.FreeSpace -gt 10737418240)
```

Turning On BitLocker

Finally, if all the previous conditions are satisfied, you can attempt to enable BitLocker on the computer. A couple of WMI methods are required to enable BitLocker; so when you're using PowerShell, you need to use the same approach. Let's walk through the minimum steps required to enable BitLocker on a computer that has a prepared TPM.

To begin, normally you get an instance of the BitLocker WMI class as shown in the following script:

```
Get-WMIObject -Class Win32_EncryptableVolume -namespace "root\
CIMV2\Security\MicrosoftVolumeEncryption"
```

However, you're going to turn on BitLocker for a specific volume, so you need to instantiate a specific instance of the class for the volume that you want to encrypt. In this example, you want to enable BitLocker on the C: volume. This script accomplishes that (note that we've changed the return variable to $FVE to denote an instance of a volume):

```
$FVE=Get-WMIObject -class Win32_EncryptableVolume -namespace
"root\CIMV2\Security\MicrosoftVolumeEncryption" -Filter
 "DriveLetter='C:'"
```

Now that you have an instance of the volume to be encrypted, the next thing you need to do is create a key protector that will protect the volume. The primary key protector that you want to use to protect the operating system volume is the TPM. The following script shows how to create a TPM key protector for C::

```
$FVE.ProtectKeyWithTPM();
```

Notice that you call the ProtectKeyWithTPM method without specifying any input variables. By default, when this method is called without any input variables, the TPM uses default Platform Configuration Register (PCR) values for PCRs 0, 2, 4, 5, 8, 9, and 10. If you prefer to customize the PCR values to use, you can specify them in the input parameter for the method call.

TPM PLATFORM CONFIGURATION REGISTERS

The TPM includes registers to store platform measurements referred to as Platform Configuration Registers (PCRs). By default, BitLocker uses PCRs 0, 2, 4, 5, 8, 9, and 10 when configured for use with the TPM. It's also possible to specify the registers to be used by BitLocker. For more information about PCRs and their use by BitLocker, refer to http://msdn.microsoft.com/en-us/library/aa376470(v=vs.85).aspx.

Next, you need to create alternative key protectors that will be used to access the encrypted volume in case the computer goes into BitLocker recovery mode. If the Group Policy has been configured to automatically back up recovery passwords to AD, then a recovery password will be automatically generated and backed up. In this example, you'll create two key protectors that perform this function.

The two methods you'll use are the following:

- `ProtectKeyWithExternalKey`
- `ProtectKeyWithNumericalPassword`

Note that what we refer to as the *BitLocker recovery password* is also called the *numerical password* when you're working directly with the BitLocker WMI class. They're the same object, and we'll use both terms throughout the chapter.

The script to create these key protectors is as follows:

```
$FVE.ProtectKeyWithExternalKey()
$FVE.ProtectKeyWithNumericalPassword()
```

When you call the method `ProtectKeyWithNumericalPassword` without specifying any input parameters, it automatically generates a recovery password that is stored securely on the computer. If you do this, you may want to retrieve this password from the computer unless it's automatically backed up to AD. Use the method `GetNumericalPassword` to retrieve the password. You'll need to provide the `VolumeKeyProtectorID`, which looks something the following from the method:

```
VolumeKeyProtectorID : {9626485F-E13D-4BC3-BD52-EB0FF4633F85}
```

Now that you've created the key protectors you'll use to protect the operating system volume of this computer, all that remains is to start the encryption. Before you do this, it's important to note that methods are available to verify that a computer is capable of supporting BitLocker as well as verify that the computer disk drive has been prepared for BitLocker conversion. It's a good idea to include these checks and options in any comprehensive script you create for enterprise use. This example simply starts encrypting the volume using the following one line of script:

```
$FVE.Encrypt()
```

BitLocker automatically uses the key protectors you've created on the instantiated class for the operating system volume: `C:` in this case. You can check conversion status using the following line of script:

```
$FVE.GetConversionStatus()
```

`GetConversionStatus` contains output variables that report the `ConversionStatus` as well as `EncrytionPercentage`, which allows you to monitor progress and determine when encryption has completed. If you need to pause encryption at any point, you can do so with the following:

```
$FVE.PauseConversion()
```

WINDOWS COMMAND-LINE INTERFACE FOR BITLOCKER

A command-line tool called `manage-bde.exe` is available for BitLocker; it allows for the status and configuration of BitLocker. The advantage of calling WMI directly using PowerShell is that robust error reporting and handling are available. However, `manage-bde.exe` does streamline several aspects of gathering status and enabling BitLocker. For more information about the `manage-bde.exe` command-line interface, see `http://technet.microsoft.com/en-us/library/dd875513(WS.10).aspx`.

This concludes our discussion of the minimum steps required to enable BitLocker for an operating system volume using the TPM key protector. Now that you understand the fundamental workflow, you can combine these steps into a single script that can be run against a computer or group of computers. It's important to note that the BitLocker WMI interface has a very rich error-reporting framework and that any comprehensive script should include error handling to process and log the errors that may and will arise when you attempt to enable BitLocker on a large collection of computers.

Storing TPM Information in Active Directory

Storing TPM information in AD is an essential step in order to manage the TPM on computers in the enterprise after the TPM has been activated. Because the TPM password isn't stored on the local computer, there is one chance to store this password when the TPM is enabled in Windows.

Why do you need to store the TPM owner password in the first place? TPM vendors follow the TCG specification when engineering a TPM. Each vendor that builds a TPM has its own implementation based on the TCG specification. Due to this, you may observe differences in the behavior of one computer manufacturer versus another depending on the TPM that is included on the computer. Specifically, lockout behavior may vary from one TPM manufacturer to the next for failed PIN entry attempts. If the TPM needs to be reset, the TPM owner password is required.

The TPM owner password—actually the hash of the owner password—is stored under the computer object in AD. Only one owner password is stored per computer, and it's stored in the attribute with the CN msTPM-OwnerInformation. Next we'll discuss the policy and steps required to store TPM owner information in AD.

Setting Policy to Require TPM Owner Information to Be Stored in Active Directory

The policy to require that BitLocker recovery passwords be archived in AD can be found in the Local Group Policy Editor or the Group Policy Management Console (GPMC) under Computer Configuration ➤ Administrative Templates ➤ System ➤ Trusted Platform Module Services. Navigate to the policy "Turn on TPM backup to Active Directory Domain Services."

To configure this policy, select the Enabled radio button to configure the options in the dialog box. Next, select the Require TPM Backup To AD DS check box to complete the configuration. This configuration doesn't require that computers contact AD DS in order to back up the TPM owner password.

As described in the policy, once the TPM owner password is configured, you can't set or change it if the computer isn't connected to the domain or if the backup should fail if the computer is unable to contact the domain.

Preparing Active Directory to Store TPM Owner Information

You must add an ACE to enable a computer to back up the TPM owner information into the computer object in AD. This must be done before you configure computers with activated and owned TPMs in the environment to ensure that the TPM owner password hash is backed up to AD.

SELF-WRITE ACE FOR TPM INFORMATION IN ACTIVE DIRECTORY

Microsoft provides script that demonstrates how to ensure that AD permissions are correctly configured to store the TPM owner information for computers. Refer to http://technet.microsoft.com/en-us/library/cc749026(WS.10).aspx for more information about setting the SELF-write ACE.

Protecting Your Investment in Active Directory

PART III

Enabling and Taking Ownership of the TPM

As we've mentioned, the TPM has three distinct states: *activated*, *enabled*, and *owned*. You saw earlier an example script that demonstrated how TPM status can be checked as a condition of enabling BitLocker. You can use a similar script to enable the TPM as well as to take ownership of it. It's important to note that in current TPM implementations, a physical presence is required to activate the TPM, so it may not be possible to carry out that function without having physical possession of the computer.

When you turn on BitLocker for the first time on a computer, it is a good idea to clear the TPM completely unless you can establish a clear chain of custody of the computer. Some enterprises may elect to have the TPM preconfigured when shipped from the original equipment manufacturer (OEM) to simplify deployment. In that case, the TPM may already be activated and the root keys associated with the TPM (in particular, the TPM endorsement key pair) available for use. It's possible to reset these keys, although we won't go into those details here.

Let's assume you have an OEM-configured machine that has an activated TPM, although that TPM isn't enabled and isn't owned. The Windows TPM WMI interface allows you to query and configure these aspects of the TPM in order to use it with BitLocker. Let's look at the steps you need to complete to prepare the TPM for use:

1. Verify that the TPM on the computer is enabled and that it has an endorsement key (EK) pair available for use. You can use the following script to verify that the TPM is enabled:

   ```
   # Get an instance of the TPM Class to work with
   $TPM=Get-WMIObject –Class Win32_Tpm –namespace "root\CIMV2\
   Security\MicrosoftTpm"
   # Check to see if the TPM is enabled
   $TPM.IsEnabled()
   ```

When you run this script, the method return tells you whether the method succeeded. To check the TPM status, you need to evaluate the Boolean return variable IsEnabled, which is either True or False. When you run the script without specifying that, as you did here, the IsEnabled return variable is displayed on the console.

To check whether the TPM has an EK you can use, you use a line of script like this with the same $TPM instance:

```
$TPM.IsEndorsementKeyPairPresent()
```

Similar to the previous example, the return variable is a Boolean value for `IsEndorsementKeyPairPresent`. If it evaluates to True, then you have a good key pair to use.

2. Now that you've verified that the TPM is enabled and you have a good EK to work with, you can begin the process of activating the TPM. I say the *process* because you must complete a few steps in this phase. Before you begin, it's a good idea to check to make sure the TPM will allow you to take ownership of it:

```
$TPM.IsOwnershipAllowed()
```

Assuming all is well, you're ready to activate the TPM. The TCG specifies that activating the TPM should follow specific state transitions. You can use the following WMI methods to transition these states and ultimately activate the TPM:

- `SetPhysicalPresenceRequest`
- `GetPhysicalPresenceTransition`
- `GetPhysicalPresenceResponse`

You set the physical presence request using the `SetPhysicalPresenceRequest` method, which is the key method in this process. A number of options are available when performing this transition, and it's possible to perform multiple steps in one method call.

Table 9.2 lists what we believe to be the most common options.

TABLE 9.2 TPM Options

Option	Description
1	Enable TPM
3	Activate TPM
6	Enable and activate TPM
14	Clear, enable, and activate TPM

You're interested only in activating the TPM in this step, so you choose option 3. The following line of script performs that operation:

```
$TPM.SetPhysicalPresenceRequest(3)
```

Immediately after the method call returns, you call `GetPhysicalPresenceTransition` to determine the next step. The script to perform that step looks like this:

```
$TPM.GetPhysicalPresenceTransition()
```

In this example, let's assume that the return value from the method is 1, which indicates that a reboot is required. Keep in mind that when rebooting the computer during a TPM transition, a user presence check may be required. These few lines of script reboot the computer:

```
$Computer=Get-WMIObject Win32_OperatingSystem
$Computer.reboot()
```

When the computer reboots, you (or the computer user) may see a BIOS-level screen that looks like Figure 9.1.

FIGURE 9.1   TPM BIOS confirmation screen

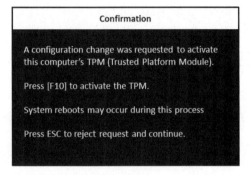

In this example, the user presses F10 to accept the change to activate the TPM, and Windows loads. You're almost finished. Finally, you need to check to see whether there's anything else you need to do. You do so by calling the method GetPhysicalPresenceResponse:

```
$TPM.GetPhysicalPresenceResponse()
```

The return value of the method informs you that there are no pending actions. You confirm that the TPM is indeed activated by checking it with the following script:

```
$TPM.IsActivated()
```

Again, the Boolean return variable informs you that the TPM is now activated.

3. Now that the TPM has been activated, you can take ownership of it. Earlier you verified that the TPM is available for ownership, so you won't check that again. Before you take ownership of the TPM, you need to choose a passphrase that will be used to protect the TPM secrets. You can use a method to convert the passphrase into a TPM owner authorization value that you'll use to take ownership. Taking ownership in this sense is a two-part process. The script to convert the passphrase into a 20-byte owner authorization value is the following:

```
$TPM.ConvertToOwnerAuth("password")
```

This line of script returns a string that you'll use for the `OwnerAuth` input variable for the method to take ownership. The actual return of our example passphrase converts to `6Pl/upEE0epQR5SObftn+s2fW3M`, which you use in the following line of script:

```
$TPM.TakeOwnership("6Pl/upEE0epQR5SObftn+s2fW3M=")
```

Finally, you verify that the TPM is now owned:

```
$TPM.IsOwned()
```

Verify that that the output Boolean variable is True to ensure that the TPM is indeed owned. Note that the initial value of `IsOwned_InitialValue` still shows False. However, if you create a new instance of the TPM class, it returns True if you perform that query against the new instance.

That was a long section, although you should now have a sense of the steps required to properly prepare a TPM for use with BitLocker. There are more methods available that we didn't cover, which are worth consideration when building your own script to configure TPMs for use with BitLocker in your own environment.

Resetting the Authorization Lockout of the TPM

As we discussed earlier, if a user has attempted to enter their BitLocker PIN too many time incorrectly, the TPM may enforce a lockout or timing delay. In order to reset the TPM, you can use the TPM owner password with this script:

```
$TPM=Get-WMIObject -Class Win32_Tpm -namespace
  "root\CIMV2\Security\MicrosoftTpm"
$TPM.ResetAuthLockOut(OwnerPassword)
```

Viewing TPM Recovery Information

The primary information stored in AD for the TPM is the TPM owner password, as we just discussed. This password is useful to update a computer without having to clear the TPM, which could have major operational impacts such as resetting BitLocker.

As we discussed earlier, TPM owner passwords aren't stored locally on the computer that the TPM belongs to. Therefore, to use the TPM owner password to manage a TPM, it's critical that you remember that password. As a backup, you can store the owner password hash in AD and subsequently use it to manage the TPM if necessary.

Protecting Your
Investment in
Active Directory

PART III

The following script demonstrates how to view TPM owner password information for computers in AD:

```
Get-ADObject -Filter 'ObjectClass -eq "msTPM-OwnerInformation"
-SearchBase 'DC=Contoso,DC=com'
```

Manage BitLocker Recovery Passwords

BitLocker is a very effective means to protect data using volume encryption for Windows computers. Given the effectiveness of the solution, it's imperative that enterprise administrators have a well-defined strategy for performing recovery of systems if issues arise that require the BitLocker-protected systems to be recovered. The first part of defining this strategy is to understand the common scenarios in which BitLocker users will need to recover their computers. If those computers are commonly used by a mobile workforce, then the most obvious solution is to take advantage of BitLocker recovery passwords.

BITLOCKER RECOVERY INFORMATION

Windows Group Policy allows backups of BitLocker recovery information to include recovery passwords and key packages. BitLocker recovery passwords are 48-digit readable passwords that are used to facilitate recovery of BitLocker-protected Windows computers. BitLocker recovery key packages are used to help recover a BitLocker volume that has corruption in the metadata section of the volume. A key package is essentially a copy of the lock that is used to protect the BitLocker volume. If that lock is corrupted, then a recovery key package is a copy of the lock that can be used to access the volume.

Configuring Active Directory to Store BitLocker Recovery Passwords

Since Windows 2008, AD has been preconfigured to store BitLocker recovery passwords. The BitLocker recovery password is stored in the computer object. Windows Server 2008 provides a Group Policy that lets you back up the BitLocker recovery information to AD. Through this Group Policy, it's possible to require backup of recovery passwords and key packages. By default, computers can use the SELF computer account to create the necessary objects in AD under the computer object to store the BitLocker recovery information, including recovery passwords and key packages. No additional configuration work regarding AD permissions is required to enable BitLocker to store recovery information in AD.

By default, the AD administrator has access to BitLocker recovery passwords and key packages. In some cases, the administrator will want to delegate permissions to another user or group to perform the function. You can use the same method discussed earlier in the chapter of creating a prototype template with the desired permission model, which you can then apply to the BitLocker recovery information objects in the directory.

Storing BitLocker Recovery Passwords in Active Directory

Windows provides a Group Policy to enable BitLocker recovery passwords to be stored in AD for each volume that is encrypted using BitLocker. The recommended approach is to ensure that this policy is enabled to require that BitLocker recovery passwords be stored in AD prior to computers having BitLocker enabled. This approach ensures that all computers that have volumes encrypted with BitLocker are recoverable. The following script shows the BitLocker recovery information object that the permissions will be applied to:

```
Get-ADObject -Filter 'ObjectClass -eq
"msFVE-RecoveryInformation"
```

Protecting Your
Investment in
Active Directory

PART III

ACTIVE DIRECTORY SCHEMA EXTENSIONS FOR BITLOCKER

When you're using a Windows Server 2008 R2 for AD, the schema is already prepared for BitLocker. However, in Windows Server versions prior to Windows Server 2008, the AD schema must be extended in order to store BitLocker recovery information. Refer to the TechNet article at `http://technet.microsoft.com/en-us/library/dd875529(WS.10).aspx` for information about how to extend an AD schema that hasn't been prepped for BitLocker.

Setting Policy to Require BitLocker Recovery Passwords to Be Stored in Active Directory

The policy to require that BitLocker recovery passwords be archived in AD can be found in the Local Group Policy Editor or the GPMC under Computer Configuration ➤ Administrative Templates ➤ Windows Components ➤ BitLocker Drive Encryption. You'll notice in the root folder of the Group Policy the policy

"Store BitLocker recovery information in AD Domain Services (Windows Server 2008 and Windows Vista)." As it suggests, this policy covers only computers with Windows Server 2008 and Windows Vista operating systems. It's still a good idea to configure this policy even if you don't have Window Vista computers to protect against inadvertent data loss.

For Windows 7 and Windows Server 2008 R2 computers, you can apply policy for the different volume types for operating system volumes, fixed data volumes, and removable data volumes. Each of these policies must be separately configured. To set the policy to require backup of operating system volumes, navigate to the policy "Choose how BitLocker-protected operating system drives can be recovered" under Operating System Drives. Select the Enabled radio button, and select the "Save BitLocker recovery information to AD DS for operating system drives" check box. In addition, you can specify that the BitLocker recovery information be backed up to AD DS. You can choose to store recovery passwords and key packages, or just recovery passwords.

Now that the policy is set, any computer that is a member of the domain will require a connection to AD in order to enable BitLocker. The reason is to guarantee that a backup of the BitLocker recovery password will be stored on the domain in AD. Without that policy, computers could have BitLocker enabled when not connected to the domain, resulting in potential loss of access and data if those computers went into recovery and the user didn't have a copy of the recovery password or a recovery key stored on a USB drive. In the next section, we'll discuss how to handle the situation where computers don't have BitLocker recovery passwords stored in AD.

Retroactively Storing BitLocker Recovery Passwords in Active Directory

In certain circumstances, some computers in the enterprise may have had BitLocker enabled while the machines were off the domain. This may occur either because those computers weren't joined to the domain or were working remotely (offline) when the policy to require BitLocker recovery passwords was put in effect. In these situations, AD administrators can connect to those computers using PowerShell and retroactively have the BitLocker recovery password escrowed into AD.

Let's look at the PowerShell script to connect to a computer and force the computer to send the BitLocker recovery password to AD:

1. Get the instance of the volume that you'd like to back up the recovery password:

```
$FVE=Get-WMIObject -class Win32_EncryptableVolume
-namespace "root\CIMV2\Security\MicrosoftVolumeEncryption"
-Filter "DriveLetter='C:'"
```

2. Now that you have an instance of the C: volume for BitLocker, you need to determine the recovery password key protector. To do so, you first need to retrieve the list of key protectors on the volume:

```
$FVE.GetKeyProtectors()
```

The output looks something like the following when multiple key protectors have been created for a volume:

```
VolumeKeyProtectorID : {{D0C23F2B-182A-4F1D-BC4A-52CDFC00E537},
{196986F0-621C-4384-B463-08D26093E644}, {EA2BB027-DC4F-4CCC-BC6A
-D8BAB9328E6F}, {9626485F-E13D-4BC3-BD52-EB0FF4633F85}}
```

3. Determine the recovery password protector identifier. For illustrative purposes, let's interrogate the first volume key protector ID:

```
$FVE.GetKeyProtectorType("{D0C23F2B-182A-4F1D-BC4A
-52CDFC00E537}")
```

In this example, the expected output looks like this:

```
KeyProtectorType : 1
```

The key protector types we're concerned with are listed in Table 9.3. For this example, it's the TPM key protector. You can find the complete list in the BitLocker WMI Win32 documentation.

TABLE 9.3   BitLocker Key Protector Type Name/Value Pairs

Value	Name
0	Unknown
1	TPM key protector
2	External key
3	Numerical password (recovery password)

Evaluate each of the volume key protector identifiers until you find the identifier of type value equal to 3.

4. Back up the recovery password to AD:

```
$FVE.BackupRecoveryInformationToActiveDirectory(
"{9626485F-E13D-4BC3-BD52-EB0FF4633F85}")
```

Protecting Your
Investment in
Active Directory

PART III

In this example, if the script returns 1, then Group Policy hasn't been enabled to allow BitLocker recovery information to be backed up to AD. Group Policy must be configured for BitLocker recovery information to be backed up.

In the next section, we'll discuss how to view BitLocker recovery passwords in AD. A useful script would combine the techniques discussed in the next section with this section to ensure that all of the computers in the enterprise that have BitLocker enabled are able to be recovered. For example, you may want to determine which computers that have BitLocker turned on don't have recovery passwords stored in AD, or you might want to check to see what computers that have BitLocker enabled don't have the correct recovery password stored in AD. You can do this using the PowerShell techniques in these sections.

Reading a Recovery Password in Active Directory

As we've illustrated, when Group Policy has been enabled, Windows will back up BitLocker recovery passwords in AD and store the passwords along with the volume identifier for each volume that is encrypted with BitLocker in the computer object of the computer that the volumes are associated with. We'll now examine the workflow associated with retrieving the recovery password for a computer that is encrypted with BitLocker when it goes into recovery.

We discussed earlier that by default, BitLocker recovery passwords are protected to the AD administrator using the confidentiality attribute. We described how permissions can be delegated to enable a specific user or group to read the BitLocker recovery password to help facilitate BitLocker recovery. In order to search for and retrieve a BitLocker recovery password from AD, the administrator or user performing that task must have permissions to read the recovery password in the computer object. In the example, we assume the account being used to access the recovery password has the correct read permissions on the computer object's BitLocker recovery passwords.

Finding Computers with BitLocker Recovery Information

In order to read a BitLocker recovery password, you need to find the computer object in AD on which you're looking to recover a BitLocker enabled volume. BitLocker provides some information on its recovery console that will assist in this process. One of the pieces of information is the recovery password identifier assigned to the encrypted volume that the user is attempting to recover. The CN of the BitLocker recovery object is `msFVE-RecoveryInformation`, and the attributes for the specific recovery data are `msFVE-RecoveryPassword` and `msFVE-RecoveryGuid`.

Let's look at what a script needs to do to accomplish this. Consider a line of script to search AD for the objects that have BitLocker recovery information. Keep in mind that the number of objects to be returned is limited, so this is for illustrative purposes only:

```
Get-ADObject -Filter 'ObjectClass -eq
"msFVE-RecoveryInformation" -SearchBase 'DC=Contoso,DC=com'
```

Finding a BitLocker Recovery Password in Active Directory

Now that you've seen how easy it is to locate the objects with BitLocker recovery information, let's look at how you can find a single recovery password using script. Let's say the user reads the recovery identifier to be {4AA81B4B-24E1-42C1-86CD-2713C2E9832E}. You can do a wildcard search of the first eight characters of the string to search AD. Here's the script that searches for the BitLocker recovery information based on the recovery identifier that the user reads from the recovery console:

```
Get-ADObject -Filter 'ObjectClass -eq
"msFVE-RecoveryInformation" -SearchBase 'DC=Contoso,DC=com'
-Properties msFVE-RecoveryPassword | Where-Object
{$_.Name -like "*4AA81B4B*} | FT msFVE-RecoveryPassword, Name
```

Deleting a Recovery Password from Active Directory

One of the limitations of the BitLocker implementation of archiving recovery passwords in AD is that when a new BitLocker recovery password is created and stored in AD, the old recovery password isn't deleted. There are a number of reasons why a new BitLocker recovery password may be created, including creating a new one using the BitLocker WMI management interface, or turning BitLocker off on a volume and then turning it back on again.

Regardless of why additional recovery passwords were created, you may want to prune from the directory the former recovery passwords that are no longer valid. The following scripts demonstrate how to delete a recovery password from Active Directory.

Using the previous example, you can search for a specific recovery password based on the identifier to determine its ObjectGUID:

```
Get-ADObject -Filter 'ObjectClass -eq
"msFVE-RecoveryInformation" -SearchBase 'DC=Contoso,DC=com'
-Properties msFVE-RecoveryPassword | Where-Object
```

```
{$_.Name -like "*4AA81B4B*} | FT ObjectGUID
ObjectGUID

-----------------

e6342712-eff9-4c8e-a244-e12f88aae78f
```

From this output, you determine that the `ObjectGUID` is e6342712-eff9-4c8e-a244-e12f88aae78f. Now you can use the following script to delete the recovery password:

```
Remove-ADObject "e6342712-eff9-4c8e-a244-e12f88aae78f"
-Confirm:$false
```

This operation should be used with great caution, because deleting active BitLocker recovery passwords may render computers unrecoverable. In the unfortunate event that a recovery password is accidentally deleted, if the computer it belonged to is online, you can use the following script to create a new recovery password for the computer:

```
$FVE=Get-WMIObject -class Win32_EncryptableVolume -namespace
"root\CIMV2\Security\MicrosoftVolumeEncryption" -Filter
 "DriveLetter='C:'"
$FVE.ProtectKeyWithNumericalPassword()
```

CHAPTER 10

Backing Up Data and Recovering from Disasters

IN THIS CHAPTER, YOU WILL LEARN TO:

I n this chapter, we're going to focus on Active Directory backup and restore. It's crucial to any AD environment to ensure successful backups to allow for restores in the event of a disaster, accidental or not. Using PowerShell and scripts can help automate backups and speed the process of restoration. They can also help with testing restores to ensure your backups are good.

Back Up Active Directory Data

Active Directory Domain Services (AD DS) is a critical service that many other services rely on in an AD-centric network. It's crucial to plan for disasters and ensure proper and consistent backups. Doing so will assist you in preventing a minor issue from turning into a calamity, such as an accidental OU deletion.

Throughout the following pages, we'll discuss the proper steps to back up AD DS via PowerShell and command-line tools.

Back Up the Directory Database

Windows Server 2008 includes a new backup application called Windows Server Backup; NtBackup no longer exists. Windows Server Backup isn't installed by default and is a feature of Windows Server. Using PowerShell in Windows Server 2008 R2, you can install the feature. You have to import the ServerManager module to get the Add-WindowsFeature cmdlet. It's recommended that you use the -IncludeAllSubFeature parameter to install the Windows Server Backup command-line tools and PowerShell module:

```
Import-Module ServerManager
Add-WindowsFeature –Name Backup-Features –IncludeAllSubfeatures
```

The only method to properly back up AD DS on a domain controller (DC) is to conduct a System State backup. It's recommended that you use the System State backup because it contains only system-state data, which minimizes the size of the backup. Table 10.1 lists the components in a System State backup in Windows Server 2008 and R2. Additional data may be included depending on which server roles are installed, but you should include the items in the table at a minimum.

TABLE 10.1   Components that Make Up a System State Backup

Component	Component
Registry	COM+ class registration database
Boot files	Cluster service information
Active Directory database (NTDS.dit)	SYSVOL directory
Active Directory Certificate Services (AD CS) database	Microsoft Internet Information Services (IIS) metabase
System files that are under Windows Resource Protection	

Windows Server Backup supports two types of backup: manual and scheduled (see Table 10.2). A scheduled backup can only be created by a member of the Administrators group because backup operators don't have the right to create Scheduled Tasks.

TABLE 10.2   Windows Server Backup Types

Type	Notes
Manual	A member of the Administrators or Backup Operators group can initiate a manual backup. The target volume can be a local hard drive or remote network share.
Scheduled	A member of the Administrators group can schedule backups. The target volume can be a local hard drive or remote network share.

Windows Server Backup introduces PowerShell cmdlets. Table 10.3 lists the Windows Server Backup cmdlets and a brief usage description.

TABLE 10.3   Windows Server Backup Cmdlets

Cmdlet Name	Cmdlet Use
Add-WBBackupTarget	Adds the WBBackupTarget object, which specifies backup storage locations, to the backup policy (WBPolicy object)
Add-WBBareMetalRecovery	Adds the needed items to the backup policy to enable you to perform a bare-metal recovery later with backups created using that policy

(continues)

Protecting Your Investment in Active Directory

PART III

TABLE 10.3   *(continued)*

Cmdlet Name	Cmdlet Use
Add-WBFileSpec	Adds the WBFileSpec object, which specifies the items to include or exclude from a backup, to the backup policy
Add-WBSystemState	Adds the items needed to the backup policy so that later you can use backups created with this policy to perform a system-state recovery
Add-WBVolume	Adds the list of source volumes to the backup policy
Get-WBBackupSet	Gets the list of backups (WBBackupSet objects) that were created for a server and stored at a location that you specified
Get-WBBackupTarget	Gets the locations for storing backups that you specified as part of the backup policy
Get-WBBareMetalRecovery	Gets the value that indicates whether the ability to perform bare-metal recoveries from backups has been added to the backup policy
Get-WBDisk	Gets the list of internal and external disks that are online for the local computer
Get-WBFileSpec	Gets the list of WBFileSpec objects that are associated with the specified backup policy
Get-WBJob	Gets the operation that is currently running (WBJob object)
Get-WBPolicy	Gets the current backup policy that is set for the computer
Get-WBSchedule	Gets the current schedule for backups in the backup policy
Get-WBSummary	Gets the history of the backup operations performed
Get-WBSystemState	Gets a Boolean value that indicates whether the ability to perform system-state recoveries with the backups has been added to the backup policy
Get-WBVolume	Gets the list of source volumes for the backup that is included in the backup policy
Get-WBVssBackupOptions	Gets a setting that specifies whether the backups created using the backup policy will be Volume Shadow Copy Service (VSS) copy backups or VSS full backups
New-WBBackupTarget	Creates a new WBBackupTarget object
New-WBFileSpec	Creates a new WBFileSpec object
New-WBPolicy	Creates a new WBPolicy object
Remove-WBBackupTarget	Removes the backup storage locations (defined by the WBBackupTarget object) from the backup policy
Remove-WBBareMetalRecovery	Removes the request to include all items needed for a bare-metal recovery from the current backup policy

Cmdlet Name	Cmdlet Use
Remove-WBFileSpec	Removes the list of items to include or exclude from a backup (as specified by the WBFileSpec object) from a backup policy
Remove-WBPolicy	Removes the backup policy that is currently set
Remove-WBSystemState	Removes the request to include all items needed for a system-state recovery from the current backup policy
Remove-WBVolume	Removes the volume to back up (specified by the WBVolume object) from the backup policy
Set-WBPolicy	Sets the WBPolicy object as the backup policy that will be used for scheduled backups
Set-WBSchedule	Sets the times to create daily backups for the backup policy
Set-WBVssBackupOptions	Sets a value that specifies whether the backups that are created using the backup policy are VSS copy backups or VSS full backups
Start-WBBackup	Starts a one-time backup operation

Creating a One-Time Backup of Active Directory

One-time backups allow you to create a backup out of schedule as required. It's a good practice to create these backups before and after major AD DS changes, such as creation or deletion of OUs or sites. To back up using Windows Server backup cmdlets, you must first import them using the Add-PSSnapIn cmdlet:

```
Add-PSSnapIn windows.serverbackup
```

You then create a Windows Backup policy and add options to the policy for the backup you're about to run. You create a blank policy in editable mode using the New-WBPolicy cmdlet:

```
$WBPolicy = New-WBPolicy
```

You then add the system-state option using the Add-WBSystemState module:

```
Add-WBSystemState –Policy $WBPolicy
```

You now have to add a target for the backup. Windows Server Backup supports using a disk, network path, or volume for backup. Use the Get-WBDisk cmdlet to return a collection of disks in the system. Then, use the New-WBBackupTarget cmdlet to specify a disk to be used for the backup. Finally, add the target to the policy using the Add-WBBackupTarget cmdlet:

```
$WBDisks = Get-WBDisk
$backupTarget = New-WBBackupTarget –Disk $WBDisks[2]
Add-WBBackupTarget –policy $WBPolicy –Target $backupTarget
```

You can store the backups on a remote network share to centralize your backups. You use the `–Network` parameter of the `New-WBBackupTarget` cmdlet to specify the share path. It's recommended that you use the `–Credential` and `–NonInheritAcl` parameters when using `–NetworkPath`. `–Credential` is the username and password for the user account that has access to the location where the backup will be stored. `–NonInheritAcl` applies permissions using the credentials supplied. This limits the folder access to the credentials specified or the Administrators/Backup Operators group of the computer hosting the share. If you don't use this option, users who have access to the shared folder will have access to the backup as well:

```
$psCred = Get-Credential
$backupTarget = New-WBBackupTarget –NetworkPath '
\\<server>\<share> –Credential $psCred –NonInheritAcl
Add-WBBackupTarget –policy $WBPolicy –Target $backupTarget
```

If you want to use the volume option, you can get a collection of volumes on the system using the `Get-WBVolume` cmdlet with the `–AllVolumes` parameter:

```
$WBVolumes = Get-WBVolume –AllVolumes
$backupTarget = New-WBBackupTarget –Disk $WBVolumes[3]
Add-WBBackupTarget –policy $WBPolicy –Target $backupTarget
```

The last option for backup targets is using a string for the volume path. You do so using the `–VolumePath` parameter of the `New-WBBackupTarget` cmdlet:

```
$backupTarget = New-WBBackupTarget –VolumePath M:
Add-WBBackupTarget –policy $WBPolicy –Target $backupTarget
```

Now that you've created the policy and added the system-state option and backup target, it's time to execute the backup using the `Start-WBBackup` cmdlet:

```
Start-WBBackup –Policy $WBPolicy
```

Then, put it all together into a reusable script, as shown in Listing 10.1.

LISTING 10.1: *Backup-ADDS.ps1*

```
## File Name: Backup-ADDS.ps1
## Description:
## This script is used to create a system state backup of
##   a domain controller.   The script prompts for backup target.
##
```

```
## Imports the windows server backup snap-in
Add-PSSnapin windows.serverbackup
## Creates the blank policy
$WBPolicy = New-WBPolicy
## Add the system state option
Add-WBSystemState -Policy $WBPolicy
# Prompts for backup target
$caption = "Backup Target"
$message = "Please select the backup target type"
$disk = New-Object `
System.Management.Automation.Host.ChoiceDescription `
"&Diks","help"
$network = New-Object `
System.Management.Automation.Host.ChoiceDescription `
"&Network Share","help"
$volume = New-Object `
System.Management.Automation.Host.ChoiceDescription `
"&Volume","help"
$volumepath = New-Object `
System.Management.Automation.Host.ChoiceDescription `
"Volume&Path","help"
$choices = `
[System.Management.Automation.Host.ChoiceDescription[]]`
($disk,$network,$volume,$volumepath);
$answer = $host.ui.PromptForChoice($caption,$message,$choices,0)
## Set the backup target after prompt
switch ($answer){
     0 {
     Get-WBDisk | select DiskName,DiskNumber,Volumes
     $WBDisks = Get-WBDisk
     $WBDisk = Read-Host "Which disk number would you like `
       to use: 0,1,2..."
     $backupTarget = New-WBBackupTarget -Disk '
       $WBDisks[$WBDisk]
          Add-WBBackupTarget -policy $WBPolicy -Target `
          $backupTarget
     }
     1 {
```

(continues)

LISTING 10.1 *(continued)*

```
$netPath = Read-Host "Please enter the network path to `
  use: \\<server>\<share>"
Write-Host "Please enter the credentials to use."
$psCred = Get-Credential
$aclInherit = Read-Host "Do you want to use the `
  NonInheritAcl option? Y or N"
If ($aclInherit -eq "Y")
{
        $backupTarget = New-WBBackupTarget `
        -NetworkPath $netPath -Credential $psCred `
        -NonInheritAcl
        Add-WBBackupTarget -policy $WBPolicy `
        -Target $backupTarget
    }
    Else
    {
        $backupTarget = New-WBBackupTarget `
        -NetworkPath $netPath -Credential $psCred
        Add-WBBackupTarget -policy $WBPolicy `
        -Target $backupTarget
    }
}
2 {
Get-WBVolume -AllVolumes | select `
  VolumeLabel,MountPath,FileSystem
$WBVolumes = Get-WBVolume -AllVolumes
    $WBVolume = Read-Host "Please enter the volume `
        number you would like to use: 0,1,2..."
    $backupTarget = New-WBBackupTarget -Volume `
        $WBVolumes[$WBVolume]
    Add-WBBackupTarget -policy $WBPolicy -Target `
        $backupTarget
}
3 {
$volPath = Read-Host "Please enter the volume path to `
  use: D:,M:..."
$backupTarget = New-WBBackupTarget -VolumePath $volPath
    Add-WBBackupTarget -policy $WBPolicy -Target `
```

```
                    $backupTarget
        }
}
## Displays the Backup Policy and runs the backup
$WBPolicy
Start-WBBackup -Policy $WBPolicy
```

Creating a Snapshot Backup of Active Directory

Windows Server 2008 introduced the ability to create and mount AD DS snap-shots. This feature allows you to mount a snapshot to view the data contained in the backup. Doing so can save time when you're choosing which backup to use for restore by letting you compare the backup data. You can mount and view multiple snapshots at the same time. AD DS and Active Directory Lightweight Directory Services (AD LDS) can be snapshotted and mounted without requiring a restart of the DC or AD LDS server. The snapshot is a copy, created by the VSS, that contains the database and log files.

To create a snapshot of AD DS, you must log on as a member of Enterprise Admins or Domain Admins. Then you use the `ntdsutil.exe` tool. In the tool, you enter the snapshot context, activate an instance, and create the snapshot. You use the NTDS parameter to activate the active instance of AD DS:

```
Ntdsutil.exe
Snapshot
Activate Instance NTDS
Create
```

The command returns "Snapshot set {GUID} generated successfully". You can use the List All command to view the current available snapshots on the DC. Backups made with Windows Server Backup are also listed, as shown in Figure 10.1. The output shows the creation of a snapshot and a list of the available snapshots. As you can see, there is a snapshot available on the `M:` drive that is from a Windows Server backup that was made earlier.

Enabling the Active Directory Recycle Bin

Windows Server 2008 R2 introduces yet another new and useful feature related to backup and restore of AD DS: the AD Recycle Bin. In the past, when an object was deleted, most of the attributes were removed, so it required a restore from backup. If the object had link-valued attributes such as group membership, a second restore was sometimes required. The AD Recycle Bin preserves all the link-valued and non-link-valued attributes of deleted AD objects. By preserving all of the object's information, a typical AD restore isn't required, which saves you lots of time.

FIGURE 10.1   The output from an `ntdsutil.exe` snapshot listing

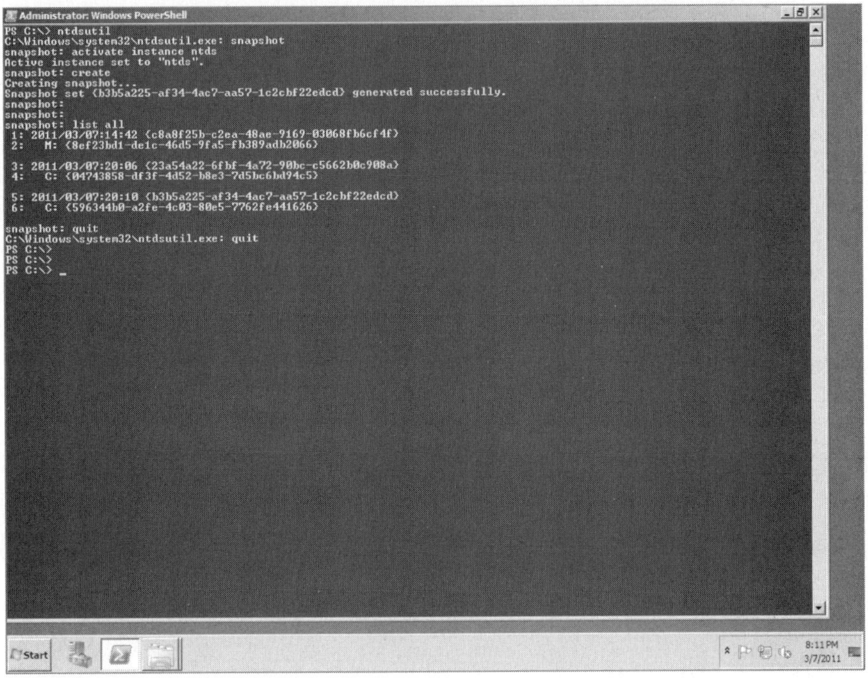

To enable the AD Recycle Bin, your AD or AD LDS forest functional level must be at Windows Server 2008 R2. Understand that enabling the AD Recycle Bin is irreversible—you can't disable it after it's enabled. When all your DCs are running Windows Server 2008 R2, you can raise the forest functional level using the `Set -ADForestMode` cmdlet. Remember to import the AD module:

```
Import-Module ActiveDirectory
$ADForest = Get-ADForest
Set-ADForestMode -Identity $ADForest -ForestMode `
Windows2008R2Forest
```

After raising the forest level, you can enable the AD Recycle Bin. You must be a member of the Enterprise Admins group to complete this step. You can then use the `Enable-ADOptionalFeature` cmdlet. The cmdlet requires a few parameters. You must provide the `-Identity` of the optional feature, which you can get using the `Get-ADOptionalFeature` cmdlet. You must also provide the `-Scope`, which is shown in the `Get-ADOptionalFeature` output, and the `-Target` forest fully qualified domain name (FQDN):

```
$RecycleBin = Get-ADOptionalFeature -Filter * | where `
{$_.Name -like "Recycle*"}
Enable-ADOptionalFeature -Identity $RecycleBin -Scope `
ForestOrConfigurationSet -Target <domain.com>
```

Back Up Other Essential Data

In this section, we'll discuss backing up other essential AD data. It may be necessary to restore only partial components of AD, such as a GPO, other files and folders, and so on. Some of these components are included in the System State backup, but you may want to back them up separately for reasons such as changes being made to GPOs, import/export of GPOs, and backing up non–AD related programs on the DC.

Creating a Backup of SYSVOL

You may need to restore a single file from your SYSVOL in the event of accidental deletion. Restoring the system state may be more work than is required if someone just deleted a startup or logon script. You can use the Windows Server Backup New `-WBFileSpec` and `Add-WBFileSpec` cmdlets to specify particular files and folders to back up:

```
$WBPolicy = New-WBPolicy
$WBFileSpec = New-WBFileSpec -FileSpec C:\Windows\SYSVOL
Add-WBFileSpec -Policy $WBPolicy -FileSpec $WBFileSpec
$WBBackupLocation = New-WBBackupTarget -VolumePath D:
Add-WBBackupTarget -Policy $WBPolicy -Target $WBBackupLocation
Start-WBBackup -Policy $WBPolicy
```

Backing Up Group Policy Objects

You now have the ability to manage GPOs via the PowerShell command line. This can be done on a Windows Server 2008 R2 DC, a Windows Server 2008 R2 member server with GPMC installed, or a Windows 7 workstation with Remote Server Administration Tools (RSAT) installed, so you don't necessarily have to wait until you have 2008 R2 DC.

Protecting Your Investment in Active Directory

PART III

You can use the `Backup-GPO` cmdlet after you import the Group Policy module. The cmdlet requires `-All`, `-GUID`, or `-Name` to specify which GPO(s) to back up. It also requires `-Path` for the folder to back up to. The path must exist, so you may need to create the folder first. Figure 10.2 shows the return output from these commands:

```
Import-Module GroupPolicy
Backup-GPO -All -Path C:\GPOBackup
```

FIGURE 10.2 The output from `Backup-GPO`

The `Backup-GPO` cmdlet can save you time from having to do a system-state restore in the event of a deleted or corrupt GPO. It also does not require that you mark the `SYSVOL` as authoritative to restore the GPO. Listing 10.2 shows a script that backs up all GPOs and stores them in a dated folder.

LISTING 10.2: *Backup-AllGPOs.ps1*

```
## File Name: Backup-AllGPOs.ps1
## Description:
## This script is used to back up all GPOs in a forest and
##   store them in a dated folder by domain.
```

```
##
## Backup path to store the GPOs
$GPOBackupDir = "C:\GPOBackups"
## Imports the Active Directory and Group Policy Modules
Import-Module ActiveDirectory
Import-Module GroupPolicy
## Get the date and create a folder
$date = Get-Date -Format yyyyMMdd
New-Item C:\GPOBackups\$date -ItemType Directory
## Get all domains in the forest
$ADDomains = Get-ADForest | select Domains
## Execute the backup for each domain
foreach ($Domain in $ADDomains.Domains)
{
        [string]$DomainToBackup = $Domain
        New-Item C:\GPOBackups\$date\$DomainToBackup
        Backup-GPO -All -Domain $DomainToBackup -Path `
        C:\GPOBackup\$date\$DomainToBackup
}
```

Backing Up Domain Controller Certificates

It's important to back up DC certificates if you're using them in your network.
Again, the system-state backup contains these certificates, but it's much easier
to restore them without using a system-state restore. PowerShell provides a way
to connect to the certificate store for both user and machine using the certificate
provider. The provider lets you navigate the stores as if they were folders on a volume. You gain access by using the cert: drive in Windows PowerShell. Using dir
cert: shows the CurrentUser and LocalMachine store in Figure 10.3:

```
dir cert:[
```

Using the cert: provider and the .NET framework, you can export the certificates
to .pfx files. You can change the number in the second line of the following snippet
to select which certificate to export. The certificate that you want to export must be
exportable for the script to work:

```
$pfxFile = "C:\CertBackup\Cert.pfx"    #Update this path
$cert = (dir cert:\LocalMachine\My)[0]
$type = `
[System.Security.Cryptography.X509Certificates.X509ContentType]`
::pfx
```

```
$password = Read-Host "Please enter the password to secure the `
file with" -AsSecureString
$bytes = $cert.export($type,$password)
[System.IO.File]::WriteAllBytes($pfxFile,$bytes)
```

FIGURE 10.3   The output from `dir cert:`

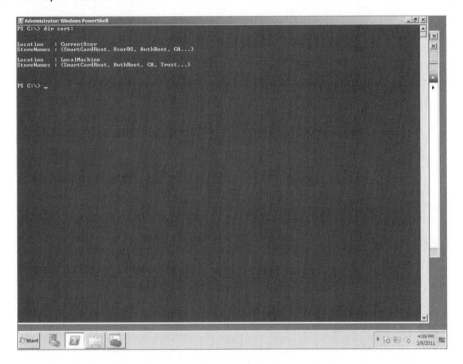

Backing Up Non-Active Directory Data on Domain Controllers

There may be other critical applications and files that you need to back up on your DCs. Using the script below the SYSVOL section shows you how to back up particular files and folders. You can add multiple selections, exclusions, nonrecursion, and wildcards to a backup policy. The following example backs up C:\Windows\SYSVOL, .jpgs under C:\Pictures, and the C:\otherstuff folder but not subfolders, while excluding .mp3 files in the C:\otherstuff folder:

```
$WBPolicy = New-WBPolicy
$WBFileSpec = New-WBFileSpec -FileSpec C:\Windows\SYSVOL
Add-WBFileSpec -Policy $WBPolicy -FileSpec $WBFileSpec
$WBFileSpec2 = New-WBFileSpec -FileSpec C:\pictures\*.jpg
Add-WBFileSpec -Policy $WBPolicy -FileSpec $WBFileSpec2
$WBFileSpec3 = New-WBFileSpec -FileSpec C:\otherstuff `
-NonRecursive
Add-WBFileSpec -Policy $WBPolicy -FileSpec $WBFileSpec3
$WBFileSpec4 = New-WBFileSpec -FileSpec C:\otherstuff\*.mp3 `
-Exclude
Add-WBFileSpec -Policy $WBPolicy -FileSpec $WBFileSpec4
$WBBackupLocation = New-WBBackupTarget -VolumePath D:
Add-WBBackupTarget -Policy $WBPolicy -Target $WBBackupLocation
Start-WBBackup -Policy $WBPolicy
```

One other consideration regarding backing up non-AD DS files is the system itself. Windows Server Backup supports a bare-metal recovery (BMR) option, which lets you perform a BMR using Windows Recovery Environment. When you use the `Add -WBBareMetalRecovery` cmdlet, the system-state option is automatically added:

```
$WBPolicy = New-WBPolicy
Add-WBBareMetalRecovery -Policy $WBPolicy
$WBBackupLocation = New-WBBackupTarget -VolumePath D:
Add-WBBackupTarget -Policy $WBPolicy -Target $WBBackupLocation
Start-WBBackup -Policy $WBPolicy
```

Make Backups Easier

Now that we've covered the basics of backups, we'll wrap it all together in this section. We'll discuss backup plans, how to back up to system volumes, and how to create a backup script.

Creating a Backup Plan

It's important to define a backup plan for your AD DS. To create the backup plan, you should define your recoverability goals. Because AD is a multimaster service with data replicated to multiple DCs, this isn't as hard as it would be for, say, Microsoft Exchange. Table 10.4 shows some possible goals.

TABLE 10.4   Examples of AD Recoverability Goals

Scenario	Goal
Entire DC fails	Restore the DC through BMR.
Database corruption on DC	Restore the database using a system-state backup.
Deletion of an OU	Use Recycle Bin to restore the OU and objects.
Deletion of a GPO	Restore using PowerShell cmdlets.

The plan should include what servers the backup will run on, how often it will run, what will be backed up, and where the backup will be stored. It should also take into consideration Flexible Single Master of Operation (FSMO) roles and the tombstone lifetime. It's recommended that you not recover a FSMO role holder, but instead rebuild and promote back into AD, if possible, using a new name.

Tombstone lifetime is also an integral factor. A backup is only good for the length of time defined by the tombstone lifetime. Table 10.5 lists the default tombstone lifetime by operating system.

TABLE 10.5   Default Tombstone Lifetime

Operating System	Lifetime
Windows Server 2003 SP1 Windows Server 2003 SP2 Windows Server 2008 Windows Server 2008 R2	180 Days
Windows 2000 Server Windows Server 2003 Windows Server 2003 R2	60 days

Note that if your domain was upgraded from 2000, 2003, or 2003 R2, then your tombstone lifetime is still 60 days; it's recommended that you change it to 180 days. Use Get-ADObject to check the value of the tombstone lifetime. If the attribute is set to <null>, then the default is used, as listed in Table 10.5:

```
Get-ADObject -Identity "CN=Directory Service,CN=Windows NT, `
CN=Services,CN=Configuration,DC=<mydomain>,DC=<com>" `
-Propteries tombstoneLifetime
```

The AD Recycle Bin has a deleted-object lifetime of 180 days. You can check the value with Get-ADObject. You can also set both of these values using Set-ADObject:

```
Get-ADObject -Identity "CN=Directory Service,CN=Windows NT,`
CN=Services,CN=Configuration,DC=<mydomain>,DC=<com>" `
-Properties msDS-DeletedObjectLifetime
Set-ADObject -Identity "CN=Directory Service,CN=Windows NT,`
CN=Services,CN=Configuration,DC=<mydomain>,DC=<com>" `
-Partition "CN=Configuration,DC=<mydomain>,DC=<com>" `
-Replace:@{"tombstoneLifetime" = <value>}
Set-ADObject -Identity "CN=Directory Service,CN=Windows NT,`
CN=Services,CN=Configuration,DC=<mydomain>,DC=<com>" `
-Partition "CN=Configuration,DC=<mydomain>,DC=<com>" `
-Replace:@{"msDS-DeletedObjectLifetime" = <value>}
```

It's important to understand these two settings, because your backup's lifespan is only as long as the lower of the two values. If one is set to 90 days and the other to 180, then your backups can only be used if they were made in the last 90 days.

Using the Operating System Volume on a Domain Controller for Backups

By default, Windows Server 2008 R2 doesn't allow system-state backups to the operating system volume. It isn't recommended that you store backups on the OS volume because if the volume fails, you lose the backups too. However, in some situations, it may be necessary to do so. If that is the case, you can add a Registry entry to override the default behavior by creating the SystemStateBackup key and AllowSSBToAnyVolume value:

```
New-Item HKLM:\System\CurrentControlSet\Services\wbengine\`
SystemStateBackup
Set-ItemProperty HKLM:\System\CurrentControlSet\Services\`
wbengine\SystemStateBackup -Name "AllowSSBToAnyVolume" `
-Type DWORD -Value 1
```

It's recommended that you use the Full Copy option when storing system-state backups on the OS volume. You do so using the Set-WBVssCopyOptions cmdlet with the -VssFullBackup option:

```
$WBPolicy = New-WBPolicy
Add-WBSystemState -Policy $WBPolicy
$WBBackupLocation = New-WBBackupTarget -VolumePath C:
Add-WBBackupTarget -Policy $WBPolicy -Target $WBBackupLocation
Set-WBVssCopyOptions -Policy $WBPolicy -VssFullBackup
Start-WBBackup -Policy $WBPolicy
```

Automating Backups with a Script

After a backup plan is in place, it takes only a few lines to implement a scheduled backup. The `Set-WBSchedule` cmdlet takes the –Schedule parameter in 24-hour format and accepts multiple schedules. The following example backup is set to run at 11:00 a.m. and 5:30 p.m. every day. When you have all your settings, you save the policy using the `Set-WBPolicy` cmdlet:

```
$WBPolicy = New-WBPolicy
Set-WBSchedule -Policy $WBPolicy -Schedule 11:00, 17:30
Add-WBSystemState -Policy $WBPolicy
Add-WBBareMetalRecovery -Policy $WBPolicy
$WBBackupLocation = New-WBBackupTarget -VolumePath M:
Add-WBBackupTarget -Policy $WBPolicy -Target $WBBackupLocation
Set-WBPolicy -Policy $WBPolicy
```

If you decide later to make changes, such as the backup target, times, or options, you can use the `Get-WBPolicy` cmdlet with the –Editable parameter:

```
$WBPolicy = Get-WBPolicy -Editable
```

This may be suitable for most organizations, but if you need a more comprehensive backup you can use the script in Listing 10.3 via a scheduled task. The script provides some additional steps to back up the GPOs and add them to the backup.

LISTING 10.3: *Backup-DomainController.ps1*

```
## File Name: Backup-DomainController.ps1
## Description:
## This script is used to back up all the GPOs for this
##   domain and back up the DC with SystemState and BMR.
##
## Backup path to store the GPOs
$GPOBackupDir = "C:\GPOBackups"
## Imports the Group Policy and Backup Modules
Import-Module GroupPolicy
Add-PSSnapin windows.serverbackup
## Back up the GPOs
Backup-GPO -All -Path C:\GPOBackups
## Run the backup
$WBPolicy = New-WBPolicy
Add-WBSystemState -Policy $WBPolicy
```

```
Add-WBBareMetalRecovery -Policy $WBPolicy
$WBFileSpec = New-WBFileSpec -FileSpec C:\GPOBackups
Add-WBFileSpec -Policy $WBPolicy -FileSpec $WBFileSpec
## Modify below for Backup Target
$WBBackupLocation = New-WBBackupTarget -VolumePath M:
Add-WBBackupTarget -Policy $WBPolicy -Target `
$WBBackupLocation
Start-WBBackup -Policy $WBPolicy
```

Restore Data

In this section, we'll discuss how to properly restore a DC, AD data, and other data. Most restore procedures don't offer a scripted method to recover data. This is for a good reason: It prevents a script from running and restoring bad data into the environment.

Restore Directory Data

There are different disaster scenarios and recovery processes, depending on what you need to recover. Multiple processes exist for some scenarios. It's important to understand the options you have when a disaster strikes, so you can make the best decision about how to proceed. Table 10.6 cover some scenarios you may encounter when managing AD (it isn't an all-inclusive list).

TABLE 10.6   Disaster Scenarios and Recovery Processes

Scenario	Process
DC failure with other DCs available	Perform a BMR and non-authoritative restore. *or* Reinstall Windows and promote back into the AD DS domain into AD DS.
DC failure holding FSMO role	Seize the FSMO role to a different DC, and reinstall Windows / promote back into AD DS domain.
Deletion of an AD object (site, OU, user) with AD Recycle Bin	Restore from AD Recycle Bin.
Deletion of an AD object (site, OU, user) without AD Recycle Bin	Perform an authoritative restore from backup.
Deletion of a GPO	Use PowerShell to restore the GPO.

Using the AD Recycle Bin to Restore Data

With the addition of the AD Recycle Bin, it's much easier to restore objects in AD DS. Using the `Get-ADObject` and `Restore-ADObject` cmdlets, you can restore an object in one line:

```
Get-ADObject -Filter {string} -IncludeDeletedObjects `
 | Restore-ADObject
```

In the `-Filter` parameter, you specify what you're looking for using PowerShell Expression Language. For example, if you want to find a user with the `displayName` Mary, you use `{displayName -eq "Mary"}`:

```
Get-ADObject -Filter {displayName -eq "Mary"} `
 -IncludeDeletedObjects | Restore-ADObject
```

Figure 10.4 shows an HR OU with two users and a group, and an Admins OU with one user and one group. The groups contain their respective members.

FIGURE 10.4   OUs, users, and groups to restore

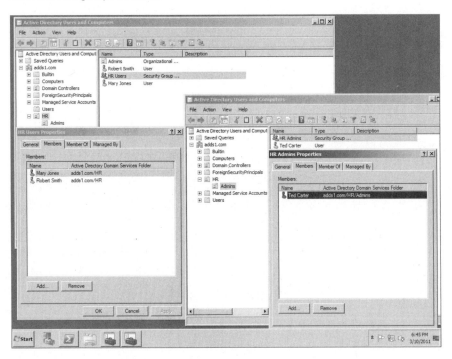

Suppose it's Monday morning, and you get a call from Mary Jones saying that she can't log in. You do a find in AD, and no objects are returned. So, you jump to PowerShell:

```
Get-ADObject -Filter {givenName -eq "Mary"} `
-IncludeDeletedObjects
```

The output returns an object with CN=Mary Jones\0ADEL..., so you realize the object is deleted. You check its last known parent:

```
Get-ADObject -Filter {givenName -eq "Mary"} `
-IncludeDeletedObjects -Properties lastKnownParent
```

The lastKnownParent is OU=HR\0ADEL.... Someone deleted an OU. To ensure that the HR OU is the highest object deleted, you search the Deleted Objects container, looking for msDs-lastKnownRDN:

```
Get-ADObject -SearchBase "CN=Deleted Objects,DC=<domain>,`
DC=<com>" -ldapFilter:"(msDs-LastKnownRDN=HR)" `
-IncludeDeletedObjects -Properties lastKnownParent
```

Now that you know HR was the highest object deleted in the tree, you can restore starting there. Restore the OU, then the objects under that OU, and finally the objects under the Admins OU:

```
Get-ADObject -ldapFilter:"(msDS-LastKnownRDN=HR)" `
-IncludeDeletedObjects | Restore-ADObject
Get-ADObject -SearchBase "CN=Deleted Objects,DC=<domain>,`
DC=<com>" -Filter {lastKnownParent -eq "OU=HR,DC=<domain>,`
DC=<com>"} -IncludeDeletedObjects | Restore-ADObject
Get-ADObject -SearchBase "CN=Deleted Objects,DC=contoso,DC=com" `
-Filter {lastKnownParent -eq "OU=Admins,OU=HR,DC=<domain>,`
DC=<com>"} -IncludeDeletedObjects | Restore-ADObject
```

Figure 10.5 shows these steps and a successful restore.

Restoring Deleted Objects Without the AD Recycle Bin

If you don't have the Recycle Bin enabled, you can restore AD objects using a process called *tombstone reanimation*. This process provides a way to recover objects without having to take the DC offline. It also restores the objectGUID and `objectSID`, thus saving you time because you don't have to fix all the Access Control Lists (ACLs) that pointed at the SID. There is no way to complete this process using built-in tools at the command line, so we'll step through using `ldp.exe`:

FIGURE 10.5   Output from an AD Recycle Bin restore

1. Log onto a DC as an Enterprise Admin.

2. Open `ldp.exe` on the DC.

3. Choose Connection ➤ Connect. Click OK.

4. Choose Connection ➤ Bind. Click OK.

5. Choose Browse ➤ Search. Enter **CN=Deleted Objects,DC=<domain>,DC=<com>** in the BaseDN box. Enter **(objectClass=user** in the Filter box. Select One Level for Scope. Click Options.

6. Select Extended for Search Call Type. Click Controls.

7. Select Return Deleted Objects from the Load Predefined drop-down menu. Click OK.

8. Click OK. Click Run to run the search.

9. The results are returned, and you must examine them for the account that was deleted. Copy the DN from the results of the object you want to restore, such as `DN=<user>\0ADEL:<GUID>,NC=Deleted Objects,DC=<domain>,DC=<com>`.

10. Choose Browse ➢ Modify.

11. Paste the copied DN into the DN box. Enter **isDeleted** in the Attribute box. Select Delete for Operation. Click Enter. Enter **distinguishedName** in the Attribute box. Enter the original DN from where the object was deleted. Select Replace for Operation. Click Enter. Click Run.

12. You should get the result `Modified CN=<user>\0ADEL:<GUID>, NC=Deleted Objects,DC=<domain>,DC=<com>`.

13. Look at the AD object. Most of the attributes must be repopulated, but the `objectSID` is still the same, which is important.

Now that you know how to use built-in tools, there are free tools to do this through the command line. You can download ADRestore from the SysInternals Suite and enter **adrestore.exe** with a search string to return matching results. The search string can be just the user's first name. Use `-r` to restore the object. If more than one object is found, you're prompted to restore each object:

```
Adrestore.exe Nicholas
Adrestore.exe -r Nicholas
```

Restoring Data from a Snapshot Backup

If you're making proper backups or snapshots of your AD, you can restore an object's attributes by hand from the mounted snapshot. A good example is when an account is deleted: You can use `ADRestore.exe` to restore the object and mount a snapshot to get any account attributes that ADRestore doesn't recover.

You use the `ntdsutil.exe` command to list and mount available snapshots. Once mounted, you can use `dsamain.exe` to mount the snapshot. You must provide the `dbpath` to the mounted snapshot and `ldapport`. It's recommended that you use a port like 50001. `dsamain.exe` will remain running in the command prompt. Minimize the window to keep it going:

```
Ntdustil.exe
Snapshot
```

```
List all
Mount <#>
Quit
Quit
Dsamain.exe /dbpath C:\$SNAP_<YYYMMDDHHMM>_VOLUME<drive>$\
Windows\NTDS\ntds.dit /ldapport <PortNumber>
```

After `dsamain.exe` has mounted the database, you can view it through Active Directory Users and Computers. Right-click your domain, select Change Domain Controller, and enter **DC:50001** to connect. You can also mount a PowerShell drive using `New-PSDrive`. Doing so allows you to use any of the AD cmdlets to read the objects in the snapshot. Remember, the snapshot is read-only, so you can't use any of the `Set-` cmdlets. From here, you can get the properties of an object and manually copy or enter them back into the restored object:

```
New-PSDrive -Name ADSnap -PSProvider ActiveDirectory -Root `
"" -Server <server>.<domain>.<com>:<portnumber>
Cd ADSnap
dir
Get-ADUser <user> -Server <server>.<domain>.<com>:<portnumber>
```

Figure 10.6 shows a mounted snapshot object on the left, the restored object with missing attributes on the right, and the properties from the `Get-ADUser` cmdlet at the bottom. Notice that the mounted snapshot's attributes are greyed, indicating that they're read only. Also notice that the restored object doesn't have any populated objects.

Remember to clean up using `Remove-PSDrive`, press Ctrl+ to kill the `dsamain.exe` running, and unmount the snapshot:

```
Remove-PSDrive ADSnap
Ntdsutil.exe
Snapshot
List Mounted
Unmount <#>
Quit
Quit
```

FIGURE 10.6   Object properties

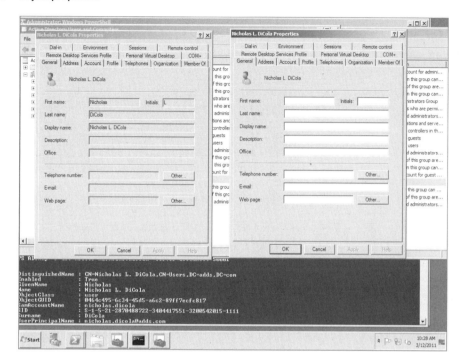

Restoring Data from a System-State Backup

In the unfortunate event that you can't use the AD Recycle Bin, you must perform an authoritative restore of the objects that were deleted. This is a bit more complicated, and we hope it will entice you to enable the AD Recycle Bin as soon as possible. To restore objects, you must first boot into Directory Services Restore Mode (DSRM). You can force the server to boot into DSRM using the bcdedit command. It may be a good idea to reset the DSRM password before rebooting to ensure that you have the correct password:

```
Bcdedit /set safeboot dsrepair
Ntdsutil.exe
Set DSRM Password
Reset Password on server localhost
```

```
<Enter the password>
<Confirm the password>
Quit
Quit
Shutdown /r /t 000
```

After you've rebooted into DSRM, log in using the `.\Administrator` username and DSRM password. You then can use the Windows Server Backup console or `wbadmin` to perform the non-authoritative restore. Because we're focused on the command line, `wbadmin.exe` is the tool of choice. Using the `get versions` parameter, you can list the available backups to restore. When you've determine which version to restore, you must use the `start systemstaterecovery` parameter, and the version must be exact:

```
Wbadmin get versions -backuptarget:<targetDrive>:
-machine:<computername>
Wbadmin start systemstaterecovery -version:<MM/DD/YYYY-HH:MM>
-backuptarget:<targetDrive> -machine:<computername> -quiet
```

Now you have a DC that has been non-authoritatively restored. The database contains the object(s) that were deleted. You must mark them authoritative so that when you reboot, the objects are replicated back out. Use `ntdsutil.exe` to mark the objects authoritative. You must run `activate instance NTDS` and then enter the Authoritative Restore menu. You can use `restore object` for one object or `restore subtree` for an entire OU:

```
Ntdsutil.exe
Activate instance NTDS
Authoritative Restore
Restore object "CN=<user>,OU=<OU>,DC=<domain>,DC=<com>"
Quit
Quit
```

The following shows the output from the command:

```
Successfully updated 1 records.

The following text file with a list of authoritatively restored
objects has been created in the current working directory:
ar_YYYMMDD-HHMMSS_objects.txt

One or more specified objects have back-links in this domain.
The following LDIF files with link restore operations have been
```

```
created in the current working directory:   ar_YYYYMMDD-HHMMSS_
links_<domain>.<com>.ldf
```

```
Authoritative Restore completed successfully.
```

Restart the server into normal operations. Then, use bcdedit to set the boot options:

```
Bcdedit /deletevalue safeboot
Shutdown /r /t 000
```

After you reboot, you'll need to restore the back-links if the restore found any. Use the ldifde.exe utility to import the created back-link LDAP Data Interchange Format (LDIF) file:

```
Ldifde.exe -i -k -f ar_YYYYMMDD-HHMMSS_links_<domain>.<com>.ldf
```

Remotely Puting a Domain Controller into Recovery Mode

In some scenarios, it may not be possible to be physically at the DC during a system-state restore. In such cases, you can use the Remote Desktop Client to remote into the server. Run the bcdedit and shutdown commands to reboot the server into DSRM:

```
Bcdedit /set safeboot dsrepair
Shutdown /r /t 000
```

After the server reboots, you can use the Remote Desktop Client to remote into the DC. You must use the <servername>\administrator format to log into the server. Figure 10.7 shows the RD client and authentication. This is a great solution when your DC is offsite in a branch office or datacenter.

Restore Other Essential Data

It may be necessary to restore other AD data that doesn't use the AD Recycle Bin or can be restored without a system-state restore. This section will discuss how to restore these other data sets.

Restoring SYSVOL from Backup

Before you can restore SYSVOL, it's imperative to know which replication system is being used. You use the dfsrmig.exe command to determine the status of SYSVOL:

```
dfsrmig.exe /getglobalstate
```

FIGURE 10.7 Remotely connecting into DC in DSRM mode

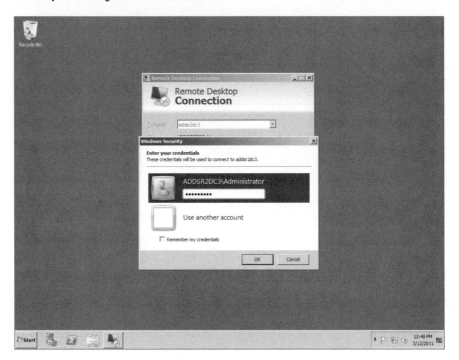

Table 10.7 lists the different states.

TABLE 10.7 SYSVOL States

State	What is used for replication
Start (state 0)	File Replication System (FRS) is servicing requests; no Distributed File System Replication (DFSR).
Prepared (state 1)	FRS is servicing; DFSR is replicating.
Redirected (state 2)	FRS is replicating; DFSR is servicing.
Eliminated (state 3)	No FRS; DFSR is servicing.

When you determine which state you're in, you can decide which process to use to restore SYSVOL. If you're using FRS, set the BUR flag and restart the FRS service to perform a non-authoritative restore. The Set-ItemProperty and Restart-Service cmdlets get this done quickly. The FRS service replicates from another DC, restoring the data:

```
Set-ItemProperty "HKLM:\System\CurrentControlSet\Services\NtFrs`
\Parameters\Backup/Restore\Process at Startup" -Name BurFlags `
```

```
-Value 210
Restart-Service ntFrs
```

To perform an authoritative restore, you must determine whether the DC has the correct data. If the data is good, you must stop FRS on all other DCs in the domain, set the BUR flag to D4, restart FRS, set the BUR flag to D2 on all other DCs, and restart FRS. If the data isn't good, you may need to restore the data from a backup. You can stop SYSVOL, use the Windows Server Backup console to restore SYSVOL, mark the BUR flag to D4, and start FRS. You still need to set all other DCs to D2 and restart FRS:

```
$
Name = $env:COMPUTERNAME
$colDCs = Get-ADComputer -SearchBase "OU=Domain Controllers,`
DC=<domain>,DC=<com> -Filter 'Name -ne $Name'
Invoke-Command -InputObject $colDCS -ScriptBlock {Stop-Service `
ntFRS -Force}
Invoke-Command -InputObject $colDCS -ScriptBlock {Set-Service `
ntFRS -StartupType Disabled}
Stop-Service ntfrs
Wbadmin.msc #Restore the SYSVOL Folder if needed
Set-ItemProperty "HKLM:\System\CurrentControlSet\Services\`
NtFrs\Parameters\Backup/Restore\Process at Startup" `
-Name BurFlags -Value 212
Start-Service ntfrs
Invoke-Command -InputObject $colDCS -ScriptBlock `
{Set-ItemProperty "HKLM:\System\CurrentControlSet\Services\`
NtFrs\Parameters\Backup/Restore\Process at Startup" `
-Name BurFlags -Value 210}
Invoke-Command -InputObject $colDCS -ScriptBlock `
{Start-Service ntfrs}
```

Restoring Group Policies from Backup

You should be using the Backup-GPOs cmdlet to back up all your GPOs before running Windows Server Backup. You can restore a GPO using the Restore-GPO cmdlet as long as a GPO with the same name still exists in the domain. Doing so restores a GPO's settings if someone makes an accidental change:

```
Restore-GPO <GPOName> -Path <LocationOfGPOBackups>
```

Protecting Your
Investment in
Active Directory

PART III

If someone deletes the GPO, you can use the `New-GPO` cmdlet to create a blank GPO; then, restore the original and delete the blank. The GPO links aren't restored, but all the settings are:

```
New-GPO <GPOName>
Restore-GPO <GPOName> -Path <LocationOfGPOBackups>
```

You can also import a backed-up GPO's settings using the `Import-GPO` cmdlet. You must specify `-TargetName`, `-BackupGPOName`, and `-Path`.

```
Import-GPO -TargetName <TargetGPO> -BackupGPOName <GPOName> `
-Path < LocationOfGPOBackups>
```

Restoring Domain Controller Certificates from Backup

Using .NET Framework and PowerShell, you can import certificates back into the certificate store. You can easily convert the following code into a prompting script:

```
$pfxFile = "C:\CertBackup\Cert.pfx"    #Update this path
$cert = New-Object `
System.Security.Cryptography.X509Certificates.X509Certificate2
$password = Read-Host "Please enter the password to secure `
the file with" -AsSecureString
$cert.Import($pfxFile,$password,[System.Security.Cryptography.`
X509Certificates.X509KeyStorageFlags]"Exportable")
$store = New-Object System.Security.Cryptography.`
X509Certificates.X509Store -argumentlist "MY", LocalMachine
$store.Open([System.Security.Cryptography.X509Certificates.`
OpenFlags]"ReadWrite")
$store.Add($cert)
```

Monitoring Health and Performance

IN THIS CHAPTER, YOU WILL LEARN TO:

I n this chapter, we'll focus on perhaps the most important aspect of Active Directory administration: ensuring that your Domain Controllers are healthy and performing well. A variety of tools and mechanisms are available to help you accomplish this. But because this book is focused on PowerShell, we're going to show you how to do a lot of the health and performance checks using PowerShell cmdlets and scripts. Often, when managing the health and performance of DCs, you're required to configure settings on a per-DC basis. When situations like this arise, using a script can make your life much easier. Throughout this chapter, we've provided scripts that you can use verbatim to ensure the health and performance of your AD environment.

Keep Active Directory Healthy

What does it mean to keep AD healthy? The health of AD (or any computer system, for that matter) is really broken into two parts: the proactive and the reactive. When you're keeping your AD proactively healthy, you're regularly performing tasks that monitor and maintain your domain to ensure that nothing unexpected happens. This includes things like keeping an eye on system events and proactively monitoring for free disk space.

No matter how good a job you do proactively with AD, you'll always be forced into reactive mode every now and then. In reactive mode, you're trying to determine why something is broken or not working as expected, and then you're figuring out what to change to resolve the issue. In this section, we'll provide you with guidance scripts for maintaining AD health from both the proactive and reactive perspectives.

Enable Logging

Enabling logging on DCs is really more of a reactive event. The type of logging we're talking about in this section you'll only want to enable when you're troubleshooting a problem. These logging mechanisms can give you some detailed information about various components of AD and make your troubleshooting go a lot more smoothly.

Enabling Kerberos Event Logging

When authentication is negotiated in Windows, the Kerberos authentication protocol is the preferred choice. The NT LAN Manager (NTLM), the second choice, is a weaker protocol that takes the direct client-to-server approach of generating a message hash and verifying it. Kerberos, on the other hand, uses three parties: a client, a server, and a Kerberos Key Distribution Center (a DC in AD). The KDC is trusted by both the client and the server, so it has the ability to issue tickets for each. When a client accesses a server, the KDC gives the client a ticket, which it can give to the server. The server uses the information inside the ticket to securely communicate with the client.

Because multiple parties are involved in this exchange, troubleshooting Kerberos problems can be tough. Typically, you can determine whether an authentication problem is caused by Kerberos issues by examining the system-event log and the security-event log of a DC. Because Kerberos is preferred and NTLM is the fallback authentication mechanism, a successful NTLM logon event may indicate problems with Kerberos. If there are any Kerberos errors, you'll find a Kerberos error code in the system log, and the source of the event will include the word *Kerberos*, *KDC*, or *LsaSrv*, as shown in Figure 11.1.

FIGURE 11.1   An example of a Kerberos error reported in the system log

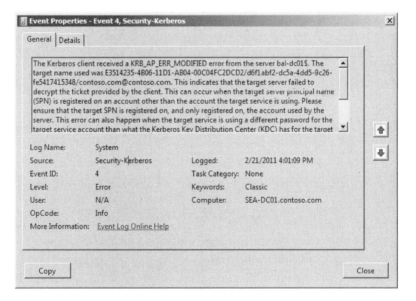

In the security log, you'll want to look for account logon and account logoff events, which indicate whether Kerberos or NTLM was used (see Figure 11.2).

FIGURE 11.2   A Kerberos account logon event recorded in the Security log

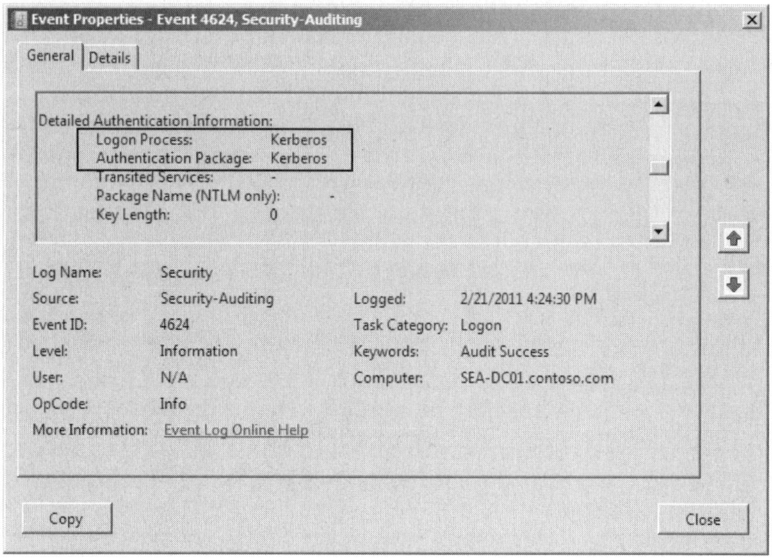

You can enable the Kerberos error log by setting the `LogLevel` key in following Registry path:

```
HKLM\System\CurrentControlSet\Control\Lsa\Kerberos\Parameters\
```

The `LogLevel` key is a `DWORD` value, and you can set it to 1 to enable the Kerberos event logging.

If the key doesn't already exist, you can create it from scratch. The change takes effect immediately, so there is nothing more to do after the key is set. Keeping the Kerberos log enabled can cause excessive error logging and negatively impact the performance of your DC. Therefore, you'll only want to enable it when you need to troubleshoot Kerberos problems.

When troubleshooting Kerberos errors, there is the potential for some false positive event log entries. Some events that show up in the log as an error can be safely ignored. In particular, event logs with Event ID 3 and that contain either a KDC_ERR_BADOPTION or KDC_ERR_PREAUTH_REQUIRED error code can probably be ignored if the user can still successfully log in. There are several error codes, however, that you shouldn't ignore. Table 11.1 lists error codes and potential resolutions for some of the common problems that you may encounter.

TABLE 11.1 Potential Kerberos Error Codes

Error Code	Description
KDC_ERR_C_PRINCIPAL_UNKNOWN	The DC can't find the user in the domain. Make sure the account exists.
KDC_ERR_S_PRINCIPAL_UNKNOWN	The DC can't find an account for the computer to which the user is requesting a ticket. Ensure that the service principal name (SPN) exists for the service.
KDC_ERR_PRINCIPAL_NOT_UNIQUE	The SPN of the server for which the user is requesting a ticket exists on multiple accounts. SPNs must be unique and therefore can only be tied to one computer object.
KDC_ERR_PADATA_TYPE_NOSUPP	The user is attempting to log on with a smart card, and the certificate can't be found. Ensure that the certificate for the user is valid and that the certificate authority (CA) can be contacted.
KDC_ERR_CLIENT_REVOKED	The user account is probably disabled, expired, or locked out.
KDC_ERR_KEY_EXPIRED	The user's password has expired and must be changed before the Kerberos ticket can be received.
KDC_ERR_PREAUTH_FAILED	The user probably entered the wrong password.
KRB_AP_ERR_SKEW	The clock on the user's computer differs from the DC's clock by more than 5 minutes. Ensure that time synchronization is working correctly.
KRB_AP_ERR_MODIFIED	Ensure that an SPN is set on the service the user is trying to access. Also ensure that DNS is configured correctly.
KRB_ERR_RESPONSE_TOO_BIG	The Kerberos ticket is too big to be transferred over UDP. The DC will fall back to TCP. If the client is a non-Windows client that doesn't support TPC fall-back (such as a Java application), you may have to force the DC to use TCP instead of UDP.

You can enable the Kerberos error log via PowerShell with the Set-ItemProperty cmdlet. If the LogLevel key doesn't yet exist, the following command will create it and set its value to 1. Otherwise, it will modify the key's existing value and change it to 1:

```
Set-ItemProperty HKLM:\System\CurrentControlSet\Control\LSA\
    Kerberos\Parameters -Name "LogLevel" -Type DWORD -Value 1
```

To disable Kerberos logging, you can either delete the key or set its value to 0. Again, this change takes effect immediately, so there is no need to reboot or restart any services. The following PowerShell cmdlet removes the key:

```
Remove-ItemProperty HKLM:\System\CurrentControlSet\Control\LSA\
    Kerberos\Parameters -Name "LogLevel"
```

One of the nuances of Kerberos event logging is that it must be enabled on each DC independently. However, Kerberos logons can potentially occur on any DC in the site or even in the domain. Therefore, if you're capturing logs to troubleshoot an issue, you'll probably want to enable the logs on multiple DCs. As with anything that requires some level of repetition, PowerShell can make this process easier. You can use the following PowerShell commands to enable Kerberos event logging on remote DCs. The following example enables the logs on BAL-DC01:

```
$reg = [Microsoft.Win32.Registry]::OpenRemoteBaseKey( ↵
    'LocalMachine', "BAL-DC01")
$key = $reg.OpenSubKey("System\CurrentControlSet\Control\Lsa\ ↵
    Kerberos\Parameters", $true)
$key.SetValue("LogLevel", 1, "DWORD")
```

The first line calls the OpenRemoteBaseKey method, which is a method in the .NET RegistryKey class. This method takes the name of the hive as its first parameter (LocalMachine means HKEY_LOCAL_MACHINE [HKLM] in this case) and the name of the server that you're remotely connecting to as the second parameter. Table 11.2 lists the other hives that you can use with this command:

TABLE 11.2   Registry Hives for Use With the OpenRemoteBaseKey Method

Hive Name	Name to Use in the Method
HKEY_CLASSES_ROOT	ClassesRoot
HKEY_CURRENT_USER	CurrentUser
HKEY_LOCAL_MACHINE	LocalMachine
HKEY_USERS	Users
HKEY_PERFORMANCE_DATA	PerformanceData
HKEY_CURRENT_CONFIG	CurrentConfig
HKEY_DYN_DATA	DynData

After the base Registry hive is opened, you can then use the OpenSubKey method to open a specific Registry subkey path. The previous example opens the path straight to the subkey where the LogLevel value should be created. When you opened the subkey, you passed in $true as the second parameter. This is necessary when you need to open the subkey for editing. If you omit this parameter, you'll receive an error when attempting to write a Registry value to the subkey.

The last line of the example creates the LogLevel value by using the SetValue method. In this case, you create the value as a DWORD by specifying it as the method's third parameter. For the second parameter, you specify that `LogLevel` should contain the value of 1, which enables Kerberos event logging.

To disable Kerberos event logging on a remote DC, you need to delete the `LogLevel` value. The following PowerShell commands will accomplish this:

```
$reg = [Microsoft.Win32.Registry]::OpenRemoteBaseKey( ↵
  'LocalMachine', "BAL-DC01")
$key = $reg.OpenSubKey("System\CurrentControlSet\Control\Lsa\ ↵
  Kerberos\Parameters", $true)
$key.DeleteValue("LogLevel")
```

In this case, the first two lines are the same as when you are creating the `LogLevel` value. The third line, however, uses the `DeleteValue` method to delete the `LogLevel` value.

Now that you know how to enable or disable Kerberos event logging on each DC, let's put it all together. The script in Listing 11.1 will allow you to either enable or disable Kerberos logging on one or all DCs in the domain. This script uses the AD module for PowerShell to enumerate the DCs in the domain, so you need to ensure that you run this on a Windows 7 or Windows Server 2008 R2 client and have a Windows Server 2008 R2 DC or a DC with the Active Directory Management Gateway installed.

Protecting Your Investment in Active Directory

PART III

LISTING 11.1: *set_kerb_logging.ps1*

```
## File Name: set_kerb_logging.ps1
## Description:
## Enables or disables Kerberos event logging on one or all
##  Domain Controllers in the current domain.
##
param([switch]$Enable, [switch]$Disable, [string]$DCName="")
# Import the AD Module if it isn't already imported
Import-Module ActiveDirectory
# Removes Kerberos logging from the specified Domain Controller
function DeleteLogLevel($dc_name)
{
    $reg = [Microsoft.Win32.RegistryKey]::OpenRemoteBaseKey(
      "LocalMachine", $dc_name)
    $key = $reg.OpenSubKey("System\CurrentControlSet\Control\"+
      "Lsa\Kerberos\Parameters", $true)
```

(continues)

LISTING 11-1 *(continued)*

```
        $val = $key.GetValue("LogLevel")
        if ($val -ne $null)
        {
            $key.DeleteValue("LogLevel")
        }
        Write-Host "Disabled on: " $dc_name
}
# Enables Kerberos logging on the specified Domain Controller
function CreateLogLevel($dc_name)
{
        $reg = [Microsoft.Win32.RegistryKey]::OpenRemoteBaseKey(
          "LocalMachine", $dc_name)
        $key = $reg.OpenSubKey("System\CurrentControlSet\Control\"+
          "Lsa\Kerberos\Parameters", $true)
        $key.SetValue("LogLevel", 1, "DWORD")

        Write-Host "Enabled on: " $dc_name
}
# If the name of a Domain Controller was specified, enable or
# disable logging on that specific Domain Controller
if ($DCName.Length -gt 0)
{
        if ($Enable)
        {
            CreateLogLevel $DCName
        }
        else
        {
            DeleteLogLevel $DCName
        }
}
# Otherwise, enumerate all Domain Controllers in the domain
else
{
        $objForest = Get-ADForest
        $colDomains = $objForest.Domains
        foreach ($strDomain in $colDomains)
```

```
{
    $objDomain = Get-ADDomain $strDomain
    $DCCN = $objDomain.DomainControllersContainer
    $colDCs = Get-ADComputer -SearchBase $DCCN -Filter *
    foreach ($objDC in $colDCs)
    {
        if ($Enable)
        {
            CreateLogLevel $objDC.DNSHostName
        }
        else
        {
            DeleteLogLevel $objDC.DNSHostName
        }
    }
    Write-Host
}
}
```

Enabling Diagnostic Logs

You may have noticed that DCs contain a Directory Service event log. But often, when AD problems arise, this log doesn't contain much information about what problem may be happening. By default, this log is only configured to contain high-level information about warnings and errors that occur in the Directory Service. Because of this, each DC has the ability to adjust the level of diagnostic detail that is logged for specific components of AD. Table 11.3 lists each component in which diagnostic logging can be enabled.

TABLE 11.3   Active Directory Components That Can Be Enabled for Diagnostic Logging

Component	Description
1 Knowledge Consistency Checker	Events about the component in Active Directory that creates connection objects between DCs.
2 Security Events	Security events recorded by DCsAD.
3 ExDS Interface Events	Diagnostic events pertaining to Exchange clients interfacing with AD.
4 MAPI Interface Events	Events for Messaging API (MAPI) clients that communicate with AD in older versions of Exchange Server and Outlook.

(continues)

TABLE 11.3   *(continued)*

Component	Description
5 Replication Events	Events pertaining to replication of directory data between DCs.
6 Garbage Collection	Events about the garbage collection process, which is used to remove Active Directory data that is no longer needed.
7 Internal Configuration	Events that are related to the internal configuration of AD. If there are internal errors, they may be logged when this diagnostic log is enabled.
8 Directory Access	Events pertaining to read and write operations to directory objects.
9 Internal Processing	Events that are often paired with other diagnostic logs to enable more specific information about the error encountered.
10 Performance Counters	Detailed events about performance-counter information.
11 Initialization/Termination	NTDS initialization and termination events, which are recorded when the directory services are started and stopped.
12 Service Control	Events pertaining to the AD services.
13 Name Resolution	Events that relate to resolving host names to IP addresses.
14 Backup	Events that are encountered when backing up AD.
15 Field Engineering	Events that are often used for troubleshooting inefficient LDAP queries.
16 LDAP Interface Events	Events about LDAP errors with additional detail.
17 Setup	Events related to AD setup errors.
18 Global Catalog	Events related to the Global Catalog.
19 Inter-site Messaging	Events related to inter-site messaging.
20 Group Caching	Events related to group caching.
21 Linked-Value Replication	Events pertaining to linked-value replication (LVR), which was a feature added in Windows Server 2003 to allow a subset of a multivalued linked attribute to be replicated instead of the entire attribute.
22 DS RPC Client	Events in this category are valid when the DC is acting as an RPC client. This may include events such as RPC errors, cancelled calls, failures with name resolution, and operations involving service principal names (SPNs).
23 DS RPC Server	Events that are valid when the DC is acting as an RPC server. Some of the events recorded in this log might be for outbound replication, replication setup, cross-domain moves, group membership queries, or lookups made by clients.
24 DS Schema	Schema-related events, such as additions, deletions, modifications, lookup, and caching errors.

This diagnostic logging is enabled on each DC independently. When working with diagnostic logs, sometimes you may have to enable diagnostic logging on multiple DCs in order to understand the problem that is occurring. Enabling these logs puts additional strain on the performance of the DC. Therefore, it's important to ensure that you only enable diagnostic logging when you need it. These logs are all disabled by default. The Registry key that houses these logs is

```
HKLM\System\CurrentControlSet\Services\NTDS\Diagnostics
```

These values are displayed in Figure 11.3.

FIGURE 11.3   The diagnostic log values are already present in the Registry.

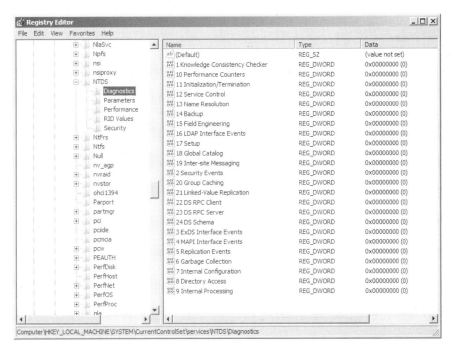

To enable the diagnostic logs, you can set the Registry value that corresponds to the component listed in Table 11.3. Each of these Registry values can be a DWORD value between 0 and 5, where 0 means the log is disabled and 5 means the diagnostic reporting is the most verbose. We recommend that when you're troubleshooting events using the diagnostic logs, you begin by setting the necessary components to 1 and then work your way up in detail as you need more information.

To enable or disable these logs, you can modify the Registry using the methods we've been discussing throughout this book. We've provided a few scripts to help you when you're working with the diagnostic logs. The first script, set_ntds_ log.ps1, allows you to enable a diagnostic log by its number on the DC that you specify (see Listing 11.2).

LISTING 11.2: *set_ntds_log.ps1*

```
## File Name: set_ntds_log.ps1
## Description:
## Sets the diagnostic logging level of a particular Domain
##   Controller.
##
param([string]$LogNumber="", [string]$LogLevel,
  [string]$DCName="")
if ($LogLevel -eq "") { $LogLevel = 0 }
if ($DCName -eq "") { $DCName = "." }
$reg = [Microsoft.Win32.RegistryKey]::OpenRemoteBaseKey(
  "LocalMachine", $DCName)
$key = $reg.OpenSubKey("System\CurrentControlSet\Services\"+
  "NTDS\Diagnostics", $true)
$value_name = "1 Knowledge Consistency Checker"
if ($LogNumber -eq "2") {
  $value_name = "2 Security Events" }
if ($LogNumber -eq "3") {
  $value_name = "3 ExDS Interface Events" }
if ($LogNumber -eq "4") {
  $value_name = "4 MAPI Interface Events" }
if ($LogNumber -eq "5") {
  $value_name = "5 Replication Events" }
if ($LogNumber -eq "6") {
  $value_name = "6 Garbage Collection" }
if ($LogNumber -eq "7") {
  $value_name = "7 Internal Configuration" }
if ($LogNumber -eq "8") {
  $value_name = "8 Directory Access" }
if ($LogNumber -eq "9") {
```

```
    $value_name = "9 Internal Processing" }
if ($LogNumber -eq "10") {
  $value_name = "10 Performance Counters" }
if ($LogNumber -eq "11") {
  $value_name = "11 Initialization/Termination" }
if ($LogNumber -eq "12") {
  $value_name = "12 Service Control" }
if ($LogNumber -eq "13") {
  $value_name = "13 Name Resolution" }
if ($LogNumber -eq "14") {
  $value_name = "14 Backup" }
if ($LogNumber -eq "15") {
  $value_name = "15 Field Engineering" }
if ($LogNumber -eq "16") {
  $value_name = "16 LDAP Interface Events" }
if ($LogNumber -eq "17") {
  $value_name = "17 Setup" }
if ($LogNumber -eq "18") {
  $value_name = "18 Global Catalog" }
if ($LogNumber -eq "19") {
  $value_name = "19 Inter-site Messaging" }
if ($LogNumber -eq "20") {
  $value_name - "20 Group Caching" }
if ($LogNumber -eq "21") {
  $value_name = "21 Linked-Value Replication" }
if ($LogNumber -eq "22") {
  $value_name = "22 DS RPC Client" }
if ($LogNumber -eq "23") {
  $value_name = "23 DS RPC Server" }
if ($LogNumber -eq "24") {
  $value_name = "24 DS Schema" }
$key.SetValue($value_name, $LogLevel, "DWORD")
Write-Host $value_name "set on " $DCName
```

The next script, in Listing 11.3, lets you get a list of the diagnostic logs that are enabled on a DC. You can run the script against the DC you're currently logged in at or specify the DC via the DCName parameter.

LISTING 11.3: *get_ntds_log_settings.ps1*

```
## File Name: get_ntds_log_settings.ps1
## Description:
## Retrieves the diagnostic logging level of a particular
##  Domain Controller.
##
param([string]$DCName="")
Write-Host "NTDS Diagnostic Settings on " $DCName
Write-Host
$reg = [Microsoft.Win32.RegistryKey]::OpenRemoteBaseKey(
  "LocalMachine", $DCName)
$key = $reg.OpenSubKey("System\CurrentControlSet\Services\"+
  "NTDS\Diagnostics")
$values = $key.GetValueNames()
foreach ($value in $values)
{
    $level = $key.GetValue($value)
    if ($level -ne "0")
    {
        Write-Host $value "enabled at level " $level
    }
}
Write-Host
```

The last script we're providing for diagnostic logging combs through the DCs in your domain and disables the diagnostic logs on every DC (see Listing 11.4). This script uses the AD module for PowerShell, so you need to make sure you're running it on a Windows 7 or Windows Server 2008 R2 client. You also need to have a Windows Server 2008 R2 DC or an older DC that is running the Active Directory Management Gateway.

LISTING 11.4: *disable_ntds_logging.ps1*

```
## File Name: disable_ntds_logging.ps1
## Description:
## Combs through every Domain Controller in the domain and
##  disables NTDS diagnostic logging on the DC.
##
```

```
# Import the AD Module if it isn't already imported
Import-Module ActiveDirectory
# Enumerate the domains in the forest
$objForest = Get-ADForest
$colDomains = $objForest.Domains
foreach ($strDomain in $colDomains)
{
    $objDomain = Get-ADDomain $strDomain
    $colDCs = $objDomain.ReplicaDirectoryServers
    # Enumerate the Domain Controllers in each domain
    foreach ($dc in $colDCs)
    {
        # Reset the NTDS Diagnostic logging values on each DC
        $obj_dc = Get-ADDomainController $dc
        $reg = [Microsoft.Win32.RegistryKey]::OpenRemoteBaseKey(
          "LocalMachine", $obj_dc.Name)
        $key = $reg.OpenSubKey("System\CurrentControlSet\"+
          "Services\NTDS\Diagnostics", $true)
        $values = $key.GetValueNames()
        foreach ($value in $values)
        {
            $key.SetValue($value, 0, "DWORD")
        }
        Write-Host $obj_dc.Name ": NTDS Diagnostic logs "+
            "disabled"
    }
    Write-Host
}
```

Check the Health of Domain Controllers

One of the key things you can do to ensure that your DCs are healthy is proactively stay on top of certain key aspects of the DCs. In this section, we'll walk you through using PowerShell to check the following factors of health on DCs in your domain, both locally and remotely:

► Ensuring that the essential services are running

► Verifying that you have adequate disk space to meeting your future growth needs

▶ Monitoring events thrown by the DC's event logs

▶ Reporting on operating system version, service pack version, and hotfix level

Determining Whether the Required Services Are Running

In order for a DC to operate correctly, a number of services must be running on the DC. It's important to check the services listed in Table 11.4 on each DC.

TABLE 11.4   Important DC Services

Service Name	Description
COM+ Event System	Used for components that are based on the Component Object Model (COM).
Remote Procedure Call (RPC)	Used to perform Remote Procedure Calls (RPCs) for COM and DCOM services.
Active Directory Domain Services	The service under which AD runs.
DNS Client	The client component of DNS. Without this service, the DC can't resolve queries to locate other DCs.
DFS Replication	Replaces the File Replication System (FRS) for SYSVOL replication. Without this service, SYSVOL won't be replicated to or from the DC.
Intersite Messaging	Allows DCs to send and receive messages with DCs in other sites.
Kerberos Key Distribution Center	The Authentication Service and Ticket Granting Service that distributes Kerberos tickets to clients. Without this service, Kerberos won't work.
Security Accounts Manager	Used for local accounts on the DC. If this service is disabled, other services may not start.
Server	Provides host services from the DC. If the Server service isn't started, file sharing, print sharing, and named-pipe sharing won't work.
Workstation	Used for establishing client-side SMB (Server Message Block) connections. This is required for SMB communication to other DCs.
Windows Time	Used to synchronize time throughout the domain. This is particularly important on DCs because time synchronization is used for replay detection in Kerberos authentication. Also, DCs serve as a time-synchronization source in the domain. Clients who authenticate against this DC will have their clocks synchronized by it.
Netlogon	Performs many duties, but is primarily responsible for maintaining secure channel connections for this DC.

It's important to ensure that all these services are enabled. You can do this on the DC that you're currently logged in at by running the Get-Service cmdlet in PowerShell. You'll probably want to check these services on all DCs in your domain or forest. In order to check a service remotely, you need to use the ComputerName parameter. For example, to check the status of the AD Domain Services (NTDS) service on BAL-DC01, you can run the following command:

```
Get-Service -ComputerName BAL-DC01 ntds
```

The following script in Listing 11.5 will enumerate all of the DCs in the forest and check to see if the critical services are running on them.

LISTING 11.5: *check_dc_services.ps1*

```
## File Name: check_dc_services.ps1
## Description:
##   Enumerates every Domain Controller in the forest and ensures
##   that the services are running that are critical to the
##   operation of Active Directory.
##
# Imports the Active Directory Module if it hasn't already been
# imported
Import-Module ActiveDirectory
# An array of each service that is checked
$services = "EventSystem",      # COM+ Event Service
    "RpcSs",                     # Remote Procedure Call (RPC)
    "NTDS",                      # Active Directory Domain Services
    "DnsCache",                  # DNS Client
    "DFSR",                      # DFS Replication
    "IsmServ",                   # Intersite Messaging
    "kdc",                       # Kerberos Key Distribution Center
    "SamSs",                     # Security Accounts Manager
    "LanmanServer",              # Server
    "LanmanWorkstation",         # Workstation
    "w32time",                   # Windows Time
    "NETLOGON"                   # Netlogon
# Checks the services on the specified DC
function check_services($dc_name)
{
    $any_stopped = $false
    Write-Host
    Write-Host "$($dc_name): " -NoNewLine
```

Protecting Your Investment in Active Directory

PART III

```
        # Check the status of each service in the list
        foreach ($svc in $services)
        {
            $status = Get-Service -ComputerName $dc_name $svc
            if ($status.Status -ne "Running")
            {
                $any_stopped = $true
                Write-Host
                Write-Host "Service Stopped: $svc" -NoNewLine
            }
        }
        if ($any_stopped -eq $false)
        {
            Write-Host "OK"
        }
        else { Write-Host }
    }
    # Enumerate each of the domains in the current forest
    $objForest = Get-ADForest
    $colDomains = $objForest.Domains
    foreach ($strDomain in $colDomains)
    {
        $objDomain = Get-ADDomain $strDomain
        $DCCN = $objDomain.DomainControllersContainer
        $colDCs = Get-ADComputer -SearchBase $DCCN -Filter *
        # Enumerate each Domain Controller in the domain
        foreach ($objDC in $colDCs)
        {
            check_services $objDC.DNSHostName
        }
        Write-Host
    }
```

Viewing the Available Disk Space across All Domain Controllers

As with any other Windows server, AD requires that adequate disk space be available on each DC. For a DC, there are various aspects to determine how much space you need to have available. The DC stores the AD data to a database file called

NTDS.DIT, which uses the Extensible Storage Engine (ESE) to read data from and write data to the database. The ESE requires that adequate space be available for writing database transaction logs and to grow the database as necessary. The amount of space required for future growth depends on how many objects you plan to add, the type of objects, and the number and length of attributes that you'll be populating for each attribute. AD allocates space in the database on demand for each attribute that is populated, so the database will grow according to the data that is held within it.

As a general rule of thumb, most people gauge the amount of needed disk space by allocating 400 MB of space for every 10,000 users. Therefore, if you plan to grow your domain by 20,000 accounts, for example, you should ensure that at least 800 MB of space is available on the partition that holds the directory database.

One thing that affects this calculation is whether the DC is also a Global Catalog server. If the DC is a GC, it holds data from other domains as well, so you'll need to ensure that there is enough space for growth across all the domains in your forest. GCs require an additional amount of space equal to about 50% of the size of other domains. Therefore, if Domain A requires 2 GB of space and Domain B requires 1 GB of space, a GC in Domain A will require at least 2.5 GB of space plus free space for additional growth. A GC in Domain B will require 2 GB of space plus free space for additional growth.

Another factor for calculating necessary disk space is to ensure that there is adequate space for the drive hosting the SYSVOL folder. The rule of thumb that most people follow here is to ensure that at least 500 MB is available in the partition, although in reality SYSVOL shouldn't be any larger than necessary. You should make sure there is enough disk space to not trigger any low-disk-space alerts and to account for any expected SYSVOL growth. Because SYSVOL is replicated among DCs, you'll want to make sure every DC in the domain meets the minimum amount of space that you determine is necessary.

For the OS partition, make sure at least 2 GB of space is available. The reason for this is to ensure that there is adequate space on your DCs for service packs and hot-fixes that you may be installing in the future.

To check the disk space using a PowerShell script, you'll need to do a couple of things. First, determine which local drives on the DC house the OS partition, NTDS.DIT, and SYSVOL. This data is accessible via Registry values on the DC. Table 11.5 shows which Registry values contain this information.

TABLE 11.5   Registry Locations for the Disk Information of Various DC Components

	Location
OS location	HKLM\Software\Microsoft\Windows NT\CurrentVersion\SystemRoot
NTDS.DIT	HKLM\System\CurrentControlSet\Services\NTDS\Parameters\DSA Working Directory
SYSVOL	HKLM\System\CurrentControlSet\Services\Netlogon\Parameters\SysVol

You can use the remote Registry commands discussed earlier in this chapter to connect to a DC and gather this information. For example, the following commands gather the location of NTDS.DIT on DC BAL-DC01:

```
$reg = [Microsoft.Win32.RegistryKey]::OpenRemoteBaseKey( ↵
  "LocalMachine", "BAL-DC01")
$key_ntds = $reg.OpenSubKey("System\CurrentControlSet\Services\ ↵
  NTDS\Parameters")
$ntds_dir = $key_ntds.GetValue("DSA Working Directory")
```

The contents of the $ntds_dir variable are the working folder used for NTDS .DIT. This value is a folder path, such as C:\Windows\NTDS. To get the drive letter for this folder, you can parse the folder path by splitting the string at the forward slashes. To split off the drive letter and store it in a separate variable, you can use the following command. The value of the resulting variable ($ntds_drive) is C:, which you'll use in a WMI query to the DC remotely:

```
$ntds_drive = $ntds_dir.Split("\")[0]
```

Now that you have the drive letter, you can perform a WMI query to the DC and ask for the information on that specific drive. To do this, you use the Get -WmiObject cmdlet and specify the Win32_LogicalDisk class.

In the command, you use a filter to ensure that you only return the drive letter of the drive you're looking for. The filter matches up the DeviceID property with the drive letter in Windows. So if $ntds_drive contains the value of "C:", the WMI query looks like this:

```
Get-WmiObject Win32_LogicalDisk -ComputerName "BAL-DC01" -Filter ↵
  "DeviceID='$ntds_drive'"
```

Putting these techniques together, Listing 11.6 enumerates all the DCs in the forest and checks the drive space on each one. This script doesn't dynamically determine how much drive space is needed on each DC. The minimums you want to check for are specified as variables at the beginning of the script; you can adjust these variables to meet the needs of your environment. By default, the script checks for the following minimums:

- OS drive: 2 GB free space

- SYSVOL drive: 500 MB free space

- NTDS drive for DCs that don't host the Global Catalog: 400 MB free space

- NTDS drive for Global Catalog Servers: 600 MB free space

LISTING 11.6: *check_drive_space.ps1*

```
## File Name: check_drive_space.ps1
## Description:
## Enumerates every Domain Controller in the forest and checks
##   the amount of free space on the OS drive, the NTDS drive,
##   and the SYSVOL drive. The minimum amounts of space are
##   specified as variables at the beginning of this script.
##
# The minimum amount of space to check for, specified in MB
$os_space = 2048       # Free space on OS Partition
$sysvol_space = 500    # Free space on SYSVOL Partition
$ntds_space = 400      # Free space on NTDS Partition for non-GCs
$ntds_space_gc = 600   # Free space on NTDS Partition for GCs
# Import the Active Directory Module if it's not loaded
Import-Module ActiveDirectory
# Enumerate each of the domains in the current forest
$objForest = Get-ADForest
$GCs = $objForest.GlobalCatalogs
$colDomains = $objForest.Domains
foreach ($strDomain in $colDomains)
{
    $domain = Get-ADDomain $strDomain
    $colDCs = $domain.ReplicaDirectoryServers
    # Enumerate each Domain Controller in the domain
    foreach ($dc in $colDCs)
    {
        Write-Host
        Write-Host "Checking Space on $($dc)"
```

(continues)

Protecting Your
Investment in
Active Directory

PART III

LISTING 11-6 *(continued)*

```
# Check the space in the NTDS Partition
$obj_dc = Get-ADDomainController $dc
$reg = [Microsoft.Win32.RegistryKey]::OpenRemoteBaseKey(
  "LocalMachine", $dc)
$key_ntds = $reg.OpenSubKey("System\CurrentControlSet\"+
  "Services\NTDS\Parameters")
$ntds_dir = $key_ntds.GetValue("DSA Working Directory")
$drive = $ntds_dir.Split("\")[0]
$disk = Get-WmiObject -ComputerName $dc -Class `
  Win32_LogicalDisk -Filter "DeviceID = '$drive'"
$mb_space = $disk.FreeSpace / 1024 / 1024

# The NTDS space check depends on the whether or not the
# DC is a GC
if (!$obj_dc.IsGlobalCatalog -and `
    $mb_space -gt $ntds_space)
{ Write-Host "  NTDS Partition:   OK" }
if (!$obj_dc.IsGlobalCatalog -and `
    $mb_space -lt $ntds_space)
{ Write-Host "  NTDS Partition:   Low" }
if ($obj_dc.IsGlobalCatalog -and `
    $mb_space -gt $ntds_space_gc)
{ Write-Host "  NTDS Partition:   OK" }
if ($obj_dc.IsGlobalCatalog -and `
    $mb_space -lt $ntds_space_gc)
{ Write-Host "  NTDS Partition:   Low" }

# Check the free space in SYSVOL
$key_sysvol = $reg.OpenSubKey("System\CurrentControlSet\"+
  "Services\Netlogon\Parameters")
$sysvol_dir = $key_sysvol.GetValue("SysVol")
$sysvol_drive = $sysvol_dir.Split("\")[0]
$sysvol_disk = Get-WmiObject -ComputerName $dc -Class `
  Win32_LogicalDisk -Filter "DeviceID = '$sysvol_drive'"
$sysvol_mb_space = $sysvol_disk.FreeSpace / 1024 / 1024
if ($sysvol_mb_space -gt $sysvol_space)
{ Write-Host "  SYSVOL Partition: OK" }
```

```
            if ($sysvol_mb_space -lt $sysvol_space)
            { Write-Host "  SYSVOL Partition: Low" }
            # Check the free space in the OS Partition
            $key_os = $reg.OpenSubKey("Software\Microsoft\"+
               "Windows NT\CurrentVersion")
            $os_dir = $key_os.GetValue("SystemRoot")
            $os_drive = $os_dir.Split("\")[0]
            $os_disk = Get-WmiObject -ComputerName $dc -Class `
               Win32_LogicalDisk -Filter "DeviceID = '$os_drive'"
            $os_mb_space = $os_disk.FreeSpace / 1024 / 1024
            if ($os_mb_space -gt $os_space)
            { Write-Host "  OS Partition:     OK" }
            if ($os_mb_space -lt $os_space)
            { Write-Host "  OS Partition:     Low" }
        }
      Write-Host
}
```

Retrieving a List of Critical Events from a Domain Controller's Event Logs

AD logs its critical events in the Windows event logs. These logs contain informational events, warnings, and errors related to the operation of AD and the DC itself. Therefore, it's important to monitor these logs and regularly take action in order to maintain a healthy AD. Generally speaking, the events that are most critical are the error events. Warning events can indicate problems as well, but they may not require immediate action.

You should monitor event logs every day. Some organizations use tools such as the Microsoft Audit Collection Service or other third-party tools to monitor and report on these event logs. In this section, we offer a cheap and quick way to monitor for critical events on your DCs.

Event logs can be read natively in PowerShell using the Get-EventLog cmdlet. This cmdlet can be used to connect to a local or remote computer and grab either all or a subset of event logs from that system. The following command demonstrates its use. Here you're connecting to BAL-DC01 and retrieving a copy of all the error events in the eystem event log:

```
Get-EventLog -ComputerName BAL-DC01 -LogName System ↵
   -EntryType Error
```

To automate this a bit, you can build a script that queries each DC for critical events and generates a report (see Listing 11.7). You can use the techniques discussed in Chapter 1, "Using PowerShell with Active Directory," to run this script as a nightly scheduled task and have the scheduled task email the report to the administrator. To ensure that you deal only with recent events, you only look at the logs that were generated within the past 24 hours.

LISTING 11.7: *report_events.ps1*

```
## File Name: report-events.ps1
## Description:
## Enumerates every DC in the forest and pulls error and
##  warning events from the System and Directory Service
##  event logs.
##
# Imports the Active Directory Module if it's not loaded
Import-Module ActiveDirectory
# Set the HTML file that you want to write the report to
$output_file = "c:\dc_log_report.html"
# Defines the style of the HTML output
$style = "<style>BODY{background-color:lightgrey}" +
"TABLE{border-width: 1px;border-style: solid;" +
"border-color: black;border-collapse: collapse}" +
"TH{border-width: 1px;padding: 0px;border-style: " +
"solid;border-color: black;background-color:#333; color: " +
"white}TD{border-width: 1px;padding: 0px;border-style: solid;" +
"border-color: black;background-color:#EFF4FB}</style>"
# Gets the current date minus 1 day for the search filter
$current_date = Get-Date
$past_days = New-Timespan -Days 1
$yesterday = $current_date.Subtract($past_days)
# Enumerate each of the domains in the current forest
$objForest = Get-ADForest
foreach ($strDomain in $objForest.Domains)
{
    $domain = Get-ADDomain $strDomain
    # Enumerate each Domain Controller in the domain
```

```
foreach ($dc in $domain.ReplicaDirectoryServers)
{
    $system_warning = Get-EventLog -ComputerName $dc `
        -LogName System -After $yesterday | `
        where {$_.EntryType -eq "Warning"}
    $system_error = Get-EventLog -ComputerName $dc `
        -LogName System -After $yesterday | `
        where {$_.EntryType -eq "Error"}
    $ds_warning = Get-EventLog -ComputerName $dc -LogName `
        "Directory Service" -After $yesterday | `
        where {$_.EntryType -eq "Warning"}
    $ds_error = Get-EventLog -ComputerName $dc -LogName `
        "Directory Service" -After $yesterday | `
         where {$_.EntryType -eq "Error"}
    if ($system_error.Count -gt 0)
    {
        $formatted_obj = $system_error | Select-Object `
            EventID, Source, Message -Unique
        $html_out += "<H2>$dc System Errors</H2>" +
            ($formatted_obj | ConvertTo-HTML -Fragment)
    }
    if ($ds_error.Count -gt 0)
    {
        $formatted_obj = $ds_error | Select-Object `
            EventID, Source, Message -Unique
        $html_out += "<H2>$dc DS Errors</H2>" +
            ($formatted_obj | ConvertTo-HTML -Fragment)
    }

    if ($system_warning.Count -gt 0)
    {
        $formatted_obj = $system_warning | Select-Object `
            EventID, Source, Message -Unique
        $html_out += "<H2>$dc System Warnings</H2>" +
            ($formatted_obj | ConvertTo-HTML -Fragment)
    }
```

Protecting Your
Investment in
Active Directory

PART III

(continues)

LISTING 11-7 *(continued)*

```
                    if ($ds_warning.Count -gt 0)
                    {
                        $formatted_obj = $ds_warning | Select-Object `
                            EventID, Source, Message -Unique
                        $html_out +=  "<H2>$dc DS Warnings</H2>" +
                            ($formatted_obj | ConvertTo-HTML -Fragment)
                    }


                }
            Write-Host
        }
        # Write the HTML file
        ConvertTo-Html -PostContent $html_out -Head $style | `
            Out-File $output_file
        # Display the HTML report
        Invoke-Expression $output_file
```

Reporting the Service Pack and Hotfix Status for All Domain Controllers

In AD, it's important that the configuration of DCs is as similar as possible. That way, you limit potential problems that may arise. If one DC is running a different Service Pack level than another, then queries to that specific DC may differ from the others. Therefore, it's a good idea to ensure that you periodically check the Service Pack and hotfix status of each DC.

You can view this information using the Get-ADDomainController cmdlet. This cmdlet returns the following OS-specific information for the DC:

- ► OperatingSystem

- ► OperatingSystemHotfix

- ► OperatingSystemServicePack

- ► OperatingSystemVersion

You can run the following command against a single DC to get this information. This command connects to the DC labeled BAL-DC01 and returns all properties starting with the word *Operating* in a list:

```
Get-ADDomainController "BAL-DC01" | fl Operating*
```

Using this command in a script to collect this information on your DCs is as simple as enumerating each DC and running the `Get-ADDomainController` cmdlet against it. The script in Listing 11.8 gathers this OS information from all the DCs in your forest.

LISTING 11.8: *get_os_info.ps1*

```
## File Name: get_os_info.ps1
## Description:
## Enumerates every Domain Controller in the forest and gets
##  information about the operating system version, service
##  pack, and hotfixes installed.
##
# Imports the Active Directory Module if it isn't loaded
Import-Module ActiveDirectory
# Enumerate each of the domains in the current forest
$objForest = Get-ADForest
foreach ($strDomain in $objForest.Domains)
{
    $domain = Get-ADDomain $strDomain
    # Enumerate each Domain Controller in the domain
    foreach ($dc in $domain.ReplicaDirectoryServers)
    {
        Get-ADDomainController $dc | `
            Select-Object Name, Operating*
    }
    Write-Host
}
```

Track Domain Controller Performance

In addition to ensuring that your DCs are healthy, you should also take measures to make sure that they're performing well. There are multiple performance counters on DCs that can help you determine how your DCs are doing. Throughout this section, we'll walk you through the important performance counters on which to measure your DCs. We'll provide explanations as to what the performance metrics mean, and if possible, we'll provide you with some recommended limits on these metrics.

Monitor Active Directory Performance

In the first part of this section, we'll focus on the performance of AD itself. This means we'll look at AD as a network service and help you understand some of its performance characteristics. In doing so, we'll look at the following areas:

- ► Measuring logon statistics for the various authentication protocols supported by AD

- ► Reviewing LDAP queries and determining if they need to be optimized

- ► Examining the performance of the AD database engine

Measuring Domain Logon Statistics

AD has the ability to authenticate people using a variety of authentication protocols. Generally speaking, you'll likely see the following protocols used for authentication against AD:

- ► NTLM authentication

- ► Kerberos authentication

- ► LDAP bind authentication

NTLM Authentication

NTLM authentication is based on a challenge and response mechanism. When a user authenticates with NTLM, a piece of data is encrypted using the user's password and sent to a DC. The DC encrypts the data with the copy of the user's password that it contains in the directory; if the two match, then the password that the user entered must be correct. There are some security vulnerabilities around the use of NTLM, and compared to Kerberos, NTLM is considered the weaker protocol. Therefore, NTLM isn't chosen by default in most authentication scenarios between Microsoft clients and AD.

NOTE AD uses a negotiation to determine which protocol should be used to authenticate the user. By default, Kerberos is preferred during this negotiation cycle. However, the client may not always choose Kerberos. If Kerberos isn't used, then the fall-back protocol is NTLM. Therefore, if you see a lot of NTLM authentication traffic on your DCs, that could indicate a problem with Kerberos authentication.

You can measure NTLM authentication traffic using the NTLM Authentications performance counter. This counter keeps track of the number of NTLM authentications that occur per second. During a busy load (such as the start of a workday), you can query for this counter to determine how many times the DC is using NTLM instead of Kerberos. You can use PowerShell to get a snapshot of the current number of NTLM authentications per second. The following PowerShell commands only provide you with a look at what is happening right now. If you want a more accurate picture, you should measure NTLM authentications over a period of time, such as one or two hours during peak load:

```
$ntlm = New-Object System.Diagnostics.PerformanceCounter( ↵
  "Security System-Wide Statistics", "NTLM Authentications")
$ntlm.NextValue()
```

Kerberos Authentication

As mentioned earlier, Kerberos is the preferred authentication protocol used in AD. A client will authenticate to the Kerberos KDC service on the DC and obtain a ticket-granting ticket (TGT). This TGT is used for requesting session tickets to services in the domain. Therefore, when measuring Kerberos traffic, you may not want to measure just Kerberos authentications, but also how many tickets are being requested. This gives you an idea of how many people are authenticating and how often resources are accessed.

To measure Kerberos authentication traffic, you use the Kerberos Authentications counter in addition to the KDC AS Requests counter and the KDC TGS Requests counter. The following PowerShell commands present this information as a snapshot in time. In a manner similar to NTLM authentications, you should measure this information over a period of time in order for it to be accurate:

```
$kerb = New-Object System.Diagnostics.PerformanceCounter( ↵
  "Security System-Wide Statistics", "Kerberos Authentications")
$kerb.NextValue()

$as_req = New-Object System.Diagnostics.PerformanceCounter( ↵
  "Security System-Wide Statistics", "KDC AS Requests")
$as_req.NextValue()

$tgs_req = New-Object System.Diagnostics.PerformanceCounter( ↵
  "Security System-Wide Statistics", "KDC TGS Requests")
$tgs_req.NextValue()
```

Protecting Your Investment in Active Directory

PART III

LDAP Bind Authentication

Lightweight Directory Access Protocol (LDAP) bind authentication is an authentication type in AD that can't be used for network logon. Rather, LDAP bind authentication is used only when you're connecting to a directory with the LDAP protocol. If you have third-party applications that use AD as an LDAP server, then you'll have LDAP binds occurring on your DCs.

LDAP binds are inherently very insecure. When used over an open, non-SSL protected channel, your credentials are sent to the LDAP server in clear text for verification. The only way to protect your credentials in this case is to use an SSL connection over which to pass LDAP credentials. However, for AD, this requires that each DC have a certificate installed, so it's often not used.

You can measure LDAP bind authentication statistics by using the LDAP Successful Binds/sec counter. The following PowerShell commands illustrate the use of this counter:

```
$ldap_bind = New-Object System.Diagnostics.PerformanceCounter( ↵
  "NTDS", "LDAP Successful Binds/sec")
$ldap_bind.NextValue()
```

Measuring Active Directory Query Statistics

As an LDAP-compliant directory service, AD can service LDAP requests from any source that is authorized to perform them. Because users can read permissions to AD by default, any user can perform an LDAP query. Queries that aren't optimized can greatly affect DC performance. If you suspect that the performance of your DCs is suffering due to inefficient queries, you can determine what queries are taking place and who is executing them.

If you have an application that you think is a culprit, you can see exactly what queries are being performed. To do this, you first need to enable diagnostic logging on field engineering events. We discussed how to do this earlier in this chapter in the section "Enabling Diagnostic Logs." In that section, we gave you a script that you can use to enable diagnostic logging on DCs remotely. To enable the field engineering events, enable logging for component number 15. If you set this log level to 4, it will log inefficient and expensive queries every 12 hours when garbage collection takes place. If you set the log level to 5, it will log inefficient and expensive queries as they occur. We only recommend enabling this log when you're looking into a specific situation; never leave it enabled in the long term. Doing so will add several events into your event logs and also negatively impact DC performance. The following command uses the script earlier in this chapter to enable this logging:

```
set_ntds_log.ps1 -LogNumber 15 -LogLevel 4 -DCName "BAL-DC01"
```

After you enable the log, the next question you may have is, "What kind of query is considered inefficient and expensive?" By default, an *expensive* query is a query where more than 10,000 objects are visited during the search operation. If your AD domain contains 50,000 users and you perform a query to list those users, that query is considered expensive because it touches more than 10,000 objects. That doesn't mean the query is bad or wrong, it just means the DC has to do some work to answer it. You shouldn't equate an "expensive" query with a "bad" query. There are many legitimate cases where you'll need to search more than 10,000 objects.

If your idea of expensive is different than 10,000 objects, then the good news is that you can modify this 10,000-object threshold. You can set a Registry key on a per-DC basis to control what the DC considers expensive. Modifying this Registry key doesn't increase the performance of the DC; rather, it's only used to determine under which criteria it should log a query as expensive. The key you can set to adjust this is at

```
HKLM\System\CurrentControlSet\Services\NTDS\Parameters\ ↵
    Expensive Search Threshold
```

Just set the Expensive Search Threshold value to a DWORD value that you want to be considered expensive. The following command uses the New-ItemProperty cmdlet to set this value to 5,000. As a side note, if you set this value to 1, the DC will log every LDAP query that it performs:

```
New-ItemProperty HKLM:\System\CurrentControlSet\Services\NTDS\ ↵
    Parameters -Name "Expensive Search Threshold" -PropertyType ↵
    DWORD -Value 5000
```

Now that you know what is considered expensive, the other question you may have is what kind of query is considered *inefficient*. By default, the DC considers any query that returns fewer than 1,000 of the objects it touches to be inefficient. For example, if you search across 50,000 users for every user in the Sales department, and only 200 users are returned in the query, then that query is considered inefficient. Similar to how you can modify what the DC considers expensive, you can also modify what the DC considers inefficient. To do so, modify the following Registry key:

```
HKLM\System\CurrentControlSet\Services\NTDS\Parameters\ ↵
    Inefficient Search Results Threshold
```

Protecting Your
Investment in
Active Directory

PART III

The following example sets this value to 5,000, which may be appropriate for an environment with 50,000 users. The determination of what should be considered inefficient is subjective, so this is something you should define based on your experience and knowledge of your AD environment.

```
New-ItemProperty HKLM:\System\CurrentControlSet\Services\NTDS\↵
    Parameters -Name "Inefficient Search Results Threshold" ↵
    -PropertyType DWORD -Value 5000
```

Once these Registry values are set, logging will occur for as long as you have the Field Engineering diagnostic value enabled. To help make enabling and disabling these settings easier, you can use the script in Listing 11.9. This script allows you to enable or disable LDAP query logging on a specific DC. To use the script, specify either the Enable or Disable parameter and the name of the DC in the DCName parameter. If you're enabling LDAP query logging, then you can optionally specify the Expensive and Inefficient keywords to adjust what the DC considers expensive and inefficient. For example, the following command uses the script to enable LDAP query logging on the DC BAL-DC01:

```
PS C:\> .\set_ldap_logging.ps1 -Enable -DCName BAL-DC01


BAL-DC01: LDAP Query Logging Enabled
```

LISTING 11.9: *set_ldap_logging.ps1*

```
## File Name: set_ldap_logging.ps1
## Description:
## Enables LDAP query logging on the specified DC
##
param([switch]$Enable, [switch]$Disable, [string]$Expensive="",
    [string]$Inefficient="", [string]$DCName="")
if ($DCName -eq "") { $DCName = "." }
$reg = [Microsoft.Win32.RegistryKey]::OpenRemoteBaseKey(
    "LocalMachine", $DCName)
if ($Disable)
{
    $key = $reg.OpenSubKey("System\CurrentControlSet\"+
        "Services\NTDS\Diagnostics", $true)
    $key.SetValue("15 Field Engineering", 0, "DWORD")
    Write-Host "$($DCName): LDAP Query Logging Disabled"
```

```
}
else
{
    ## Enable the Field Engineering events
    $key = $reg.OpenSubKey("System\CurrentControlSet\"+
      "Services\NTDS\Diagnostics", $true)
    $key.SetValue("15 Field Engineering", 4, "DWORD")
    ## Configure the values for Expensive and Inefficient
    $key = $reg.OpenSubKey("System\CurrentControlSet\"+
      "Services\NTDS\Parameters", $true)
    if ($Expensive -ne "")
    {
        $key.SetValue("Expensive Search Threshold", $Expensive,
          "DWORD")
    }
    if ($Inefficient -ne "")
    {
        $key.SetValue("Inefficient Search Results Threshold",
          $Inefficient, "DWORD")
    }
    Write-Host "$($DCName): LDAP Query Logging Enabled"
}
```

Measuring the Performance of the Active Directory Database

The AD database (NTDS.DIT) is the file the DC uses to store all the configuration and domain data for AD. This database uses the ESE, which is based on Microsoft's Joint Engine Technology. The database engine uses a series of transaction logs in a lazy-commit fashion to write data to the database. This means that when data needs to be written to the database, it isn't written directly to the NTDS.DIT file. Instead, it's first written to a log file on disk and simultaneously held in memory. When this data is queried, the results are returned from memory first. The data is also streamed to disk so that if the DC crashes before it has time to update the NTDS.DIT file, the log file can be used to write that data to the database. The log file is written to sequentially in a very fast manner as data comes in. The database file, on the other hand, is written to randomly as data is placed in specific places in the database. The lazy-commit system means data is not written to the database immediately. Rather, the DC commits the data to the database when it has some free cycles to do so.

The ESE database system employed by AD can be rather complex. It's important to monitor the performance of this database to ensure that the DC functions properly and that it can store the data it needs to. You should pay attention to the following five database performance counters included with the DC:

Database Cache % Hit   This is the percentage of page requests for the database file that were filled by the cache rather than a file operation of the database. The higher this number, the better.

Database Page Fault Stalls/sec   This is the number of page faults per second that can't be serviced due to the limited memory.

Database Page Evictions/sec   This counter describes the memory pressure on the database cache. When this counter is high, the DC needs more memory.

Database Cache Size   This counter contains the current amount of memory that the directory service is using to cache the database. Ideally, this number should be as high as possible. This would indicate that database operations are mostly occurring out of memory instead of having to be paged from the disk.

Log Threads Waiting   This contains the number of threads that are waiting for data to be written to a transaction log file. Transaction commits to the database can't occur until they're first written to the transaction log. If this number is high, then data isn't being streamed to the log file fast enough, and you probably need a faster hard drive or a different RAID configuration on the DC.

The following PowerShell commands use the counters discussed to display information about the DC's database performance. Ideally, you should examine these counters over a period of time in order to get an accurate picture. These commands provide only a snapshot of the current state:

```
$db_cache_pct = New-Object System.Diagnostics.PerformanceCounter ↵
  ("Database", "Database Cache % Hit", "lsass")
$db_cache_pct.NextValue()
$db_pf_stalls = New-Object System.Diagnostics.PerformanceCounter ↵
  ("Database", "Database Page Fault Stalls/sec", "lsass")
$db_pf_stalls.NextValue()
$db_pg_evicts = New-Object System.Diagnostics.PerformanceCounter ↵
  ("Database", "Database Page Evictions/sec", "lsass")
$db_pg_evicts.NextValue()
$db_cache_sz = New-Object System.Diagnostics.PerformanceCounter ↵
```

```
    ("Database", "Database Cache Size", "lsass")
$db_cache_sz.NextValue()
$log_threads = New-Object System.Diagnostics.PerformanceCounter ↵
    ("Database", "Log Threads Waiting", "lsass")
$log_threads.NextValue()
```

Monitor Domain Controller Hardware

In this part of this section, we'll look at various aspects of DC hardware. The performance of DCs depends heavily on the processors, memory, hard disks, and network adapters used by the server. Therefore, we'll look across these various components so you'll understand what to watch out for in each one. In doing so, we'll teach you how to use PowerShell to gather some of the data associated with the performance of this hardware, so you can automate DC hardware reporting and stay on top of your DC's performance.

Generating a Report of CPU Utilization

The CPU in a DC is only one of the components that must be monitored to ensure that the DC isn't overburdened. CPUs execute one or more threads inside a process. While threads are being executed, the processor is being used. Therefore, the first measure of CPU utilization that we'll look at is % Processor Time. This indicates what percentage of time the processor spends executing threads in the active processes. You really should look at this metric over a period of time, perhaps monitoring it every second for an hour or two during the day when the DCs are used heavily. When examining your processor utilization over a period of time, you should rarely see % Processor Time exceed 80 to 85%. There will be occasional spikes, but they should be the exception rather than the norm. If you regularly see your processor sitting above 85% utilization, it's time to add additional processors or additional DCs to scale out the load. This might also be a good time to turn on LDAP query logging to help determine why your processor utilization is so high.

You can use PowerShell to give you a snapshot of the current value of the % Processor Time metric. To do so, use the following PowerShell commands:

```
PS C:\> $pct_proc_time = New-Object System.Diagnostics. ↵
    PerformanceCounter("Processor", "% Processor Time", "_Total")
PS C:\> $pct_proc_time.NextValue()
2.582036
```

The second CPU metric to keep an eye on is Interrupts/sec Counter. It measures the number of hardware interrupts that are being received from the DC's I/O devices. A DC in normal operation could be processing thousands of interrupts per second. To understand what is healthy for your environment, you should establish a baseline number by monitoring your DCs when they're healthy for a period of time and then comparing the ongoing monitoring results to the baseline. If there is a sudden spike in interrupt requests, it could mean that a bad piece of hardware in the DC is throwing excessive interrupts. The following PowerShell commands display a snapshot of the current number of interrupts per second. Remember that this is only a point-in-time snapshot, so you should use it in a script to monitor the DC over a period of time to get an accurate assessment:

```
PS C:\> $interrupts = New-Object System.Diagnostics. ↵
  PerformanceCounter("Processor", "Interrupts/sec", "_Total")
PS C:\> $interrupts.NextValue()
129.0122
```

The final metric of a DC's CPU utilization is the processor queue length. The processor-run queue holds the threads that are waiting to be executed. When the queue length is high, that means the processor can't keep up and isn't processing the threads quickly enough. When this happens, the processor becomes the bottleneck. Ideally, this queue length should be zero, but it's normal for it to have one or two threads waiting. We recommend ensuring that the queue length doesn't exceed two threads waiting for execution per processor. So if you have two processors, the processor queue length should be less than 4. As with the other counters, you should monitor this over time, but the following PowerShell commands give you a snapshot of your current processor queue length:

```
PS C:\> $cpu_queue = New-Object System.Diagnostics. ↵
  PerformanceCounter("System", "Processor Queue Length")
PS C:\> $cpu_queue.NextValue()
2
```

Generating a Report of Memory Usage

Memory usage in Windows is a tough topic to comprehend, partly because the terminology used has changed over the years. Therefore, it's important to first give you a quick understanding of how memory works in Windows; this will help you understand how a DC uses memory and how much it should have.

The first thing to point out is that there is a distinct difference between virtual memory and physical memory. When a process uses memory, it doesn't address physical memory directly. Instead, it addresses virtual memory, which acts as a layer of obfuscation on top of physical memory. The address space of physical memory is completely different from the address space of virtual memory. For example, if a process allocates 1 page of memory at address 28, that page may physically reside at address 96 in physical memory.

The size of the virtual address space varies depending on the version of Windows that is in use. For example, the virtual address space is different in 32-bit Windows, 64-bit Windows, and Itanium. The connection between physical and virtual address spaces is very weak. In fact, the address space that a process can use is sometimes larger than the amount of physical memory in the system. This ensures that the process can address its own memory in any way it sees fit without impacting other processes. With this architecture, process 1 using a memory page at address 28 doesn't impact process 2 using a memory page at address 28. This is because address 28 in process 1 may map to address 54 in physical memory, and address 28 in process 2 may map to address 103 in physical memory.

In 32-bit Windows, 4 GB of memory is addressable. By default, this is split down the middle for applications (user-mode memory) and for the OS (kernel-mode memory). Each gets 2 GB of addressable memory, unless a specific startup switch is used that allows applications to use more than 2 GB. In 64-bit Windows, however, there is a theoretical limit of 16 EB (that's exabytes) of addressable memory. In reality, though, Windows will allow you to address up to 16 TB. This 16 TB address space is also split in half (8 TB for applications and 8 TB for the OS). So even if only 8 GB of memory is installed on the computer, applications can address up to 8 TB.

To allow applications to use the same address space, Windows uses context switches, which swap out the address space between different processes. For example, if the processor is executing a thread in the notepad.exe process, it first ensures that it's using Notepad's address space. If you switch over to Microsoft Word, the processor will swap out the active address space with Word's address space. This doesn't mean memory pages are moved around; it just means the memory map is adjusted. The kernel, on the other hand, always occupies the same address space and isn't swapped out like applications.

Now that you understand how memory works in Windows at a high level, let's look at some common terminology. We can separate the common memory terms into two buckets: terms that pertain to virtual memory and terms that pertain to physical memory. Table 11.6 describes the common terms for virtual memory.

TABLE 11.6   Common Terminology for Virtual Memory

Term	Description
Reserved	Memory that has been allocated for use by a process when it asks for a contiguous block of addresses in its address space. This memory isn't backed by physical memory (in RAM or on disk), so nothing can be stored at these addresses yet.
Committed	Memory that has been allocated by a process and is backed by physical memory in RAM or on disk. This memory can be used because when something is written to it, the data can be stored in RAM, a memory mapped file, or a paging file.
Free	Memory in the address space that is currently not being used.
System commit limit	The total amount of memory that can be committed by the system. Calculated by adding together the amount of physical RAM in the system plus the sizes of the paging files.
Current system commit charge	The total amount of memory that is currently committed for use.

Table 11.7 describes the common memory terms for discussing physical memory.

TABLE 11.7   Common Terminology for Physical Memory

Term	Description
Zeroed pages	Memory pages that have been zeroed out (previous data in this page has been written over with all zeroes). When a page is zeroed out, it's ready to be reused.
Free pages	Memory pages that aren't being used but haven't yet been zeroed out. Before they can be used, they must first be zeroed out.
Modified pages	Memory pages that haven't been used in a while. Before the space can be reused for another process, the existing data first needs to be written to disk.
Standby pages	Memory pages that haven't been used in a while but have already been written to disk. If the process that was using the memory pages needs them back, it can reuse them. Otherwise, these memory pages can be freed, zeroed out, and reused if they're needed.
Working set	Amount of committed memory being used by a process that is currently physically in RAM.
Active	Amount of memory that is currently used in process working sets.

When examining memory usage on a DC, there are a few main areas that you should look at:

▶ The amount of available memory

▶ The frequency at which page faults are occurring

▶ How heavily the paging files are used

▶ Local Security Authority Subsystem Service (LSASS) memory usage

The amount of available memory can be determined by using the Available MBytes counter. This value is a combination of memory from the free list, the zeroed list, and the standby list. According to Table 11.7, these pages are available for reuse, although they may need to be zeroed out first. The following PowerShell commands grab a snapshot of the current amount of available memory:

```
PS C:\> $mem_avail = New-Object System.Diagnostics. ↵
   PerformanceCounter("Memory", "Available MBytes")
PS C:\> $mem_avail.NextValue()
398
```

There are two types of page faults in Windows: hard page faults and soft page faults. A soft page fault occurs when the memory page is still in physical memory but is in the working set of the process. A hard page fault occurs when a process requests a memory page that is no longer kept in physical memory. In this case, the page was previously moved to a paging file on the hard disk and must first be retrieved back into physical memory before it can be used. Page faults are a normal occurrence, so don't be alarmed to see them happening. Memory is regularly paged out even if there is plenty available. The Virtual Memory Manager in Windows performs this process continuously as a measure of efficiency. You can use the Page Faults/sec counter to determine how frequently page faults are occurring in your DC:

```
PS C:\> $page_faults = New-Object System.Diagnostics. ↵
   PerformanceCounter("Memory", "Page Faults/sec")
PS C:\> $page_faults.NextValue()
66.9549
```

Ultimately, the thing that will probably slow down memory usage the most is excessive reading from the paging file. Windows tries not to make a regular habit of writing frequently used memory pages to the paging file. Therefore, if data is being paged out to disk excessively, that's a really good indication that your DC needs more memory. There are two counters to look out for when examining the paging file:

▶ *% Usage*—Shows the current usage of the paging file

▶ *% Usage Peak*—Shows the peak usage of the paging file

Protecting Your
Investment in
Active Directory

PART III

The following commands demonstrate how to query the %Usage and the %Usage Peak counters:

```
PS C:\> $pf_usage = New-Object System.Diagnostics. ↵
  PerformanceCounter("Paging File", "% Usage")
PS C:\> $pf_usage.NextValue()
9.453583
PS C:\> $pf_usage_peak = New-Object System.Diagnostics. ↵
  PerformanceCounter("Paging File", "% Usage Peak")
PS C:\> $pf_usage_peak.NextValue()
9.453583
```

When you're monitoring DCs, there is one process that it's very important for you to keep an eye on: the LSASS process. LSASS is the process in which the Local Security Authority operates, and it's the process from which AD is primarily serviced. With regard to memory, the LSASS process has a variable memory usage model. The idea is that LSASS should consume a baseline amount of memory; if any additional memory is left, it can be used for caching AD data in order to service requests more quickly. Looking at the LSASS process as a whole, you'll notice that it grows over time as it caches more and more information. However, the private (nonshared) memory for LSASS won't grow significantly over time. Therefore, you should monitor private bytes to detect an LSASS memory leak:

```
PS C:\> $lsass_priv = New-Object System.Diagnostics. ↵
  PerformanceCounter("Process", "Private Bytes", "lsass")
PS C:\> $lsass_priv.NextValue()
3.601613E+07
```

Generating a Network Bandwidth Report

Over the years, as networking hardware has steadily improved, network bandwidth has become less of a problem. However, it's still important to monitor the bandwidth used by your DC, for a few reasons. First, you could have a malfunctioning network card, and a lack of data sent or received could indicate to you that there are problems. Second, you could be receiving excessive amounts of data, which could mean that you're experiencing unusually heavy traffic or are in the midst of a Denial of Service attack. Also, there is always the possibility of a misconfiguration of the network settings, which could also be causing problems. If you have multiple network adapters in the DC, then you may not even notice that one of them is misbehaving.

To monitor network bandwidth, look at two primary performance counters:

► Bytes Sent/sec

► Bytes Received/sec

You can use these counters to determine whether there is an unusually heavy or light network load on your DCs. The amount of network traffic that your DC sends and receives is subjective. Therefore, you should take a baseline of a healthy DC over a period of time (a couple of days or possibly a week or more). The longer the period over which you can take a baseline, the more accurate the picture of your bandwidth usage will be. The following PowerShell commands provide a snapshot of current network utilization:

```
PS C:\> $bytes_in = New-Object System.Diagnostics. ↩
  PerformanceCounter("Network Interface", "Bytes Received/sec", ↩
  "Local Area Connection")
PS C:\> $bytes_in.NextValue()
864.7373
PS C:\> $bytes_out = New-Object System.Diagnostics. ↩
  PerformanceCounter("Network Interface", "Bytes Sent/sec", ↩
  "Local Area Connection")
PS C:\> $bytes_out.NextValue()
1173.977
```

Generating a Hard-Disk Report

The hard disk is often the slowest component in a DC. Because of the way memory is used (as discussed earlier in this chapter in the section "Generating a Report of Memory Usage"), the hard disk serves as a temporary backup for storing memory pages that aren't used very often. If memory pages that are frequently used are cached to disk, then that indicates that the DC needs more memory.

The performance of the hard disks in the DC is of great importance to the performance of AD. To monitor the performance of the disks, you need to keep an eye on the disk usage and the disk response time. You can measure the amount of disk time with the % Disk Time counter. As a general rule of thumb, we recommend that you only host AD on DCs and don't install additional applications for hosting. If your DC only services AD, then the % Disk Time counter should not exceed 70%. However, if you're hosting other services on your DC, such as a SQL server, then you can expect % Disk Time to be higher.

Protecting Your
Investment in
Active Directory

PART III

If it's above 90%, you should consider reconfiguring your disks into a different RAID configuration. The following PowerShell commands grab a point-in-time look at % Disk Time on the DC:

```
PS C:\> $disk_time = New-Object System.Diagnostics. ↵
  PerformanceCounter("PhysicalDisk", "% Disk Time", "_Total")
PS C:\> $disk_time.NextValue()
0.466341
```

Another set of counters that is important to look at for hard-disk health are Disks Reads/sec and Disk Writes/sec. These counters track how much data is being read from and written to the disk in one second. Note that DCs generally read more than they write. Therefore, it's not uncommon to notice that your read operations are more intensive than your write operations. The following PowerShell commands illustrate how to gather disk read and write data:

```
PS C:\> $disk_read = New-Object System.Diagnostics. ↵
  PerformanceCounter("PhysicalDisk", "Disk Reads/sec", "_Total")
PS C:\> $disk_read.NextValue()
0
PS C:\> $disk_write = New-Object System.Diagnostics. ↵
  PerformanceCounter("PhysicalDisk", "Disk Writes/sec", ↵
  "_Total")
PS C:\> $disk_write.NextValue()
0
```

You should also measure the length of the disk queue. This indicates how many requested operations are outstanding on the disk. If this number builds up, that's an indication that your disk can't keep up with demand. Generally speaking, you want no more than two operations in the queue for each disk that you have installed. So if you're running two drives in a RAID configuration, the disk queue length should be four or less. You can use the following PowerShell commands to get a snapshot of the disk queue length:

```
PS C:\> $disk_queue = New-Object System.Diagnostics. ↵
  PerformanceCounter("PhysicalDisk", ↵
  "Current Disk Queue Length", "_Total")
PS C:\> $disk_queue.NextValue()
```

The final aspect of disk health that you want to keep an eye on is the amount of free disk space available on the DC. We discussed this topic in detail earlier in this chapter in the section "Viewing the Available Disk Space across All Domain Controllers." We recommend that you go back and read that section if you haven't already done so.

Protecting Your Investment in Active Directory

PART III

INDEX

Note to the Reader: Throughout this index **boldfaced** page numbers indicate primary discussions of a topic. *Italicized* page numbers indicate illustrations.

F

O

P